2/91

# Computers and the Imagination

## Visual Adventures Beyond the Edge

Clifford A. Pickover

ST. MARTIN'S PRESS
NEW YORK

First published in the United States of America in 1991
Printed in the United States of America

Library of Congress Cataloging-in-Publication Data

Pickover, Clifford A.
      Computers and the imagination / Clifford A. Pickover.
         p.   cm.
      Includes bibliographical references and index.
      ISBN 0-312-06131-5
      1. Computers.   2. Computer simulation.   3. Computer
graphics.
      I. Title.
      QA76.P465   1991
      004—dc20                                      91-12058
                                                        CIP

*To Elahe*

# Preface

*The Buddha, the Godhead, resides quite as comfortably in the circuits of a digital computer or the gears of a cycle transmission as he does at the top of a mountain or in the petals of a flower; to think otherwise is to demean the Buddha -- which is to demean oneself.*                    Robert Pirsig, *1975*

This book is meant to be a stimulus for the imagination – an energizing elixir for scientific creativity. This book is also about some of the many things which researchers do with a computer: *simulating, visualizing, speculating, inventing, and exploring.* However, if a researcher's primary investigative effort is considered as the trunk of a tree, then many of this book's topics are the offshoots, branches, and tendrils. Some of the topics in the book may appear to be curiosities, with little practical application or purpose. However, I have found all of these experiments to be useful and educational, as have the many students, educators, and scientists who have written to me during the last few years. It is also important to keep in mind that throughout history, experiments, ideas and conclusions originating in the play of the mind have found striking and unexpected practical applications. I urge you to explore all of the topics in this book with this principle in mind.

*Computers and the Imagination* will appeal to the educated layperson with a curious or artistic streak, as well as students and professionals in the sciences, particularly computer science. Some of the patterns in this book can be used by graphic artists, illustrators, and craftspeople in search of visually intriguing designs, or by anyone fascinated by optically provocative art. The book is not intended for mathematicians looking for a formal mathematical treatise. As my previous book, *Computers, Pattern, Chaos, and Beauty* (St. Martin's Press, 1990), the purposes of this book are:

1.  to present several novel graphical ways of representing complicated data,

2.  to promote and show the role of aesthetics in mathematics and to suggest how computer graphics gives an appreciation of the complexity and beauty underlying apparently simple processes,

3.  to show the beauty, the adventure, and the potential importance of creative thinking using computers, and

4.  to encourage the use of the computer as an instrument for simulation and discovery.

"Lateral thinking" has been employed in the development of many of the topics of this book. This is a term discussed by writer/philosopher Robert Pirsig (author of *Zen and the Art of Motorcycle Maintenance*). As he explains it, lateral thinking is reasoning in a direction not naturally pointed to by a scientific discipline. It is reasoning in an unexpected direction, given the actual goal one is working toward (also see de Bono, 1975). In this book, the term "lateral thinking" is used in an extended way, and indicates not only action motivated by unexpected results, but also the deliberate shift of thinking in new directions to discover what can be learned.

Imagery is at the heart of much of the work described in this book. To understand what is around us, we need eyes to see it. Computers with graphics capability can be used to produce visual representations from myriad perspectives. In the same spirit as Martin Gardner's book *Mathematical Circus* or Theoni Pappas' book *The Joy of Mathematics*, *Computers and the Imagination* combines old and new ideas – with emphasis on the fun that the true scientific explorer finds in doing, rather than in reading about the doing.

This book is a collection of some of my papers published since *Computers, Pattern, Chaos, and Beauty*. With just a few exceptions, all of the described research and computer graphics in the book are my own. However, the *Introduction* and various one-page *Interlude* sections describe some unusual work by other researchers in related fields. The *Interlude* sections and some of the appendices also contain further information, images, and futuristic products to stimulate the imagination.[1]

*Computers and the Imagination* includes topics such as scientific visualization, simulation, number theory, and computer art, and you will be urged to explore in greater depth the ideas presented. You should be forewarned that some of the material presented involves sophisticated concepts (e.g. "Irregularly Oscillating Fossil Seashell"); other chapters (e.g. "The Cancer Game") require little mathematical knowledge in order to appreciate the subject. You are encouraged to pick and chose from the smorgasbord of topics. Many of the articles are brief and give you just a flavor of an application or method. Often, additional information can be found in the referenced publications. In order to encourage your involvement, computational hints and recipes for producing some of the computer-drawn figures are provided. For many of you, seeing pseudocode will clarify concepts in ways mere words cannot.

---

[1] *Note*: Although all of the products listed in this book provide a stimulus for the imagination, they are listed for illustrative purposes only. *The author does not endorse any particular software or product*, nor does he accept responsibility for the selection of any products by the reader. The opinions expressed in this book are the author's and do not represent the opinions of any organization or company.

The book is organized into nine main sections:

1. **Simulation**. In the quest for understanding natural phenomena, we turn to several simple computer simulations. These experiments are the easiest in the book for students to implement and explore, and include butterfly curves and cancer growth simulations.

2. **Exploration**. In this section, the interesting weave of "mathematical fabric" is explored. Topics include the Lute of Pythagoras, earthworm algebra, number theory, super-large numbers, and the elusive cakemorphic integers.

3. **Visualization**. Computer graphics has become indispensable in countless areas of human activity. Presented here are experiments using graphics in biology, mathematics, and art. Topics include pain-inducing patterns, seashells, and voltage sculptures.

4. **Speculation**. In this section are several speculative survey articles. Topics include "Who are the ten most influential scientists in history?" and "What is the social and political impact of a soda-can-sized supercomputer?"

5. **Invention**. This section describes several inventions. Topics include anti-dyslexic fonts and speech synthesis grenades.

6. **Imagination**. Discussed here are computer-generated poetry and stories.

7. **Fiction**. Presented in this section are a few short stories dealing with computers and scientific experiments.

8. **Exercises for the Mind and Eye**. This section presents imaginative unsolved puzzles and curiosities. There are also serious experiments for future research. Described in this section are Grasshopper sequences and the Amazon skull game.

9. **Computers in the Arts and Sciences**. This last section treats you to a list of unusual resources on the subject of computers in science and art. Listed are individuals and companies distributing computer art, music, and films, and also some references to unusual literature.

In deciding how to organize the material within these sections of *Computers and the Imagination*, I considered a number of divisions – computer- and non-computer-generated forms, science and art, nature and mathematics. However, the lines between these categories become indistinct or artificial, and I have therefore arranged the topics randomly within each section to retain the playful spirit of the book, and to give you unexpected pleasures. Throughout the book, there are suggested exercises for future experiments and thought, and directed reading lists. Some information is repeated so that each chapter contains sufficient background information, and you may therefore skip sections if desired. Smaller type fonts, as well as the symbols [[ and ]], are used to delimit material which you can skip during a casual reading, and a glossary is provided for some of the technical terms used in the book.

At the beginning of many chapters of *Computers and the Imagination* are large computer-generated "sculptures" constructed with tiny black dots. These images are actually created from simple mathematical formulas, and each contains precisely one-million dots. Background information, as well as algorithmic recipes for these sculptures, can be found in "Million-Point Sculptures" on page 285. Other frontispiece figures include grotesque *Digital Monsters* which are discussed in "Descriptions of Color Plates and Frontispieces" on page 393.[2]

The basic philosophy of this book is that creative thinking and computing are learned by experimenting. I conclude this preface with a quote from Morris Klein (*Scientific American*, March 1955) that encompasses the general theme of this book:

> *The creative act owes little to logic or reason. In their accounts of the circumstances under which big ideas occurred to them, mathematicians have often mentioned that the inspiration had no relation to the work they happened to be doing. Sometimes it came while they were travelling, shaving, or thinking about other matters. The creative process cannot be summoned at will or even cajoled by sacrificial offering. Indeed it seems to occur most readily when the mind is relaxed and the imagination roaming freely.*

## For Further Reading

1. De Bono, E. (1970) *Lateral Thinking: Creativity Step by Step.* Harper and Row: New York.

2. Gardner, M. (1979) *Mathematical Circus.* Penguin: England. (A collection of interesting puzzles, paradoxes, and games.)

3. Gardner, M. (1978) *Aha! Insight.* Freeman: New York. (A collection of puzzles which encourages creative leaps of thought, leading to solutions of seemingly impossible problems.)

4. Pappas, T. (1989) *The Joy of Mathematics.* Wide World Publishing: California. (A collection of mathematical puzzles and concepts for the layperson.)

5. Pickover, C. (1990) *Computers, Pattern, Chaos, and Beauty.* St. Martin's Press: New York.

6. Pirsig, R. (1975) *Zen and the Art of Motorcycle Maintenance.* Bantam: New York. (A philosophical story dealing with humans and technology.)

---

[2] *Book cover*: The cover of this book shows an image of a creature which the author rendered using an IBM RISC System/6000 computer. Many aspects of the figure, including color, lighting, and shading, are controlled by a computer program. The creature's body was created using formulas which produce three oscillating spiral shapes. The intricate background and diffuse collection of tiny spheres toward the back of the figure were also generated by simple formulas. Information on other color plates can be found in "Descriptions of Color Plates and Frontispieces" on page 393.

*"Thinking is more interesting than knowing,
but less interesting than looking."*

Wolfgang von Goethe

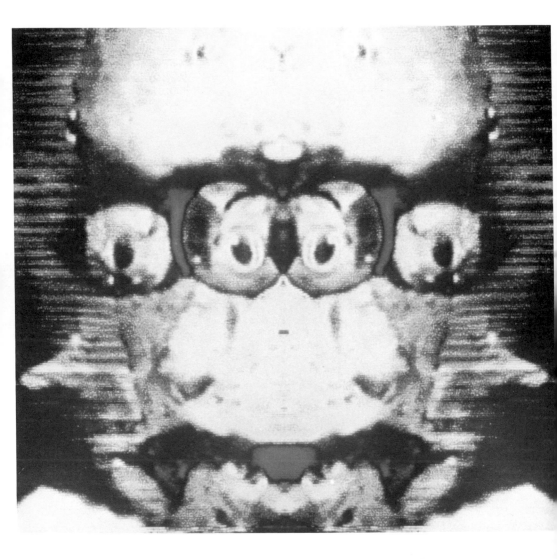

# Contents

**PART IX**
**CONCLUSION**

**PART X**
**APPENDICES**

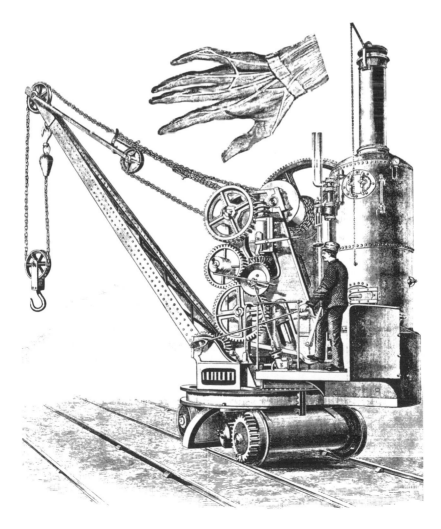

# Part  I

# INTRODUCTION

# Chapter 1

# Computers and the Unexpected

$$\frac{\mathcal{T}^2}{\eta^{35}}\ \mathcal{R}^9$$

*"The explosive freedom we gain from describing reality in mathematical metaphors is breathtaking. We can discover truths about ourselves that we could never have learned as poets writing in English."*

Paul Rapp, *Get Smart: Controlling Chaos, 1989*

Computers, mathematics, and freedom – three words which may never before have appeared together in a single sentence. However, computers and computation are now providing humankind with an unlimited landscape for exploration, and unparalleled aid for the imagination. The picture above, drawn in the 1800s, is entitled "The Secret of Celestial Mechanics." Like the old wizard blowing bubbles as he creates strange new worlds, computers allow modern-day explorers to invent and study artificial worlds through simulation and computer graphics.

Since their rapid growth following the Second World War, computers have changed the way we perform scientific research, conduct business, create art, and spend our leisure time. *Computers and the Imagination* was written to illustrate the eclectic nature of computer territory. It contains a collage of topics, some which can be effectively explored using a computer, and some which deal with the

**Figure 1.1.** *Visualization of a twisted torus (bagel shape).* This work, produced by Russian mathematician/artist A. T. Fomenko, is one piece in a large collection of mathematically inspired artwork. He calls the piece a "two-adic solenoid," a mathematical term which indicates an infinite series of tori embedded in each other. Each torus becomes thinner and thinner as it winds twice around the axis of the previous torus. Only nine tori are drawn, and for convenience of the viewer, each torus is cut so that successive tori can be seen through the holes. This is an example of what Fomenko calls "hidden symmetry." "Visualizing Cantor Cheese Construction" on page 141 has more information on this kind of object. (Figure reprinted with permission from *Computers and Mathematics with Applications*, Volume 17, 1989, page 304, Pergamon: NY. See also Hargittai, I. (1989) *Symmetry 2: Unifying Human Understanding.* Oxford: NY.)

impact of the computer on society. This introduction presents a collection of some unusual, and perhaps unexpected, facts related to computing and computer art. I would like to start by describing what this book is *not* about. It does not contain the standard number-crunching problems found in scientific texts – most often these do not stimulate creativity, nor do they have artistic appeal. Also, the problems and topics in this book are not of a "linear" variety, where variables are fed into an equation and a succinct answer is returned. In fact, many of the exercises

**Figure 1.2.** *Stewart Dickson's 3-D mathematical object in polymer-resin.* Through a new process called stereolithography, artists and engineers can create 3-D models in plastic from computer data. Sculptors using computer graphics can discover new aesthetic forms in the mathematical fabric of undulating surfaces and twisting shapes. (Image © 1989 by Stewart Dickson, courtesy of The Post Group.)

are of the "stop-and-think" variety, and can be explored without using a computer.

Many topics in this book have a visual appeal and belong in the general category of scientific visualization. Scientific visualization refers to the use of both simple and advanced computer graphics to help understand complicated data. The idea of visually presenting information and ideas dates back many centuries. During the Ice Age – 60,000 to 10,000 B.C. – cave dwellers in France, Spain, Africa, and Scandinavia painted animals on walls of their caves. More recently, intricate artifacts such as 9th century B.C. Assyrian stone carvings, 18th century Tibetan tankas, and 16th century celestial maps from Germany all indicate humankind's fascination with the visual representation of information and abstract ideas. Today's visual media are somewhat less exotic; they include television and computer graphics. However, it's the comic strip – not film, computer graphics, or television – that reaches one-third of humanity every day. (You can read more about scientific visualization in Part IV.)

In modern science and computer art, random number generators have proven invaluable in simulating natural phenomena and in sampling data, and several chapters in this book rely on the use of random numbers for a variety of purposes. The generation of random numbers also has a long history. Since antiquity, societies have had a need to generate and use chance events in a variety of settings. Prehistoric people used dice much like ours, played dice games similar to our own, and sometimes cheated opponents with loaded dice! Before dice became useful in

**Figure 1.3.** *Horned Sphere.* Mathematicians sometimes invent bizarre objects to test their ideas. Alexander's horned sphere is one example of an intricate, intertwined surface for which it is difficult to define an inside and an outside. (Image from Peterson (1990*b*).)

games, cubes with numbers were used as magical aids for divining the future.[3] Primitive man probably used cubical knucklebones or the anklebones of sheep for dice-like gaming pieces (Manchester, 1980).

Like the generation of random numbers and the development of visual pres-

entations, computers have also undergone significant development since their early incarnations. One example of an early computing machine is Blaise Pascal's wheel computer. In 1644, at the age of 20, this French philosopher and mathematician built a calculating machine to help his father compute business accounts. The machine, called a Pascaline (pictured at left), used a series of spinning numbered wheels for adding large numbers. Unfortunately problems with reliability and service caused Pascal's Pascaline business to fail. The Indians of North and South America also made use of a primitive computing "machine." In 1590 a Jesuit, Joseph de Acosta, recorded the following information regarding the Inca culture:

*In order to effect a very difficult computation for which an able calculator would require pen and ink ... these Indians make use of their kernels of*

---

[3] The practice of divination by means of dice is called "Astragalomancy."

**Figure 1.4.** *Metallic sculptures by John Robinson.* Mathematical sculptures and tapestries inspired by formulas, knots, DNA, bundles, and beautiful ovoids comprise the large artwork collection of John Robinson. For more information, contact Mathematics and Knots, University of Wales, Dean Street, Bangor, LL57 1UT, UK. Also see "Products, Classroom Aids, Art, Games, Distributors" on page 384.

*grain. They place one here, three somewhere else, and eight I know not where. They move one kernel here and three there and the fact is that they are able to complete their computation without making the smallest mistake. As a matter of fact, they are better at calculating what each one is due to pay or give than we should be with pen and ink.*

A final example of an ancient computing device is the abacus, consisting of a series of beads which move along rods. The abacus is not a toy. In 1947, Kiyoshi Matsuzake used a soroban (the Japanese version of the abacus) to defeat Private Tom Wood of the United States Army of Occupation, who used the most modern electro-mechanical calculating machine of the day. Their contest consisted of a series of addition, subtraction, and multiplication problems.[4]

Today our computing machines can perform many billions of operations in a second. Of course, these modern machines have far fewer moving parts than their

---

[4] The abacus in its present form was introduced into China about 1200 A.D. It exists in many different "flavors" and under several names. The Turks call it a *coulba*, the Armenians a *choreb*, and the Russians, who still use it today, call it a *stchoty*.

**Figure 1.5.** *Metallic sculpture by John Robinson.* See previous figure for additional information.

ancient progenitors. As a result, a user's finger will not become stuck in a gear, lever, or wheel. Computers today are generally safe. However, in 1981, Kenji Urada, a repairman at Kawasaki Heavy Industries in Japan, became the first person in history to be killed by a robot. His death occurred at an automobile gear processing line. The robot came up from behind and crushed him to death.

Our reliance on computers in the 1990s is quite heavy. According to scientists surveyed recently, the sudden 24-hour failure of all microprocessors on earth would result in a loss of several million lives and 100 billion dollars – even if all systems returned to normal after the 24-hour period.[5] Operations hit hardest would be finance, banking, communications, transport, factories, airplanes, emer-

---

[5] I conducted this informal survey and found that the average number of predicted lost lives was 1,400,000. (Numbers ranged from a low of one thousand to a high of five million lives lost.) The average predicted international money loss was 520 billion dollars. (Numbers ranged from a low of nine billion dollars to a high of two trillion dollars.)

gency dispatching, submarines, automobiles, and telephones.[6] It is not surprising that respondents indicated the countries most affected would be the USA and Japan.[7]

I would like to add one final note on how topics were chosen for this book. Many chapters attempt to embody the special sense of beauty that mathematicians experience when exploring complicated shapes in accessible forms that anyone can see and touch. From a personal perspective, computer graphics is a powerful vehicle for artistic expression. However it is notable that some artists and scientists have attempted to squeeze some of this beauty out of dry formulas without the aid of a computer. One early example is Dutch graphics artist M.C. Escher, who represented many complex and repeating geometrical forms by hand. Escher's preoccupation with symmetry is well known, and his periodic plane-filling patterns have been analyzed by many mathematicians. Escher's 20th-century counterpart is Russian mathematician A. T. Fomenko, whose algebraic surfaces and crystal structures are hand-drawn in mystical and surreal settings (Figure 1.1). Other fine examples of modern-day artists inspired by mathematics are John Robinson, from the United Kingdom (Figure 1.4 and Figure 1.5), and Helaman Ferguson, a Professor at Brigham Young University. Ferguson creates mathematically inspired stone sculptures as a way of conveying the beauty of theorems. His pure white marble sculptures have rather exotic-sounding names like "trefoil knots" and "horned spheres." Some resemble the twisted computer graphics forms displayed in the Color Plate section of this book. If you are interested in other examples of physical sculpture inspired by geometrical formulas you should consult the sections "Scherk's Surface" on page 363, "Products, Classroom Aids, Art, Games, Distributors" on page 384, and "Notes for the Curious" on page 371. For instance, Stewart Dickson is an artist who represents mathematical forms in plastic. The process he uses, called stereolithography, employs laser-based tools and photosensitive liquid resins which harden as they form beautiful, computer generated 3-D sculpture (Figure 1.2).

At this point you are set to proceed further in *Computers and the Imagination*. Grab a pencil and paper, and a calculator or personal computer if handy, and turn the page. If you do not have an interest in computing, there are ample thought puzzles and artistic graphics to stimulate your imagination. A quote by John Steinbeck, in collaboration with marine biologist Edward Ricketts, sets the tone for the organization of this book.

---

[6] Other areas affected by the 24-hour microprocessor failure would include: clocks and watches, household appliances, television and radio stations, organizations with a computer-based working environment, railways, air traffic control, stock markets, satellite and space equipment, elevators, military equipment, weather forecasting, and environmental control systems.

[7] When the surveyed scientists were asked to speculate about imaginative causes of the 24-hour failure, some gave both serious and wild answers. Here is a sampling: solar/astronomical activity, a biological anti-computer virus, a massive electromagnetic field resulting from an out-of-control fusion reactor, a prelude to alien invasion, a nano-mechanical anti-computer virus, an accidental firing of a new field effect weapon, computer design sabotage, divine intervention, an H bomb, and an ionized meteor.

*"The design of a book is the pattern of reality controlled and shaped by the mind of the writer. This is completely understood about poetry or fiction, but is too seldom realized about a book of facts. "*          John Steinbeck

## 1.1 For Further Reading

1.  Peterson, I. (1990*a*) Equations in Stone. *Science News.* September, 138(10): 152-154. (Describes mathematically inspired sculptures made of bronze, onyx, and marble.)

2.  Peterson, I. (1990*b*) *Islands of Truth.* Freeman: New York. (Describes recent research in mathematics and computer graphics.)

3.  Manchester, R. (1980) *Mammoth Book of Fascinating Information.* Hart: New York. (Describes extraordinary facts about commonplace objects, from automobiles to eyeglasses.)

4.  Newman, J. (1956) *The World of Mathematics.* Simon and Schuster: New York. pgs. 463-464. (Contains information on the Jesuit priest Joseph de Acosta.)

5.  Williams, M. (1990) Early Calculators, in *Computing Before Computers.* Aspray, W., ed. Iowa State University Press: Ames, Iowa. (A survey of computing technology prior to the development of the modern computer.)

6.  MacGillavry, C. (1986) The symmetry of M. C. Escher's "impossible" images. *Computers and Mathematics with Applications.* 12B(1/2): 123-138. (An overview of the Dutch artist's work, as it relates to geometric symmetry.)

7.  Fomenko, A. (1989) Visual and hidden symmetry in geometry. *Computers and Mathematics with Applications.* 17(1-3): 301-320. (Contains Fomenko's beautiful and surreal images representing mathematical objects.)

8.  Dickson, S. (1990) Manufacturing the impossible soap bubble. *IRIS Universe: The Magazine of Visual Processing.* 12: 24-29.

9.  Kurzweil, R. (1990) *The Age of Intelligent Machines.* MIT Press: Cambridge, Massachusetts. (This book covers contains information on pattern recognition, the science of art, computer-generated poetry, and artificial intelligence.)

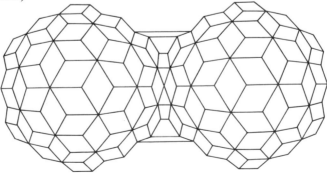

# Part II

# SIMULATION

Tromba Marina

Chapter 2

# Simulation: Introduction

"*From the standpoint of Taoist philosophy natural forms are not made but* grown, *and there is a radical difference between the organic and the mechanical. Things which are made, such as houses, furniture, and machines, are an assemblage of parts put together, or shaped, like sculpture, from the outside inwards. But things which grow shape themselves from within outwards. They are not assemblages of originally distinct parts; they partition themselves, elaborating their own structure from the whole to the parts, from the simple to the complex.*"                                      Alan Watts, *1958*

In their quest to understand the world around us, scientists turn increasingly to computer simulation.[8] Whether the system is natural or artificial, we can design simple computer models for a variety of phenomena.  Computers are already being used to simulate the tiny forces binding molecules, the operation of complex instrumentation, the support structures of huge skyscrapers, the stability of aircraft designs, the behavior of mathematical functions, and the behavior of the

---

[8] If you have no interest in actually programming a computer you may wish to skip the *Simulation* section and proceed to *Speculation*.

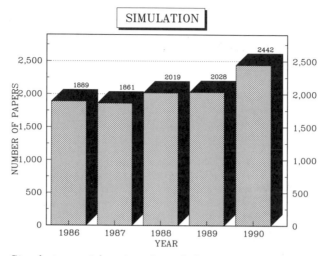

**Figure 2.1.** *Simulation articles.* A review of the world scientific literature shows the number of simulation articles hovering around 2000 for each of the years 1986 to 1990.

economy. Instead of building an expensive physical model for experimentation and testing, a mathematical model can often be substituted and a computer used for evaluation purposes.[9]

Many introductions to simulation in physics and mathematics are so formalized, so steeped in arcane terms and symbols, that it is difficult for the beginner to know how to start. Therefore my goal is to encourage students and professionals to start with the simple examples in this book which are easily implemented on a personal computer. Of all the parts of this book, *Part 1: Simulation* contains some of the simplest computer experiments to implement. Simulations such as *Growing Your Own Font, Butterfly Curves,* and *A Leaning Tower of Books* should be of interest to students wishing to quickly experiment with a few sample simulations in physics, biology, psychology, and art. The most complicated simulation to implement in this part of the book concerns molecular evolution (last chapter in *Simulation*), and you may wish to skip this section upon a first reading of this book.

Each chapter is self-contained, so that this part of the book can be used as a tutorial for motivated students. The exercises might also be used to provide additional problems for secondary school and undergraduate seminar courses. Advanced students and professionals will find new material here as well. Many suggestions for future research problems are scattered throughout the text.

---

[9] It may interest you to know that in 1989 the world's scientific journals published 2028 articles with the words "simulation" or "simulations" in the title. Figure 2.1 shows the number of papers with titles containing either of these two words for the years 1986-1990, the 1990 value estimated from data for January-June 1990. (The data for this and similar graphs in the book result from computer searches through data bases such as *Science Citation Index*.)

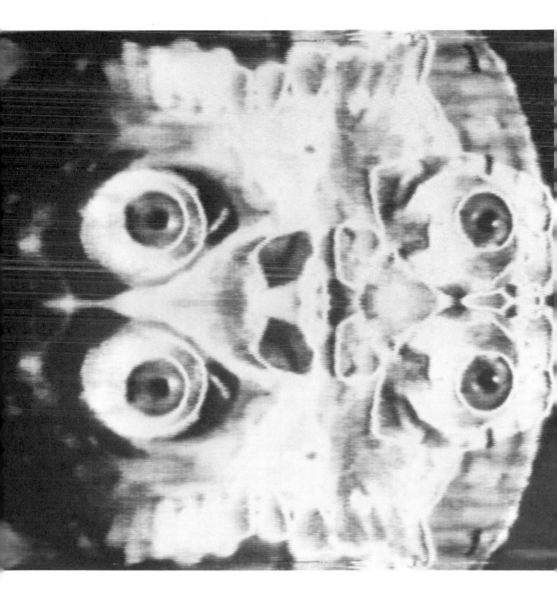

# Chapter 3

# Butterfly Curves

*"Philosophers and great religious thinkers of the last century saw evidence of God in the symmetries and harmonies around them – in the beautiful equations of classical physics that describe such phenomena as electricity and magnetism. I don't see the simple patterns underlying nature's complexity as evidence of God. I believe that is God. To behold [mathematical curves], spinning to their own music, is a wondrous, spiritual event."*

Paul Rapp, *1990*

Let us begin the **Simulation** section of this book with an introduction to a graceful,  yet easy-to-program, geometric curve which resembles a butterfly or moth. One of the most beautiful aspects of geometry is the variety of forms found in the plane algebraic and transcendental curves. Many of these curves express beauty in their symmetry, leaves and lobes, and asymptotic behavior. Butterfly curves, developed by Temple Fay at the University of Southern Mississippi, are one such class of beautiful, intricate shapes. These curves can be easily used for experimentation, even on personal computers.

**Figure 3.1.** *Butterfly Curves.* Curves produced by implementing Equation (3.1) on page 20 on an IBM 3090 mainframe. You should be able to compute and draw these curves using personal computers.

The equation for the Butterfly Curve can be expressed in polar coordinates by[10]

$$\rho = e^{\cos(\theta)} - 2\cos(4\theta) + \sin^5(\theta/12) \tag{3.1}$$

This formula describes the trajectory of a point as it traces out the butterfly's body. $\rho$ is the radial distance of the point to the origin. Pseudocode 3.1 gives an algorithmic description of how this curve can be implemented in a computer program. Figure 3.1 is a drawing made using the formula for a range of $\theta$ values (see Pseudocode 3.1). Butterfly curves with a longer period of repetition can be created using

---

[10] Polar curves are represented on a coordinate system that looks a little like a polar view of the earth, with the North Pole at the graph's center.

```
┌─────────────────────────────────────────────────────────────────────┐
│                                                                       │
│   ALGORITHM: How to Create a Butterfly Curve                          │
│  ─────────────────────────────────────────────────────────────────   │
│   OUTPUT: Plot points at locations specified by                       │
│           variables xx and yy.                                        │
│   NOTE:   Assume screen goes from 0 to 100 in x and y directions.     │
│  ─────────────────────────────────────────────────────────────────   │
│                                                                       │
│    1  pi = 3.1415;                                                    │
│    2  DO theta = 0 to 100*pi by .010;                                 │
│    3    r = exp(cos(theta))   2*cos(4*theta) + (sin(theta/12))**5;    │
│    4    x = r * cos(theta);    /* convert from polar coordinates */   │
│    5    y = r * sin(theta);                                           │
│    6    xx = (x * 6) + 50;     /* scale factors to enlarge and        │
│    7    yy = (y * 6) + 50;         center the curve */                │
│    8    IF theta = 0 THEN MovePenTo(xx,yy);                           │
│    9               ELSE DrawTo(xx,yy);                                │
│   10  END;                                                            │
│                                                                       │
└─────────────────────────────────────────────────────────────────────┘
```

**Pseudocode 3.1.** *How to create a Butterfly Curve.*

$$\rho = e^{\cos(\theta)} - 2.1 \cos(6\theta) + \sin^7(\theta/30) \qquad (3.2)$$

Other butterfly-like curves can be created by adding terms or modifying the values of the constants.

## 3.1 Stop and Think

1.  Plot the behavior of $\rho = e^{\cos(2\theta)} - 1.5 \cos(4\theta)$. How does this contrast with the standard Butterfly Curve?

2.  The $100\pi$ value for the iteration loop in Pseudocode 3.1 is actually much larger than necessary to compute a complete Butterfly Curve. That is, the curve loops back on itself when such large "theta" values are used. How is the repetition period of the butterfly dependent upon the periods of the individual summed trigonometric curves in line 3 of the program code?

## 3.2 For Further Reading

1.  Fay, T. (1989) The Butterfly Curve. *American Math. Monthly.* 96(5): 442 - 443.

2.  Lawrence, J. (1972) *A Catalog of Special Plane Curves.* Dover: New York.

3.  Whitney, C. (1990) *Random Processes in Physical Systems: An Introduction to Probability-Based Computer Simulations.* Wiley: New York.

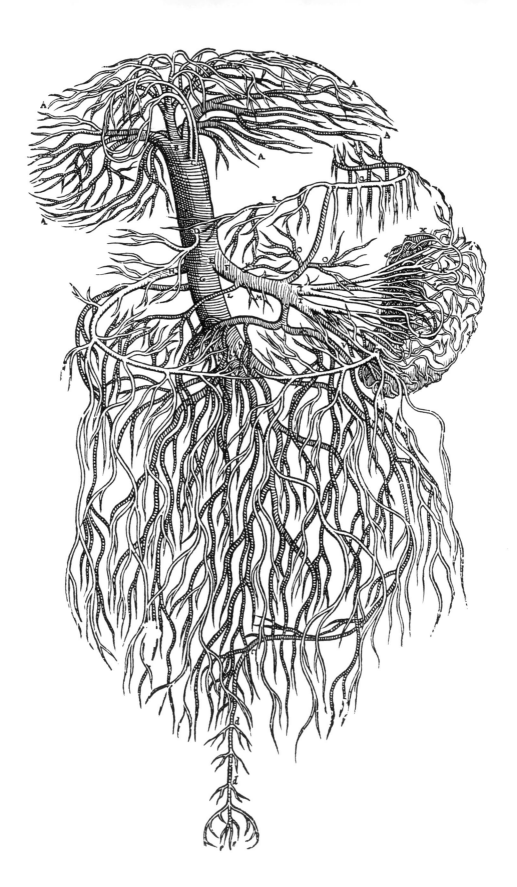

Chapter 4

# The Cancer Conundrum

*"Each of us is a mobile museum. The fluid in our bodies is a perfect replica of that ancient sea in which we grew to fruition following our liberation from the clay."*
Lyall Watson

DNA (deoxyribonucleic acid) contains the basic genetic information of all living cells. The sequences of bases of DNA (adenine, cytosine, guanine, and thymine – A, C, G, and T) hold information concerning protein synthesis as well as a variety of regulatory signals. The DNA molecule, supported by a twisting sugar-phosphate backbone, contains millions of such bases. In fact, the DNA strings in a single cell would measure up to six feet in length if stretched out, but an elaborate packing scheme coils it to fit within a cell only 1/2500 of an inch across. Special enzymes copy the genetic information. Additional enzymes check to make sure the copying process is correct. You might think of these enzymes as zealous police inspectors, and as a result of their meticulous patrol, the genetic data-processing makes only about one error in a billion copy steps.

You may be interested in studying a "game" which is an artificial genetics model. I call this game the "Cancer Conundrum" because the simple genetic rules can produce both stable behavior and uncontrolled growth of the DNA segments. I use the letters G, C, A, and T to represent the four chemical bases which make up the hereditary material of living cells. As an example, you can use just two bases, and start with a single base "G." A "C" is added to the next generation. Each succeeding generation repeats the previous two generations, in order, as you can see in the following diagram. Whenever two C's occur in a row, the sequence splits, and the generation process continues in each branch as before. This splitting is a metaphor for enzymatic cleavage at a particular recognition pattern. In the table which follows, the dash indicates a split.

```
Generation          Sequence
    1                  G
    2                  C
    3                  GC
    4                  CGC
    5                GC-CGC
    6            CGCGC CGC-CGC
    7        GC-CGCGC CGC-CGC CGC-CGC
```

In generation 5 the sequence splits due to "CC." In generation 6 the right sequence splits due to the "CC."

[[ Note that in the above system, without the concept of splitting, the number of bases in each generation would form a Fibonacci sequence. In this scenario it is easy to predict whether the $n$th base is G or C. If we associate with G the number 1 and C the number 2, the following equation defines the $n$th base of the sequence:

$$a_n = [kn] - [k(n-1)] \tag{4.1}$$

where $k = (\sqrt{5} + 1)/2$ and the bracket symbols indicate that values are to be truncated to an integer value; for example, $[x]$ is the greatest integer not exceeding $x$. ]]

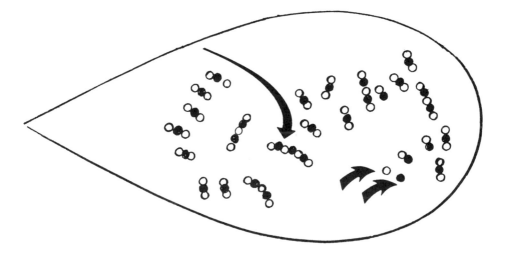

**Figure 4.1.** *Uncontrolled growth (snapshot after 8 generations).* The genetic "soup" shown here represents the growth and fragmentation of primitive genetic strands reproducing according to the rules described in this chapter. Filled and unfilled circles denote G and C respectively. The two original progenitors are denoted by the two small arrows. The large arrow indicates the largest strand (CGCGCGC) produced in 8 generations. The child strands are placed near their parents, producing a random diffusion of particles away from the progenitor.

## 4.1 Stop and Think

Questions arise in the Cancer Conundrum simulation which starts with the two bases, G and C. For example, what is the largest strand produced with no splits? Does the system grow out of control and rapidly produce super-huge strands (cancer), or does it limit itself to small chunks? What is the relative frequency of all the different species floating in the primoridal soup after $n$ generations? (A colleague, Bill McCormick, has used a computer program to determine that the 18th generation contains 8192 CGC pieces floating in the genetic "soup.") Is it possible for the strands to grow larger and larger for a few generations and then to "disintegrate" into small strands of only one or two bases?

Our genetic code is similar to a large computer program. There are about six billion bits used to describe a human, in contrast to tens of millions of bits in very complicated computer programs. Using the rules given in this chapter, how much time would it take a computer program to generate a genetic sequence as large as a human's? I hope you share my pleasure in studying a number of these systems starting with different sequences, and even introducing mutations.

You may wish to modify the Cancer Conundrum so that it becomes more of an "Evolution Game," where the different segments of genetic material may interact or combine in interesting manners. In addition, a graphics interface whereby the genetic pieces actually code for distinct computer graphics representations of primitive organisms may allow researchers to look at the primordial soup to determine how the evolution process is progressing (Figure 4.1).

The frontispiece diagram for this chapter shows a dissection of the entire portal (liver) vein system in a human, and all the veins which feed into this system from the intestines and other organs. Those of you who have sophisticated programming expertise may wish to extend the cancer game in this chapter to model the spread of the genetic segments throughout a complicated network of vessels.

## 4.2 For Further Reading

This section lists some books with information on simple biological simulations and models.

1. Langton, C. (1989) *Artificial Life*. Addison-Wesley: New York.

2. Eigen, M., Winkler, R. (1983) *Laws of the Game: How the Principles of Nature Govern Chance*. Harper Colophon: New York. (A fascinating book on all kinds of simulations in science.)

3. Dawkins, R. (1986) *The Blind Watchmaker*. W.W. Norton: New York.

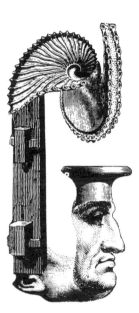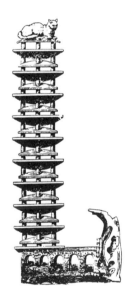

# Chapter 5

# Growing Your Own Font

*"The chess board is the world, the pieces are the phenomena of the universe, the rules of the game are what we call the laws of Nature."*
Thomas Henry Huxley, *A Liberal Education*

 ecorative type fonts have been used before the invention of moveable type to catch the eye and ornament the page. With computers it is now possible to store a great many fonts, decorative or not, and to create entirely new ones. My own favorites are "grown" on the spot. Starting from a skeletal framework entered by hand, certain growth processes will produce fonts that appear rustic, weedy, bushy or, in a word, organic.

As a glance at Figure 5.1 and the frontispiece for this chapter attests, there is no end to the inventiveness that has been employed in ornamental fonts in the past. In her delightful book, *Bizarre and Ornamental Alphabets*, Carol Grafton has catalogued all manner of whimsical letters. Some of these sport growths of one kind or another. Why not turn the computer loose to grow its own?

## 5.1 From Frame to Font

I will now present the means for doing just this. If you are interested in the science behind the process, the technique employs kinetic growth models in a two-dimensional space. Similar methods model polymerization and aggregation processes that occur far from equilibrium. This means that the user begins the growth process by defining a skeletal font of tiny adjacent dots from which growth can occur. Conceptually it is useful to think of the font as growing upon a chess board using rules which mimic certain physical growth processes. The term "growth" simply means that more dots are added next to the original dots in the skeleton. Figure 5.2 shows such frames for the letters F and E.

**Figure 5.1.** *Ornamental font from C. Grafton's collection.*

The frame for a grow-your-own font is placed upon a two-dimensional grid, the lines of the frame being strips of adjacent cells in the grid. In the computer the grid will be an array in which letter cells will contain ones (for black). Other cells will contain zeros (for white). To start the growth a black site on the grid is selected by a random number generator. The program then examines an adjacent site in the neighborhood of this one and, if the new site is not black, the program makes it so. Another random site is now selected and the procedure is repeated.[11]

The more iterations the font growing program allows, the thicker the letter becomes (see the sequence in Figure 5.3). The user may control the density and structure of the growth by employing more complicated rules. For example, a new site may be disallowed from turning black if it is surrounded by more than a certain number of occupied sites. Figure 5.4 shows an interesting but not too useful font obtained by allowing growth only at some of the tips and corners of the letters. Figure 5.5 shows a bushy letter which has encouraged growth that is downward and to the left.

[[ Up to this point, the growth I have discussed selects adjacent sites using random +1's and -1's in order to grow to the right, left, up or down in relation to the growth site. Two random numbers can be used to control the growth in the $x$ and $y$ directions, respectively. In other words, if the growth site has coordinates $(i, j)$, the first random +1 or -1 might determine whether the new site will be at $(i + 1, j)$ or at $(i - 1, j)$, while the second random number would determine a new site at $(i, j + 1)$ or at $(i, j - 1)$. But rather than use independently random

---

[11] The process (technically known to physicists as "Eden growth" or "reaction-limited monomer cluster growth") is repeated many times.

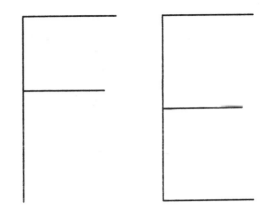

**Figure 5.2.** *Beginning skeletal frame for the letters F and E.*

-1's and +1's to control directions, you can make the present choice of +1 or -1 depend on the previous choice. (This is known as a *Markov process*. Pseudocode 5.1 shows you how to generate such numbers.) This deviation from randomness can cause the hairy fonts to favor a certain direction of growth.

The algorithm I call FONTGRO uses two arrays, *skelx* and *skely*, which hold the *x* and *y* data. The array index *i* runs from 1 to *num*, where *num* is the current number of black cells, the ones where growth has occurred. If *skelx(i)* = 6 and *skely(i)* = 5 there will be a black dot at (6,5). FONTGRO is shown in Pseudocode 5.2.

The algorithm assumes that the arrays *skelx* and *skely* already contain the points of the skeletal framework from which the font will be grown. Consequently, FONTGRO begins with a value for *num* equal to the number of points that the programmer has already used in setting up the frame. Line 2 specifies 100 generations. In other words, 100 new points will be added to the frame in the course of its elaboration into an organic-looking font. You may find this number too small for some applications; you are, of course, free to change it to suit the size of your letters.

In the next two lines a random number between 0 and 1 is selected, multiplied by *num*, rounded down and incremented by 1. This process yields a random number between 1 and *num*, effectively selecting a point in the current font to grow from.

In the next few lines, *num* is incremented and two new random numbers, *g* and *h*, are selected as the basis for the direction of the new growth. According to whether these numbers are less than 0.5 or not, the increments *xinc* and *yinc* become +1 and -1 respectively. Finally, in the last lines, the increments are added to the point with coordinates *skelx(r)* and *skely(r)* to produce a new point at *skelx(num)* and *skely(num)*. Note that for the sake of simplicity, I did not have FONTGRO check whether a newly created point happened to sit on top of one already in the growing letter. The net effect is very similar to what the algorithm would generate if it did check, however. ]]

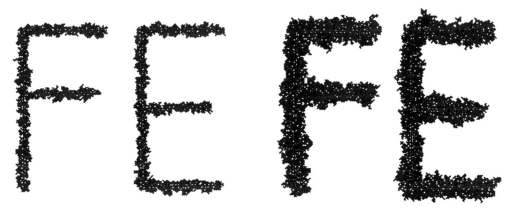

**Figure 5.3.** *An evolving font.*

A great deal of fun can be had with such fonts. For example, write a little horror story and invite some children to read a scary tale told by your computer. The title might be: **THE THING IN THE ATTIC.** Even as you read, the letters appear to be growing fatter and hairier. With any luck, you won't have to finish the story because the children will be nowhere in sight when your computer finishes the frightening title.

## 5.2 For Further Reading

1.  Grafton. C. (1981) *Bizarre and ornamental alphabets.* Dover: New York.
2.  Pickover, C. (1989) Markov aggregation on a sticky circle. *Computers in Physics.* July/August 3(4): 79-80.

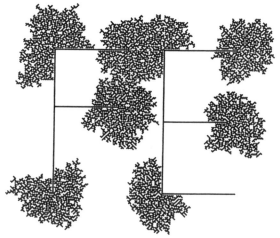

**Figure 5.4.** *Experiment using more restrictive growth rules.*

**Figure 5.5.** *Fonts with directional growth.*

3. Pickover, C. (1990) Growing your own font. *Algorithm*. July/August 1(5):11-12.

The font at the end of this chapter is an architectural font from Grafton (1981). See her book for a 3-D drawing of some of the houses constructed from these floor-plans.

```
ALGORITHM: Markov Numbers
```
Note: if p(-1), denoted by pm1, and p(+1), denoted by pp1,
are 0.5, then the usual random numbers are generated. xinc
is the increment to the x coordinate. Repeat this concept
to determine the y-direction step.

```
result = random /* result is a random number on (0,1) */
if oldxinc = -1 then if result < pm1 then xinc = -1
                                     else xinc = 1
if oldxinc = 1 then if result < pp1 then xinc = 1
                                    else xinc = -1
oldxinc=xinc
```

**Pseudocode 5.1.** *How to create Markov numbers.*

```
ALGORITHM: FONTGRO - an algorithm for growing ornamental fonts
1   num = number of points in frame
2   FOR 100 generations do
3       r = random
4       r = int (r * num) + 1
5       num = num + 1
6       g = random; h = random
7       if g < 0.5
8           then xinc(num) = xinc(num)+1
9           else xinc(num) = xinc(num)-1
10      if h < 0.5
11          then yinc(num) = yinc(num)+1
12          else yinc(num) = yinc(num)-1
13      skelx(num) = skelx(r) + xinc
14      skely(num) = skely(r) + yinc
15  END
```

**Pseudocode 5.2.** *FONTGRO - an algorithm for growing ornamental fonts.*

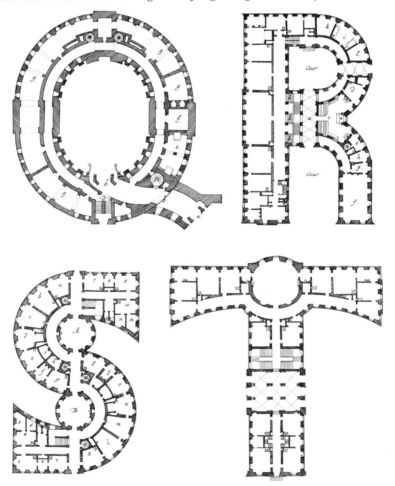

# Chapter 6

# Experiments with a Leaning Tower of Books

*"The distinction between art and science is contrived. Both are processes of discovery and both use a variety of tools and techniques."*
Computer Graphics World, *1989*

One day while walking through a library you notice a stack of books leaning over the edge of a table. It seems as if it is about to fall. A question comes immediately to mind: Would it be possible to stagger a stack of many books so that the top book would be far out into the room – say 20 or 30 feet? Or would such a stack fall under its own weight? You ask several friends, and each gives a different answer.

Simple as this question sounds, there have nonetheless been several discussions on this topic in prestigious physics journals. In this section I report on some of the remarkable findings, and encourage your involvement by including computer pseudocode. Fortunately for computer programmers, the simulation of the book-stacking is relatively easy on a personal computer.

As Jearl Walker points out in *The Flying Circus of Physics*, the stack of books will not fall if the following rule is met: the center of mass of all the books above any particular book must lie on a vertical axis that cuts through that particular book. This must be true for each book in the stack. Whether or not a stack falls can be determined by a computer simulation of a stack of books, where the

```
ALOGRITHM: Test for the stability of a leaning stack of books.
/* ------------- Data Entry ------------------------*/
Print('How many books do you wish to stack?');
Get(NumBook);
Do i = 1 to NumBook;
 Display('Enter left, right coordinates for book number',i);
 Get (left(i),right(i));
end;

/* -------Will the stack topple ? ------------------*/
Do i = 1 to NumBook-1
 /* initialize ctr. mass for all books above test book */
 CmAbove=0
 Do j = i+1 to NumBook
  CmAbove=CmAbove + (right(j)+ left(j))/2
 End   /* j */
 /* compute composite center of mass */
 CmAbove=CmAbove/(NumBook-i)
 If CmAbove > right(i) then do
   Display ('Stack topples')
   Print(i,CmAbove, right(i))
 end   /* if */
end    /* i */
```

**Pseudocode 6.1.** *Test for the stability of a leaning stack of books.*

centers of mass of the books are computed. This is easy to calculate: Assuming we are only concerned with a stack leaning in a single direction, the center of mass of a single book is simply $(r + l)/2$, where $r$ and $l$ are the left and right coordinates corresponding to the edges of each book. (For simplicity, we assume that each book has the same thickness.) The composite center of mass for an entire stack of books is the average of all the individual centers of mass. Pseudocode 6.1 outlines the necessary computation. Users enter the right and left coordinates of each book they wish to stack.

To make the problem more interesting, the user can get an idea about how sturdy the stack is by providing small lateral vibrations to each book and seeing if the stack falls. To do this simply add a small random number to each book's center of mass. Execute Pseudocode 6.1 several hundred times to see if the stack is still standing. For a slightly more complicated model, the displacement of each book's movement can be simulated by a spring undergoing simple harmonic motion. Given a slight random force $F$ applied to each book, and a force constant $k$, the displacement of the book's center of mass is given by $k = -F/x$. $k$ need not be constant for each book.

**Some Science**

Is it possible to make the stack jut out several feet? A mile? Is there any limitation as to how far the top book can be beyond the edge of the table? Several papers in the *American Journal of Physics*, and other journals, point out that there is no such limit. For example, the top book in a stack can be made to clear the table if there are 5 books in the stack (identical book sizes are assumed). For

---

ALGORITHM - Compute the harmonic series in Equation (6.1).
Determines the amount of overhang attainable with n books.

```
sum=0
Do i = 1 to n     /* n = number of books */
 sum = sum + 1/float(i)
end
sum = sum*0.5; Print(sum)
```

---

**Pseudocode 6.2.** *Compute the amount of book overhang.*

an overhang of 3 book lengths, you need 227 books! For 10 books, you need 272,400,600 books. And for 50 book lengths you need more than $1.5 \times 10^{44}$ books! Therefore, although there is no limit as to how far out one can "travel" with the book stack, a great many books are required to do so. (We exclude complications such as the earth's gravity not being constant, the effect of the moon, etc.) A formula for the amount of overhang attainable with $n$ books, in book lengths, can be used:

$$1/2(1 + 1/2 + 1/3 + \cdots + n^{-1}).  \qquad (6.1)$$

This harmonic series diverges very slowly, so a modest increase in book overhang requires many more books. This equation can be implemented in Pseudocode 6.2.

## 6.1 Stop and Think

Pseudocode 6.1 can be used as the foundation for several fascinating and educational computer games for students. For example, with a simple graphics interface two players can be presented a small group of books to stack. The players' goal is to make their stack (which appears on the screen) jut out as far as possible beyond the edge of the table without having the stack fall. They are each given a minute to arrange the books! For the scientifically minded experimenter, the program can display the exact point at which the stack was made to fall by graphically highlighting the "bad" book and by displaying the various centers of mass. If you wish to take the game further, more complicated shapes can be used, such as triangles and circles. In another experiment, the computer can "throw" down books with random positions, and only those stacks that can physically stand up (as tested by Pseudocode 6.1) will be displayed. Throw several thousand books, and see what remains on the table.

## 6.2 For Further Reading

1.  Walker, J. (1977) *The Flying Circus of Physics*. Wiley: NY.
2.  Boas, R. (1973) Cantilevered books. *American Journal of Physics*. 41: 715.
3.  Pickover, C. (1990) Some experiments with a leaning tower of books. *Computer Language*. May 7(5): 159-160.
4.  Johnson, P. (1955) Leaning tower of Lire. *American Journal of Physics*. 23: 240.
5.  Sutton, R. (1955) A problem of balancing. *American Journal of Physics*. 23: 547.

Shown facing this page is an engraving of St. Patrick's Cathedral. The spires, 330 feet tall, were finished in 1888. If you had a tower of books as high as these spires, how many feet could the books be made to travel in a horizontal direction.

Chapter 7

# Building Your Own Artificial Webs

*"If all mankind were to disappear, the world would regenerate back to the rich state of equilibrium that existed 10,000 years ago. If insects were to vanish, the environment would collapse into chaos."*

Edward O. Wilson, *1990*

A few years ago, while walking through a Connecticut woodlot, I became curious about the variety of spider web structures in the forest. Some webs were vertical, others horizontal, some large, some quite small. To understand which of these webs might be most effective in catching insects, Dr. Gary Login and I designed unusual artificial webs which are explained in the next paragraph. You can design your own computer-generated webs, as described in the "Stop and Think" section.

Spiders are one of the most diversified groups of organisms in terrestrial envi-

ronments. There are presently over 22,000 described species, and the list may easily reach 50,000 with further study. Because of their predatory nature and tremendous numbers, spiders play ecologically important roles in the food chains of many ecosystems.[12] Spider webs come in all sizes, shapes, and orientations. The largest of all webs are the aerial ones spun by tropical orb weavers of the genus *Nephila* – they can grow to 18 feet in circumference! Some spiders, such as the trap-door spider, don't even use traditional webs to capture their prey (Figure 7.1).

Studies of potential prey of various spiders provide new insight into the efficiency of webs as a function of their structures, heights, and sizes. In order to

---

[12] It may interest you to know that in 1989 the world's scientific journals published 148 articles with the words "spider" or "spiders" in the title. Figure 7.2 shows the number of papers with titles containing these words for the years 1986-1990, the 1990 value estimated from data for January-June 1990.

**Figure 7.1.** *Trap-door spider.*

learn more about the abundance and activity of prey available to spiders, and to learn about the efficiency of different webs, we constructed artificial webs made of plexiglass coated on both sides with a sticky resin called "Tanglefoot." Different sizes, positions, and locations of traps were used to simulate webs found in nature. Nine webs (five horizontal and four vertical) were placed in different habitats to simulate natural locations of ground- and tree-dwelling spiders. Horizontal traps were mounted above the ground on stakes. Vertical traps were suspended with strings and would sway slightly with the wind. Over a sampling period of two weeks, we trapped about 1400 arthropods (mostly insects). We found that for horizontal traps, the webs caught between 0.7 and 1.8 arthropods per square centimeter, and in the vertical traps the web capture ranged from 0.3 to 1.1 arthropods per square centimeter. In horizontal traps, the side of the web away from the ground captured about twice as many insects as the side toward the ground, although the diversity of insects on both sides was nearly the same.

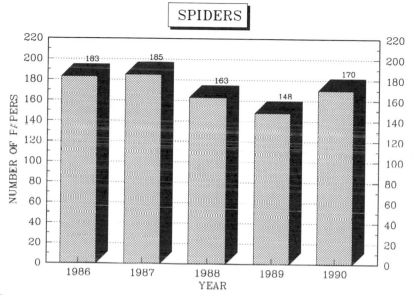

Figure 7.2. *Spider articles.* A review of the world scientific literature shows the number of spider articles hovering around 170 for each of the years 1986 to 1990.

For those of you who would like to learn about the causes of these differences, see our paper.[13]

## 7.1  Stop and Think

In order to better understand how web shapes and positions may alter their efficiency in trapping insects, you can design computer webs which simulate web orientations in nature. For example, construct a computer-drawn horizontal grid, or wireframe, and launch artificial insects with parabolic trajectories from a hypothetical ground. Your insects can be represented by little squares, circles, cubes, or spheres of different sizes. For starters, you may wish to consider a two-dimensional case where the web is simply represented as a horizontal line. "Insect" launches can be modeled using formulas for projectile motion found in introductory physics texts. [[ Here is a simple example computation for an insect jumping off a rock onto the ground. Suppose that an insect jumps upward from a rock at an angle of

---

[13] For the more entomologically-minded reader:  Diptera and Homoptera were the most common insects caught.  The breakdown is as follows:  1170 Diptera, 142 Homoptera, 52 Coleoptera, 19 Hymenoptera, 4 Orthoptera, 3 Lepidoptera, 3 Aranae, 2 Opilone.  For many more details of this study, including the insect activity according to plant microhabitat zone, see our paper referenced at the end of this section.

37 degrees to the horizontal, with a velocity of 10m/sec. The rock is 20 meters high. Where will this insect land? To solve this, resolve the initial velocity into $x$ and $y$ components. The following projectile motion equations can be used to determine the time of flight: $y = v_{0_y}t + 0.5a_yt^2$ and $v_y = v_{0_y} + at$. The variable $y$ is the height of the rock, which is 20 meters. The acceleration due to gravity $a_y$ is $9.8m/sec^2$. $v_{0y}$ turns out to be $-6m/sec$ (negative since down is positive). Knowing the time of flight, you can compute the motion in the $x$ (horizontal) direction using $x = v_xt$. In this example, the insect lands 22 meters away from the rock! ]]

1.  In your simulation, which side of the web captures more electronic insects? A "capture" may be defined as taking place every time one part of the insect body intersects a web strand.

2.  How does the web efficiency change with the spacing of the strands of the web?

3.  In your simulation, how does the web efficiency change with size and orientation of the webs? Do real spiders follow what your simulation suggests?

4.  Try introducing a velocity factor which allows the high-speed insects to rip through the web and not be captured. Our sticky plexiglass webs did not capture large beetles and other large flying insects because only a thin coat of Tanglefoot was applied. This is consistent with natural webs, which do not capture powerful or streamlined insects such as *Scarabaeidae* and *Buprestidae*.

5.  Use other curves to represent the strands of the web, e.g. sine waves, fractals, etc.

6.  Write a program that follows the recipe of construction for a typical real orb web. The details of real web construction, which involve bridges, frames, and spirals, are diagramed in Savory's *Scientific American* article. These webs are a nice form of computer art.

7.  Abnormal webs are spun by spiders under the influence of sleep-inducing drugs. The abnormality consists of the omission of the longest threads. Marijuana causes spiders to leave a large space between framework threads and peripheral turns of the internal spirals. Benzedrine causes the spider to produce an erratic spiral, and scopolamine causes the spiral to run smoothly but in false directions (Witt, 1954). Write a program to mimic these effects. (See "Notes for the Curious" on page 371 for additional information on spiders.)

## 7.2 For Further Reading

1.  Login, G., Pickover, C. (1977) Sticky traps and spider prey. *Carolina Tips*. June 15(7): 25-28.

2.  Bristowe, W. (1958) *The World of Spiders*. Collins: London.

3.  Staples, R., Allington, W. (1959) The efficiency of sticky traps in sampling epidemic populations of the eriophyid mite (Aceria Tulipae K.), vector of wheat streak mosaic virus. *Annals of the Entomological Society of America.* 52: 159-164.

4.  Turnbull, A. (1973) Ecology of the true spiders (Araneomorphae). *Annual Review of Entomology.* 305-348.

5.  Savory, T. (1960) Spider webs. *Scientific American,* April 202: 115.

6.  Witt, P. (1954) Spider webs and drugs. *Scientific American.* December 191: 80.

# Chapter 8

# A Wiring Problem

*"Rarely [do I solve problems] through a rationally deductive process. Instead I value a free association of ideas, a jumble of three or four ideas bouncing around in my mind. As the urge for resolution increases, the bouncing around stops, and I settle on just one idea or strategy."*

Heinz Pagels, *Dreams of Reason*

The task of interconnecting electrical components in circuits is an important one, and a problem which computers are increasingly being used to solve. I have studied the following wiring problem, not with a computer, but rather with 450 scientists in order to test their ability to solve a seemingly simple looking geometric problem. The problem is stated as follows. Given the six boxes (represented by enclosed regions A, B, C) in Figure 8.1, is it possible to connect box A to A, B to B, and C to C with lines which do not cross or go outside the surrounding frame? Your lines may be curvy, but they cannot touch or cross each other, or touch any other line in the drawing. In my study, I asked people to time themselves as they attempted to arrive at a solution. About twenty percent of the scientists surveyed said this problem was impossible to solve. Figure 8.2 indicates the number of seconds it took the other 80% to solve the problem as a function of each person's age. The problem is in fact solvable, and the solution is left as an exercise for you. If you cannot solve the problem, don't think about it for a day, and then return to the problem. Many of the people I tested found it easier to solve this on their second attempt a day later. A computer could probably solve this class of problems faster than a human; however, humans have one advantage in that they have the ability to discard bad attempts rather quickly. (See "Notes for the Curious" on page 371 for additional information on wire problems.)

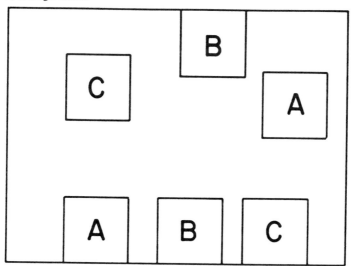

**Figure 8.1.** *Connections.* Is it possible to connect the boxes without crossing lines? Interestingly, many scientists surveyed could not solve this problem.

## 8.1 Stop and Think

1. Write a computer program to randomly place squares within Figure 8.1, in order to create new and unusual wiring problems.

2. Psychologists have long been interested in the relationship between visualization and the mechanisms of human reasoning. What is the significance of the fact that people find the puzzle easier to solve after returning to it a day later? Is there any correlation in a person's ability to solve the puzzle with sex, profession, artistic ability, etc.?

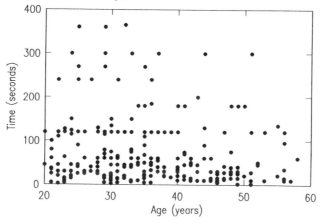

Time vs Age

**Figure 8.2.** *Time vs Age.* Results of the wiring puzzle survey. Each dot represents a single person.

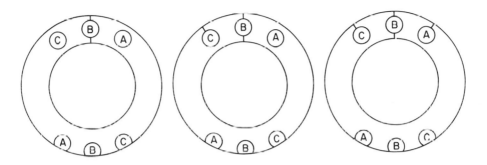

**Figure 8.3.** *Wiring on a washer.* Which of the above puzzles are possible to solve? Try to connect shape A to shape A, shape B to shape B, and shape C to shape C without crossing lines.

3.  As an additional exercise, consider the problems shown in Figure 8.3. Which of these wiring puzzles, if any, are possible to solve?

The frontispiece figure, as well as the figure below, show examples of Celtic art — ancient "wiring problems" where interlacing bands often form one continuous line.

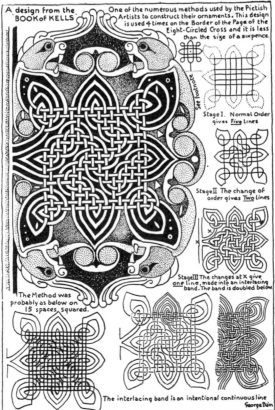

Chapter 9

# Desktop Evolution

*"The earth of 4 billion years ago was an RNA world, in which RNA molecules carried out all the processes of life without the help of either proteins or DNA. "*                               M. Waldrop, *1989*

*"'These are the main simulation computers,' Copernick said. 'Each of these can simulate the entire life-cycle of an organism. With a fifty-gigahertz clock, I can take a human being from a fertilized cell to an octogenarian in eleven hours. They are our most important single tool we use in bioengineering.' "*                               Leo A. Frankowski, *Copernick's Rebellion*

The simulation which follows will be the most difficult in the *Simulation* section

for you to implement. If you are not interested in the complexities of genetic structures and sequences, you should probably skip to the next chapter. Here the purpose is to give an informal background to several computer experiments which model the evolution of primitive biological structures. In particular, the experiments start with artificial chains of RNA (ribonucleic acid) with random sequence. RNA is described in more detail later. A computer program can gradually introduce mutations and allow users to observe the resultant folded RNA sequences and connections. The simulations here are obviously very simple models for the complex processes which actually occurred through biochemical evolution; however, the results do provide interesting educational insights and a stimulus for fascinating future experiments.

To understand the origin and evolution of life at the molecular level is a fundamental pursuit which, among other things, may help to provide insight into the remarkable panoply of living forms on earth today. Not too long ago inquiry into

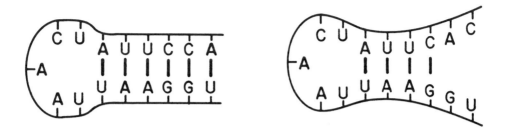

**Figure 9.1.** *RNA stability.* Stability of RNA depends on how well a strand bonds to itself, which depends in turn on the extent to which the two sections of strand are composed of complementary base sequences. These bonds, which connect adjacent strands like rungs on a ladder, are called hydrogen bonds. In this figure, the molecule at left is more stable than the molecule at right, which has fewer complementary base pairs.

the molecular genesis of living things was considered to be a matter of pure armchair speculation, but with scientific advances made in the last 20 years, at least some of the steps in the origin of biomolecules can be simulated in the laboratory. In the present section, computer simulations with accompanying graphics provide a means with which to simulate and understand some of these processes.

## Background

Nucleic acids, such as DNA (deoxyribonucleic acid) and RNA (ribonucleic acid),

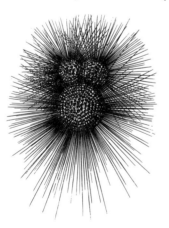

contain the basic genetic information of all life forms (for background, see "The Cancer Conundrum" on page 23.) This information is expressed as a sequence of four different chemical bases. In this chapter, single-stranded RNA structures are the biomolecules under investigation. RNA's four bases are designated G, C, A and U – standing for guanine, cytosine, adenine, and uracil. These molecules are thought by some to be the most primitive "life" forms that first evolved: they spontaneously fold into complex secondary structures, and reproduce given the right conditions. Today we know that the folding patterns of RNA affect their function and survival in the presence of enzymatically or biochemically harsh conditions.

## Biochemical Evolution

The period of chemical evolution on earth, whereby organic compounds gradually accumulated in the primitive seas, probably began about 4,000 million years ago. Hydrogen cyanide (HCN) is central to most of the reaction pathways

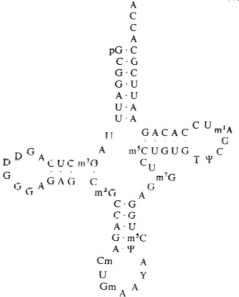

**Figure 9.2.** *A folded molecule of an 80-base RNA sequence from a bacterium.* Non-standard characters, such as Ψ and m⁷G, stand for slight variations on the usual G, C, A, U bases.

leading to abiotic formation of these simple nitrogen-containing organic compounds. HCN is readily formed by reactions such as:

$$2CH_4 + N_2 \rightarrow 2HCN + 3H_2 \tag{9.1}$$

$$CO + NH_3 \rightarrow HCN + H_2O \tag{9.2}$$

HCN is the precursor of organic molecules such as purines and pyrimidines, which make up molecules such as DNA and RNA.

It has been postulated by a number of researchers that RNA was the original protogene, the first informational macromolecule, and the first structure at the threshold of life. The arguments for this hypothesis are too many for this section to discuss, but it is interesting that researchers today our attempting to induce RNA strands, in a suitable environment, to reproduce themselves, and undergo adaptation by evolution. In addition, the genetic information of many viruses lies encoded in a single-stranded RNA molecule.

**RNA Folding**

The folding of the linear RNA polymer into secondary structures is a consequence of hydrogen bonding between complementary base pairs (G binds to C strongly, with three hydrogen bonds; A binds to U with two hydrogen bonds). The stability of the folded RNA structure depends on how well the bases at one section bond to bases at another (Figure 9.1). The final folded structure in turn is thought to influence RNA's function and interaction with proteins, and to protect RNA from destruction by certain enzymes. Figure 9.2 shows a typical folded structure for a bacterial RNA strand containing 80 bases. The molecule is called transfer RNA since it transfers amino acids during the

**Figure 9.3.** *Several typical artificial molecules of length around 80 units.* These have evolved after about 5000 generations of simulated evolution. The dots represent bases. Dots connected across the chain are those which are bonded.

process of protein synthesis. The endpiece figure for this chapter shows a folded RNA strand for a much longer sequence (see "Stop and Think" on page 56 for details).

In this chapter I outline a simple program used to perform experiments in molecular evolution by generating artificial RNA sequences, introducing mutations, and allowing the user to observe the folded RNA sequences and connections. The program is a teaching tool allowing researchers and students to follow the evolution of hypothetical RNA molecules of their own choosing in both a qualitative and quantitative fashion.

An RNA sequence consisting of G, C, A, and U bases serves as input to a folding program. How may possible RNA folding patterns exist? The total number of the theoretical base pairs and their likely topological combinations are immense, and the actual number can be written as:

$$\frac{N!}{2^{N/2}\left(\dfrac{N}{2}\right)!} \tag{9.3}$$

where $N$ is the number of bases. For example, a strand with four bases numbered 1, 2, 3, and 4 can fold into three different fully-bonded structures (1 bonds 4, 2 bonds 3 vs. 1 bonds 2, 3 bonds 4 vs. 1 bonds 3, 2 bonds 4). Not all of these bonding patterns, however, are biochemically possible. Therefore, we must introduce several biochemical constraints to allow the computer to narrow down the immense number of possibilities to just a few realistic folded molecules.

***Rule 1) Steric Constraints*** - Because the formation of base pairs between different sections of an RNA strand can only be accomplished by folding the chain on a plane, loops will naturally result (see Figure 9.2 and Figure 9.3). However, we place the constraint that no base pairs may be bonded if they are fewer than five bases apart, since this would form too "strained" a molecule. In other words, if loops form, they must consist of five or more bases.

***Rule 2) Planarity*** - The molecule is kept planar. We are interested only in secondary structures. Researchers often assume that the nucleic acid secondary-structure interactions are so large that they will strongly constrain possible tertiary structures.

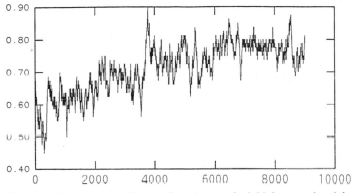

**Figure 9.4.** *GC fluctuations.* Fluctuations in a typical 80-base molecule's GC percentage (*y*-axis) as a function of time.

*Rule 3) Complementarity* - Only G-C pairs and A-U pairs are considered. Other bonds are not biochemically favored and will not "stick" together. (This rule can be broken if you desire, as described later.)

*Rule 4) Cooperativity* - A bond will be made only if several adjacent bonded pairs can also be made. One fairly realistic way of implementing this constraint is to assign point values to different patterns. Specifically, if one section of bases is to stick to another, a 6-point rating must be achieved where the stronger G-C bonds are given a point value of 2 and weaker A-U bonds are given a point value of 1. For example, CGA at one part of the molecule bonding with GCU at another part of the molecule yields only 5 points, and therefore the connections are not made.

### Assessment of Overall Goodness of a Structure

Once a folded structure has been generated, how can you determine if the final structure is better than another? When producing and checking the structures which evolve through time, you must estimate the relative stability of a structure. In general, the more bonds the better the structure. A fairly accurate measure can be computed if the bases are considered two pairs at a time. For example, two adjacent GC pairs in a row are significantly more stable than two GC base pairs separated by an AU base pair. Cantor and Schimmel (1980) give a complete listing of stability values. These relative thermodynamic values are summed for an entire RNA structure and are followed and plotted as a function of time and mutation.[14]

### Programming Details: How to Start

The program may use any real or artificially generated (random) RNA sequences as input. The user enters a threshold value for the acceptance of a cooperative interaction (see Rule 4). I typically use a point value of 6 since it excludes many low-energy structures and predicts many published secondary structures. G-U pairs, which can sometimes occur

---

[14] You can estimate the relative stability of a structure by incrementing a "goodness" value $g$ by a different amount for each bonded pair. If there are two adjacent A bases at one section of the strand bonded to two U bases at another, $g$ gets incremented by 1.2 units ($g = g + 1.2$), since these bonds are energetically favorable. More favorable are AU to UA pairs ($g = g + 1.5$). For GC to CG, $g = g + 4.3$. For GG to CC, $g = g + 4.8$. For all other permitted pairs, such as CA to GU, $g$ is incremented by 2.1.

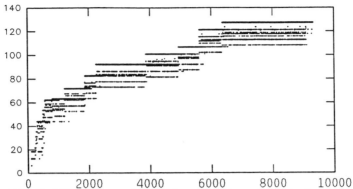

**Figure 9.5.** *Stability of a typical 80-base structure through time.* In this figure, the higher the value on the *y*-axis, the more stable the structure.

in nature, may be permitted if the user desires (i.e., Rule 3 can be broken). If a random sequence is selected, the user may skew the random distribution to favor the occurrence of one base over another in an artificial input sequence.

Mutation capability can be enabled in the program, and this permits the introduction of random mutations at random positions in the strand. For example, an A may be changed to a G somewhere in the strand. A mutation is incorporated if the RNA is thermodynamically more stable than the non-mutated form. (The user can also have the mutation incorporated if it is merely neutral rather than favorable.) The program cycles through a user-determined number of mutation trials. In the program, this parameter is called "years" to give the user the valid sense that these mutations take place through time. The user is able to monitor the mutation positions and thermodynamic stability as a function of time, as well as the G-C percentage as a function of time.

In a computer program, the input sequence is scanned by a double do-loop so that bases $b_i$ and $b_j$ in the molecule are selected and tested to determine if they fulfil Rules 1-4. This approach is capable of catching both nearby and long-range pairings. In order to determine whether this simple approach gives a reasonable estimate of secondary structure, I tested the program on several sequences in the literature, and my folded structures were usually identical to the published ones.

### Observations

As would be expected, through the gradual introduction of mutations, a variety of complicated and conspicuous folding patterns spontaneously result from a given input sequence, and these consist of hairpin structures reminiscent of true biological molecules. While the artificial RNAs resemble natural RNAs only in spirit rather than details, a number of remarkable similarities exist. For example, for $N = 80$ (where $N$ is the number of bases) with mutations, three- and four-loop patterns often result, and these are forms which sometimes resemble real RNA structures called transfer RNAs (Figure 9.2) Another similarity is that both the artificial RNAs (e.g. those shown in Figure 9.3) and bacterial transfer RNAs have about 25 percent of their bases hydrogen bonded. Also, many of these artificial "evolved" RNAs contain a short tail in the last 3 or 4 bases; this is reminiscent of the 3- or 4-base long protrusion from the acceptor sequence in natural transfer RNAs. On the other hand, if the intial random RNAs are folded, *without mutations*, these kinds of patterns do not form. Therefore, mutations are necessary to form these more life-like structures. The fascinating aspect of this game is how closely it reflects a certain aspect of reality. Random substitutions and structures that "win" in the simu-

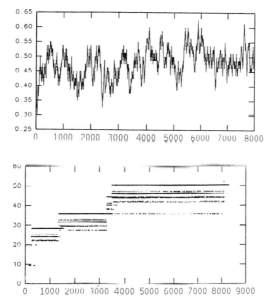

**Figure 9.6.** *GC fluctuations and stability for 80 bases.* A) (Top) Another typical example of the fluctuations in an 80-base molecule's GC percentage (*y* axis) as a function of time (see Figure 9.4). B) (Bottom) Stability plot for A.

lation are the very ones that have also "won" in evolution. In pre-biotic conditions, these folding patterns were particularly resistant to being broken down and were therefore advantageous.

Let me list some additional observations. If the user starts with an RNA sequence which has slightly more G's and C's for $N = 80$) than occur in a random sequence, then the sequence has better pairing and the GC content continues to rise slightly through time (and through the introduction of mutations). Starting from purely random sequences, for $N = 80$, the GC content seems to rise to a lesser extent through time. Note that it is thought that GC-rich strands were the first to arise spontaneously in pre-biotic conditions. Another observation is that most mutations don't help, and are discarded. Also note that if neutral mutations are allowed, there are more changes in the bases through time. For $N = 1000$, with a purely random sequence, there is a definite upward GC trend through time.

Some interesting questions come to mind: Do the RNA structures evolve to a final energetically "best" form where additional mutation does not improve the stability of the molecule? If so, how long does it take to reach this final "omega" point? Or do the molecules simply get better and better with time? The answer is that with $N = 80$, and with GC content initially slightly favored, the omega point is reached after about 5000 to 7000 generations. The resulting structures often contain 3 (and sometimes 4) hairpin loops. When starting with a purely random sequence, an omega point is still around 5000 generations, but only 2 hairpin loops are usually formed.

Figure 9.3 shows several typical 80-base molecules which have evolved after about 5000 generations. Figure 9.4 shows the change in GC percentage over time for an 80-base molecule. "0.5" on the *y*-axis indicates equal amounts of G's or C's compared with A's or T's. For this particular simulation, GC content was slightly favored initially. Why is the plot jagged? The evolution program may introduce a G or C (causing a momentary upward spike on the chart), but then the connection may be discarded if the molecule is not thermodynamically better off than its predecessors in the simulation. The plot therefore gives a record of the program's "attempt" to evolve a molecule, even though some of the attempts are discarded. Note that there is a gradual rise in G/C content with a final plateau around 75% in Figure 9.4

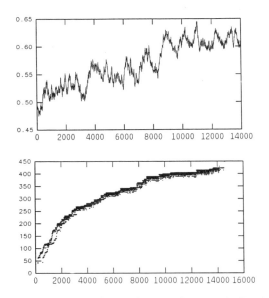

**Figure 9.7.** *GC fluctuations and stability for 400 bases.* A) (Top) Fluctuations in a typical 400-base molecule's GC percentage (*y*-axis) as a function of time. B) (Bottom) Stability plot for A.

Figure 9.5 shows how stable the structures are though time. If you have a background in biochemistry, Figure 9.5 shows the thermodynamic "goodness" of the molecule which gives a relative measure of the free energy (in units of negative kcal). On this chart, the higher the number, the more

stable the structure. Notice a rapid initial rise in the curve as the molecule quickly finds good connections. Sometimes the program will introduce a mutation in an already-bonded base and this configuration is discarded. This causes a momentary decrease in the stability, which is in turn reflected by a transient decrease in the plot. The various plateaus in Figure 9.5 indicate locally stable configurations in the molecule's evolution. For comparison, Figure 9.6 and Figure 9.7 show charts for $N = 80$ and $N = 400$ starting from a random initial sequence (GC not initially favored).

This chapter can only be viewed as introductory and speculative; however, it is hoped that the techniques will provide useful tools and stimulate future, more sophisticated, studies in the generation of life-like molecular structures produced by relatively simple generating rules. Perhaps computer simulations such as these may help scientists better understand the fundamental rules underlying the apparent complexity of biochemical structures, since they can now visualize, predict, and define some of these shapes in precise scientific terms.

## 9.1 Stop and Think

[[ A provocative problem for future research is to start with different statistical distributions of bases (Gaussian, Brownian, etc.) and determine what folded structures evolve. In addition, students and teachers may wish to model the initial artificial sequence as a Markov process. For example, consider a sequence of 1's and 0's which represent GC and AT pairs. A Markov model is easily achieved with a computer program using binary values $\{B_i, \ i = 1,2,3, \ldots , N\}$ where the 0/1 sequence is not "completely random" but can be described as a stationary Markov process with the transition matrix $P$:

$$P = \begin{bmatrix} P_0 & 1 - P_0 \\ 1 - P_1 & P_1 \end{bmatrix}$$

(9.4)

$P_0$ and $1 - P_0$ are the probabilities that $B_i$ is equal to zero or one, respectively, if $B_{i-1}$ is equal to zero. $P_1$ and $1 - P_1$ are the probabilities that $B_i$ is equal to one or zero, respectively, if $B_{i-1}$ is equal to one. When $(P_0, P_1 \neq 0.5)$ the data contain correlations since the values of $B_i$ depend on the values at $B_{i-1}$. The modeling of genetic sequences by Markov processes has been mentioned previously (Pickover, 1987). The conversion of genetic sequences to a binary waveform and subsequent signal processing analysis has been discussed in the literature (Pickover, 1984). ]]

Note that the evolution process described here did not involve the concept of a *population* of RNA molecules that interact, nor does the population size increase with time. It would be interesting for you to incorporate these ideas into your simulations. (See "Notes for the Curious" on page 371 for additional information on genetics.)

The endpiece figure for this chapter is a folded RNA sequence for a long RNA strand from the bacterium *E. coli*. 1,542 bases are represented. The diagram is courtesy of R. Gutell. For further reading see: Woese, C., Winker, S., Gutell, R. (1990) Architecture of ribosomal RNA. *Proceedings of the National Academy of Sciences.* November 87: 8467-8471.

## 9.2 For Further Reading

1. Cantor, C., Schimmel, P. (1980) *Biophysical Chemistry, Part III.* W. H. Freeman: San Francisco.

2. Eigen, M., Winkler, R. (1983) *Laws of the Game. How the Principles of Nature Govern Chance.* Harper Colophon: New York. (A fascinating book on all kinds of simulations in science.)

3. Pickover, C. (1991) DNA and protein tetragrams: biological sequences as tetrahedral movements. (IBM RC 16522). Request copies from: ITIRC, Irene Sacco, 500 Columbus Avenue, Thornwood, NY 10594. Also see: Pickover, C. (1987) DNA Vectorgrams: representation of cancer gene sequences as movements along a 2-D cellular lattice. *IBM J. of Research and Development.* 31: 111-119; Pickover, C. (1984) Frequency representations of DNA sequences: Application to a bladder cancer gene. *J. Molecular Graphics.* 2: 50; Pickover, C. (1990) On genes and graphics. *Speculations in Science and Tech.* 12(1): 5-15. Pickover, C. (1984) Computer-drawn faces characterizing nucleic acid sequences. *J. Molecular Graphics.* 2: 107-110.

4. Tinoco, I., Borer, P., Dengler, B., Levine, M., Uhlenbeck, O., Crothers, D., Gralla, J. (1973) Improved estimation of secondary structure in ribonucleic acid. *Nature New Biol.* Nov. 246: 40-41.

5. Waldrop, M. (1989) Catalytic RNA wins chemistry Nobel prize. *Science.* Oct. 246:325.

6. Pickover, C. (1990) Some experiments in molecular evolution. *Speculations in Science and Technology.* 13(3): 181-191.

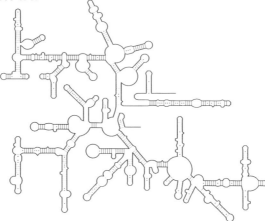

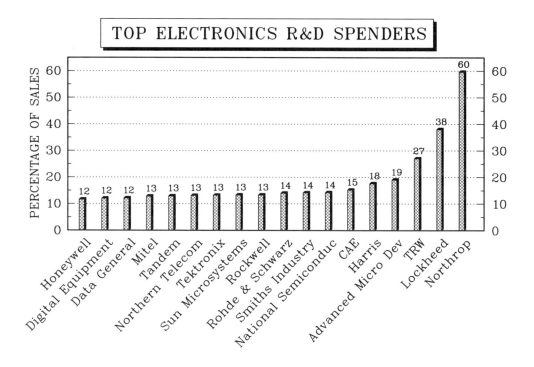

**TOP ELECTRONICS R&D SPENDERS**

Chapter 10

# Interlude: Research and Development

*[Except for a few industries such as computers,] the relationship between R&D intensity of industries and profit growth is generally insignificant.*
Graham Morbey, business consultant

As a result of technological developments such as the transistor, integrated circuit, and microprocessor, the United States dominated electrotechnology since the 1940s. Today many of the commonly used measures of successful research and development – total paper citations, overall R&D spending, and number of patents – indicate a rough parity with Japan. All of the companies on the chart shown here are U.S. companies, except for CAE (Canada), Rhode & Schwarz (Germany), Northern Telecom (Canada) and Mitel (Canada). You should compare this chart with the chart in "Interlude: Research and Development" on page 101 which shows the top spenders in terms of U.S. dollars rather than percentage of sales. Data for this chart comes from: Kaplan, G., Rosenblatt, A. (1990) The expanding world of R&D. *IEEE Spectrum.* October 27(10): 33.

# Part III

# SPECULATION

Organo Portatile

# Chapter 11

# Speculation: Introduction

"*Every man gets a narrower and narrower field of knowledge in which he must be an expert in order to compete with other people. The specialist knows more and more about less and less and finally knows everything about nothing.*"
                                                                    Konrad Lorenz

"*Descended from monkeys? My dear let us hope that is not true! But if it is true, let us hope that it not become widely known!*"
         The wife of the Bishop of Worcester, upon hearing Charles Darwin's theory of evolution through natural selection

This part of the book presents speculations by a number of scientists on various topics. In fact, all of the informal surveys within *Speculation* present the answer to various questions that I posed to approximately sixty interested scientists, lawyers, engineers, technicians, and programmers. Contributions were solicited through personal contact and through electronic mail.

The purpose of these speculative chapters is to provide entertainment, education, and stimuli for future listmaking. This section can be viewed as part of a series of speculative survey articles and books in science and computing (see references). Some of the international contributors are from research and development laboratories and have their doctorates in chemistry, mathematics, computer science, physics, or the humanities. You are forewarned that since the number of contributors was small, and these respondents were primarily localized to one laboratory, this survey will not represent the views of the scientific community as a whole. I urge you to experiment by composing your own lists, which will no doubt differ from the ones presented here. Note also that opinions expressed in this part of the book are representative of the individual scientists surveyed, and do not represent the opinions of any organization or company.

## 11.1 For Further Reading

1. *Speculations in Science and Technology*. A journal filled with interesting speculative papers in the physical, mathematical, biological, medical and engineering sciences. Science and Technology Letters, PO Box 81, Northwood, Middlesex HA6 3DN England.

2. *21st Century Science and Technology*. A journal dedicated to providing information on advanced technologies and science policies. *21st Century Science*, 60 Sycolin Road, Suite 203, Leesburg, VA 22075.

3. Platt, C. (1989) *When You Can Live Twice as Long, What Will You Do?* William Morrow: New York.

4. Feingold, S. (1989) *Futuristic Exercises: A Workbook for Emerging Lifestyles and Careers in the 21st Century and Beyond*. Garrey Park Press: Maryland.

5. Mel, B., Omohundro, S., Robinson, A., Skiena, S., Thearling, K., Robison, A., Young, L., Wolfram, S. (1988) Tablet: A personal computer in the year 2000. *Communications of the ACM*. 31(6): 639-646.

6. Pickover, C. (1990) Who are the ten most influential scientists in history? *The History and Social Science Teacher*. 25(3): 158-161.

7. Luke, T., Thearling, K., Skiena, S., Robision, A., Omohundro, S., Mel, B., Wolfram, S. (1988) Academic computing in the year 2000. *Academic Computing*. May/June 1-13: 8.

Chapter 12

# A Soda-Can-Sized Super-Super Computer

*"This is my prediction for the future: whatever hasn't happened will happen, and no-one will be safe from it. "*
          J.B.S. Haldane

*"Why, sometimes I've believed as many as six impossible things before bre-akfast. "*
          Lewis Carroll

This section presents speculations by a number of scientists on the scientific and social impact of a tiny computer with near-infinite computational power and memory.

If humankind were given a soda-can-sized computer with near-infinite computational power and memory – free of charge to all individuals who requested such a device – how would humanity be affected from both a scientific and sociological standpoint? The precise question I posed to scientists is stated in the following:

*If there existed a soda-can sized computer with infinite memory and infinite speed, what would be the scientific and sociological impact of such a machine? Would there be tremendous scientific gains within a year of distributing this computer, or would science plod along at its current rate? What fields would benefit? How would mankind change?*

*In formulating your opinion, please consider the following: the computer is given to every individual who requests it, free of charge. The computer is programmed in a standard language such as Fortran or C. Standard peripherals can be attached. I/O speeds are infinite. Of course, peripherals such as printers and displays and networks work at standard rates. No special graphics hardware comes with the machine.*

There was no universal agreement on whether or not tremendous scientific gains would be made in one year, but given five years, a majority of the respondents felt that there would be large scientific gains. Some researchers were not confident that such a computer would be good for humanity. As expected, many respond-

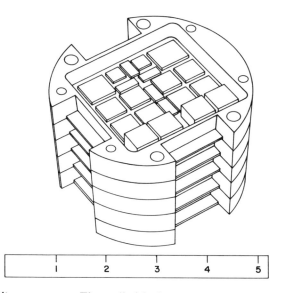

**Figure 12.1.** *Aladdin processor.* The cylindrical, compact Aladdin digital processor, which will achieve one billion floating point operations per second processing speed in a cylindrical volume only 4 inches in diameter and six inches long.

ents suggested that various supercomputing applications would flourish. Also, many of those surveyed noted that the soda-can supercomputer is not constrained at all by programming efficiency. Future programmers need only precisely define a method, any method, to solve a problem. For example, problems with an iterative solution could be calculated to arbitrarily fine precision in arbitrarily short time periods. Since the soda can computer will be I/O (peripheral) constrained to current technologies, the new computer is most naturally targeted for computation intensive applications.

It is interesting to point out that the notion of consolidating a large amount of processing power within a soda-can-sized enclosure is not entirely fanciful. The February 1990 edition of *SIGNAL*, the Official Publication of the Armed Forces Communication and Electronic Association, contains a picture of the Aladdin digital processor. It resembles a soda can and is intended to achieve 1 billion floating point operations per second processing speed in a cylindrical volume only 4 inches in diameter and 6 inches long. A rough sketch of the computer in shown in Figure 12.1. Another interesting example of impressive technology is a device called "Deep Thought." The hardware "heart" of this recently designed chess computer fits on a circuit board the size of a large pizza. It has two processors which can search 500,000 positions per second. In 1989, Deep Thought defeated grandmaster Bent Larson, a former contender for the world chess title.

You may also be interested to know that in 1989 the world's scientific journals published about 100 articles with the words "supercomputer" or "supercom-

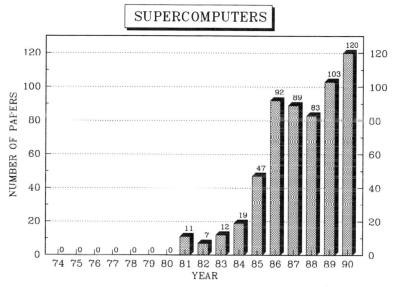

**Figure 12.2.** *Supercomputer articles.* A review of the world scientific literature shows the number of supercomputer articles growing rapidly after 1980.

puters" in the title. Figure 12.2 shows the number of papers with titles containing the word "supercomputer" for the years 1974-1990.

Survey contributors noted that this computer would be of interest in neural network research. To create a neural network, a precise description of a single node (neuron) and how it relates to neighboring nodes (synapse model) is provided. The network could be iterated to whatever complexity is desired; the complexity itself could be made flexible. This gives researchers a "brain the size of a planet in a soda can." The memory available gives humanity a massive data base (for example, the entire Library of Congress) rapidly searchable for any desired knowledge.

You will find no conclusion in this chapter. However, humankind is moving rapidly to the point where straightforward technological advances − not to mention exotic advances such as nanotechnology and biomolecular computers − could provide us with a machine very like the one described in this article. In some ways, the Aladdin computer is the first step towards the hand-held super-super computer with near-infinite speed and near-infinite memory. On the other hand, some have pointed out that true expert systems which simulate complex decisions across many disciplines are resistant to computerization. As one scientist put it, "No amount of speed or memory is going to make an iota of difference in creating the software that will be able to accomplish these heroic feats of the mind."

## 12.1  General, Commonly Reported Answers

What follows is a condensed list of some of the predictions held in common by a significant number of the respondents and deemed to have major impact on humankind.

1. Numerical weather prediction capabilities are enhanced.
2. Certain robotic hardware is enhanced.
3. Computer industry is destroyed or drastically changed.
4. Software industry flourishes.
5. Military use flourishes.
6. Various artificial intelligence applications flourish.

## 12.2  Summary Statements on Impact Assessment

The following is a list of other impacts of the machine on science and the world as a whole. Where possible, these predictions are sorted by subject matter. Naturally, many of the subject areas overlap.   Many of the predictions are explained or justified in the later sections of this chapter which give a sampling of detailed responses. Predicting the future is not a well-defined task, and you may take exception to some of the imaginative answers. Nonetheless, it is certain that such a device would have major impact on industrialized societies.

### 12.2.1  Sociopolitical Impact

1. Current cryptographic systems are destroyed, thereby destroying world banking.
2. India flourishes.  (The explanation for this is given in the detailed response section.)
3. There is a diversion of funds from information processing activities to information gathering.
4. Many book, and other paper, publishers find difficulty surviving.
5. There are enhancements to education, using digital images of historical teachers. (The explanation for this is given in the detailed response section.)
6. Robots substitute for humans in many economically important functions.
7. Humans become extinct. (The explanation for this is given in the detailed response section.)
8. There are cyborg-like humans, with can-computer implanted in abdomen.
9. There are highly effective assignment of crews and resources to airline flights.
10. Foreign language translation skyrockets.

11. There is a decay of society into video game addicts.

12. Demographics change as more people work from home.

13. Military confiscates soda can computers.

14. There is a destruction of primitive and indigenous cultures.

15. There is an enhanced stock market efficiency, with accompanying changes. Arbitrage advantages vanish.

16. There is multi variate real-time forecasting (weather, stocks, wars).

17. Economy is guided to optimal use.

18. Postal system is eliminated or severely reduced.

19. There is extensive espionage and counterespionage.

20. There is an establishment of a police state that can keep track of the population from a centralized location.

21. Paper and coin currency is abolished.

22. There are totally synthetic movies.

23. Photographs are no longer admissible as evidence in court because they are so easily faked.

24. There is an immediate and major impact on games.

25. Hypertext novels flourish.

26. Sports gambling flourishes.

27. Education systems are revolutionized – less stress on memorization.

### 12.2.2 Programming/Information Impact

1.  Research on algorithm optimization declines. There will be no more papers in SIGGRAPH about improving ray-tracing performance.

2.  Computer viruses cause greater problems.

3.  Software bugs become more evident.

4.  There is a movement to less efficient programming languages, like Prolog.

5.  Cryptography dies.

6.  There is a race between code makers and code breakers.

7.  Existing communications networks are swamped.

8.  Computers are used as tape recorders (due to their infinite memory), for espionage purposes.

9.  The analog tape recording industry dies.

10. Saturday morning cartoons are created using a computer.

11. Computer analysis of world radio broadcasts is commonplace.

12. Data security, if possible, is provided by digital signatures and biometric security devices.

### 12.2.3 Scientific/Technical Impact

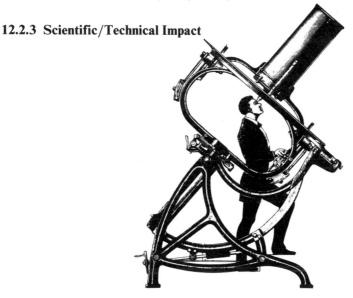

1.  Automated search for extraterrestrial life is improved.
2.  There is a better understanding of galaxies, black holes, oceans, and chemical reactions.
3.  There are improved telescopes and imaged-processed images from outer space.
4.  Computer peripheral industry is enhanced.
5.  Computer chess player immediately beats all humans players for all time.
6.  Many brute-force math problems are solved.
7.  Tremendous expansion in all kinds of simulation modeling, e.g. numerical predictions of nuclear explosions and vehicle crashes.
8.  There is a major impact on neural net research.
9.  Major impact on database applications.
10. There are enhancements to animation, with impact on entertainment industry.
11. There are enhancements in flight simulators and similar training tools.
12. Communication field is enhanced.
13. Household products are made smart; voice recognition is provided to all appliances.
14. Speech recognition problems, in general, are solved.
15. NP-complete problems are answered. (See Glossary.)
16. Quantum chemistry research is enhanced; theory leaps ahead of experiment.
17. Computer vision research is enhanced.
18. Robots become available with superb feature extractors.
19. Scientific Monte Carlo applications are enhanced.

20. There are enhancements to airplane, car, and furnace design. (See CAD in Glossary.)

21. There is improved load analysis on physical systems, e.g. airplane wings.

22. There are new chemical compounds, medical procedures, genetic discoveries.

23. Instantaneous financial transactions are possible.

24. There is rapid handling of conventional batch processing jobstreams.

25. Military or destructive use is enhanced.

26. Military security is compromised.

27. There are intelligent sensors for weather, space, geology applications.

28. All research is enhanced by intelligent language parsers.

29. Speech synthesis is enhanced.

30. There are intelligent vehicles.

31. There are human health monitoring machines.

32. Hologram-like TV is made possible.

33. There are smart weapons which can target without human intervention.

34. There are extreme advances in TV, video, ornamental art.

35. Genetic research is enhanced.

36. New theorems in logic and mathematics are proved.

37. CAM (see Glossary), computer art, music, music synthesis, and animation are improved.

38. "Zillionth digit" of $\pi$ is found.

39. There are instantaneous language translations – any two humans could communicate.

40. There is a green revolution – as a result of weather forecasts.

41. Many areas of consumer electronics collapse. (This is explained in the detailed response section.)

42. Unified field theory becomes a reality.

43. High energy physics research is improved.

44. An information world ties together all cultures.

45. All books, television, radio and other programs are stored in computer.

46. There is more harm than good: massive resources stolen and not noticed.

47. Molecular dynamics simulations are improved.

48. Protein folding programs are improved.

49. Particle physics research is enhanced.

50. Complicated cellular automata, starting from initial random conditions, on a huge grid, produce life-like behavior as complex "societies" of particles evolve.

51. Fractal and complex dynamics theory is enhanced. Researchers and computer artists immediately explore strange new worlds deep within the Mandelbrot set.

52. There are instantaneous graphic ray-tracing techniques.

53. All medical images stored in computer memory rather than on film.

54. DNA sequence and pattern-matching analysis are improved.

55. Superconductor theories are improved.

56. Military submarine sonar information interpretation is improved.

57. The need for special-purpose computers, such as vector processors, vanishes.

58. Some present functions of medical doctors are replaced by can.

59. Ther are fewer human fatalities due to mechanical failure of imprecisely machined parts.

60. Goldbach's Conjecture and Fermat's Last Theorem are proven by computation. Number theorists love this.

61. Searches are conducted for messages deep within the decimal expansion of certain irrational numbers, such as $\pi$, $e$, $\phi$ (the golden ratio), etc.

62. Engineering of huge construction projects is enhanced.

## 12.3  A Sampling of Correspondence from Contributors

The following are excerpts from imaginative, colorful, or even cynical comments regarding the impact of the powerful computing machine described in this chapter.

### 12.3.1  General Supercomputing

"The soda can computer would fling us into a new age and a strange age. Science would make some tremendous immediate gains as existing software is ported with arbitrarily large array bounds. This would most likely be first seen in engineering, where existing tired, old FORTRAN programs would suddenly be sped up to a point where parametric optimization problems would never again be problems. However, this initial surge would soon level off as the limits of existing software are reached. It would take many years before new software paradigms which exploit the hardware supplant the old methods."

"There would be tremendous scientific gains within a year, even if the device were not soda-can-sized. A battleship-sized computer with infinite speed will still enable many scientific gains since there will be no waiting for the 'what-if' results. The most obvious early benefits would occur in those fields now using supercomputers involving large calculations. The programs and seed data already exist, so the startup delay would be small. Gains would be seen in computer science since performance constraints could be removed from algorithms. "

The most immediate beneficiaries of this device are the somewhat obvious supercomputing areas relating to aerodynamics, DNA mapping, and weather forecasting. In addition, atomic weapons and medical and pharmaceutical research will be helped since the algorithms and programs have been previously developed, albeit on a smaller scale. Now the results will be instantaneously known and used by anyone with access to the research or the programs. Since any cryptocode could instantly be broken the only barriers to information exchange will be physical.

"Would there be true scientific advances? Most assuredly, but these will pale in comparison to the role these computers will play in the new society that they will make possible."

### 12.3.2  Robotics, Artificial Pets

"Robotics will benefit as a result of the size of the computer. Since the computer is available  free of charge, it will be economically feasible to incorporate it in many places where a computer cannot currently be justified. This will give rise to infinitely fast computers being assigned to trivial tasks. Many simple mechanisms will no longer need to be implemented in hardware since they could be replaced by this computer and off-the-shelf software."

"One can speculate that these small super-powerful computers can be implanted in mammals to monitor various biometric parameters. Also, scientists will probably design artificial animal pets, such as robot rabbits or cats, which respond in life-like ways to their environment and owners."

### 12.3.3  Economic and Social Impact

"Free access to a valuable tool will be a new experience for mankind. The computer industry will be destroyed, of course. Computer hardware companies will have to switch over to peripherals. CPU maintenance as an enterprise or as a user concern disappears since a replacement CPU could be had for the asking. There will be a new software race. Those who currently develop hardware will switch over to software thus bolstering the software ranks. Countries like India which have software talent but are short on hardware will find themselves newly competitive. Countries in which the human investment has not already been made will find themselves behind in this new race also. Humankind will definitely benefit, provided that the government is aware of and is prepared to circumvent the various dangers related to giving every citizen virtually unlimited computing power. Networks of every kind will spring up across the world, creating security issues as vexing as battling the AIDS epidemic."

### 12.3.4 Games

"There will be an immediate impact on all games, and some of the romance will disappear from games like chess since everyone's computer would outplay the world champion."

### 12.3.5 Minimal- or Negative- or No- Impact Statements

The following responses indicate that there will be minimal gains from the super-fast device. Some individuals suggested that there will be a negative impact on the world.

"The scientific gains will be minor. There are three reasons for this. First, although many scientific projects now depend on computers, only a very small amount of scientific work depends on having very fast ones. Science is largely experimental, not computational. Second, anyone working on the leading edge of a science, even its computational aspects, is heavily involved in exploring new ideas. This means new methods, new understanding. In truly novel work the bulk of time lies in the preparation for the experiment (computer experiment or otherwise) and trying to understand the results, not in the execution of the 'experiment.' Third, most true scientific advances occur via serendipity, accidents or just plain dumb luck. Computers are not likely to aid these activities much – even artificially intelligent ones. Progress in less well understood areas might be disappointing. Until we can communicate at close to infinite speed, we will lack the connection to the information needed to use in the computer."

"There will be little impact on society as a whole because at least 60 percent of the world's population will be unable even to use the computers. Most of the major problems facing the world involve far more than data processing. For example, environmental issues (waste disposal, water purity, air purity) need large investments in infrastructure to resolve, as do problems such as feeding the hungry, clothing the naked, curing the ill and sheltering the homeless. Better computers might help with some of these issues, but will have little real impact."

"The human race is not always responsible with new and possibly dangerous technology. Every minute of every day we have enough destructive force hanging over our heads to turn the earth into a cloud of dust. Who's to say what type of biological or chemical weapons could be created with unlimited computing power?"

"More harm than good will come from this machine. It will be possible to solve, via brute force, a lot of otherwise difficult password encodes, and other crypto-algorithms. If such machines are networked, it goes without saying that people could hack their way in, steal massive resources, and scientific results, and not be noticed. Who will notice speed problems using a machine with infinite speed?"

"The proposed can creates a Tower of Babel for the way these machines will talk to each other, write books which distill experience, interact, reproduce, etc. It will take fifteen years for these babies to mature to the point where we're getting a lot more out of them than we're putting in."

### 12.3.6 Heat

"For various reasons associated primarily with some rather fundamental theories, we know that flipping a bit must generate some heat. We can reduce the amount of heat per bit flip perhaps to the fundamental limits of quantum mechanics, but we should still expect some heat. Therefore, flipping a very, very large number of bits in a very, very small time will generate a sizeable amount of heat in a very small space and time. We will expect about a 12 megaton yield from each of the little machines.  This will definitely produce a few changes.  There will be an increased emphasis on bug-free. programming – you certainly don't want one of these units going off accidentally."

### 12.3.7  Satellites

"NASA is deploying an 'earth resources' satellite in the next few years.  This satellite will send several terabytes of data to earth every single day.  The can could be used as a space-probe pre-processor for this data, so that unnecessary data is not transferred to earth."

### 12.3.8  Impact on the Home

"Household appliances will become very smart; vacuum cleaners will work independently – although we may not trust unsupervised lawn mowers.  This appliance revolution is also enhanced with voice recognition."

"If the proposed device existed with graphics, there is a niche which will allow the average consumer to exploit the power of this fantastic computer – the electronic camera. The computer industry and the electronic camera are already on a collision course with each other.  The weak link in the system is the requirement that the consumer go to the photo processing center to perform the image customization. Ideally, the consumer should be allowed to perform this image processing in the comfort of his or her own home.  A

super-graphics computer could provide this platform. The consumer will benefit in other ways.  Since the digital images are already 'in the computer,' they will also be available for other software packages.  For instance, the images could be transferred to desktop publishing documents, word processing documents, or painting programs, or simply downloaded to the laser printer for immediate printing."

### 12.3.9  Education

"Tremendous growth and opportunities will occur in the field of education.  Today's computers and educational software do not even come close to providing the same level of education as real, live teachers provide.  However, if this device were attached to a graphics screen, a whole new class of educational software could be created.  Instead of being greeted with either a text menu or a graphical interface, like HyperCard, when initially sitting down at the computer, imagine seeing Walter Cronkite (or some other dignitary of your choice) on the screen.  With the speed and resolution proposed, animation programs will exist which could draw these complicated objects (e.g., people) 'on the fly' and their voices could be digitally generated from voice patterns stored in memory.  The software will interact with the user, tune the lesson for the intended audience and take them on numerous educational journeys, complete with actual video footage, photo stills, sounds and even background music.  Think of the possibilities: Churchill will teach about World War II, Einstein about nuclear physics, or Joe Dimaggio about the Yankees.  The student's interest will be maintained because the person teaching the subject will be someone the student will want to learn from."

"The educational systems will be turned upside down.  For example, the concept of spending years in 'busy work' and memorization will have to be turned into how to retrieve that information from your soda can.  A high school education will teach one how to make decisions and draw conclusions from the available data."

### 12.3.10  Business

"The soda can computer will have tremendous scientific impact, but this is predicated upon a stable society, or at least a relatively ordered society.  Unfortunately, a good part of society as we know it would certainly crumble.  Where would IBM, Digital, or Apple fit in a world with unlimited free computing – can they convert that part of their now obsolete workforce into a functioning part of society, or would the unemployment lines suddenly swell with millions of ex-executives?  Would Japan retain its competitive edge in a world where the software developer reigns supreme?  Can the environment handle new threats from an even more rapidly advancing technology, or will the technological advances solve the ecological crisis?"

### 12.3.11  Human-Machine Interface

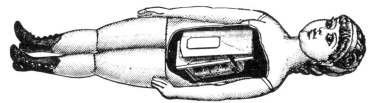

"The proposed device will bring computer-augmented humans (cyborgs) closer to reality. There is room inside the abdominal cavity to place a soda-can-sized item.  The scene in Star Wars, where R2D2 sticks an extension probe into a wall socket to interface with a ship's CPU, could be a human sticking his finger in a socket instead.  With infinite memory, and finger-hookup between people, I/O devices will not be needed.  The CPU will be wired into one's brain (if not directly, then onto one's optic/auditory/speech nerves).  To cure psychoses resulting from information overload, the CPU will be slowed down.  Computer viruses will be a greater problem, even if the CPU were not used to create a cyborg.  Computer viruses are enough of a problem with semi-PC-literate users – just imagine if every person had a PC at no cost."

### 12.3.12  Natural Language

"Though initially programmed in FORTRAN or C, other languages which are easier for the non-computer literate would soon become available, allowing many others to access the vast amount of data that could be stored in the computer.  Foreign language phrase books with very advanced parsers will understand both English and the foreign language and will be voice based as well.  A 'book of everything' will exist which will contain all the data ever written in all books.  A few search routines are provided to extract references.  Combined with an intelligent parser from the phrase book, the can will be very useful for carrying out research."

### 12.3.13  Graphics

"Special graphics hardware will not be required to make use of the proposed device, if the device can quickly carry out all of the processing. The proposed device will work with bit maps and produce HDTV (high-definition TV) images, or normal monitor output. Currently special graphics hardware serves to lift CPU load from the main processor. This is no longer needed. Hologramatic TV will be possible, by giving the computer control of three LCD plates, each filtering red, green, or blue and letting it set up the holes needed to re-construct the image. Achieving sufficient resolution will be difficult, but the Japanese can produce a reasonably large LCD TV that shows a good picture today. This may also have implications for telecommunications."

"The thought of performing volume tracing with minuscule voxels at a speed only limited by how fast rendered images can be pumped onto a peripheral is quite appealing."

### 12.3.14  Military

"In the military field the proposed device will have interesting applications, allowing the development of 'smart' weapons that could correctly identify and track their targets without the need for human intervention."

"This powerful device will have great value aboard submarines. The government requires better SONAR imaging systems. A tremendous amount of data is gathered by submarines when they are merely listening (passive mode). It takes time to identify the threat submarine against the background of ocean life and other manmade noise. A faster minicomputer could make this target identification go more quickly and accurately. *Improving the SONAR capabilities of our Navy's submarine fleet is the most important application of the can computer.* Presently there is so much SONAR equipment in the bows of our subs, that torpedoes are launched from the sides of the hull. This will change rather quickly."

### 12.3.15  Finance

"The result of providing everyone with the proposed device will be a leap forward in market efficiency. Note that if everyone could look for arbitrage opportunities, such opportunities will vanish. I know several Finance Professors that this will please to no end!"

### 12.3.16  Paradox

"The use of the word 'infinite' in the description of the proposed devices presents a problem. If the memory were infinite it would be impossible to search through it to retrieve data. If the I/O speed were infinite, then output would exist simultaneously with input, an impossibility. For something to have infinite speed, it would have to exist outside of time. Outside of time, motion is impossible. The result of this would be stasis. It may be hard to construct a business case for this device."

"It would be interesting to give a specific definition for the term *near-infinite* posed in the stated problem, and then determine what difference this makes. For example, if the can had googolplex[15] memory locations and could perform googolplex calculations (sequentially, not necessarily in parallel) within one second, the can could perform a cellular-automaton simulation of the entire universe at the level of the Planck length. With $10^{googolplex}$ memory locations, it could perform a simulation of all possible universes of the same size as our own universe."

---

[15] *Googolplex* is defined in 'Results of the Very-Large-Number Contest' on page 207.

### 12.3.17 Consumer electronics

"Many areas of consumer electronics will collapse. Audio, video and game electronics are variations of information processing. These functions will be done with various attachments to the supercomputers. The computers will even perform the signal processing associated with broadcast media (TV and radio). The antenna will be just another computer peripheral."

### 12.3.18 Society

"The really large impacts on society will come later. Eventually, there will be software which would allow the computer to effectively see, hear, speak, and pass the Turing test. When that finally becomes generally available, computers would become permanent, omnipresent companions and advisors. Getting dressed in the morning will include grabbing your pants, shoes, and computer. Society would polarize into those who let the computer do the thinking for them, and those who use the computers as incredibly powerful tools. The latter users will approach the realms where a sufficiently advanced technology would resemble magic. It would be some of these sociological changes that I believe would have the most far-reaching effects. For example, consider instantly diagnosed (free) medical advice, or instant language translation so that any two humans could communicate. Consider weather forecasting so precise that the proper crop could be planted at the proper time with optimally timed application of fertilizers and pesticides. Perfect efficiency in everything, from the cars we drive to the factories that produce them, to the smokestack scrubbers that clean the air."

"The proposed device would become the great equalizer with the only barrier being in the distribution of new software. People and governments would be able to simulate policy decisions before their implementation, hopefully to the good of the world populace."

Given cellular phone technology, all of these soda cans will be networked. Let us assume that there is an adequate method of arbitration between all of these soda cans talking to each other. The first sociological change would be in demographics: people who deal with information and other non-hands-on types could work from anywhere they pleased (e.g., at home in Hawaii)."

### 12.3.19 Neural Networks

"Infinitely large neural networks, which perform instantaneous evaluations of data, could detect correlations in the data, leaving humans free to do the intuitive side of analysis. The can could detect correlations between all manner of 'unrelated' things: for example, it might 'realize' that the rate of cabbage root-growth was related to the 180-year sun-cycle: any data and all data could be put into the computer, and ALL data could be tested for correlation, however unlikely."

### 12.3.20 Medicine

"Such a computer could perform an enormous barrage of tests: many scientists will simply turn to thinking up tests to implement on this machine, and append these suggestions to an endless list of suggestions. A very good use would be in the medical world: simply drop into the local hospital once a year and provide a blood sample. The doctor takes a color image and sends it through the computer which immediately scans and checks your blood for thousands of possible diseases. There would be time to check everybody."

"A similar system could be used to monitor a human for health and fitness, perhaps providing warnings and vital clues in the event of the human's ceasing to function normally. This warning is achieved with a cheap radio transmitter, a self-contained, light weight power source, and a powerful air horn."

### 12.3.21  Database and Libraries

"The proposed device, used simply as a database, will advance all scientific disciplines. A small computer with infinite memory and infinite speed will allow anyone to gather vast amounts of data. The most readily available data would be books from the Library of Congress as they become available in soft-copy, and television and radio programs converted to binary and saved in memory."

"The real use of this capability would require several years' evolution of the means to control this vast amount of data to be able to obtain any desired information without difficulty. Over time, hierarchical structures and binary-type search patterns would enable a more structured view of this data."

"If everybody had one of the proposed devices, everybody in the world could have the entire British library in their bedrooms. Publishers will find business more difficult."

### 12.3.22  Music

"The can computer will have a tremendous impact on music, musical instruments, and music appreciation. Who knows what weird portable instruments and futuristic sounds will be created? All traditional instruments could be retrofit with the can computer for digital processing."

"All of the great, and not-so-great, works of music from all of earth's cultures can be stored in the can computer. This should revolutionize music education and music analysis."

"If a keyboard, as well as digital-to-analog and analog-to-digital converters, were attached to a soda can, then one has a truly general synthesis system. If a musician wants to do subtractive synthesis, he just loads the subtractive synthesis program. If additive synthesis were desired, he just loads the program. Realtime resynthesis, which is currently a computational nightmare, becomes easy. Also, there is no limit on the number of voices."

### 12.3.23 Legal

"The proposed device could function as an audio and video recorder, turned on all the time. This could be useful in certain legal situations, such as when the police ask 'Where were you on the night of January 20th?' However, security would be a big issue. One wouldn't want to let just anyone view the personal data."

### 12.3.24 Optical Computers

"It may interest you to know that for the past 30 years engineers have been building smaller and smaller silicon chips through which electrons pass. In 1990, however, researchers at AT&T Bell Laboratories in Holmdel, New Jersey, developed the first optical digital processor that uses not electrons but laser beams to carry information. Perhaps this is the first step to building the soda-can computer postulated in this chapter. The Bell Labs machine may lead to computers in which the only limit to computing power will be the speed of light. In 1987, Bell Labs' physicist David Miller replaced silicon transistors on a microchip with infinitesimal mirrors. In 1990, Michael Prise was able to combine 128 of these 'optical transistors' onto a single processor (pictured below). Prise used four arrays of 32 optical transistors – each array small enough to fit into the typed letter O." (Photograph reprinted with permission of AT&T. ©1990 AT&T.)

### 12.3.25   Evolving Intelligences

"With infinite speed and memory, research on 'evolving' programs will succeed.  We will evolve an artificially intelligent being inside of a can.  A being with nominally human (or better) intelligence that were capable of accessing an infinite amount of data at infinite speeds would be close to a god.  (We had better not connect this unit to a network until we make sure that the god in question isn't Cthulhu.)  If this being were benign enough to tell us how to migrate our minds over to the soda cans, then we will then become gods, too."

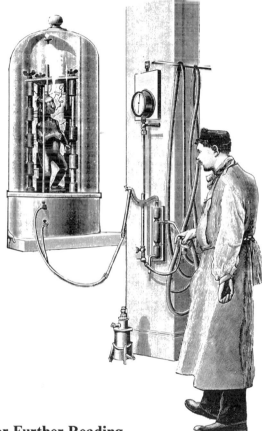

## 12.4  For Further Reading

1.   Dereska, S. (1990) DARPA's advances provide basis for rapid progression. *SIGNAL*, the Official Publication of the Armed Forces Communication and Electronic Association. February Issue. pgs. 29-33.

2.   Hsu, F., Anantharaman, T., Campbell, M., Nowatzyk, A. (1990) A grandmaster chess machine. *Scientific American*. October 263(4): 44-54.

3.   Pickover, C. (1991) A soda-can-sized supercomputer. *Computers in Physics*, May/June, in press.

GALILEO GALILEI LINCEO FILOSOFO E MATEMATICO DEL SER.<sup>MO</sup> GRAN DVCA DI TOSCANA

# Chapter 13

# Who are the Ten Most Influential Scientists in History?

Of the thousands of famous and important scientists who have influenced the course of human history, which scientists have most influenced our lives and our thoughts? This survey presents a composite ranking, computed from the respondents' individual rankings of the top ten scientists. This chapter admittedly has little to do with computers. However, today's modern computer is a result of advances made by the work of pioneering and influential scientists in the fields of electronics, physics, and chemistry during the last century. In this chapter, these scientists and others are ranked in a survey conducted in 1989.

A note on eligibility of scientists on the list: Anonymous persons, such as the inventor of the wheel and inventor of writing, or the discoverer of fire, were disqualified from the list. Where two individuals, in very close collaboration, have produced a joint accomplishment, a joint entry is provided (e.g. Watson and Crick, or the Wright brothers). Inventors were considered as scientists.

I was surprised at the remarkable agreement between many contributors' lists. Personally, I might have included Jack Kilby (pictured at end of chapter), inventor of the integrated circuit chip, and Gregory Pincus, inventor of the birth control pill. Only a single contributor suggested either of these two names.

I urge you to experiment by composing your own list, which will no doubt differ from the one presented here.

In order to account for the relative ordering of scientists in contributors' lists, the final ranking was determined by summing reciprocal weights:

$$R_{tot} = \sum 1/W_i \tag{13.1}$$

where $W$ is the rank from 1 to 10 in an individual's list, and $R$ is the total final rank. For example, a scientist ranked 10th by ten people is equivalent to a scientist ranked first by one person. In either case, the weighted sum, $R$, is "0.1."

Given the above scoring system and criteria, the following is a ranking of the ten top scientists as determined by IBM scientists and technicians.

**Figure 13.1.** *Isaac Newton (1642-1727)* Newton, an English physicist and mathematician, invented calculus, discovered the compound nature of white light, and constructed the first reflecting telescope. In addition, he worked out the laws of motion and the theory of universal gravitation. He was ranked number 1 by contributors.

## 13.1  The Top Ten

1. **Isaac Newton (1642-1727)  Rank: 29.5**
   English physicist and mathematician. Calculus, optics, gravitation.

2. **Albert Einstein (1879-1955)  Rank: 16.5**
   German-Swiss-American physicist. Quantum theory, relativity.

3. **Galileo (1564-1642)  Rank: 13.8**
   Italian astronomer and physicist.  Motion of falling bodies, quantitative measurement, use of the telescope.

4. **Charles Darwin (1809-1882) Rank: 8.8**
   English naturalist. Evolution.

5. **Aristotle (384-322 B.C.) Rank: 8.3**
   Greek philosopher.  Codification of all ancient knowledge. Classification of living species.

6. **Euclid (300 B.C.)  Rank 6.1**
   Greek geometer. Self-consistent geometry.

7. **James C. Maxwell (1831-1879) Rank: 4.7**
   Scottish physicist. Equations for electromagnetism. Kinetic theory of gasses.

8. **Louis Pasteur (1822-1932) Rank: 4.52**
   French chemist. Germ theory of disease. Inoculation. Stereochemistry.

9. **Thomas Edison (1847-1931) Rank: 3.9**
   American inventor. Phonograph. Light bulb.  Refinement of electrical distribution network.

10. **Nicolaus Copernicus (1473 - 1543) Rank: 3.6**
    Polish astronomer.  Heliocentric theory of solar system.

**Figure 13.2.** *De Re Metallica.* A plate from Agricola's *De Re Metallica*, the first book to offer detailed technical drawings and scientific approaches to mining. The book, published in 1556, offers readers an entertaining picture of the first age of technology.

Of all the people in the "Ten," Edison received the fewest votes (11); however, he is not last on the list since the distribution of relative weights for Edison was higher than for Copernicus who received 19 votes.

For completeness, a ranking is also included based simply on the number of times a scientist appeared on people's lists, with no weighting factor applied:

1. Newton (51)

2. Einstein (48)

3. Galileo (40)

4. Darwin (29)

5. Pasteur (25)

6. Copernicus / Maxwell (19)

7. Aristotle (17)

8. Euclid (16)

9. Marie S. Curie (1867-1934) Polish-French chemist. Radioactivity. Nobel prize in physics and chemistry.
   Tied with Karl Gauss (1777-1855) German mathematician and astronomer  Mathematics of planetary orbits. Electricity. Magnetism. (13)

10. Archimedes (287?-212 B.C.) Greek Mathematician. Lever. Buoyancy. $\pi$.
    Tied with Edison (12).

## 13.2  The Runners-Up

Other scientists who did not score high enough to be included in the top 10 but who scored very favorably were: Freud, Bohr, von Neumann, Kepler, Heisenberg, Fermi, Shockley, Watson and Crick, Mendel, Bell, da Vinci, Mendeleev, and Faraday. All were on at least five people's lists.

## 13.3  Appendix 1 - Last Place

Scientists who received between two votes and five votes were:  Franklin, Leibniz, Lavoisier, Turing, Taylor, Descartes, Pythagoras, Ptolemy, Marconi, Watt, Goedel, Michelangelo, Hawking, von Braun, and Dirac.

## 13.4  Appendix 2 - The List of Michael Hart

Michael Hart, physicist, astronomer, mathematician and lawyer, gives the following ranking in his book *The 100: A Ranking of the Most Influential Persons in History*. I recommend his book wholeheartedly. His list, in order, is: Isaac Newton, Ts'ai Lun (50? - 118? A.D.) (Chinese official. Paper.), Johann Gutenberg (1400? - 1468?) (German inventor. Printing press.), Albert Einstein, Louis Pasteur, Galileo Galilei, Charles Darwin, Euclid, Nicolaus Copernicus, James Watt (first practical steam engine).

## 13.5  A Sampling of Correspondence from Survey Contributors

**From an IBM Fellow at Yorktown Heights, New York:** Here is my list of influential scientists. I've interpreted "influential" as "affecting my own personal view of the world." My list, in order, is: Newton, Boyle, Watson and Crick, Planck, Boltzmann, Fourier, Galileo, Einstein, Archimedes, Turing.

**From Lexington, Kentucky:** I wanted to also give you my list for the ten individuals best at explaining and popularizing science:
1.  Carl Sagan
2.  Isaac Asimov
3.  Stephen Jay Gould
4.  Douglas Hofstadter
5.  Martin Gardner
6.  Jearl Walker
7.  Sir James Jeans
8.  James Burke
9.  Richard Feynman
10. Baird Smith (if only more people could get to hear him!)

**From East Fishkill, New York:** The following is my top ten ranking for computer scientists: 1. Von Neumann, 2. Grace Hopper (pictured at end of chapter), 3. T. J. Watson, 4.

Clive Sinclair, 5. Wozniak and Jobs, 6. Benoit Mandelbrot, 7. Seymour Papert, 8. Bezier, 9. James Foley.

**From White Plains, New York:** I would suggest that this listmaking is as foolish a goal as finding "the most beautiful woman," "the smartest person," etc. Just think about what you asked for.  Immediately come to mind at least 15-20 scientific disciplines (Math, Optics, Biology, Chemistry, Medicine, Aeronautics, Energy, Electronics, Fluids, Mechanics, etc.). To meet your criteria, and assuming all sciences were weighted equally, one would have to select at most one person from each field of science. The most brilliant person of medicine? There have to be at least 10 candidates there alone. Does Einstein have the lead in physics? Perhaps, but I'd find it hard to come up with 1 or 2 mathematicians. A second point: what does "influential" mean? *Is the cure for Polio more influential than the discovery of gravity or the calculus?* Sorry, Cliff. I'll pass on this one.

## 13.6  Stop and Think

Perhaps teachers will conduct this poll in their classrooms. I would be interested in how the results of classroom surveys compare with the findings in this chapter.

## 13.7  For Further Reading

1.  Agricola, G. (1950) *De Re Metallica*. Dover: NY (Translated from the first Latin edition of 1556).
2.  Asimov, I. (1964) *Adding a Dimension*. Avon: NY.
3.  Cohen, I. (1985) *Revolution in Science*. Harvard University Press: Massachusetts.
4.  Hart, M. (1978) *The 100: A Ranking of the Most Influential Persons in History*. Hart Publishing: NY.
5.  Pickover, C. (1990) Who are the ten most influential scientists in history? *The History and Social Science Teacher*. 25(3): 158-161.

### GRACE HOPPER
(born 1906)

A PIONEER IN THE FIELD OF HIGH-LEVEL
PROGRAMMING LANGUAGES

### JACK ST. CLAIR KILBY

IN 1958 DEVELOPED THE FIRST
INTEGRATED CIRCUIT

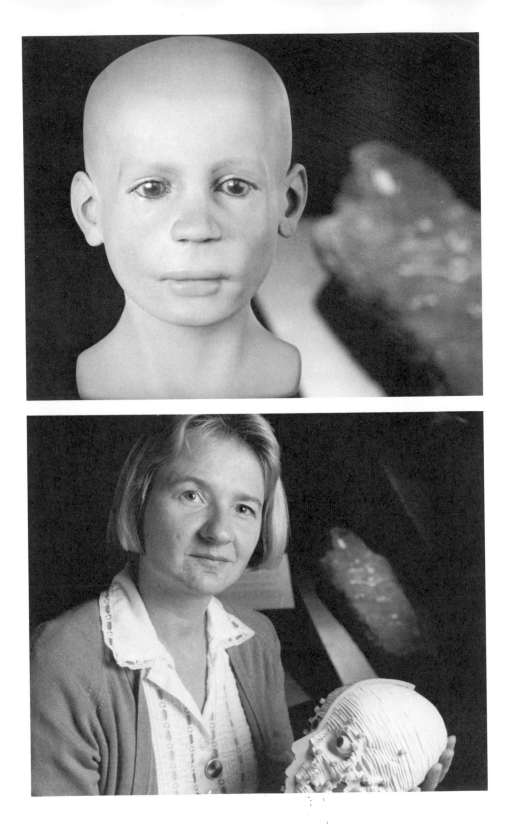

Chapter 14

# Interlude: The Mummy Project

Imagine a slightly decayed, 2000-year-old mummified child being probed by the most advanced computer instrumentation and computer graphics equipment. This is not some grotesque scene from a Steven King novel, rather this is precisely what an interdisciplinary research team at the University of Illinois is excited about. In the early 1990s, using two supercomputers (a CRAY 2S and a Connection Machine CM-2) to construct 3-D video animations from 2-D CAT scan "slices," David Lawrence hopes to unravel the identity of the small Egyptian child within the mummy's ancient wrappings. In a related project, Ray Evenhouse uses various computers to carefully reconstruct the mummy's skull from head scan information. He "builds" the flesh back on the skull (top facing figure), and then, with a special computer program used in updating old photos of missing children, he "ages" the mummy's face to 18 years old. Finally, Evenhouse produces physical 3-D models of heads at various ages.

The researchers' combined tests – including radiography, CAT scans, 3-D imaging, and wood, textile, resin and insect analyses – shed light not only on the mummy, but on mummification during Egypt's Roman period. Researchers conclude that the mummy is an 8 year old who died of unknown causes around A.D. 100. Without even removing the mummy's wrappings, they can tell that at least three organs were left inside the body.

The bottom facing photograph is of Sarah Wisseman, Assistant Director of the University of Illinois Campus Program on Ancient Technologies and Archeological Materials. She holds a plastic cast of a skull model created from CAT-scan sections of the Egyptian mummy's head. She can be reached at: The University of Illinois at Urbana-Champaign, ATAM, 116 Observatory, 901 South Mathews Avenue, Urbana, IL 61801 USA. (Photos by Bill Wiegand/U. of Illinois.)

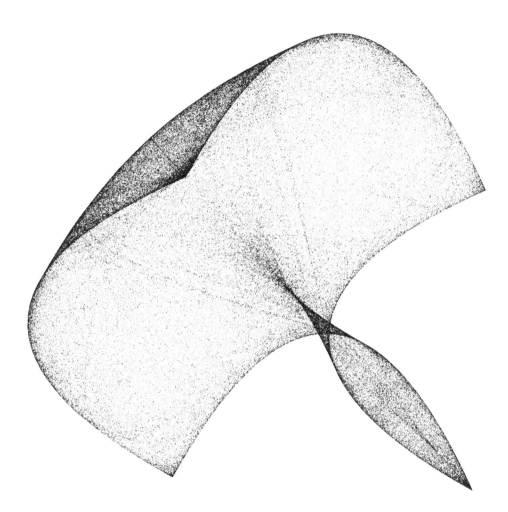

Chapter 15

# A Personal Computer Placed In the Year 1900

*"Our present world would certainly be mind-boggling to most people of any previous century. The one constant today is change itself. By facing and anticipating change, we can dilute fear of the unknown and act in ways that are most appropriate for both ourselves and society at large. "*

Edward Cornish

If humankind, in the year 1900, were suddenly given a modern personal computer, how would humanity be affected from both a scientific and sociological standpoint? I presented this question to many scientists. To bring some practical relevance to this survey, I should point out that in humankind's past there are actual historical examples of the sudden, unexpected arrival of a technology, and it's fascinating to follow the effect of such events on the history of humankind and also to contemplate future technologies which may appear "before their expected time" (i.e., they are chronologically misplaced). (See the Appendix for examples of some past technological anachronisms.) The precise question posed to people is stated in the following:

*The year is 1900. A single IBM Personal Computer PS/2, or similar personal computer, is given to scientists at Harvard University by some anonymous benefactor. With the computer come: 1) A power source that will allow the unit to be used for one year, and 2) manuals enabling scientists to operate the computer and manuals for FORTRAN programming. Assume that the system will run trouble-free for a year. After a year, when the computer power source has died, scientists are still free to analyze the hardware. Question: what would be the effect on the world in the 1900's, and on the world today, if the described scenario actually took place? As a reminder as to what was happening around 1900: the British Empire was near its peak, automobiles (Daimler, Benz) were first commercially sold, the motion picture was invented, Roentgen discovered X-rays, Marconi invented the radio, Becquerel discovered radioactivity, and the Wright brothers invented the airplane. Other famous scientists of the day were Freud, Planck, and Einstein.*

After reading through the responses of those surveyed, I was most interested to note the degree to which the opinions of computer professionals differed. Some of those surveyed said there would be almost no effect, since scientists in 1900 had little framework in which to understand programming concepts. On the other hand, some contributors indicated that a useful program would be running within 3 days of receiving the machine and manuals. Many indicated that the scientists, in their attempt to understand the machine, would destroy it. Others predicted that the US government (and the government of other countries) would attempt to obtain the personal computer. Some respondents went as far as to suggest that there would be very little commercial benefit and only minor scientific and engineering benefit.

Many scientists suggested that the computer would be used to generate large tables of functions, much like those seen today in the back of mathematical handbooks. Some speculated that the real impact of this event would be on the development of the electronics and computer *industry*, because scientists would now have a demonstration of what is possible and have the clues on how to achieve these possibilities. This would result in having solid state electronics and computer industries develop much sooner than they did in our world. For example, some said that our current (1990's) state of electronics and computer development would occur in the late 1950's. However, research in other areas may even be slowed, as a large portion of the brightest people went to work on this project. As a result, some scientists indicated that the US may never have developed the atomic bomb by the end of World War II. Also, today's large multi-million-dollar mainframes with proprietary operating systems would not be viewed as the "proper way to go," and would never be dominant. There would be one clear standard defined by this computer, which everyone would try to work toward. The resulting computer industry would be very much affected.

Finally, some of the scientists polled indicated that if the computer were placed just a decade or two later, incredible strides could have been made in quantum theory; however, 1900 would have been too early for the device to have much effect.

## 15.1 Summary Statements on Impact Assessment

Those surveyed had many ideas as to the impact of the chronologically misplaced personal computer on science and the world as a whole. A summary of some of their statements is listed below. Where possible, these predictions are sorted by subject matter. Naturally, many of the subject areas overlap. Many of the predictions are explained or justified in the later sections of this chapter which give a sampling of detailed responses. Predicting a new future as a result of an anachronism is not a well-defined task, and you may take exception to some of the imaginative answers. Nonetheless, I am certain that the misplaced personal computer would have a major impact on humankind.

### 15.1.1 Programming/Information Impact

1. The concept of "programming languages" takes the academic world by storm and simpler computers (Babbage Engines) are produced, primarily to automate industrial technology.
2. The academic world develops the science of theoretical computing.
3. Computer has almost no effect since scientists in 1990 do not fully understand programming concepts.
4. Three days after computer received, a program is running.
5. Two months after computer received, major simulations are running.
6. Future computers have fonts and a "look" similar to that found in the misplaced personal computer.

### 15.1.2 Scientific/Technical Impact

1. Chaos and fractal theory accelerated. Computer graphics of fractals in the 1920s.
2. Miracle drugs designed early; DNA structure discovered earlier.
3. "Cure for cancer" in the 1960s.
4. Power source duplicated, and computer works for a time greater than a year.
5. Power supply disassembled, rendering computer inoperable.
6. Computing technology hastened by several years.
7. Computer-targeted field guns are available in World War I.
8. Computer navigation equipment available in World War II.
9. As a result of the early introduction of computers, today we use technology that would not have existed until the year 2020-40.
10. Computer put to use in computing orbital parameters, ballistic tables for artillery, and in hydrodynamic ship design.
11. Fortran used to solve various differential equations that describe thermal gradients and Maxwell's equations.
12. If a printer were supplied: a rush to produce tables of mathematical functions and actuarial tables.
13. The desire to understand the insulation materials drives the world to extensive materials technology investigations.
14. Study of the ferrites in the transformers will expand 1900 technologies.
15. Television device development accelerated.
16. In trying to understand an IC's function, scientists blow it out.
17. Fluid mechanics problems solved.

18. Since the manuals are printed on better paper than a contemporary paper mill can produce, this leads to competition between various paper houses and printers. Better paper manuals are available today.

19. Patent activity and excitement over the corrugated cardboard shipping materials.

20. Analysis of plastic bags, bubblewrap, cable ties, software cases: with major impact on humanity.

21. Existence of complex-number data types aids mathematical research.

22. Within 3 weeks, $\pi$ to 5000 decimal places.

23. Floppy disks accidentally destroyed.

24. Realizing that magnetism was involved in the floppy disks leads to iron disk players instead of record players, and the early development of magnetic storage technologies.

25. Analysis of the CRT fragments, after the vacuum tube imploded under examination, reveals useful details about electronics (resistors, capacitors, transformers).

26. Early development and better funding for much of the electronics industry.

27. Plastics industry enhanced.

### 15.1.3 Sociopolitical Impact

1. Scientists learn to type.

2. The world population will be higher in the 1990s.

3. The first world will be wealthier, the second and third worlds hungrier and more in debt.

4. The first world's wealth distribution will be more concentrated than today.

5. Mass unemployment common.

6. Educational standards will be lower for the vast majority.

7. Enhanced US prestige, partly due to US placing the first man on moon in the 1940s or 1950s.

8. The US government learns of the personal computer's existence and impounds it.

9. Various industrial countries learn of the personal computer's existence and steal or copy the manuals.

10. Various industrial countries learn of the personal computer's existence and destroy it because it appears to be a military or industrial threat.

11. The personal computer is kept secret by Harvard as they study it, and once the power source dies, they publish a multitude of papers.

12. The finely etched circuit boards and chips are treated like rare gems, with the university's endowment enriched by the sale and display of the artifacts.

13. A mythology, perhaps even a religion, develops.

14. Intense political fights regarding who gets to study the machine.

15. World War II does not occur, due to early development of atomic technology.

16. Rapid technological changes lead to severe and irreversible pollution problems.

17. SETI research increases as we search the universe for our benefactors. The Creationism paradigm will strengthen.

18. Science fiction book and movie industry enhanced, with more of the general populace interested in science fiction.

## 15.2  Typical Zero-Impact Statements

The following are typical statements from scientists who thought that the chronologically misplaced computer would have little or no impact on the scientific world.

"The misplaced personal computer will have almost no effect on science. The tasks we accomplish with computers today are the cumulative product of over 100 years of developing ideas. It is doubtful that the 1900 user of a PS/2, or any other computer, would have achieved very much more with it than the census did ten years before with the first Hollerith machine. Indeed, they probably would have accomplished a great deal less, as understanding FORTRAN well enough to write in it would entail a much larger conceptual leap than rods and punch cards did."

"Today, it can take a good programmer many months to acquire anything close to true proficiency at a new programming language. And this is only with help from books and instructors with literally decades of the accumulated knowledge. In a completely new technical field the startup time would be considerable – surely more than a year – especially given only limited access to a single machine. There would be a buzz around the immediate vicinity of the computer, but it would be treated more as a curiosity than as a tool. Very few people would even have access to it. Probably the best benefits would come from studying it to try to understand its principles of operation."

"Note that the science of 1900 was too immature to take full advantage of the misplaced personal computer. Quantum physics was having its first primal scream in 1900. This was the year that Planck published his first papers on black body radiation. Not until around 1905 did Einstein propose that this could imply that light came in lumps called photons, and explain the photo-electric effect in that context. Semiconductor technology is strongly influenced by the way that impurities modify the electrical behavior of the band structure of semiconductor crystals – a completely quantum phenomenon. A chemical assay of the chips would certainly not reveal the quantum behavior of these structures. Scientists of the day could not conceive of the micro-electronic engineering involved: actually laying down the impurities in geometrical patterns at the micron level to build circuits! In other words, scientists of the time could not grasp the significance of the way this finished product was constructed."

"Little actual computing will be accomplished. The science and engineering of the day was too heavily geared toward pencil-and-paper theory instead of numerically intensive, blood-and-guts computing. Perhaps fluid mechanics could have benefitted. The theory of computing (i.e., dependence on Boolean algebra) could be deduced from the FORTRAN manuals, which would have dramatic effects on the history of the computer."

"Little would be learned by examination of the computer's carcass. No schematics come with the computer, so it is doubtful that the components would reveal much. Even if they knew what the chips were ('the heart of this device is that tiny thing?'), there would be almost no way for them to disassemble or otherwise analyze them. The CRT, if they could figure it out, might tell them more about electronics than the entire CPU. Understanding the disk drives would be more difficult."

"In the 1900s there were not many computationally intensive problems pressing on the minds of scientists. The census, a few statistical issues, not much else. Everything was still done by craftsman and hands-on workers. The few engineers and scientific types had their own rule-of-thumb ways of doing things and were not computationally limited.   Many brilliant ideas languish for a long time before getting rediscovered when society is ready to accept them."

"The computer will break quickly; it will become the basis of some new quasi-religious movements; it will not be believed, but the inspiration for applied mathematics will be considerable. However, this computer will prove to be so distracting that intellectuals may stop working on other problems, so the sum effect may be zero. The donation of the computer could have a bigger impact than the computer itself; the biggest effect of all is that people, even at Harvard, will lose their assertiveness and will just wait for the next gift."

"The power in the machine would give out probably just as they were gearing up to make full use of it. This would lead to arguments between those who had wanted to dismantle it from the beginning and those who didn't. Unless there was someone really powerful who wanted it kept intact on the off chance that the power might come back, it would eventually be dismantled."

## 15.3  Religion

"The effects of having the equipment to analyze is difficult to assess. Analysis would be difficult with the tools of the day, and scientists will destroy the machine in their attempt to understand the electronics.  If some form of logic probe were invented, perhaps the computer age would have been accelerated somewhat.  It is more likely, however, that the finely etched materials would be treated like rare gems, with the university's endowment enriched on the sale and display of the artifacts.  Who knows, we may be doing the same thing now: Perhaps today's geodes (see Glossary) were the supercomputers of some lost prior civilization.  Another good possibility: Some mythology, perhaps even a religion, is likely to grow up around such an unusual, out-of-nowhere device.  Who knows what the effects of such a gift from aliens or gifts from the future shamanism might be today."

"Though the machine is put together properly most academics of the time will be unable to understand how it works and denounce it as a hoax.  It may feature as a side show for a little while before the power runs out and it is eventually dismantled in a junk shop somewhere and thrown away."

"This is a common science fiction theme, the dropping of some advanced machine into a primitive society.  Most of the time, if the society is very primitive, the advanced machine is broken and/or then worshipped as some God.  If the advanced machine is very advanced, like the monoliths in the movie 2001, the machine can defend itself and pulls the primitive society into some accelerated development.  A personal computer is not self-protective and I am sure that after a short period of time, the Harvard folks will break it in some way.  So nothing wonderful will be calculated."

"The secondary effects might be greater than the impact of the computer itself. People and governments could become obsessed with finding the benefactor. New religions could get started and congregants would start praying and looking for the next gift. Power plays at various levels of government and academia would take place to determine control of the gift. New fields of philosophy and law will develop about the meaning and use of sudden presents from mysterious entities."

"The machine will collect a group a believers and form the core of a small religious cult which may still be active today, and these people will be surprised when today's companies started to sell working versions of their most holy relic!"

## 15.4  Some Predicted Time-Tables

"At about noon on the third day after the placement of the personal computer, scientists will have a running program – perhaps a mortgage calculation. By week two, programs will be reasonably large, but still not very complex.  By month two, major models will be running, but these will still be very primitive by 1990 standards.  It will not be until late fall or early winter of 1900 before there is any really useful work, except in the field of mathematics. January, 1901, will be a bleak month."

"The following is another predicted chronology involving four separate stages.  The first stage is *wonder*: everybody is wondering where it comes from, why it comes, and is shy to touch the machine because of fears of destroying it. Stage two is *exploration*: after the manuals were read, discussed, read again, and discussed again, the first sample programs would be written.  Stage 3 is *enthusiasm*: all seems solvable with this computer.  Stage 4 is *cooling down*: they realize that the base of computer science (e.g., algorithms, data-structures) is missing, and they cannot write larger programs without knowing these concepts. After the one year, there will be many more people involved with computer science. Therefore there is a theoretical base for the pioneers of calculating machines. And there will be lots of sponsored projects. The hardware will not lead to an improvement in technology, because an IC (see Glossary) is a real 'black box' for a 1900s scientist. The power source is more interesting to the engineers. The fantasy of poets and writers will be inspired. To sum up, the computer will solve some mathematical/physical problems, but the main impact is on the theoretical study of information processing, and on freeing cash for the development of simple mechanical or tube computers. Changes in technology may have occurred too fast for the current Green movement to have surfaced at an appropriate time (10-40 years ago), so the planet may have severe (irreversible) pollution problems. The major corporations today, if they existed, would have different names and may be European-based and probably wouldn't have made the machine that was sent back in time to spark the whole change off."

## 15.5  Practical Applications

"The computer will be used to compute orbital parameters and ballistic tables for artillery. It will also be used for hydrodynamic ship design. Flight equations may not have been developed enough to be useful, nor was quantum mechanics even a gleam in people's eyes. Fortran would have been used to solve some differential equations that described thermal gradients, as well as various solutions for Maxwell's equations. Many math majors in 1900 will receive jobs as 'computers', producing tables and tables of Taylor series expansions that result in small-print numbers in thick reference books. Statistics, such as used for actuarial tables, would be greatly aided."

## 15.6  Impact of Packaging Material and Manuals

"The computer manuals are printed on paper better than any contemporary paper mill can produce, with a precision greater than any contemporary printer could manage. This applies to the manuals inside the boxes as well. This will lead to competition between the various paper houses and printers to meet the standards (and emulate the fonts) that the manuals were printed with. This would be reflected today with better paper and different standard fonts and document layouts.

Corrugated cardboard may not have been available in 1900, so a patent will be given to the first company to produce a machine which make this surprisingly strong paper. This company will achieve much recognition and financial benefit.

Plastic bags, bubblewrap, cable ties, and software cases would all be studied in various chemical labs, and there would be a race to duplicate the properties of these amazing materials. In our history, plastics first occurred in Germany around 1900, but were thrown away as a failure, only to be developed further some 20 years later. With the presence of these containers the plastics industry could have advanced much further today, possibly furthering Germany (a country already interested in dies and related products), and this may have affected the outcome of the world wars."

"The main value of this chronologically misplaced workstation will be the manuals. Just seeing the manuals and the computer itself can have a major impact. The computer will become a local icon and will be a source of industrial inspiration. It will lead to a burst of inventiveness in electronics and materials. The manuals could be copied, and if Harvard or the government does not suppress wide distribution, then the concepts and ideas in the manuals would revolutionize intellectual thought. It is interesting that a FORTRAN manual is included; this is the one language that usually has good examples and good manuals, so people might really figure FORTRAN out. C would be impossible. There were just enough switching devices in existence in 1900 so some FORTRAN processors other than the donated personal computer would be made. The level of abstract mathematics in 1900 was ready for computational devices, but society would not be ready, and therefore there will not be a widespread effect."

## 15.7  Impact on Mathematics

"In a few weeks, a mathematically-minded scientist will be able to program the computer using FORTRAN. The field of mathematics as a whole will have some upheavals due to the introduction of a complex number data type. A significant amount of work would have to be done away from the computer, including dry running of programs, since CPU resource would be very constrained. Some of the classical problems (Pi to n decimal places) would be programmed, together with a few research programs (whose results might be doubted and have to be re-calculated by hand until confidence in the machine grew)."

## 15.8  Impact of Hardware

"After the power supply died and the scientists analyzed the various pieces, they would certainly recognize the CRT, transformers, and connectors, but the materials associated with the insulation, for example, would be very difficult to understand. They could analyze most of the organics, but would have difficulty in figuring out how to manufacture them. The integrated circuits would stump them for a long time. First, the silicon dopants are in concentrations too small to isolate chemically, and second, the feature sizes forming the integrated components would be unresolvable using their optical instruments."

"Research in other areas may even be slowed, as a large portion of the brightest people will work on this project. The US may never have developed the atomic bomb by the end of World War II, for example."

"Floppy disks, originally housing the software, are easily destroyed and probably rendered useless under examination by the crude technology of the times. In the best scenario, scientists will determine that magnetism was involved in recording information. This could lead to iron disk players instead of record players and the early development of magnetic storage technologies. On the other hand, this may slow their development by many years as technologists attempt to go straight there and miss out on some of the important steps in between, such as tapes."

The visual display unit is important since scientists of 1900 were already familiar with phosphorescent tubes. Therefore, this could easily lead to the early development of TVs. Analysis of the fragments after the vacuum tube imploded under examination could reveal details about electronics (resistors, capacitors, transformers). The electron guns would be salvageable and so would samples of the chemicals used to line the inside of the screen. This could lead to early development and better funding for much of the electronics industry. The results of this would be widespread. If they were able to begin to understand transistor technology, 1940 may be like 1990, and it is unlikely that World War II would have occurred, due to the development of atomic technology.

"The CPU box itself contains, among other things, lots of 'funny black rectangles of silicon' with a few impurities. They will not have had the technology to open them up and see what was inside (or even detect the impurities). This will lead to lots of professors working out how to grow perfect crystals of silicon, cutting them into rectangles, soldering wires onto them and painting them black. They will then wonder why they don't compute when electricity is added. These techniques will be very valuable when someone has developed transistor technology, and there will then begin an accelerated development of chip technology and chip manufacture. Much more of our world may be computer-controlled and we may well have a utopian society. Alternatively the rate of change we have experienced may be the fastest society will withstand without either disintegrating or reacting violently against the new technology and returning to the fields. With advances in medical science the world population could be higher, but it is doubtful that the political situation will be any better."

"The power source may lead to the earlier development of better batteries."

## 15.9  Appendix A. The Year 1900

In order to give you an appreciation for what the world was like in 1900, a few interesting events are listed here; these events occurred in 1889, 1900, or 1901

1.  History – Filipinos demand independence from U.S. William McKinley, 25th US president, is assassinated. Emperor William II visits England. Germany secures Baghdad Railroad contract. Edmund Barton is inaugurated as the first Prime minister of Australia. Treaty is negotiated on building of Panama Canal under US supervision.

2.  Literature – Oscar Wilde: "The Importance of Being Ernest." Joseph Conrad: "Lord Jim." Kipling: "Kim."

3.  Philosophy/Religion – Shintoism reinstated in Japan against Buddhist influence. Sigmund Freud: "The Interpretation of Dreams." Bertrand Russell: "A Critical Exposition of the Philosophy of Leibniz."

4.  Visual Arts – Picasso: "Le Moulin de la Galette." Cezanne: "Still Life with Onions." Renoir: "Nude in the Sun." Walt Disney born. Picasso's Blue Period.

5.  Music – Johann Strauss dies.  Richard Strauss: "Ein Heldenleben." Aaron Copland born. Dvorak: "Rusalka." Rachmaninoff: "Piano Concerto No. 2." Ragtime jazz develops in U.S.

6.  Science – Rutherford discovers alpha and beta rays in radioactive atoms. First magnetic recording of sound is made. Max Planck formulates quantum theory. American scientist R.A. Fessenden transmits human speech via radio waves.  First trial flight of Zeppelin is made. The hormone adrenaline is first isolated.  Marconi transmits telegraphic radio messages.  First motor-driven bicycles are made.

7.  Daily Life – J.P. Morgan organizes the US Steel Corporation.  Oil drilling begins in Persia. Boxing is recognized as a legal sport in England.

## 15.10  Appendix B. Unexpected Arrivals of Technology

The following are some actual historical examples of the sudden, unexpected arrival of a technology. As stated in the beginning of this chapter, it is a fascinating task to follow the effect of such events on the history of humankind and also to contemplate future technologies which would not have occurred until many years later, except for an accidental discovery.  All of the following were discovered by accident:  Velcro, penicillin, X rays, Teflon, dynamite, Scotchguard, Post-Its, Ivory soap, aspirin, polyethylene, nylon, LSD, rayon, and rubber.

As a specific example, consider the effect that rubber has had on civilization.  Europeans found no important use for rubber for more than two centuries because it became soft and sticky at high temperatures. Charles Goodyear's accidental discovery, which overcame this temperature sensitivity, came about when he allowed a mixture of rubber and sulfur to touch a hot stove. To his surprise the rubber did not melt but only charred slightly – and this temperature-insensitive rubber made by the combination of rubber and sulfur has played an important role in many industries.

As another example, consider the Friedel-Crafts reaction, named after the two chemists who observed an unexpected result of an experiment in Friedel's laboratory in 1877. Their unexpected combination of chemicals promised the possibility of synthesizing a wide variety of hydrocarbons and ketones, established a new area of research and practice in organic chemistry, and laid the foundation for one of the most important modern industrial chemical processes. Their reaction has touched our lives in many important ways. One may speculate that the superiority of Britain's fighter pilots over the Germans' was due in part to superior aviation gasoline, which came about through a direct outgrowth of Freidel-Crafts chemistry.

## 15.11  For Further Reading

1.    Feingold, S. (1989) *Futuristic Exercises: A Workbook for Emerging Lifestyles and Careers in the 21st Century and Beyond*. Garrey Park Press: Maryland.

2.    Brown, P. (1990) Metamedia and Cyberspace: advanced computers and the future of art. In *Culture, Technology, and Creativity in the Late 20th Century*. Philip Heywood, ed. Arts Council of Great Britain.

3.    Grun, B. (1975) *The Timetables of History*. Simon and Schuster: New York.

4.    Roberts, R. (1989) *Serendipity: Accidental Discoveries in Science*. Wiley: New York.

5.    Pickover, C. (1991) A personal computer placed in the year 1900. *IEEE Computer*, in press.

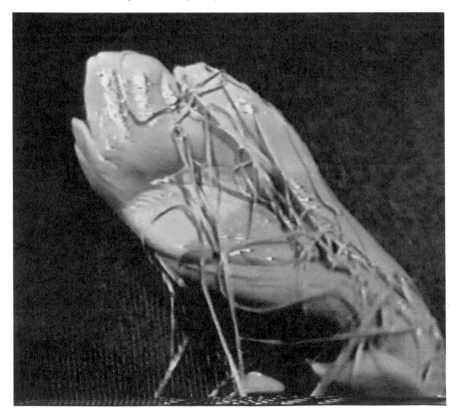

Chapter 16

# Interlude: Research and Development

The National Science Foundation estimated that, in the fiscal year 1990, the United States will spend almost $150 billion for research and development in all fields. This is more than the combined expenditures of West Germany, France, Japan, and the United Kingdom. In 1988, the United States had 77 full-time R&D professionals for every 10,000 people.

The chart shown here indicates the top R&D spenders. These companies are from the U.S. except for Siemens, which is from Germany. You should compare this chart with the chart in "Interlude: Research and Development" on page 59 which shows the top spenders in terms of percentage of sales rather than U.S. dollars. Data for this chart comes from: Kaplan, G., Rosenblatt, A. (1990) The expanding world of R&D. *IEEE Spectrum*. October 27(10): 33.

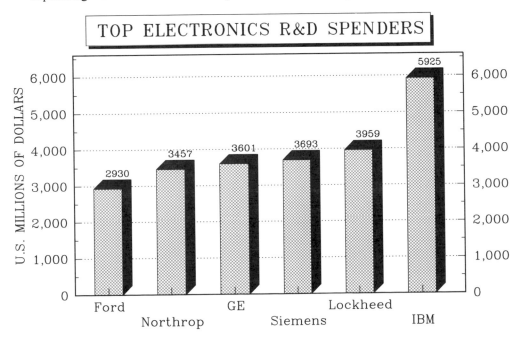

Trombetta di Canna

# Part IV

# VISUALIZATION

Tromba del Madure

Chapter 17

# Visualization: Introduction

*"The standard argument to promote scientific visualization is that today's researchers must consume ever larger volumes of numbers that gush, as if from a fire hose, out of supercomputer simulations or high-powered scientific instruments. If researchers try to read the data, usually presented as vast numeric matrices, they will take in the information at a snail's pace. If the information is rendered graphically, however, they can assimilate it at a much faster rate."*
R. Friedhoff and T. Kiely, *The Eye of the Beholder, 1990*

*"We take a handful of sand from the endless landscape of awareness around us and call that handful of sand the world."* Robert Pirsig

Computer graphics has become indispensable in countless areas of human activity – from colorful and lighthearted television commercials, to strange new artworks, to evolutionary biology, to processed images from the edges of the known universe. It is also becoming very useful to mathematicians. Long before computer graphics, pictures and physical models played an important role in mathematics. Nineteenth-century mathematicians, for instance, regularly drew pictures and sculpted bizarre plaster or wooden models to help them visualize and understand

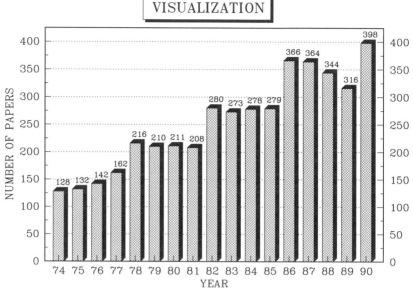

**Figure 17.1.** *Visualization articles.* A review of the world scientific literature shows the number of visualization articles rising during the years 1975 - 1990.

geometric forms. Today mathematicians use computer graphics to add a vivid new dimension to geometric investigations. One center of this kind of activity is the Geometry Supercomputer Project, based at the University of Minnesota at Minneapolis-St. Paul. Established in 1987 by a group of thirteen mathematicians and computer scientists, this project addresses various unsolved mathematical problems using powerful computers.

A recent National Science Foundation study found that the sciences were in urgent need of government support for graphic tools to view the millions of bytes of data that computers are heaping upon researchers (Wolff, 1988). The commercial world is beginning to recognize the visualization needs of the scientific community and respond to them. Graphics workstations were born more than five years ago to give investigators more comprehensible representations of their results. Manufacturers such as Stardent, Silicon Graphics, IBM, PIXAR, and many others have aimed to bridge the gap between fast computation and 3-D images.

Today, *scientific visualization* has come to mean the marriage of high-speed computation and colorful 3-D graphics. Visualization is being vigorously pursued in various university supercomputer centers and government labs.[16] In the sections to follow, we will use both simple 2-D graphics and more sophisticated 3-D graphics to help visualize a range of phenomena. The usefulness of a particular

---

[16] In 1989 the world's scientific journals published about 300 articles with the words "visualization" or "visualizations" in the title. Figure 17.1 shows the number of papers with titles containing these words for the years 1975-1990, the 1990 value estimated from data for January-June 1990.

**Figure 17.2.** *Visualization of protein shapes.* (By Henrik Bohr and Soren Brunak, The Technical University of Denmark.) This is a graphical representation of an ensemble of 3-D conformations of a small pancreatic protein from a bird.  For more information, see Borh and Brunak (1989).

graphic representation is determined by its descriptive capacity, potential for comparison, aid in focusing attention, and versatility. For background articles in the field of scientific visualization, see the reference section which follows. There are also many journals devoted to the subject of scientific visualization, including: *Computers and Graphics* (Pergamon), *The Visual Computer* (Springer-Verlag), *IEEE Computer Graphics and Applications* (IEEE Computer Society), *The Journal of Visualization and Computer Animation* (Wiley), *Computer Graphics World* (PennWell Publishing), and *Pixel* (American Association of Computing Machinery).

As mentioned in the *Introduction*, almost all of the computer graphics in this book are my own, but I would like to conclude this section with a gallery of four favorite graphics from other scientists (Figure 17.2, Figure 17.3, Figure 17.4, and Figure 17.5). More information on each of these patterns, and the insight they provide, is in the publications referenced.

**Figure 17.3.** *Visualization of a neural network.* (By Peter Desain, Utrecht School of the Arts, The Netherlands.) This is a graphical representation showing different trajectories in a neural network. Each point on the plot represents a rhythm in a net of interacting cells. For more information, see Desain and Honig (1989).

## 17.1 For Further Reading

1. Friedhoff, R., Kiely, T. (1990) The eye of the beholder. *Computer Graphics World.* August 13(8): 47-56. Also: Peterson, I. (1989) The color of geometry. *Science News.* December 23, 136: 406-410.

2. Tufte, E. (1983) *The Visual Display of Quantitative Information.* Graphics Press: Connecticut. Also see: Wolff, R. (1988) The visualization challenge in the physical sciences. *Computers in Science.* Jan./Feb. 2(1): 16-31.

3. Wainer, H., Thissen, D. (1981) Graphical Data Analysis. *Annual Review of Psychology.* 32: 191-241. Also: Friedhoff, R., Benzon, W. (1989) *Visualization: The Second Computer Revolution.* Abrams: New York.

4. Gerdes, P. (1989) Reconstruction and extension of lost symmetries: examples from the Tamil of South India. *Computers and Mathematics with Applications.* 17(4-6): 791-813.

5. Bohr, H. and Brunak, S. (1989) *Complex Systems.* 3: 9.

6. Desain, P. and Honig, H. (1989) Quantization of musical time: a connectionist approach. *Computer Music Journal.* 13(3): 56-66.

7. Rangel-Mondragon, J., Abas, S. J., (1988) Computer generation of penrose tilings. *Computer Graphics Forum.* 7: 29-37.

**Figure 17.4.** *Visualization of a Tamil ring-pattern.* (By Paulus Gerdes, Higher Pedagogical Institute, Mozambique.) These diagrams aid researchers in understanding traditional Tamil designs. Tamil women of South India use a mnemonic device for memorization of pictograms. The women form a background grid for the pattern by starting with an orthogonal net of equidistant points placed on a smooth ground. For more information, see Gerdes (1989).

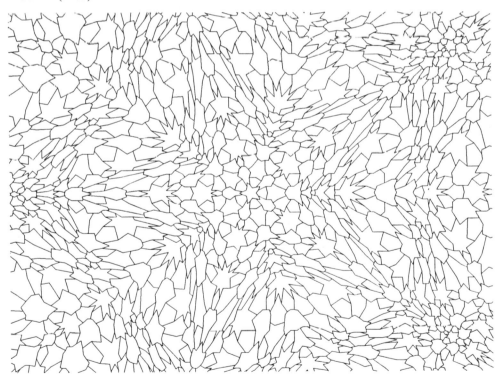

**Figure 17.5.** *Visualization of tiling patterns.* (By J. Rangel-Mondragon and S. J. Abas, University of North Wales, U.K.) Depicted here is a pattern obtained from a nonlinear transformation applied to a Penrose tiling (Glossary). Such tilings are generated using two different shapes with certain matching rules applied to their edges. For more information, see Rangel-Mondragon and Abas (1988).

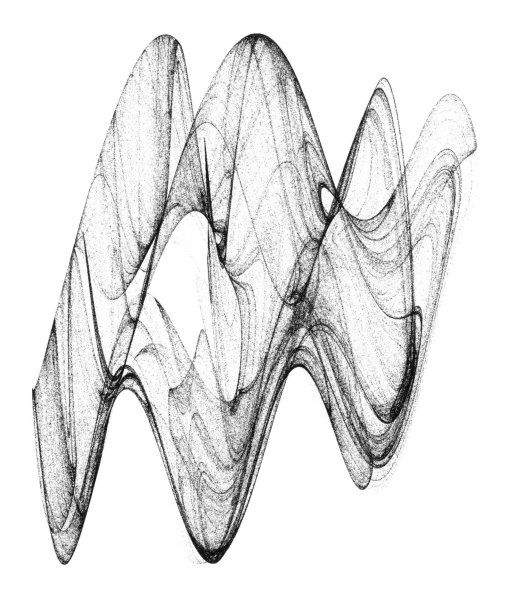

# Chapter 18

# Pain Inducing Patterns

The *Visualization* section begins with a pattern known to cause pain in viewers. Therefore, for legal reasons, this fascinating pattern is only described but not printed. Because some viewers have been known to require medical supervision after gazing at the patterns, I have called this class of patterns "painful patterns."

In 1984, several British researchers discovered that some people find a certain pattern of stripes painful to look at; moreover, stripe viewing apparently induced headache attacks in some subjects with histories of headaches. In 1989, researchers in the U.S. further demonstrated that this kind of pattern appears to help in distinguishing those people who suffer from migraine headaches from other types of headaches. Migraine sufferers, when presented with this pattern will find the pattern extremely objectionable and attempt to avert their gaze, while people who do not suffer from this type of headache will have relatively little difficulty looking at the pattern. The test pattern was designed for use by physicians as one part of an overall diagnostic test, and can be used to help distinguish migraine from non-migraine headache sufferers. It must however be used with caution, as the pattern is capable of triggering migraine headaches in some people. Certain patients with epilepsy may also suffer seizures after looking at the pattern.

Despite the potential for triggering migraine headaches, the interesting pattern has been published in the journal *Brain* in 1984. You can program this pattern on your computer using the following hint: it resembles a circle filled with alternating black and white vertical stripes. At a viewing distance of 43 cm, this grating has a spatial frequency of 3 cycles/degree of visual arc, and a Michelson contrast (*Glossary*) of about 0.7.

## 18.1 For Further Reading

1.  Marcus, D., Soso, M. (1989) Migraine and stripe-induced visual discomfort. *Archives of Neurology*. October 46: 1129-1132.
2.  Wilkins, A., Nimmo-Smith, I., Tait, A., McManus, C., Sala, S., Tilley, A., Arnold, K. Barrie, M., Scott, S (1984) A neurological basis for visual discomfort. *Brain*. 107: 989-1017.

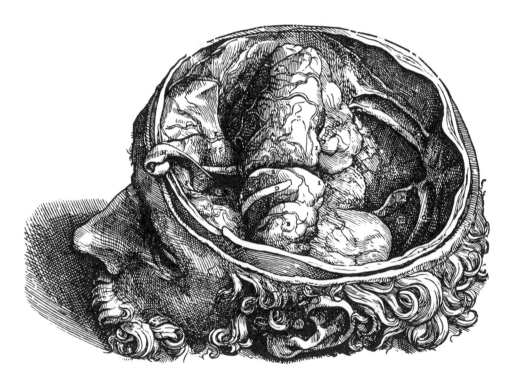

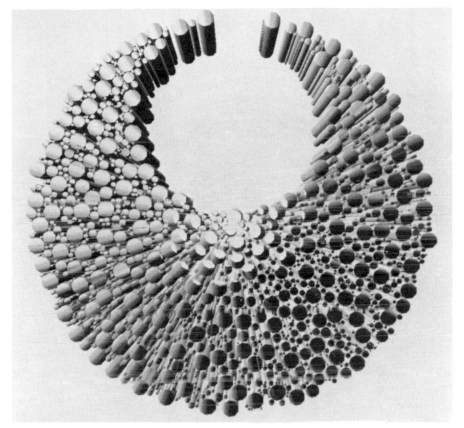

*Cleopatra's Necklace*, or *Fertile Crescent*, "grown" using the osculatory methods described in section 25.2.

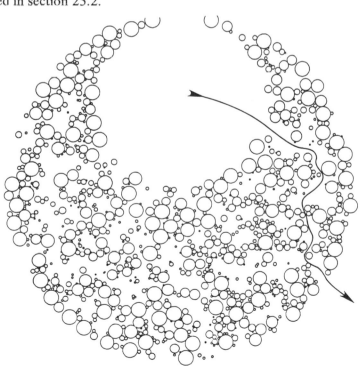

Find the longest path from the inner side of this low density crescent to the outer side. Shown is one path. Is it the longest?

# Chapter 19

# The Ikeda Attractor

A deep reservoir for striking images is the *dynamical system*. Dynamical systems are models comprised of the rules describing the way some quantity undergoes a change through time. For example, the motion of planets about the sun can be modeled as a dynamical system in which the planets move according to Newton's laws. The frontispiece diagram for this chapter represents the behavior of mathematical expressions called *differential equations*. Think of a differential equation as a machine that takes in values for all the variables at an initial time and then generates the new values at some later time. Just as one can track the path of a jet by the smoke path it leaves behind, computer graphics provides a way to follow paths of particles whose motion is determined by simple differential equations. The practical side of dynamical systems is that they can sometimes be used to describe the behavior of real-world things such as planetary motion, fluid flow, the diffusion of drugs, the behavior of inter-industry relationships, and the vibration of airplane wings. Often the resulting graphic patterns resemble smoke, swirls, candle flames, and windy mists.

The *Ikeda attractor* shown facing this page is an example of a strange attractor. As background, *predictable attractors* represent the behavior to which a system settles down or is "attracted" (for example, a point or a looping closed cycle). An example of a *fixed point attractor* is a mass at the end of a spring, with friction. It eventually arrives at an equilibrium point and stops moving. A *limit cycle* is exemplified by a metronome. The metronome will tick-tock back and forth – its motion always periodic and regular. A *"strange attractor"* has an irregular, unpredictable behavior. Its behavior can still be graphed, but the graph is much more complicated. With "tame" attractors, initially close points stay together as they approach the attractor. With strange attractors, initially adjacent points eventually follow widely divergent trajectories. Like leaves in a turbulent stream, it is impossible to predict where the leaves will end up given their initial positions.

Pseudocode 19.1 shows you how to produce the Ikeda pattern, a representation of a dynamical system. Simply plot the position of variables *j* and *k* through the iteration. The variables *scale, xoff,* and *yoff* simply position and scale

```
ALGORITHM: How to Create an Ikeda Attractor.
c1 = 0.4, c2 = 0.9,  c3 = 6.0, rho = 1.0;
for (i = 0, x = 0.1, y = 0.1; i <= 3000; i++) (
   temp = c1 - c3 / (1.0 + x * x + y * y);
   sin_temp = sin(temp);
   cos_temp = cos(temp);
   xt = rho + c2 * (x * cos_temp - y * sin_temp);
   y =   c2 * (x * sin_temp + y * cos_temp) ;
   x = xt;
   j = x * scale + xoff;
   k = y * scale + yoff;
)
```

**Pseudocode 19.1.** *How to create an Ikeda attractor.* (The program coded here is in the style of the C language.)

the image to fit on the graphics screen. The Ikeda attractor has been described in greater detail by K. Ikeda (see references).

## 19.1  For Further Reading

1.  Ikeda, K. (1979) Multiple-valued stationary state and its instability of the transmitted light by a ring cavity system. *Optical Communications.* 30: 257.

2.  Stewart, I. (1987) The nature of stability. *Speculations in Science and Technology.* 10(4): 310-324.

APPARENTLY, PROFESSOR ERK, OUR NOTIONS
ABOUT THE STATE OF ANCIENT SCIENCE WILL
HAVE TO UNDERGO SOME REVISION.

Chapter 20

# Virtual Voltage Sculptures

*"Artists can color the sky red because they know it's blue. Those of us who aren't artists must color things the way they are or people might think we're stupid."*
Jules Feiffer

Sculpture is one of the oldest and most widespread of the arts. I think you'll agree with me that it's also one of the most difficult of the arts, for it requires physical labor, patience, and complete control of the material for a long time. Today, computer graphics can help artists and scientists project their imaginations, creating unusual sculptures which are free from the physical restraints of gravity and material properties. Computer sculptures of abstract 3-D forms by both artists and computer scientists are beginning to become socially accepted, as evidenced by the display of such works in various art museums and galleries. Some beautiful past work includes the computer art of William Latham (IBM United Kingdom Scientific Center), John Lewis (New York Institute of Technology), and Donna Cox (National Center for Supercomputing Applications) (see references).

Of particular interest to me are sculptures created by computing an equal-valued surface, or "isosurface," at a particular value in a 3-D continuum of data. One can apply the same kinds of isosurface graphics that are used to represent molecular orbitals and electron densities to computer art. [[ I have defined a *continuum structure of a sculpture* by the spatial function in Equation (20.1), which is a simplification for formulas giving the voltage fields from a distribution of charges:

$$I(\vec{x}) = \int \frac{\rho(\vec{x}')}{|\vec{x} - \vec{x}'|^{\alpha}} \, d\vec{x}' \tag{20.1}$$

Don't let the complicated expression scare you away, because we will simplify this. The numerator $\rho(\vec{x})$ usually represents a 3-D continuous charge density, but here I use

**Figure 20.1.** *Sculpture created from a short segment of DNA (deoxyribonucleic acid).*

$$\rho(\vec{x}) = \sum_i a\delta(\vec{x} - \vec{x}_i) \tag{20.2}$$

to represent a collection of points.

$$I(\vec{x}) = \sum_i \frac{a}{|\vec{x} - \vec{x}_i|^\alpha} \tag{20.3}$$

where $a = 1$. This is a much simpler expression than those used for realistic voltage potential equations for molecules, but when $\alpha = 1$, $I$ is the voltage potential for a collection of point charges. Here $\rho(\vec{x})$ is simply the value 1 at specified coordinates of points in space. Equation (20.3) does define a global geometrical envelope which may be useful for artists and for scientific visualization. In a computer program, one can represent the "internal skeletal structure" of a sculpture by a collection of points $j$. A computer program places an imaginary 3-D array of grid points around the collections of point charges and computes the distance from each grid point to each of the point charges. The intensities $I_i$ are obtained by computing $\Sigma 1/d_{ij}^\alpha$ for every element $i$ in the 3-D array. The value $d$ is simply the distance from each array point (or volume element) to a coordinate of the wire frame. For the sculptures in this section, a 40x40x40 volume array was used. Equi-valued surfaces, which represent the final form the viewer actually sees, are defined by

$$I(x,y,z) = C \tag{20.4}$$

**Figure 20.2.** *Abstract sculpture.*

for a given spatial function, $I$, and user-specified constant $C$. The equi-valued surface sculptures in this chapter were computed using a program which represents surfaces as a collection of small triangular facets.]] The triangles which make up the surface are smoothed, shaded, rotated, and lighted via a general purpose display program running on a graphics workstation.

Figure 20.1 is a sculpture created from a short segment of DNA (deoxyribonucleic acid). (See "The Cancer Conundrum" on page 23 for information on DNA.) Note that the sculpture may be useful as an educational diagram since the major and minor grooves in DNA are clearly made visible, and these features are sometimes obscure to viewers who look at the molecule with all its atoms. I have also represented enzyme molecules in a similar manner in order to better see the overall surface envelope and not be distracted by the thousands of atoms. It is amusing that many viewers of this sculpture have found a resemblance of the overall form to Auguste Rodin's marble sculpture, "The Kiss." For Figure 20.2, the underlying skeletal structure consists of a row of point charges following three simple trigonometric curves that form a knot. Figure 20.3 is the same as Figure 20.2, except that the isosurface value $C$ (Equation (20.4)) is slightly higher, and more interior structures are revealed. It is as if the creature represented by the sculpture were starving; greater degrees of starvation are easily attainable. Some of the chunkiness in the figure arises from the use of a coarse grid and also the fact that isosurface values are difficult to compute for data that are either rapidly changing in value or constant in value for nearby volume elements. I hope that as these methods become generally available to artists and scientists, additional visually interesting "voltage" sculptures will be created using relatively simple underlying skeletal structures. Since the sculpture is actually a continuum of density in three space, artists can experiment with the $C$ value in order to produce the most desirable effects. In addition, $\alpha$ values in the range of 1 to 4 should be tried. I have found that $\alpha = 3$ and $\alpha = 4$, in particular, give very

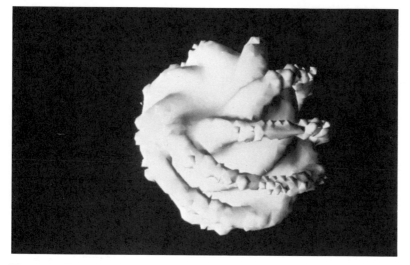

**Figure 20.3.** *Abstract starvation sculpture.* A starved version of previous figure. (As one friend remarked, "The fat melts away, and you can see its ribs.")

interesting-looking forms, even though these values do not correspond to a physically meaningful term such as voltage potential. In closing, computer scientists should note that the triangulated isosurface sculpture is "economical" for interactive graphics, because the reevaluation of the spatial function is not required for rotation, translation, and zoom once the sculpture has been generated. Also, many graphics software and hardware technologies make use of triangular input data.

## 20.1 For Further Reading

1.    Latham, W., Todd, S. (1989) Computer sculpture. *IBM Systems Journal.* 28(4): 692-699.

2.    Lewis, J. (1989) Algorithms for solid noise synthesis. *Computer Graphics (ACM-SIGGRAPH).* 23(3): 263-273.

3.    Cox, D. (1989) The tao of post modernism: computer art, scientific visualization and other paradoxes. *Leonardo Supplemental Issue: Computer Art in Context.* pgs 7-12.

4.    Cox, D. (1988) Using the supercomputer to visualize higher dimensions: an artist's contribution to scientific visualization. *Leonardo.* 21: 233-242.

5.    Koide, A. (1989) Designing molecules and crystals by computer. *IBM Systems Journal.* 28(4): 613-627.

6.    Reitz, J., Milford, F., Christy, R. (1979) *Foundations of Electromagnetic Theory.* Addison-Wesley: Reading, Mass.

7.    van Dam, A. (1988) PHIGS+ functional description, revision 3.0. *Computer Graphics (ACM SIGGRAPH).* July 22(3) (entire volume).

8.    Pickover, C. (1991) Virtual voltage sculptures, *Leonardo*, in press.

Chapter 21

# The World of Chaos

*"Except for our own thoughts, there is nothing absolutely in our own power."*
Rene Descartes

*"Fractal images are incomplete art, of course, since they are abstract and not culturally rooted. "* P.W. Atkins, *1990*

To ancient humans, Chaos represented the unknown, the spirit world – menacing, nightmarish visions that reflected man's fear of the irrational and the need to give shape and form to his apprehensions. Today, chaos theory is an exciting, growing field which usually involves the study of a range of phenomena exhibiting a sensitive dependence on initial conditions. Although chaos often seems totally "random," it can obey strict mathematical rules derived from equations that can be formulated and studied. One important research tool to aid in the study of chaos is computer graphics. From chaotic toys with randomly blinking lights to wisps and eddies of cigarette smoke, chaotic behavior is irregular and disorderly; other examples include weather patterns, some neurological and cardiac activity, the stock market, and certain electrical networks of computers. Chaos theory has also often been applied to a wide range of visual art.[17]

In physics, there are certain famous and clear examples of chaotic physical systems. A few examples are listed here: thermal convection in fluids, supersonic panel flutter in supersonic aircraft, particles impacting on a periodically vibrating wall, various pendula and rotor motions, nonlinear electrical circuits, and buckled beams. Moon's book gives many more examples.

This section of the book will provide you with a list of some new references in the chaos literature which you can add to the extensive reference list in *Computers, Pattern, Chaos, and Beauty* (Pickover, 1990). I also want to describe a

---

[17] In 1989 the world's scientific journals published about 1,200 articles with the words "chaos" or "fractal(s)" in the title. Figure 21.1 shows the number of papers with titles containing the words "chaos" or "fractal(s)" for the years 1975-1990, the 1990 values estimated from data for January-June 1990.

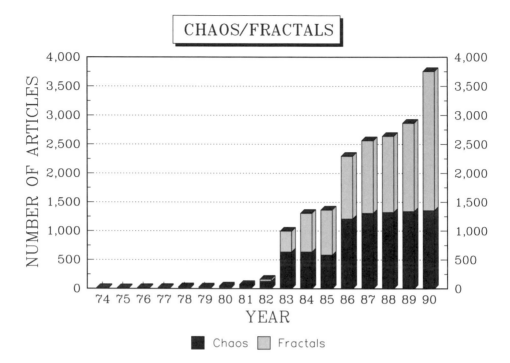

**Figure 21.1.** *Chaos and fractal articles.* A review of the world scientific literature between 1973 and 1990 shows the number of chaos and fractal articles rising dramatically between the years 1982 and 1990.

few of the color plates in this book. Other color plates are described in "Descriptions of Color Plates and Frontispieces" on page 393. For example, Color plate 10 shows a "Julia-like" set computed for the two-dimensional complex Euclidean space $f:C^2 \to C^2$. You can learn more about Julia sets by reading Mandelbrot's book or *Computers, Pattern, Chaos, and Beauty*. I computed this very high resolution image (2500x2500 pixels with 24 bits of color) using an IBM 3090 computer and a Matrix QCR-Z camera. The image represents a visually interesting quartic variant of Shigehiro Ushiki's Julia set that he calls "Phoenix." My computer program produces a quartic variation by iterating just four commands, in order:

$$z = z^2 - 0.5z + \alpha, \quad x = z^2 - 0.5y + \alpha, \quad y = z, \quad z = x \qquad (21.1)$$

where $\alpha = 0.56667$, and all variables are complex. The "level sets" (sometimes called contours) are computed as usual for Julia sets, and the colors indicate different rates of explosion for the initial complex plane values $z_0$. The various curvy stalks both within and outside of the region corresponding to bounded orbits indicate that an orbit has passed through a narrow cross-shaped aperture centered at the origin.[18] That is, points are colored if an orbit ever satisfies either of the two conditions:

$$\begin{cases} |x| < \varepsilon \text{ or} \\ |y| < \varepsilon \end{cases} \qquad (21.2)$$

where $\varepsilon = 0.01$.

Many of the color plates in this book show additional renditions of irregular behavior in physical or mathematical systems. For example, Color plates 1 and 2 show an image-processed representation of a non-Newtonian fluid. The image corresponds to a region of the fluid which is 2 cm by 2 cm in area. Art Stein helped to digitally capture my images (which were stored on a VHS video tape) using a MATROX MVP board in an IBM AT. These images were subsequently imaged-processed using an IBM 3090. (See "Notes for the Curious" on page 371 for additional information on these shapes.)

Color plate 5 was created on a graphics supercomputer by plotting the trajectory of a conical pendulum, and representing the positions of the pendulum by a collection of spheres. For artistic purposes, the figure is oriented with the "mouth" pointing to the side rather than up. This image was computed on an IBM 3090 computer and rendered using a Stellar GS2000 graphics workstation running a general-purpose scientific visualization tool. This graphics tool also runs on an IBM RISC System/6000.

## 21.1  The Lorenz Attractor

Here I want to encourage your involvement by providing a simple computer recipe. Consider, for example, the famed Lorenz Attractor. In 1962, MIT meteorologist E.N. Lorenz was attempting to develop a model of the weather. Lorenz simplified a weather model until it consisted of only three differential equations.

$$dx/dt = 10(y - x) \qquad (21.3)$$

$$dy/dt = -xz + 28x - y \qquad (21.4)$$

$$dz/dt = xy - (8/3)z \qquad (21.5)$$

$t$ is time, and $d/dt$ is the rate of change. If we plot the path that these equations describe using a computer, the trajectories seem to trace out a squashed pretzel. The surprising thing is that if you start with two slightly different initial points, e.g. (.6, .6, .6) and (.6, .6, .6001), the resulting curves first appear to coincide, but soon chaotic dynamics leads to independent, widely divergent trajectories. This is not to say that there is no pattern, although the trajectories do cycle, apparently at random, around the two lobes. In fact, the squashed pretzel shape always results no matter what starting point is used. This is the behavior to which the system is attracted.

---

[18] See "Turning a Universe Inside-Out" on page 169 for information on related topics and a definition of the term "orbit."

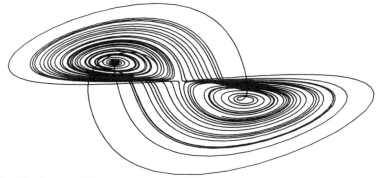

**Figure 21.2.** *The Lorenz Attractor.*

To create the Lorenz attractor, one needs to solve the system of differential equations given above. Several numerical techniques can be used that come up with an accurate value for *x,y,* and *z* as a function of time. The most straightforward approach, which I have used to get a rough idea about the Lorenz attractor, simply replaces *dx* with *(xnew - x)*, and replaces *dt* by a time step, called *h.* Other higher accuracy approaches, such as Runge Kutta methods, can be used but only with consequent increase in computer time. To create a projection of this 3-D figure in the *x-y* plane, simply plot *(x,y)* pairs of points and omit the *z*-value (Figure 21.2).

## 21.2 Lyapunov Surfaces and Volumes

Lyapunov surfaces and volumes provide an elegant way to represent the rich and complicated behavior of certain simple formulas. The mathematics of this method is somewhat technical, so I direct you to my paper for illustrations and details.[19] A few of the details are mentioned here.

[[ A number of natural phenomena can be described by one-dimensional maps of the kind $X_{t+1} = f(X_t)$, $t = 1,2,3, \ldots \infty$. As an example, consider the equation

$$X_{t+1} = \frac{\lambda X_t}{[1 + X_t]^\beta} \qquad (21.6)$$

where $\beta$ is a constant, and $\lambda$ is called a bifurcation parameter.[20] This equation has been used to fit a considerable amount of data on insect populations (See May, 1976). High-resolution bifurcation maps of this equation are presented in Pickover (1988).

How can the researcher visualize the intricate stability behavior of the 2-parameter system in Equation (21.6) and convey the results in an easy-to-understand fashion to colleagues? This section

---

[19] Pickover, C. (1990) Visualizing chaos: Lyapunov surfaces and volumes. IEEE Computer Graphics and Applications. March 10(2): 15-19.
[20] You can study the behavior of this equation using your computer by first selecting a starting value for $X_{t=1}$ of 0.3. Your choice of starting value does not matter much. The result $X_{t+1}$ is fed back into the equation as a new value for $X_t$, and the process repeated over and over again. If $\beta = 5$ and $\lambda > 59$, the $X$ values you generate will seem to behave chaotically. For $\lambda < 59$ the $X$ values will be periodic.

```
ALGORITHM: Code to Generate the Lorenz Attractor

Typical values: h=0.01, npts=4000;
Typical starting values: x,y,z = .6;

  frac=8/3;
  do i = 1 to npts;
    xnew = x + h*10*(y-x);
    ynew = y + h*((-x*z) + 28*x-y);
    znew = z + h*(x*y - frac*z);
    x=xnew; y=ynew; z=znew;
    MovePenTo(x,y);
  end;
```

**Pseudocode 21.1.** *How to generate the Lorenz attractor.*

describes the dynamics of Equation (21.6) by computing several hundred thousand Lyapunov exponents (Equation (21.7)) for a range of $\lambda$ and $\beta$ values. Lyapunov exponents tell you how "crazy" the behavior of your equation is. Stated more scientifically, it quantifies the average stability of the oscillatory modes. 3-D maps with pseudocolor can reveal the complicated behavior of Equation (21.6) in an aesthetic and useful fashion. For the dual parameter dependence in Equation (21.6), the search for useful graphical representations becomes an interesting challenge (see my paper). Note that Markus and Hess have produced several fascinating and beautiful color 2-D Lyapunov graphs for the logistic map, where the bifurcation parameter changes periodically between two different values.

In this section, for each parameter pair $(\lambda, \beta)$, one computes the Lyapunov exponent

$$\Lambda = \lim_{N \to \infty} \frac{1}{N} \sum_{n=1}^{N} \ln \left| \frac{dx_{n+1}}{dx_n} \right|, \quad x = f(\lambda, \beta) \tag{21.7}$$

where $dx_{n+1}/dx_n = \lambda[ -x\beta(1 + x)^{-\beta-1} + (1 + x)^{-\beta}]$ in our special case. As has been pointed out for other 1-D maps, the approach to the limit in Equation (21.7) can be highly irregular (Markus and Hess, 1989). However, iterating Equation (21.7) several hundred times yielded satisfactory results and useful maps.

One-dimensional maps are characterized by a single Lyapunov exponent which is positive for chaos, zero for a marginally stable orbit, and negative for a periodic orbit:

$$\begin{aligned}
\Lambda &< 0, \text{ the orbit is stable} \\
\Lambda &= 0, \text{ the orbit is neutrally stable} \\
\Lambda &> 0, \text{ the orbit is locally unstable and chaotic}
\end{aligned} \tag{21.8}$$

Any system containing at least one positive Lyapunov exponent is defined formally to be chaotic, with the magnitude of the exponent reflecting the time scale on which the system's dynamics become unpredictable.

In my work, $\beta$ is not constant but oscillates between two values as a function of $t$. Pickover (1990) shows a Lyapunov volume which can be thought of as a rectangular chunk of Swiss cheese, representing $\Lambda$, $\beta_1$ and $\beta_2$. The volume may be sliced, using interactive graphic tools, to reveal interior structures. Here a color table containing colors progressing as the colors of the rainbow is used. Blue areas are stable, and yellow and red represent chaos.

Those of you interested in both the history and mathematics of chaos should consult the papers and books listed in the following section.[21] Some interesting references for a general reading on the subject are singled out in the following list.

---

[21] I invite you to submit papers with interesting computer graphics to the "Chaos and Graphics" section of the international journal *Computers and Graphics*. I edit this section, and we publish a range of artistic and scientifically interesting images in the broad field of chaos. You are also invited to contribute to *The Pattern Book*, a catalog of visually interesting patterns from many different fields. Write to me for more details.

1.  Gleick, J. (1987) *Chaos: Making a New Science*. Viking: New York.

2.  Stewart, I. (1989) *Does God Play Dice? (The Mathematics of Chaos)*. Basil Blackwell: New York.

3.  Moon, F. (1987) *Chaotic Vibrations*. John Wiley and Sons, New York. (Moon gives many practical examples of chaos in real physical systems.)

4.  Shaw, A. (1984) *The Dripping Faucet as a Model Chaotic System*. Aerial Press: California.

5.  Pickover, C. (1990) The world of chaos. *Computers in Physics*. Sept/Oct 4(5):460-470.

## 21.3  For Further Reading

Included in the following list are some interesting references in the field of chaos, many of which are not included in the extensive chaos reference list in *Computers, Pattern, Chaos, and Beauty*.

1.  Cooper, N. (1989) *From Cardinals to Chaos*. Cambridge University Press: New York. (Topics: Stan Ulam, iteration, strange attractors, Monte Carlo methods, the human brain, random number generators, number theory, and genetics.)

2.  Milnor, J. (1989) Self-similarity and hairyness of the Mandelbrot set. In *Computers in Geometry and Topology*. M. Tangora, ed. Marcel Dekker. pp 211-257.

3.  Ushiki, S. (1988) Phoenix. *IEEE Trans. Circuits and Syst.* July 35(7): 788-789.

4.  Abraham, R., Shaw, C. (1985) *Dynamics – The Geometry of Behavior, Part 3: Global Behavior*. Aerial Press: California. (Actually, the entire book collection of Aerial Press, including the Visual Math Series, is an educational wonderland).

5.  Healy, J. (1990) Chaos on Sesame Street. *American Educator*. Winter Issue. 22-39.

6.  Chossat, P., Golubitsky, M. (1988) Symmetry-increasing bifurcations of chaotic attractors. *Physica D*. 32, 423-426.

7.  Collet, P., J.P. Eckmann. (1980) *Iterated Maps on the Interval as Dynamical Systems*. Birkhauser: Boston.

8.  Crutchfield, J., Farmer, J., Packard, N. (1986) Chaos. *Scien. Amer.* 255: 46-57;

9.  Dewdney, A. K. (1985) Computer Recreations. *Scien. Amer.* 253: 16-24.

10. Feigenbaum, M. (1979) The universal metric properties of nonlinear transformations. *J. Statistical Physics*. 21: 669-706.

11. Feigenbaum, M. (1981) Universal behavior in nonlinear systems. *Los Alamos Science*. 1: 4-27.

12. Feder, J. (1988) *Fractals*. Plenum: New York.

13. Glass, L., Mackey, M. (1988) *From Clocks to Chaos: The Rhythms of Life* Princeton Univ. Press: New Jersey.

14. Dodge, C. (1988) Profile: A musical fractal. *Computer Music Journal*. 12(3): 10-14.

15. Hassell, M. (1974) Insect Populations. *J. Anim. Ecol.* 44: 283-296.

16. Hirsch, M. (1989) Chaos, Rigor, and Hype. *Mathematical Intelligencer*. 11(3):6-9. (Pages 8 and 9 include James Gleick's response to this article.)

17. Hofstadter, D. (1981) Strange Attractors. *Sci. Amer.* 245: 16-29.

18. Lorenz, E. (1963) Deterministic nonperiodic flow. *J. Atmos. Sci.* 20: 130.

19. Mandelbrot, B. (1983) *The Fractal Geometry of Nature*, Freeman, San Francisco.

20. Markus, M., Hess, B. (1989) Lyapunov exponents of the logistic map with periodic forcing. *Computers and Graphics*. 13(4), 553.

21. May, R. (1976) Simple mathematical models with very complicated dynamics. *Nature*. 261: 459-467.

22. Reitman, E. (1989) *Exploring the Geometry of Nature*. Windcrest Books: Pennsylvania.

23. Stevens, C. (1989) *Fractal Programming in C*. M and T Books: Redwood City, California. (This book is a dream come true for computer programmers interested in fractals.)

24. Stewart, I. (1987) The nature of stability. *Speculations in Science and Tech.* 10(4): 310-324.

25. Lakhtakia, A., R. Messier (1989) Self-similar sequences and chaos from Gauss sums. *Computers and Graphics*. 13: 59-62.

26. Lakhtakia, A., M.N. Lakhtkia, (1988) Ramanujan and the Julia set of the iterated exponential map. *Z. Naturforsch. A.* 43: 681-683 .

27. Lakhtakia, A. (1988) The Bohr-Hund atom in a fractal! *Am. J. Phys.* 56. 104-105.

28. Barnsley, M. (1988) *Fractals Everywhere*. Academic Press: New York.

29. R. Devaney (1989) *An Introduction to Chaotic Dynamical Systems*. Addison-Wesley.

30. R. Devaney, L. Keen (1989) *Chaos and Fractals, the Mathematics Behind the Computer Graphics*. American Mathematical Society: New York.

31. M. Barnsley and S. Demko (1985) Iterated function systems and the global construction of fractals. *Proc. Royal Soc. London A.* 399: 243-275.

32. T. Bedford (1986) Dimension and dynamics for fractal recurrent sets. *J. London Math. Soc.* 33: 89-100.

33. F. Dekking (1982) Recurrent sets. *Advances in Mathematics*. 44: 78-104.

34. J. Curry, L. Garnett, D. Sullivan. (1983) On the iteration of rational functions: computer experiments with Newton's method. *Commun. Math. Phys.* 91: 267-277.

35. J. Hutchinson. (1981) Fractals and self similarity. *Indiana Univ. Math. J.* 30: 713-747.

36 P. Blanchard. (1984) Complex analytic dynamics on the Riemann sphere. *Bull. Amer. Math. Soc.* 11: 85-141.

37. McRobie, A., Thompson, M. (1990) Chaos, catastrophes, and engineering. *New Scientist.* 126(1720): 41-46.

38. Pickover, C. (1988) The use of image processing techniques in rendering maps with deterministic chaos. *The Visual Computer, An International Journal of Computer Graphics*. 4: 271-276.

Chapter 22

# Irregularly Oscillating Fossil Seashells

*"The ultimate in bizarre form is found in Nipponites, [an organism] which became an irregular tangle that could not swim and may not have been able even to crawl about. "*      C. Fenton and M. Fenton, *The Fossil Book, 1980*

*"In the works of Nature, purpose not accident, is the main thing. "*      Aristotle

When one says the words "scientific visualization" most graphics experts think of applications in weather, fluid flow, molecular dynamics, geology, and medicine – because it is in these areas that scientific visualization has become particularly popular and yielded new insights. This chapter of the book describes the use of scientific visualization methods to describe the onset of irregular oscillations in an animal's shape. In particular, Chris Illert (see *Acknowledgments*) and I discuss the challenges of generating and representing unusual growth patterns characteristic of certain extinct mollusks, and we present computer graphics methods. Unlike the fairly simple logarithmic-spiral forms found in many shells, such as exhibited by the marine snails facing this page, the forms we generate require a few additional parameters to specify their shape.

As background: phylum Mollusca is the second largest phylum of the animal kingdom, and is made up of such forms as clams, snails, slugs and octopuses.[22] The group has enormous diversity, both in shape and size, ranging from the twisted, wormlike solenogastrids to the baglike octopuses. Cephalopods represent the most specialized of the molluscan group and include octopuses, cuttlefish, squids and nautiluses. One group of cephalopods, the ammonoids (Figure 22.1) reached their peak in the Mesozoic era and became extinct at the end of the Cretaceous period. The word *Ammonites* means "Ammon's stones"; it was given to fossil shells whose wrinkled whorls suggest ram's horns, which often appeared on the Egyptian god, Ammon. It is known that ammonoids avoided the extensive shallows in which large dinosaurs sometimes swam and their sizes ranged from tiny shells of 1/2 inch diameter to some with a diameter of 6 to 7 feet.

---

[22] The arthropods make up the first largest phylum.

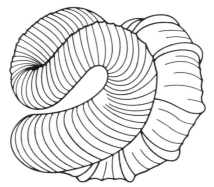

**Figure 22.1.** *Sketch of the front-facing portion of a fossil of Nipponites mirabilis.*


## 22.1 Mathematical Framework for Pattern Generation

In this section we present mathematical methods for biological pattern generation which are particularly useful for computer generation of seashells. (Many of you will wish to skip the mathematical details in this section and simply enjoy the images and methods.) There have been a number of past studies which used various simple spiral models for seashells, and some of these studies are referenced at the end of this chapter. We go beyond these simple methods by introducing more comprehensive and interesting generating formulas and parameters. The approaches may be of particular interest to computer scientists and graphics researchers. As background, the trajectory of a typical equiangular, or logarithmic, spiral through 3-D real space may be thought of in terms of a point which is rotated and whose distance from the pole varies exponentially.

[[This kind of continued similarity (scale invariance) is defined by a simple linear matrix equation:

$$\underset{\sim}{\Upsilon}(\phi) = e^{\alpha\phi}\begin{bmatrix} \cos\phi & -\sin\phi & 0 \\ \sin\phi & \cos\phi & 0 \\ 0 & 0 & 1 \end{bmatrix}\underset{\sim}{\Upsilon}(0) = e^{\zeta\phi}\underset{\sim}{\Upsilon}(0) \tag{22.1}$$

where

$$\zeta = \begin{bmatrix} \alpha & 1 & 0 \\ 1 & \alpha & 0 \\ 0 & 0 & \alpha \end{bmatrix} \tag{22.2}$$

for some real constant $\alpha$, and $0 < \phi \leq \infty$. In Equation (22.1) $\underset{\sim}{\Upsilon}(0)$ is the shape of the seashell's aperture (e.g. a circle). The matrix corresponds to a simple rotation through an angle $\phi$. The physical meaning of Equation (22.1) is this: if one takes a growth ring (generating curve) coinciding with the shell aperture, rotate it though the angle $\phi$ (via the rotation matrix), magnify all three of its space dimensions simultaneously by the same scale factor $e^{\alpha\phi}$, then one has a one-to-one mapping onto the new growth ring at location $\phi$. Because of the exponential form of this matrix transformation, and others of the kind, it is usually an easy matter to differentiate any number of times giving:

$$\left[\frac{\partial}{\partial\phi} - \zeta\right]\underset{\sim}{\Upsilon}(\phi) = 0 \tag{22.3}$$

$$\left[\frac{\partial^2}{\partial\phi^2} - \zeta^2\right]\underset{\sim}{\Upsilon}(\phi) = 0 \tag{22.4}$$

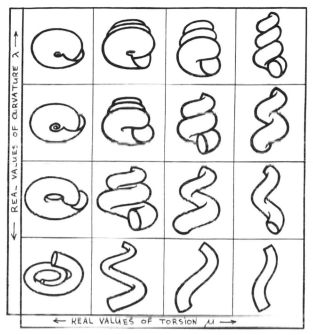

REAL VALUES OF CURVATURE λ →

← REAL VALUES OF TORSION μ →

**Figure 22.2.** *Equiangular coiled shell forms.* These satisfy the first order symmetry (Equation (22.3)). This is for various *real* values of curvature λ and torsion μ. Clearly torsion is related to axial squashing or stretching, while curvature provides a winding or coiling effect *about* the axis of symmetry. (Drawing by Illert, after Okamoto.)

$$\left[ \frac{\partial^n}{\partial \phi^n} - \underset{\sim}{\zeta}^n \right] \Upsilon(\phi) = 0 \tag{22.5}$$

where

$$\underset{\sim}{\zeta}^n = \begin{pmatrix} 0.5[(\alpha + i)^n + (\alpha - i)^n] & 0.5i[(\alpha + i)^n - (\alpha - i)^n] & 0 \\ -0.5[(\alpha + i)^n - (\alpha - i)^n] & 0.5[(\alpha + i)^n + (\alpha - i)^n] & 0 \\ 0 & 0 & \alpha^n \end{pmatrix} \tag{22.6}$$

The trajectory described by Equation (22.1) satisfies any, and all, of the differential equations Equation (22.3), Equation (22.4), and Equation (22.5). We will not deal here with fractional differentiation where *n* is not an integer. We have found it useful to combine the two lowest order equations, Equation (22.3) and Equation (22.4). Equation (22.3) and Equation (22.4) are true, therefore some Lagrange multiplier Ω can be found such that both equations are true subject to the constraint of each other, hence

$$\left[ \frac{\partial^2}{\partial \phi^2} - \zeta^2 + \Omega \left( \frac{\partial}{\partial \phi} - \zeta \right) \right] \underset{\sim}{\Upsilon}(\phi) = 0 \tag{22.7}$$

This new result (Equation (22.7)) is an improvement on Equation (22.3) with new solutions in addition to the initial transformation (Equation (22.1)). Therefore the iteration process has generated new information and higher order effects. It turns out that Ω is a simple constant for real-world seashells. It is not a scalar constant but, instead, a diagonal matrix constant:

$$\Omega = \begin{pmatrix} \lambda_1 & 0 & 0 \\ 0 & \lambda_2 & 0 \\ 0 & 0 & \mu \end{pmatrix} \tag{22.8}$$

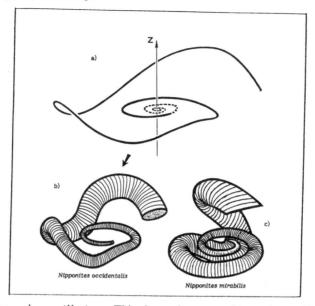

**Figure 22.3.** *Irregular oscillations.* This shows the onset of irregular oscillations perpendicular to the coiling plane. Complex values of torsion $\mu$ can produce "cylindrical" sine-spirals which increasingly oscillate perpendicular to the coiling plane, loosely approximating shells such as *Nipponites occidentalis*. This model does not account for the whole story, because, for example, the juvenile stage of *Nipponites mirabilis* demonstrates "sphericity." (a) Computer simulated "cylindrical" sine-spiral. (b) *Nipponities occidentalis*, an example of a "cylindrical" sine-spiral. (c) Juvenile stage of *Nipponites mirabilis* showing "sphericity" (after Illert, 1990).

If we assume that the constants are all real, such that $\lambda_1 = \lambda_2 = \lambda$ then it turns out that $\lambda$ is related to the fundamental curvature while $\mu$ is related to torsion. Also, curvature is related to the magnitude of the torque (the "winding force" in the *x-y* plane) about the axis of symmetry, while torsion is related to the magnitude of the axial squashing force along the axis of symmetry. Okamoto (1984) has summarized these concepts which show first-order equiangular spiral tubes possessing different values of curvature and torsion (Figure 22.2). However, not all real-world shells are this simple. Our past work in variously wound or decoiled second order "clocksprings" (satisfying Equation (22.7) when $\mu = 0$), and second order moebius elastic conoids (satisfying Equation (22.7) when $\lambda_1 = \lambda_2 = -2\alpha$) also vividly confirm the physical interpretation of the constants in the matrix $\Omega$.

In this chapter we note there is no reason to assume that the curvature and torsion constants in the matrix (Equation (22.8)) should be real. Indeed, complex values of the curvature constants $\lambda_1$ and $\lambda_2$ produce trajectory-transverse oscillations within the coiling plane (Figure 22.3), whereas complex values of the torsion-constant $\mu$ produce trajectory-transverse oscillation perpendicular to the coiling plane. Complex values of both curvature and torsion constants can produce spherical Lissajous trajectories characteristic of *Nipponites* in Figure 22.4. ]]

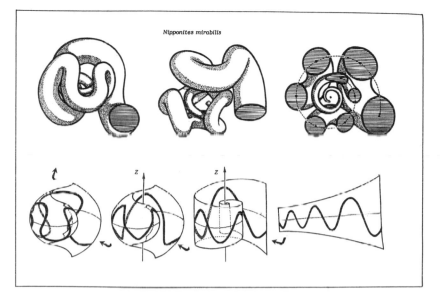

**Figure 22.4.** *The onset of irregular oscillations in Nipponites mirabilis.* A shell exhibiting both complex curvature λ and complex torsion μ oscillates both within, and transverse to, the coiling plane (after Illert, 1990).

## 22.2 Graphics

Many past papers have noted that nature and mathematics are inextricably linked. What is new here is the use of rich software tools and powerful new hardware to visualize mathematical models of nature. Our graphic goals were twofold: 1) to emphasize the role of simple graphical primitives in generating complicated aesthetic structures, and 2) to indicate the degree to which such studies are facilitated with the emergence of a new class of graphics supercomputers. The color plates in this book give you an indication of the power of modern computer graphics in verifying theoretical growth predictions. Color plate 26 shows a computer-generated representation of *Nipponites*, prior to onset of irregular oscillations. This is similar to the juvenile stage. Color plate 19 shows a computer-generated representation of the adult *Nipponites*.

For those of you interested in computer graphics: only a single graphic primitive was used for each 3-D computer graphic, namely a "polysphere" (i.e., *n* spherical surfaces at given centers with specified radii). The position of each of the spheres is determined by Equation (22.8), and the spheres penetrate one another to form the final, relatively smooth structure.

It is fascinating to note that powerful graphics workstations can be used to rotate the shells with only a few seconds' pause between images. The required computations for a similar animated sequence of shells could take hours on traditional high-powered mainframe computers. Also, note that with my simple programs, only three or four parameters are required by the user to specify the shapes in the figures. This "image compression" allows the computer artist to create a multitude of shapes with relative ease.

**Figure 22.5.** *Computer-generated fossil sea shell* (*Nipponites mirabilis*).

## 22.3 Summary and Conclusions

Despite an extensive scholarly literature dating back to classical times, the beautiful

panoply of seashell geometries has resisted rigorous theoretical analysis, leaving applied scientists and computer graphics researchers to adopt difficult empirical approaches toward classification and generation. The power of the iteration procedure described here for biological pattern generation is clearly demonstrated by various seashell geometries we have generated, and particularly by those bizarre varieties on the borderline between deterministic classical equiangular spirals on the one hand and unstable oscillations on the other. (Color plate 21 shows a rendition of the extinct *Madagascalites* using similar formulas.) We have shown that this dissipative system becomes irregular in a precise and well-defined way. Possible biological significance for this kind of iteration procedure is discussed by Illert, but the goal of this paper is to familiarize computer scientists with the intriguing computer graphics made possible by the methods described here. A chapter such as this can only be viewed as introductory; however, it is hoped that the techniques, equations, and systems will provide useful tools and stimulate future studies in the graphic characterization of morphologically rich spiral shapes produced by relatively simple generating formulas.    Computer graphics models of oscillating spiral formulas may help us better understand the rules underlying all the spirals we see in nature because we can now visualize, predict, and define these shapes in precise scientific terms.

## 22.4  For Further Reading

For those of you who wish to explore the area of morphological shape generation in general, the Fibonacci sequences, as well as a number of published papers, address the generation of mathematically derived morphological models for plants and other natural shapes (see references). Researchers have also explored the use of rules based on the laws of nature, such as two-dimensional logarithmic spirals for sea shells (Kawaguchi, 1982), or tree branching patterns determined from the study of living specimens (Aono, 1984). These and other successes provide continuing incentive for more research on the generation of biological structures. Rivlin's book *The Algorithmic Image* indicates recent advances in the computer synthesis of natural forms, while Thompson's older book *On Growth and Form* discusses various mathematical properties of biological structures, such as cells aggregates, horns, teeth, and tusks. (See "Notes for the Curious" on page 371 for additional information on seashells.)

1.    Fenton, C. Fenton, M. (1980) *The Fossil Book*. Doubleday: New York.   Also see: Cortie, M. (1989) Models for mollusc shell shape. *South African Journal of Science*. July 85(7): 454-460.

2.    Pickover, C. (1988) Mathematics and Beauty XI: A Sampling of Spirals and "Strange" Spirals in nature, science, and art. *Leonardo* May 21(2): 173-181. Reprinted in *Selected Papers on Natural Optical Activity*. (1990) A. Lakhtakia, ed. *International Society for Optical Engineering*.

3.    Pickover, C. (1989) A short recipe for seashell synthesis. *IEEE Computer Graphics and Applications*. November 9(6): 8-11.

4.    Illert, C. (1990) *Nipponites mirabilis*, a challenge to seashell theory? *Nuovo Cimento*. 12D(10): 1405-1421; Illert, C. (1983) Mathematics of Gonomonic seashells.  *Math. Bioscience*. 63(1): 21-56; Illert, C. (1987)   Part 1. Seashell Geometry. *Nuovo Cimento* 9D(7): 792-813. Part 2. Tubular 3-D seashell surfaces. *Nuovo Cimento* 11D(5): 761-780.

5.    Okamoto, T. (1984) Theoretical morphology of *Nipponites. J. Palaeneont. Soc. Japan*. 36: 37-51 (in Japanese).

6.    Jena, R. (1984) *Mathematical Approach to Pattern and Form in Plant Growth*. John Wiley and Sons: New York.

7.    Rivlin, R. (1986) *The Algorithmic Image*. Microsoft Press, WA.

8.    Kawaguchi, Y. 1982. A morphological study of the form of nature. *Computer Graphics (ACM SIGGRAPH)*. July '82 Proc.: Boston. 16(3): 223. Also: Aono, M., Kunii, L. (1984) Botanical tree image generation. *IEEE Computer Graphics and Appl*. 4: 10-34.

9.    Thompson, D. (1961) *On Growth and Form*. Cambridge: England.

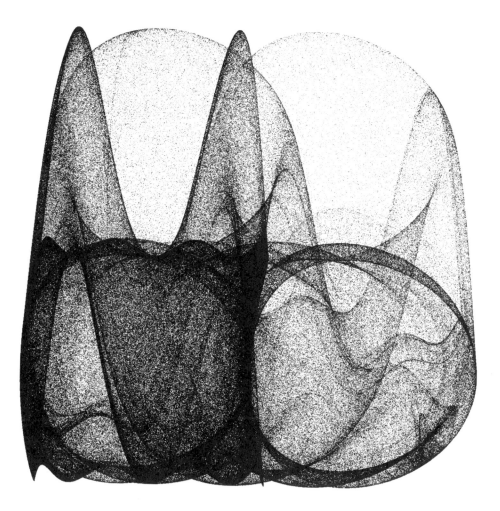

Chapter 23

# Picturing Randomness with Noise-Spheres

*"Sequences of truly patternless, unpredictable digits are a valuable commodity."*
Ivars Peterson

*"Anyone who considers arithmetical methods of producing random digits is, of course, in a state of sin."*
John von Neumann

The idea that the human visual system can be used to detect trends in complicated data is not new – and neither is the application of that idea in computer graphics. What is new is the use of rich software tools and powerful new hardware to visualize random data. This chapter provides a light introduction to a simple graphics technique which uses colored balls to visualize the output of random number generators. You can use this representation, called a *noise-sphere*, to detect "bad" random number generators with little training. You can also use it to find patterns in time series data.

In modern science, random number generators have proven invaluable in simulating natural phenomena and in sampling data (see the references at the end of this chapter). They're used by scientists for tackling a wide variety of problems, for example, developing secret codes, modelling the movement of atoms, and conducting accurate surveys. This is why it's useful to build easy-to-use graphic tools which, at a glance, help to determine whether a random number generator being used is "bad" (i.e non-uniform and/or with non-independence between various digits). Although a graphics supercomputer facilitates the particular representation described below, a simpler version would also be easy to implement on a personal computer; therefore, one of the objectives of this chapter is to stimulate and encourage programmers, students, and teachers to explore this technique in a classroom setting. You can also consider the colorful representations solely as art objects, providing another example of the link between mathematics and art.[23]

---

[23] This chapter is number 90 in a ninety-part "Mathematics and Beauty" series which emphasizes the aesthetic side of mathematics and scientific visualization. For others in the series see, for example: Pickover, C. (1988) Overrelaxation and Chaos. *Phys. Lett. A*, July 30(3): 125-128; Pickover, C.

## 23.1 Noise-sphere

The figure shown here is a representation which I call a *noise-sphere*.

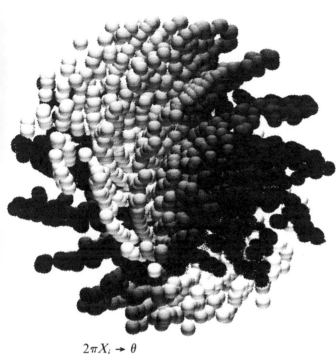

The various spiral projections are indicative of a bad random number generator. To produce the figures, you can simply map the output of a random number generator to the position of spheres in a spherical coordinate system.[24] This is easily achieved with a computer program using random numbers $\{X_i, \quad i = 1,2,3, \ldots, N, \quad 0 < X_i < 1\}$, where $X_i$, $X_{i+1}$, and $X_{i+2}$ are converted to $\theta$, $\phi$ and $r$ respectively. For each triplet, an $(r, \theta, \phi)$ is generated and these coordinates position the individual spheres. Because the initial data points range between 0 and 1, they may be scaled to obtain the full range in spherical coordinates:

$$2\pi X_i \rightarrow \theta \tag{23.1}$$

$$\pi X_{i+1} \rightarrow \phi \tag{23.2}$$

$$\sqrt{X_{i+2}} \rightarrow r \tag{23.3}$$

The square root for $X_{i+2}$ serves to spread the ball density though the spherical space and to suppress the tight packing for small $r$.

The resultant pictures can be used to represent different kinds of noise distributions or experimental data. In particular, by using this approach, "bad" random number generators can be visually detected. A standard good random number generator will produce no particular correlations in the ball positions in the noise-sphere. I have, however, found surprising results when this approach is applied to a BASIC random number generator. As the noise-sphere is rotated the

(1986) Mathematics and beauty: time-discrete phase planes associated with the cyclic system, $\{\dot{x}(t) = -f(y(t)), \quad \dot{y}(t) = f(x(t))\}$, *Comput. and Graph.*, 11(2), 217-226. Pickover, C. (1988) A note on Chaos and Halley's Method. *Commun. ACM*, November, 31(11): 1326-1329. Pickover, C. (1988) A note on rendering chaotic "repeller distance-towers." *Computers in Physics*, May/June Pickover, (1987) Blooming Integers *Comput. Graph. World* (March), 10(3): 54-57.

[24] A point can be located in spherical coordinates $(r, \theta, \phi)$ as well as rectangular coordinates $(x, y, z)$. The transformation between these coordinates is: $x = r \sin \theta \cos \phi$, $y = r \sin \theta \sin \phi$, $z = r \cos \theta$.

user can perceive various tendrils emanating from the cluster. There should be no such correlations if the distribution is truly random. The method is effective in showing that random number generators prior to release 3.0 of BASIC have subtle problems (see references).

You should take care when coloring the individual component spheres within the noise-spheres in order to help emphasize the various spiral striations. I have found that simply mapping the random number triplet values to red, green, and blue intensities helps the eye see correlated structures in 3-D.

Powerful graphics workstations can be used to rotate the representations with only a few seconds' pause between images. This is useful since correlations not visible from one viewpoint may become visually apparent when the sphere is viewed from another angle. However, if you do not have access to graphics super-computers you can render your data simply by plotting a scattering of dots and projecting them on a plane. The visual effect may be less striking without the real-time rotation, but with just a few test rotations of the noise-sphere, the user can detect a problem generator with relative computational ease. Since the noise-ball approach is sensitive to small deviations from randomness, it may have value in helping researchers find patterns in complicated data such as genetic sequences and acoustical waveforms. Interestingly, the spherical coordinate transformation used for the noise-ball *allows the user to see trends much more easily, and with many fewer trial rotations*, than an analogous representation which maps the random number triplets to three orthogonal coordinates.

## 23.2  Stop and Think

I urge you to test the approach outlined here on a variety of random number generators. For example, consider the linear congruential generator: $s(x) = (137x + 187) \bmod 256$, which is given by Knuth as an example of a bad random number generator. Generate several thousand points, map them to the noise-sphere, and view the results.

In another experiment, consider introducing a slight Markov dependence of the data points to determine how sensitive the noise-sphere is to this kind of deviation from randomness. In a computer program, generate random numbers $X_{new}$, save the previous random number in variable $X_{old}$, and execute the following code:

GenRandom($X_{new}$)
if $X_{old} < X_{new}$ then $X_{new} = \max(0, X_{new} - \delta)$
else $X_{new} = \min(1, X_{new} + \delta)$
$X_{old} = X_{new}$

$\delta$ controls the dependence of new values of the random numbers on the preceding number. $\delta = 0$ creates the standard, uncorrelated numbers.

As a last experiment, consider a uniform distribution of random numbers between 0 and 1. Take these random numbers, and round or truncate them to finite accuracy so that each is an integer multiple of $1/v$ for some given number $v$. If this is done, the scattering of points in the noise-sphere will show a regular pattern. The noise-sphere acts as a kind of microscope revealing the "grain" of the random numbers. The resulting figures for these and other experiments are left as a puzzle and surprise for you. Enjoy!

## 23.3  Why Graphics?

You may wonder why we should consider the noise-sphere approach over traditional brute-force statistical calculations. One reason is that this graphic description requires little training on the part of users, and the software is simple enough to allow users to quickly implement the basic idea (without the sophisticated lighting and shading) on a personal computer. The graphics description provides a qualitative awareness of complex data trends, and may subsequently guide the researcher in applying more traditional statistical calculations. Also, fairly detailed comparisons between sets of "random" data are useful and can be achieved by a variety of brute-force computations, but sometimes at a cost of the loss of an intuitive feeling for the structures. When just looking at a page of numbers, differences between the data's statistics may obscure the similarities. The approach described here provides a way of simply summarizing comparisons between random data sets and capitalizes on the feature integration abilities of the human visual system to see trends.

## 23.4  For Further Reading

1.  Knuth, D. (1981) *The Art of Computer Programming, Vol. 2,* 2nd ed. Addison-Wesley: Massachusetts.
2.  Mckean, K. (1987) The orderly pursuit of disorder. *Discover.* January 72-81.
3.  Gordon, G. (1978) *System Simulation.* Prentice-Hall: New Jersey.
4.  Park, S. and Miller, K. (1988) Random numbers generators: good ones are hard to find. *Commun. ACM.* 31(10): 1192-1201.
5.  Voelcker, J. (1988) Picturing randomness. *IEEE Spectrum.* August 25(8): 13.
6.  The IBM Personal Computer BASIC. Version A2.10. This is an interpreted BASIC.
7.  Richards, T. (1989) Graphical representation of pseudorandom sequences. *Computers and Graphics.* 13(2): 261-262.
8.  Pickover, C. (1988) From noise comes beauty: textures reminiscent of rug weavings and wood grains spring from simple formulas (Mathematics and Beauty X). *Computer Graphics World*, March, 11(3): 115-116.
9.  Pickover, C. (1989) Picturing randomness with Truchet tiles. *Journal of Recreational Math.*, 21(4): 256-259.
10. Pickover, C. (1990) Picturing randomness on a graphics supercomputer. *IBM Journal of Research and Development*, 34(6), in press. (Color graphics.)

Chapter 24

# Visualizing Cantor Cheese Construction

This chapter introduces you to one of the craziest shapes ever dreamed of by humankind: *Cantor cheese*. This shape is an artistically interesting analog of the *Cantor set* which I will describe in the next paragraph. We will also take a look at a related object, the *solenoid*. Computer programs are given for Cantor cheese and solenoid construction.[25]

The term *Cantor cheese* was used by Stewart, in his book *Does God Play Dice?* to describe an artistically interesting analog of the Cantor set described by Cantor (1845-1918) and later by Mandelbrot. As background, a Cantor set can be constructed by taking an interval of length 1 and removing its middle third (but leaving the end points of this middle third). This leaves two smaller intervals, each one-third as long. The middle thirds of these smaller segments are removed and the process is repeated:

This set has a "measure zero," which means that a randomly thrown dart would be very unlikely to hit a member. At the same time it has so many members that it is in fact uncountable, just like the set of all of the real numbers between 0 and 1. Many mathematicians, and even Cantor himself for a while, doubted that a crazy set with these properties could exist (Schroeder, 1986). As you have just been shown, however, such a set is possible to formulate. The dimension $D$ (see Glossary) of this particular Cantor dust after many iterations is less than one

---

[25] This chapter represents a collaboration with mathematician Kevin McCarty, ROLM Corporation, California.

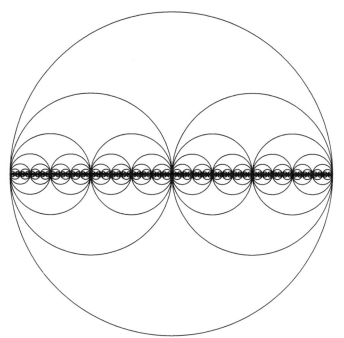

**Figure 24.1.** *Cross section of the Cantor cheese in Color Plate 15 and Fig. 24.2.*

since $D = \log 2 / \log 3 = 0.63$. You can read more about the concept of fractional dimensions, and how 0.63 was derived, in Mandelbrot (1983). Cantor dusts with other fractal dimensions can easily be created by removing different sizes (or numbers) of intervals from the starting interval of length 1. Cantor sets are highly useful mathematical models for innumerable physical phenomena, from the distribution of galaxies in the universe to the fractal Cantor-like structure of the rings of Saturn.

A topologically similar set starts with a circular disc. Everything *except* for two smaller discs is removed. Here we use pairs of circles rather than pairs of lines, and the subdivisions are repeated as with the Cantor set described above. We retain only those points inside the circles. Figure 24.1 is a picture of this Cantor cheese with each circle's radius slightly less than half of the previous

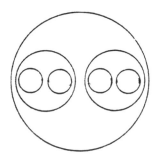

generation's radius. (The term "generation" refers to the nesting level of the circles; see Pseudocode 24.1). If we consider just the line along the diameter, the fractal dimension for the set of points is close to 1. Smaller fractal dimensions are obtained by using circles which are further shrunken and separated (as diagrammed here). Figure 24.1 is a cross section taken at the front of the object in Color plate 15. In Color plate 15, the nested circles are represented as nested cylinders for artistic purposes. (Some generations are represented by cones

```
ALGORITHM: Program 1. Program Code for Generating
           Cantor Cheese Cross-Sections
m          - a 1-D array containing the midpoints of each circle.
gen        - the number of generations.
DrawCircleAt - draws a circle at (x,y) with a given radius.
The picture boundaries go from 0 to 100 in the x and y directions.

m(1)-50;    count=1;
radius=50;  frac=1;
DrawCircleAt(m(count),50,radius);
do gen = 0 to 10;
     bot = 2**gen; top=(2**(gen+1))-1;
     radius=radius/2  ;  l=radius;
     do i = bot to top;
          m(count+1)= m(i) - frac*l;
          DrawCircleAt(m(count+1),50,radius);
          m(count+2) = m(i) + frac*l;
          DrawCircleAt(m(count+2),50,radius);
          count=count+2;
     end;
end;
```

**Pseudocode 24.1.** *Program code for generating cantor cheese cross-sections.*

to show the interior nested structures.) A graphics supercomputer, such as a Stellar GS1000, allows models of the Cantor cheese to be rotated, shaded, and magnified in real time.

For those of you who wish to display cross-sections of the Cantor Cheese, computer program pseudocode is given in Pseudocode 24.1 Note that if recursive computer program languages are used, the pseudocode for generating the cheese cross sections can be simplified (Pseudocode 24.2).

## 24.1  Description of a Variable Dimension Cheese

It is possible to create a 3-D representation of the Cantor cheese such that the fractal dimension corresponding to the cross-section continuously decreases from front to back of the figure. Instead of cylinders, nested spire-like objects can be used that taper along the $z$-direction. If one were to slice into such a figure, each cross-section has a different fractal dimension. The front face, corresponding to $D \sim 1$, looks like Figure 24.1. The back cross-section resembles the second in-line figure in this chapter. Nested circles still form the cross-sections of nested spires, but the nested circles separate as the dimension decreases. The first enclosing circle does not change size, and so it generates a cylinder. The two smaller circles inside change their sizes in direct proportion to the shrinkage factor, and so form cones. At the next level, the shrinkage factor is applied twice, so the diameters vary as the square of the shrinkage factor. This forms, instead of a cone, a conical-shaped spire similar to a surface of revolution generated by a parabola – like a tall tent. As the nesting level of circles increases, the shapes formed along the third dimension are narrower spires with profiles generated by cubics, quartics,

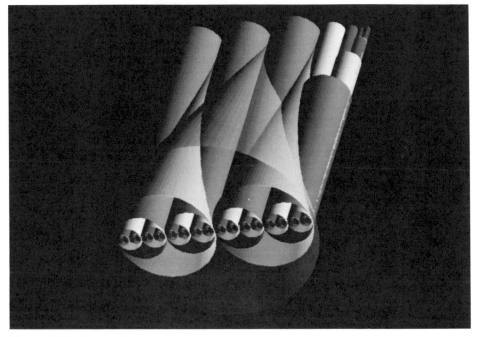

**Figure 24.2.** *Cantor Cheese.*

and so on. The spires are not, strictly speaking, surfaces of revolution. The centers of circles of cross-section, as would-be centers of rotation, are not in general straight line segments. We call these centers of the spires *spines*.

As mentioned above, the enclosing circle does not change size, so its center does follow a straight line along the $z$-axis. The centers of the two circles at the next level also lie along straight lines parallel to the $z$-axis. At each succeeding stage, the two centers of the next stage are located along a diameter, halfway between the center and the edge. Thus the centers are located according to the following scheme:

| level | center coordinate |
|-------|-------------------|
| 0 | 0 |
| 1 | $\pm 1/2$ |
| 2 | $1/2\,(\pm 1 \pm z)$ |
| 3 | $1/2\,(\pm 1 \pm z \pm z^2)$ |
| ... | |
| k | $1/2\,(\pm 1 \pm z \pm z^2 \pm ... \pm z^{(k-1)})$ |

Each choice of sign in one of these formulas locates a particular spire's center, and describes the spinal curve as a function of z. Clearly the location of the spine of a spire at level k is given by a polynomial of degree $(k-1)$ in the shrinkage factor $z$. The radius of the corresponding cross-section circle is $z^k$.

```
ALGORITHM: Program 2. Program Code for Cantor Cheese
                Cross-Sections (recursive).

The pseudocode for generating cheese cross-sections can be
simplified in a manner which more clearly reveals the
recursive nature of the construction.

    frac -          size reduction factor, < 0.5
    level -         number of generations (recursive depth)

 Procedure DoCircle(x, y, radius, level : integer);
     begin
            (* first draw the enclosing circle *)
            DrawCircleAt(x, y, radius);

            (* if there are further levels, then work      *)
            (* on the left circle, then the right circle   *)
            if (level > 1) then begin
                DoCircle(x - radius/2, y, frac * radius, level-1);
                DoCircle(x + radius/2, y, frac * radius, level-1);
            end;
     end;
                    Cross-Sections (recursive).
```

**Pseudocode 24.2.** *Program 2. Program Code for Cantor Cheese*

You can create your own 3-D representation of variable-dimension cheese, but a simple two-dimensional plot of the polynomial curves above is sufficient to give you a correct impression of the shape. Indeed, a similar figure appears in Mandelbrot (1983) (p. 81).

## 24.2 The Solenoid, a Cousin of the Cantor Set

The solenoid is a weird, twisted doughnut-like shape. It's a topological construction which arises from, and is related to, the Cantor set. It is one of the principal examples of a strange attractor in dynamical systems theory. In this chapter, we won't dwell on its interesting topological properties, which would take many pages (see references for further reading). Instead, we develop some formulas which help to elucidate its self-similar structure, and allow computer graphical generation of images which are pleasing in their simplicity and grace, yet sufficiently complex to intrigue the eye.

The starting point of the solenoid is the solid torus, and a mapping from the torus to itself. The mapping squeezes the tube of the torus to half its original diameter, stretches it out to twice its original length, and wraps this length twice around, inside the skin of the original. In wrapping around twice, one coil sits next to another one with no overlap, just as one would coil up lengths of a garden hose. The coil makes a half-twist as it wraps around once, joining back up to itself after two turns.

We have found that the representation of nested tori provides quite a visualization challenge. Our first attempts portrayed these complicated objects using various degrees of transparency, but we found that the resulting figure was too complicated to understand.

---

ALGORITHM: Program 3. Program Code for Generating Solenoid.

The following pseudocode computes (x, y, z) coordinates for the centers of the nested tubes in the solenoid construction.

```
level:           nesting level
circlepts:       number of steps around longitudinal circle
zr, zi:          longitudinal angle, as a complex number pair
wr, wi:          location inside the cross-sectional disk, as
                 a complex number pair.
```

```
circlepts = 36;
pi = 3.14159;

for i = 0 to circlepts do
        begin
        angle = 2 * pi * i / circlepts;
        x = cos(angle);                    (* initial longitudinal *)
        y = sin(angle);                    (* angular position     *)
        zr = x; zi = y;                    (* as a complex number  *)
        wr = 0; wi = 0;              (* cross-section location *)
        for j = 1 to level do
                begin
                wr = wr + zr / 4;
                wi = wi + zi / 4;
                zx = zr * zr - zi * zi; (* complex squaring     *)
                zy = 2 * zr * zi;       (* of z  *)
                zr = zx; zi = zy;
                end;
        x = zr * (1 + wr);
        y = zi * (1 + wr);
        z = wi;

        (* The radius of the cross-sectional disk centered at  *)
        (* the point (x,y,z) is 1/(2**(level+1))               *)
end;
```

**Pseudocode 24.3.** *Program Code for Generating Solenoid.*

The representation we settled on uses both shaded facets and wire meshes. The first stage is illustrated in Figure 24.3. The initial torus is shown as a mesh cage. Again note that we can rotate and shade the objects in real-time. Three colored lights were used to illuminate the object.

Like a taffy machine with no off-switch, this operation of stretching, winding and twisting is repeated indefinitely. As the mapping carries the original torus to an image of itself wrapped twice around, it also carries the twice-wrapped image to one wrapped four times around. Each iteration produces another tube nested inside the previous one. At each stage, the number of windings doubles and the thickness halves. This process converges in the limit to a connected set of infinitely thin windings, called a solenoid.

[[ The easiest way to describe the way this mapping works is to use complex numbers. A point inside the solid torus is located by a pair of complex numbers $(z, w)$. The $z$ coordinate represents the longitude angle, and locates a point on the unit circle in the complex plane which will be the center or spine of the torus. The $w$ coordinate locates a point inside a disk of radius $1/2$, considered as a piece of the complex plane. The disks are imagined to be threaded on the unit circle like a necklace. With these coordinates, the mapping which wraps the torus twice around inside itself is

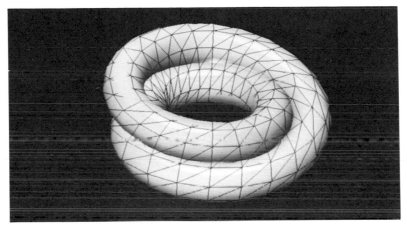

**Figure 24.3.** *Solenoid, inside initial torus (represented by a mesh).*

$$f:(z, w) \rightarrow (z^2, w/2 + z/4) \tag{24.1}$$

The term $z^2$ simply wraps the unit circle twice around itself as $z$ traverses the unit circle once. The term $w/2$ shrinks the original $w$ coordinate to half its size, while the $z/4$ term moves it away from the $w = 0$ origin so the image does not intersect itself on the second loop. The simple algebraic formula allowed by complex number representation makes it easy to compute repeated iterations of the mapping. (See Pseudocode 24.3 for an algorithm to iterate this calculation.)

The connection with the Cantor cheese is seen by considering a cross-section of the solenoid construction perpendicular to the windings. A sequence of nested disks is seen; each disk contains two smaller disks just as in the Cantor cheese construction. When the longitude angle is zero ($z = 1 + 0i$), all nested disks line up, but for other longitude angles the varying amounts of twist cause the disks to become separated. This separation can be seen in Figure 24.4 which shows the mapping iterated to the second level of nesting. ]]

## 24.3  History

The set we know today as the Cantor set was discovered by Oxford professor Henry Smith (1826-1883) in 1875. The founder of set theory, Georg Cantor (1845-1918), made use of Smith's invention in 1883. Benoit Mandelbrot has characterized and made use of this set in the field of fractal geometry, and you should consult his book *The Fractal Geometry of Nature* for some elegant drawings of this set and for some closely related curves such as the Devil's staircase. Ian Stewart's book *Does God Play Dice? (The Mathematics of Chaos)* provides an excellent introduction to the Cantor set as well as chaos theory and fractals, and the book is highly recommended. Hofstadter (1985) explains how the cross-sections of various strange attractors, such as the Henon attractor, can be considered as Cantor sets.

For those of you interested in a mathematical nomenclature for the Cantor set, see Barnsley's book *Fractals Everywhere*. For example, the Cantor set can be considered a subset of the metric space $[0,1]$. The Cantor set $C$ can then be defined as $C = \bigcap_{n=0}^{\infty} I_n$ where

$$I_0 = [0,1],$$

$$I_1 = \left[0, \frac{1}{3}\right] \cup \left[\frac{2}{3}, \frac{3}{3}\right],$$

$$I_2 = \left[0, \frac{1}{9}\right] \cup \left[\frac{2}{9}, \frac{3}{9}\right] \cup \left[\frac{6}{9}, \frac{7}{9}\right] \cup \left[\frac{8}{9}, \frac{9}{9}\right]$$

etc.

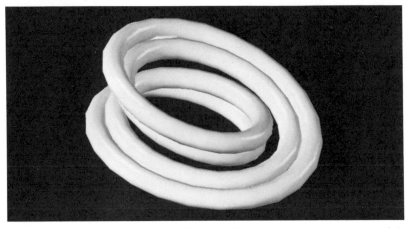

**Figure 24.4.** *Solenoid, second stage.* The mapping is iterated to the second level of nesting.

Notice that the point $x = 0$ is in the Cantor set, as well as many other points.

For additional background on the solenoid, Stephen Smale identified this kind of object as an example of a strange attractor in his seminal 1967 paper "Differentiable Dynamical Systems."

## 24.4  For Further Reading

1.    Stewart, I. (1989) *Does God Play Dice? (The Mathematics of Chaos.)* Blackwell: New York. Also: Mandelbrot, B. (1983) *The Fractal Geometry of Nature.* Freeman: New York.

2.    Pickover, C., McCarty, K. (1990) Visualizing Cantor cheese construction. *Computers and Graphics.* 14(2): 337-331.

3.    Hofstadter, D. (1985) *Metamagical Themas.* Bantam: New York.

4.    Barnsley, M. (1988) *Fractals Everywhere.* Academic Press: New York.

5.    David Ruelle (1980) Strange Attractors. *Mathematical Intelligencer.* 2: 126-137. Also: Robert L. Devaney (1989) *An Introduction to Chaotic Dynamical Systems.* Benjamin: New York.

6.    Smale, S. (1967) Differentiable dynamical systems. *Bulletin of the American Math Society.* 73: 748-817.

7.    Schroeder, M. (1986) *Number Theory in Science and Communication.* Springer: Berlin. (A goldmine of valuable information.)

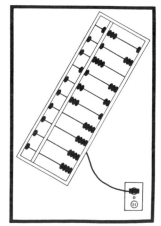

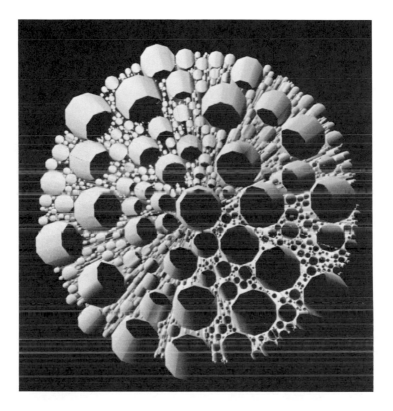

*Hyper-packed cylinders* "grown" using the methods described in section 25.2.

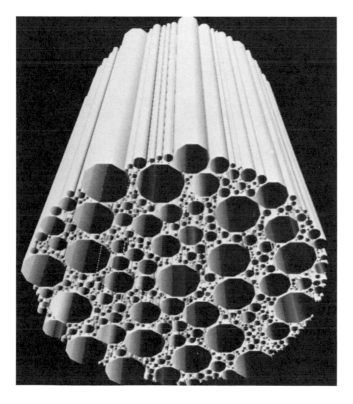

# Chapter 25

# Twisted Mirror Worlds

In this chapter you will journey through a circus of strange mirror worlds where uniform and regular shapes become perverted distortions of their former selves. In mathematical terms, the geometrical processes are known as *inversion* and *osculation*, and they both can be used to produce visually interesting patterns. The goal of this chapter is to give an informal introduction and tutorial on certain graphical aspects of these processes for the non-mathematician, and to present artistic renditions using these methods. Illustrations similar to those shown in Figure 25.11 can be found in specialized geometry textbooks, and the diagrams are included to familiarize you with graphical curiosities in these fields. All of the other illustrations are original productions.

## 25.1 Inversion

The inversion mapping technique makes use of a circle to map all of the points on a plane onto other points on the plane, except for the point at the very center of the circle. The figures will help you understand the process. Here are the details. The mapping is done as follows: a line is drawn from the center of the circle ($C$) to the point to be mapped ($P$). The new mapped point $P'$ is placed on the line $CP$ so that the product of the distances $CP$ and $CP'$ is equal to the square of the radius of the circle, $r^2$. Try drawing these lines on the figures in this chapter. Any circle which passes through the center of the reference circle $C$ maps into a straight line, and that any other circle maps into a circle. Also note that inversion is symmetric: If a figure A maps into a figure B, then figure B maps into figure A. These properties are illustrated in Figure 25.1 and Figure 25.2.

The top, left diagram in Figure 25.1 indicates inversion of a circle entirely outside the reference circle. Its image is the set of points entirely inside the reference circle. In Figure 25.1 and Figure 25.2, the reference circle is denoted by an arrow. The bottom, left diagram in Figure 25.1 illustrates the case of a circle that is tangent to the reference circle. A circle tangent externally is transformed into a circle tangent internally, and vice versa. The top, right diagram in Figure 25.1 shows inversion of a circle cutting the reference circle. The bottom, right figure

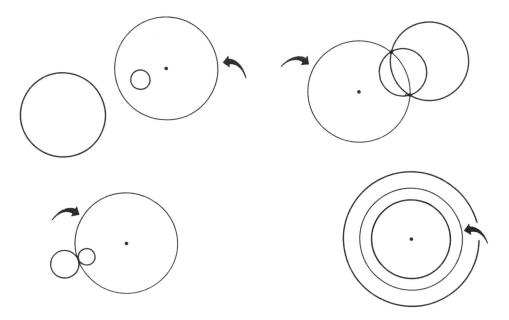

**Figure 25.1.** *Geometrical and graphical properties of inversion of circles.* The reference circle is denoted by an arrow.  See text for details.

shows inversion of a circle concentric with the reference circle. Circles which go through the center of the reference circle constitute a special case. Figure 25.2 shows how circles can be transformed to lines if the circle intersects the center of the reference circle.  Notice, in general, if the reference circle and the circle to be inverted touch at any points, then these points are fixed points and do not change upon inversion.

Figure 25.3 - Figure 25.6 indicate inversion acting upon various regular arrays. Figure 25.3 shows the results of inversion on a regular square array of equal-sized circles.  The reference circle for inversion is centered at the center of the figure.  The 4-lobed central shape is the image of the outer edges of the original square array of circles. Figure 25.4 indicates inversion acting upon a square lattice of incomplete hexagons. Figure 25.5 and Figure 25.6 show inversion operating upon overlapping hexagons and ellipses, respectively. You will no doubt create novel patterns based on inversion of other repeating shapes in a lattice.

Inversion can be used to transform more complicated pictures. Figure 25.7 and Figure 25.8 show the inversion of a regular array of insects (Figure 25.7a) (original artwork by William Rowe), and a North American Indian mask (Figure 25.8a). The original images were digitized at a resolution of 240 dots per inch.  Inversion can change the spacing of these dots, and this accounts for the varying dot density across the inverted images.

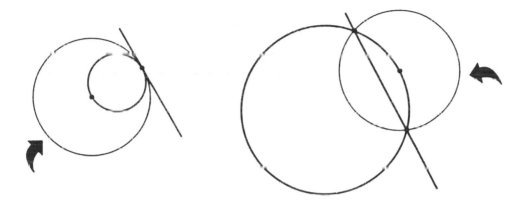

**Figure 25.2.** *Circles can be transformed to lines if the circle intersects the center of the reference circle.*

## 25.2  Osculation

In the previous sections, inversion of circles and lattices of packed circles produced graphically interesting images. Even with no inversion, adjacent circles, which are packed so that they *osculate* ("kiss," i.e., just touch), can sometimes provide a deep reservoir for striking images. This section provides several simple recipes for graphically interesting structures based on the osculatory packing of finite areas using circles. The problem of covering a finite area with a given set of circles has received frequent attention.   As background, the densest packing of non-overlapping uniform circles is the hexagonal lattice packing where the ratio of covered area to the total area (*packing fraction*) is $\phi = \pi/\sqrt{12}$ ~ 0.9069. The limiting packing fraction for nested hexagonal packing of circles, with $k$ *different* circle sizes is

$$\phi_k = 1 - (1 - 0.9069)^k \tag{25.1}$$

This applies to cases where each of the uncovered areas, or *interstices*, is also hexagonally packed by smaller circles.  For larger values of $k$, $\phi_k$ approaches unity.

Other researchers have usually defined a distribution of circles as *osculatory* if any available area is always covered by the largest possible circle.  If the original area to be covered is a tricuspid area (Figure 25.9), then the first circle to be placed must be tangent to the three original larger circles.   This kind of packing is also often referred to as *Apollonian packing*. In contrast to past work,

**Figure 25.3.** *The results of inversion on a regular array of equal-sized circles.* The reference circle for inversion is centered at the center of the figure.

the criterion for osculatory packing is relaxed here: each successively placed circle on the plane need only be tangent to at least *one* previous circle (*tangent-1 packing*). To generate Figure 25.10 a circle center is randomly placed within the available interstice. The circle then grows until it becomes tangent to its closest neighbor. The process is repeated several thousand times. One easy way to simulate this on a computer is to determine the distances $d_i$ from the newly selected circle center to all other circles $i$ on the plane. Let

$$\delta_i = d_i - r_i, \tag{25.2}$$

where $r_i$ is the radius of circle $i$. $\min\{\delta_i\}$ is then the radius of the new circle. Note that if there exists a negative $\delta_i$ then the selected center is within a circle on the plane. In this case the circle center is discarded, and a new attempt to place a circle is made. Repeated magnification of the figures reveals the self-similarity of the figures; the figures are fractal and look the same at various size scales.

## 25.3 Pappus' Arbelos, Loxodromic Sequences, Fibonacci Spirals

I will conclude by describing three gems of classical mathematics which stirred my interest in the area of circle osculation and inversion. To create Figure 25.11a, start with two circles, denoted by arrows in Figure 25.11, with a line through their centers. Next place a circle with its center on the line and

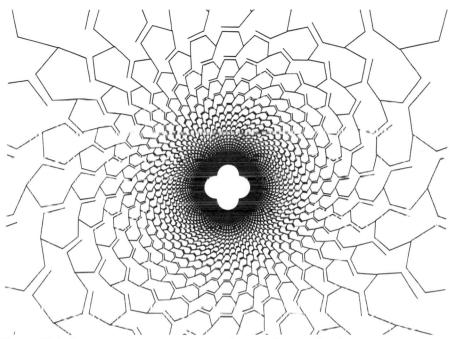

**Figure 25.4.** *Inversion acting upon a square lattice of incomplete hexagons.*

which is tangent to the two original circles. Continue to fill the crescent area with tangent circles, as shown. The first small circle, which has its center on the line, can be denoted $C_0$, the next smaller circle is denoted $C_1$, and so on. This figure is called *Pappus' Arbelos* and seems to have been known to the early Greek mathematicians. Interestingly, the vertical distances from all the small circles' centers in the crescent to the line segment is

$$2nr_n \qquad (25.3)$$

where r is the radius of each of the circles, $C_n$. Using a reference circle whose center is at the point where the 2 large circles touch, Pappus' Arbelos can be inverted, to a column of congruent circles. You can learn more about Pappus' Arbelos in Walker (1981).

Another graphically interesting example of osculating spheres is the *loxodromic* sequence. A *loxodromic* sequence of tangent spheres in n-space is an infinite sequence of *(n-1)*-spheres having the property that every n+2 consecutive members are mutually tangent (Figure 25.11b). Coxeter has shown that points of contact of consecutive pairs of spheres lie on a loxodrome. You can learn more about this sequence in Weiss (1981). If $\beta$ is a constant angle, while $\theta$ and $\phi$ are the longitude and latitude of a point on the loxodrome, the loxodrome's equation may be written $x = \sin \phi \cos \theta$, $y = \sin \phi \sin \theta$, $z = \cos \phi$, where $\theta = -\tan \beta \log \tan(\phi/2)$. Doing a little historical research, you'll find out that the loxodrome curve was actually first conceived by Pedro Nunes around 1550. Note that a loxodrome is a curve on the surface of a sphere which makes a constant angle with the parallels of latitude, e.g., a course with a constant compass bearing. It is the

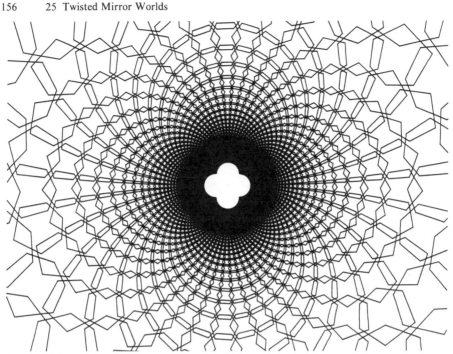

**Figure 25.5.** *Inversion operating upon overlapping hexagons.*

spherical analog of the logarithmic spiral in the plane, which makes a constant angle with concentric circles.

As a final graphical curiosity, Figure 25.12 shows a Fibonacci spiral of circles. Fibonacci spirals are involved in the patterns of phylotaxis, for example, in the arrangement of seeds in a sunflower head. We can approximate a Fibonacci spiral pattern by drawing circles which have polar coordinates with radii

$$r(i) = k\sqrt{i} \tag{25.4}$$

and angles

$$\theta(i) = 2i\pi/\tau. \tag{25.5}$$

where $\tau$ is the Golden Number $(1 + \sqrt{5})/2$. Radii increasing as the square root of the integers create a mean density of packing that is constant. The inversion of this pattern is left as an exercise for you to solve. See (Baratt and McKay, 1987) for a numerical recipe for creating Fibonacci patterns.

## 25.4  Conclusions

In this chapter we have seen additional examples of interesting graphical behavior in simple geometrical systems. Inversion seems to create the most aesthetic patterns when operating on a repeating motif (such as spheres and hexagons in a lattice) although non-repeating patterns can also create interesting shapes (such

**Figure 25.6.** *Inversion operating upon overlapping ellipses.*

as in Figure 25.8). For an excellent introductory book on inversion, see (Meder, 1967). For other work in the area of geometrical processes which create repeating and artistic patterns, see Dunham's work on repeating hyperbolic patterns (Dunham et al., 1981). Some of the first well-known repeating patterns based on geometrical transformations appeared in mathematical expositions (Fricke and Klein, 1890) which sometimes inspired artists, such as M. C. Escher, to create more complicated repeating patterns of interlocking motifs.

## 25.5  A Computer Hint

There are many ways you can program inversion on your computer. One computational suggestion is given here:

$$Q_x = \frac{P_x}{|P|^2} \tag{25.6}$$

$$Q_y = \frac{P_y}{|P|^2} \tag{25.7}$$

where $P$ is the original point (expressed in terms of its $x$ and $y$ coordinates) and $Q$ is the new inverted point. *Important:* the inversion circle has radius 1 and is located at the origin. Note that any points on the unit circle of radius 1 map to

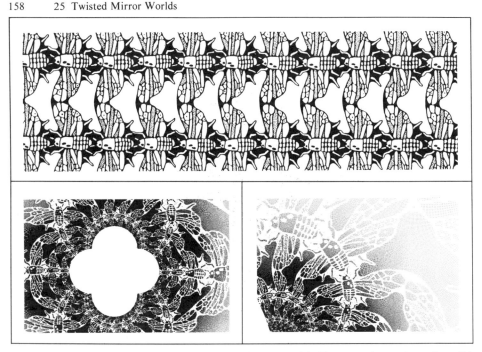

**Figure 25.7.** *Inversion of a regular array of insects.* (a) Picture prior to inversion. (b) Inversion, with reference circle centered at the middle of the 4-lobed shape. (c) Inversion, with reference circle near the lower left.

themselves. Points inside the unit circle ($|P| < 1$) map into points outside the circle.

## 25.6 For Further Reading

1.  Hill, F. (1990) *Computer Graphics*. Macmillan: New York.

2.  Kausch-Blecken, H., Schmeling, V., Tschoegl, N. (1970) Osculatory packing of finite areas with circles. *Nature.* March 225: 1119-1121.

3.  Boyd, D. (1973) The residual set dimensions of the Apollonian packing. *Mathematika.* 20: 170-174.

4.  Pickover, C. (1989) Circles which kiss: a note on osculatory packing. *Computers and Graphics.* 13(1), 63-67.

5.  Walker, J. (1981) Inversive geometry. In *The Geometric Vein*. Davis, C., Grunbaum, B., Sherk. F., eds. Springer-Verlag: New York.

6.  Coxeter, H. (1968) Loxodromic sequences of tangent spheres. *Aequationes Math.* 1: 104-121.

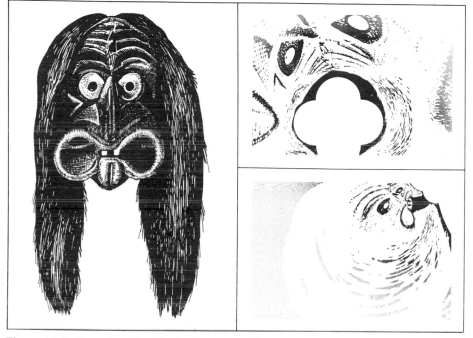

**Figure 25.8.** *Inversion of a North American Indian mask.* (a) Picture prior to inversion. (b) Inversion, with reference circle centered at the middle of the 4-lobed shape. (c) Inversion, with reference circle near the upper right. For artistic purposes, the inverted image is the negative of the one shown.

7.  Weiss, A. (1981) On Coxeter's loxodromic sequence of tangent spheres. In *The Geometric Vein.* Davis, C., Grunbaum, B., Sherk. F., eds. Springer-Verlag: New York.

8.  Barret, A., Mackay, A. (1987) *Spatial Structure and the Microcomputer.* Macmillan: New York.

9.  Peterson, I. (1987) Portraits of Equations. *Science News.* 132(12): 184-186 (and cover picture).

10. Meder, A. (1967) *Topics from Inversive Geometry.* Houghton Mifflin Co.: Boston.

11. Dunham, D., Lindgram, J., Witte, D. (1981) Creating repeating hyperbolic patterns. *ACM SIGGRAPH Computer Graphics* 15(3): 215-220.

12. Fricke, R., Klein, F. (1890) Vorlesungen uber die Theoire der elliptischen Modulfunktionen (Publisher unknown), Leipzig.

13. Series, C. (1990) Fractals, reflections and distortions. *New Scientist.* 127(1735): 54-60.

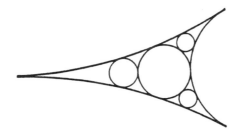

**Figure 25.9.** *Tricuspid interstices in standard osculatory packing.*

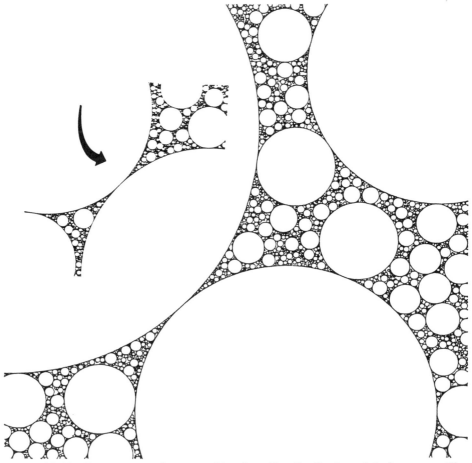

**Figure 25.10.** *Tangent-1 osculatory packing for white distribution of circle centers.* The embedded figure, pointed to by the arrow, is actually a magnification of a tiny section of the packing plot.

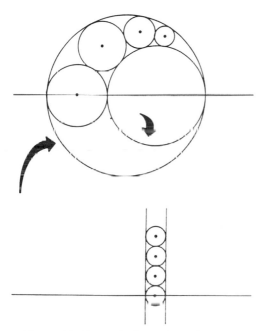

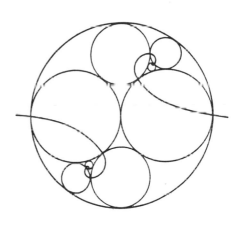

**Figure 25.11.** *Packed circles.* (a) Pappus' Arbelos. (b) A *loxodromic* sequence of tangent spheres.

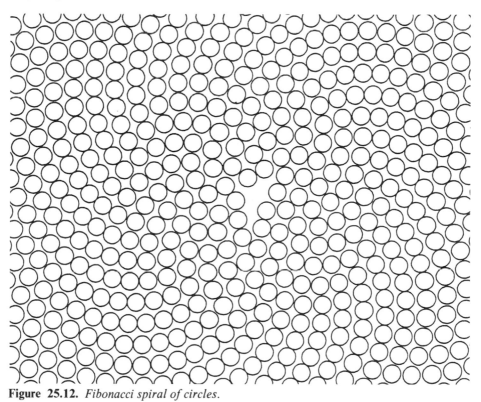

**Figure 25.12.** *Fibonacci spiral of circles.*

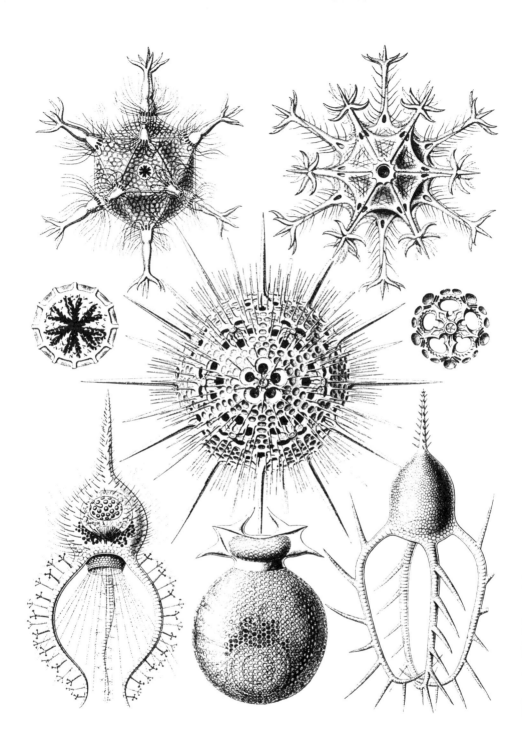

Chapter 26

# Polyhedral Paradise

In this chapter you will read about powerful graphics computers which can be used to visualize complicated geometric models of multifaceted solids called polyhedra. The ancient Greeks knew about some of the simple symmetrical polyhedra such as the cube, octahedron (whose faces are composed of eight equilateral triangles), and icosahedron (whose faces are composed of twenty equilateral triangles). In the more recent past, paper models of complicated polyhedra were hand-built and photographed in order to allow students and mathematicians to appreciate the complicated symmetries (see Wenninger, 1971, and Steinhaus, 1983). For example, Wenninger, in his beautiful book *Polyhedral Models*, describes how he constructed over 100 paper models of uniform polyhedra. Wenninger estimated that the average working time spent on each model was about eight hours, but a few of the complex models took twenty or thirty hours of work. Two of the non-convex snubs required more than one hundred hours of work each! Therefore, the main purpose of this chapter is to emphasize the degree to which geometric presentations are facilitated with the emergence of a new class of graphics supercomputers. A second goal is to demonstrate how research in polyhedral models can reveal an inexhaustible new reservoir of magnificent shapes and images.

## 26.1 Tutorial and Review

As background, a polyhedron is called *regular* if it is bounded by regular congruent polygons (Glossary), and the same number of edges meet at each vertex. A polyhedron is called *convex* if it does not contain dimples, dents or grooves. The five solids of this kind are also called *Platonic*, after Plato. These regular polyhedra include the tetrahedron, cube, octahedron, dodecahedron and icosahedron. Polyhedral shapes are quite common in various species of marine protozoa such as those illustated in the frontispiece for this chapter. Hargittai (1986) and others have noted that many primitive organisms have the shape of the pentagonal dodecahedron, and Belov suggested that the pentagonal symmetry of primi-

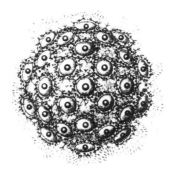

**Figure 26.1.** *Marine protozoon with polyhedral symmetry.*

tive organisms represents their defense against crystallization (Belov, 1976). Figure 26.1 shows an invertebrate organism with polyhedral symmetry.

Continuing with some defintions of terms, *Archimedean* or *semi-regular* polyhedra all have regular polygons as faces, and all vertices equal, but admit a variety of such polygons in one solid. There exist 13 semiregular polyhedra. The simplest semiregular polyhedra are obtained by symmetrically shaving off the corners of the regular solids.

*Prisms* and *antiprisms* have two congruent and parallel faces. The faces of prisms are joined by a set of parallelograms; the faces of antiprisms are joined by a set of triangles. There is an infinite number of prisms and antiprisms. *Convex uniform polyhedra* consist of the Platonic and Archimedean solids, together with prisms and antiprisms. You should remember that uniform polyhedra have the same arrangement of regular polygons at every corner; however, the polygon faces are not all of the same kind.

## 26.2  Graphics Gallery

Several polyhedral shapes are represented in (Pickover, 1990) including a snub dodecahedron with 92 faces (80 triangles and 12 pentagons). The snub form is created from the standard dodecahedron by shaving off certain corners. My 1990 *Symmetry* article illustrates these forms using color computer graphics. Stellated polyhedra are nonconvex and can be created by extending the faces of the regular polyhedra, much like a star can be formed by extending the edges of a pentagon. Detailed methods for the construction of the stellated forms (as well as for all of the uniform polyhedra) are given by Wenninger (1971). Color plate 24 is an artistic rendition of the small stellated dodecahedron with spheres placed at the vertices. To produce these artistic constructions, many triangular facets are used to tile the object. Some of the triangle vertices are actually hidden inside the poly-hedron, and some of the internal spheres placed at these points are so large that they poke out through the facets.

| Vertex | x | y | z |
|--------|-----|-----|-----|
| 1 | 0 | 1 | t |
| 2 | 0 | 1 | -t |
| 3 | 1 | t | 0 |
| 4 | 1 | -t | 0 |
| 5 | 0 | -1 | -t |
| 6 | 0 | -1 | t |
| 7 | t | 0 | 1 |
| 8 | -t | 0 | 1 |
| 9 | t | 0 | -1 |
| 10 | -t | 0 | -1 |
| 11 | -1 | t | 0 |
| 12 | -1 | -t | 0 |

**Figure 26.2.** *Vertex list for an icosahedron.* $(t = (\sqrt{5} - 1)/2.)$

A convenient computer graphics metafile was used to specify the relevant information needed to produce a figure. I used graphic workstations, such as a Stellar GS1000 or IBM RISC System/6000, to rotate and shade the objects. You will be interested to know that this class of computers can be used to rotate the models with only a few seconds' delay between images. The required computations for a similar animated sequence of models could take several minutes on traditional mainframe computers.

I trust that the ideas presented in this chapter will stimulate future studies in the graphic presentation of polyhedral models. Today, sophisticated computer graphics hardware can display shaded, interactive models of "traditional" and "nontraditional" 3-D models with high degrees of symmetry. For applications which require that real physical models be built, the computer is very useful for quickly revealing interesting shapes that can then be physically constructed. Computer tools such as these can allow students, artists, and mathematicians to visualize these shapes in ways not possible only a few years ago.

## 26.3 Stop and Think

You may wish to draw your own polyhedron. Figure 26.2 gives you the informa-

tion necessary to draw an icosahedron. Perhaps you can think of ways to decorate a stick-figure diagram of the icosahedron to make it resemble a virus or protozoan with icosahedral symmetry. The icosahedron is scaled to fit inside a unit cube. In the table, $t = (\sqrt{5} - 1)/2$. The variable $t$ is the reciprocal of a famous constant known as the golden ratio. (You will learn more about the golden ratio in "The Lute of Pythagoras" on page 203.) The 12 vertices of the icosahedron have the following values: $(0, \pm 1, \pm t)$, $(\pm t, 0, \pm 1)$, $(\pm 1, \pm t, 0)$. Following are the triplets of vertices that make up the 20 triangular faces. The first number is the face number, and the next three numbers are the vertex numbers, as given in Figure 26.2: (1,1,7,3), (2,3,7,4), (3,4,7,6), (4,6,7,8), (5,1,8,7), (6,3,4,9), (7,3,9,2), (8,1,3,2), (9,1,2,11), (10,11,2,10), (11,2,9,10), (12,4,5,9), (13,5,4,6), (14,5,6,12), (15,8,11,12), (16,8,1,11), (17,5,12,10), (18,9,5,10), (19,6,8,12), (20,12,11,10).

### 26.3.1 Buckminsterfullerene!

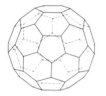

In the 1990s, one of the most interesting examples of a chemical polyhedron is the almost-spherical "soccerene," "buckminsterfullerene," or "buckyball." This molecule has 60 carbon atoms that are arranged at the vertices of a truncated icosahedron, a soccer-ball form popularized by Buckminster Fuller for use in geodesic domes. Today chemists are very excited about this cage-like molecule, and you can read more about their interest in "Notes for the Curious" on page 371.

## 26.4  For Further Reading

1.    Pickover, C. (1990) Computer renditions of polyhedral models, *Symmetry*, 1(1): 41-44.  (Color graphics.)

2.    Wenninger, M. (1971) *Polyhedral Models*. Cambridge University Press, New York.

3.    Steinhaus, H. (1983) *Mathematical Snapshots*, 3rd ed. Oxford Univ. Press: New York.

4.    Hargittai, I. and Hargittai, M. (1986) *Symmetry Through the Eyes of a Chemist*.  VCH Publishers: Weinheim.

5.    Belov, N. (1976) *Notes on Structural Mineralogy* (in Russian, *Ocherki po strukturnoi mineralogii*), Nedra: Moscow.

6.    Kappraff, J. (1990) *Connections: The Geometric Bridge Between Art and Science*. McGraw-Hill: New York.

## ROBOT INSECTS!

All kinds of advanced, insect-like robots are being developed in Rodney Brooks' lab at the Massachusetts Institute of Technology. Perhaps future houses will have dozens of these robots walking around – for amusement, protection, and housecleaning. (Photos courtesy of R. Brooks, Artificial Intelligence Laboratory, MIT.)

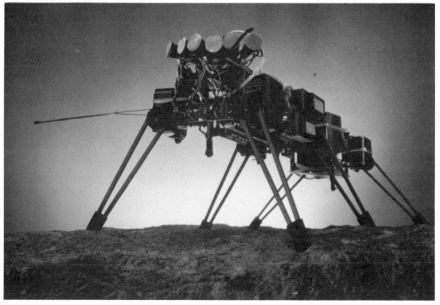

# Chapter 27

# Turning a Universe Inside-Out

Since its discovery around 1980, the Mandelbrot set has emerged as one of the most scintillating stars in the universe of popular mathematics and computer art. When most people talk about the Mandelbrot set, however, they usually mean the area just outside the set near its infinitely complicated fractal boundary. But there is also action inside the set, as some of the figures in this chapter will show. There are fractal landscapes there, infinite successions of crenellated contours, and, stranger still, fractal forests that branch both inside and outside the set. It all depends on what version of the program one writes. We'll also explore the Mandelbrot set for mappings other than the original one ($\zeta \rightarrow \zeta^2 + \mu$). The Mandelbrot set, which is the $\mu$ map for the iterative process $f_\mu$: $\zeta \rightarrow \zeta^2 + \mu$, $\mu \in C$, $\zeta \in C$, has been widely investigated in recent years. Briefly stated, the Mandelbrot set is defined as the set of complex values of $\mu$ for which successive iterates of 0 under $f_\mu$ do not converge to infinity.[26]

In pursuing the set's inner dimensions, I will not dwell on its connection with stability and chaos in dynamical systems. The connection lies in the closely-related Julia sets named after French mathematician Gaston Julia. You may delve into such matters by consulting the bibliography at the end of this chapter. In this short chapter, we examine the behavior of inverted Mandelbrot sets for the mapping

$$\zeta \rightarrow \zeta^p + \left( \frac{1}{\mu} \right)^p \tag{27.1}$$

where $p$ is a positive integer greater than 1. This particular mapping yields graphically interesting dynamical behavior with a high degree of symmetry. It also produces inverted versions of the set, where the convergence to infinity occurs at the center of these images of a rich and varied fractal universe. Figure 27.1 shows the

---

[26] If you want a gradual programming tutorial on the Mandelbrot set, try: Pickover, C. (1989) Inside the Mandelbrot set. *Algorithm*, Nov/Dec 1(1): 9-12. (This issue can be ordered from Algorithm, P.O. Box 29237, Westmount Postal Outlet, 785 Wonderland Road S., London, Ontario Canada N6K 1M6.)

**Figure 27.1.** *Mandelbrot set* This is $M(p)$ for the iterative process $\zeta \rightarrow \zeta^p + (1/\mu)^p$, $p = 2$. For this figure, $|\text{Re}(\mu)| \leq 2.0$, $|\text{Im}(\mu)| \leq 2.0$. The convergence to infinity occurs at the center of the figure.

Mandelbrot set, also called the *M*-set or $M(p)$, for the $p = 2$ case.[27] Bounded orbits, which do not explode, correspond to the black surrounding regions. Several contours (level sets) are plotted for the first few iterations. These contours indicate the rate at which the iteration explodes.

My own favorite probe of the Mandelbrot set's behavior is called the epsilon cross technique. The result of this method can be seen in Figure 27.2. Figure 27.2 is the same as Figure 27.1 except that contours are not plotted, and certain points with traditionally divergent trajectories are plotted when either of two conditions are satisfied by an orbit of $\zeta$

$$\begin{cases} |\text{Re}(\zeta)| < \varepsilon \\ |\text{Im}(\zeta)| < \varepsilon \end{cases} \tag{27.2}$$

---

[27] To create these figures, start with an array of complex values $\zeta$ and have the computer follow the outcome of the repetition process defined in Equation (27.1). Once the initial points are selected, each iteration represents a step along a path that hops from one complex number $\zeta$ to the next. The collection of all such points along a path constitutes an *orbit*. The basic goal is to understand the ultimate fate of all orbits for a given system. For example, for certain initial $\zeta$ values, the equation produces larger and larger values; i.e., the function explodes or diverges. For other values, it does not explode (it is bounded). This behavior can be characterized by computer graphics. (See Mandelbrot's book (1983) for fascinating computer graphic representations of Julia sets. Also see Brooks and Matelski (1981) for some early graphic representations of Julia and Mandelbrot sets).

**Figure 27.2.** *Mandelbrot forest corresponding to previous figure.*

(Re and Im refer to the real and imaginary parts of $\zeta$.) I have used the value of 0.01 for $\varepsilon$ with some success, as the images in this chapter make clear. Figure 27.3 is a magnification of a portion of the edge in Figure 27.2 showing self-similar structures. The tree-like structures are finer in this figure since $\varepsilon = 0.001$ was used. Figure 27.4 is a hexagonal inverted *M*-set, corresponding to the $p = 3$ case.

The test in Equation (27.2) can also be used to reveal structures in the "black" *interior* of the inverted M-set.

## 27.1 Symmetry

You should explore Equation (27.1) for larger values of $p$, which produce higher degrees of symmetry. Note that when $p = 2$, a diamond-shaped structure is produced with 4 equivalent edges. The $p = 3$ case produces a regular hexagonal shape with 6 equivalent edges. $p = 4$ produces a 12-sided figure. It is clear that the set $M(p)$ exhibits a $p(p-1)$-fold symmetry. Note that M-sets for $\zeta \rightarrow \zeta^p + 1/\mu$ exhibit only a $(p-1)$-fold symmetry. The traditional M-set for $\zeta \rightarrow \zeta^p + \mu$ also exhibits a $(p-1)$-fold symmetry and the corresponding Julia set shows a $p$-fold symmetry (Lakhtakia et al., 1988). You should consult Peitgen

**Figure 27.3.** *Magnification of a small portion of the forest in previous figure.*
$-1.21 \leq \mathrm{Re}(\mu) \leq 0.212$, $-1.19 \leq \mathrm{Im}(\mu) \leq -0.647$.

and Richter for outstanding and stimulating graphics for additional variations on
the traditional quadratic Mandelbrot sets.

## 27.2 Stop and Think

Figure 27.5 shows stalks inside of the Mandelbrot set. What are these tendrils
leading out from the centers of attraction? The tendrils branch and rebranch with
greater and greater frequency as they approach the edge of chaos represented by
the Mandelbrotian boundary. The beautiful tree-like structures exhibit self-similarity; that is, they repeat basic structural themes with increasing magnification. I
urge you to follow and explore these $M$-set stalks at various regions within the set.
The behavior of these stalks can be quite complicated and visually attractive. It is
enjoyable to ponder this forest of ribbons. Thinking about the epsilon cross test,
does it make sense, in the end, that we should see tree-like structures?

**Figure 27.4.** *Mandelbrot set*. This is for the $p = 3$ case displaying $p(p-1)$-fold symmetry. $|\operatorname{Re}(\mu)| \leq 1.2$, $|\operatorname{Im}(\mu)| \leq 1.2$.

## 27.3  For Further Reading

1.  Pickover, C. (1990) Inverted Mandelbrot sets. *Visual Computer*. 5: 377.

2.  Brooks, R., Matelski, J. P. (1981) The dynamics of 2-generator subgroups of PSL(2,C). In *Riemann Surfaces and Related Topics: Proceedings of the 1978 Stony Brook Conference*. Kyra, I. and Maskit, B. (eds.) Princeton University Press: New Jersey. (Note: this 1978 paper contains simple computer graphics and mathematical descriptions of both Julia and Mandelbrot sets).

3.  Mandelbrot, B. (1983) *The Fractal Geometry of Nature*. Freeman: San Francisco.

4.  Peitgen, H., Richter, P. (1986) *The Beauty of Fractals*. Springer: Berlin.

5.  Lakhtakia, A., Vasundara, V., Messier, R., Varadan, V. (1987) On the symmetries of the Julia sets for the process $z \to z^p + c$. *Journal of Physics A: Math. General*. 20: 3533-3535.

6.  Stevens, R. (1989) *Fractal Programming in C*. M and T Books: Redwood City: California.

**Figure 27.5.** *Mandelbrot stalks*. These stalks are within the *interior* bounded region of the Mandelbrot set for a magnification near an edge in Figure 27.1. ( $-1.28 \leq \mathrm{Re}(\mu)$ $\leq -0.823$, $-0.94 \leq \mathrm{Im}(\mu) \leq -0.561$).

Chapter 28

# From Math Comes Beauty:
# Monkey Curves and Spirals

*"Throughout the shadowy eons of man's existence there have been some men committed to the communication of the inexplicable. They have been the philosophers, the scientists, and, always, the artists. Some have opted for words, some chose music, and happily for the rest of us, a battery of geniuses attempted to convey just what they felt – visually."*     David Larkin, *1973*

Over the last few years, mathematicians have begun to enjoy and present bizarre mathematical patterns in new ways – ways sometimes dictated as much by a sense of aesthetics as by the needs of logic. Moreover, computer graphics allows non-mathematicians to better appreciate the complicated and interesting graphical behavior of simple formulas.

Once again, I think you will be excited to know that complicated and artistic surfaces can be fully computed and rendered in just a few seconds using the new class of graphics supercomputers that have become readily available in the 1990s. This new breed of computer can typically plot more than 50,000 shaded triangular facets in a second. This speed may make such hardware and software systems of interest to both artists and computer graphics scientists.

Here are some recipes for producing a beautiful graphics gallery. I hope you enjoy trying these with your own machines, or changing the formulas slightly to see the graphic and artistic results. The generating formulas for the surfaces in this chapter are of the form

$$z = \alpha + \beta \cos\left(6\pi\sqrt{(x^2 + y^2)} + arctan(y/x)\right) \tag{28.1}$$

where

$$\alpha = 3y(3x^2 - y^2)/4 \tag{28.2}$$

or

$$\alpha = 5\sqrt{|x| - |y|} + \frac{2|xy|}{\sqrt{(x^2 + y^2)}} \tag{28.3}$$

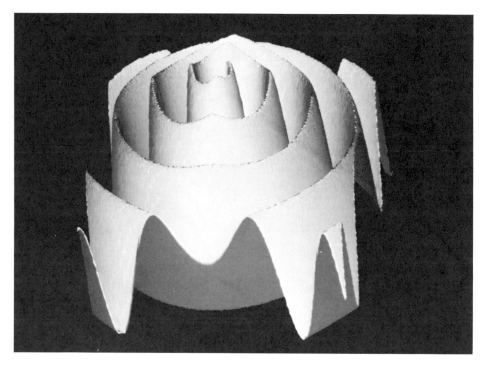

**Figure 28.1.** *An intricate mathematical surface.* This was produced using Equation (28.3), where the "5" is replaced by "1."

You may wish to experiment with other values of $\alpha$ such as

$$5xy^2/(x^2 + y^4). \tag{28.4}$$

The $\alpha$ term creates a surface upon which a 3-D spiral form sits. When $\alpha = 3y(3x^2 - y^2)/4$, I call the surface a *Ricard surface* after the IBM programmer who mentioned this spiral in a newsletter (Ricard, 1989). Equation (28.2) produces a modified hyperbolic saddle surface. The use of Equation (28.3) produces another interesting and artistic surface – a spiral atop a base with 4 creases (Color Plate 12). Equation (28.4) produces a more intricate base. For the figures here, $\beta = 1$ was used. However, you may wish to try a cosine term for $\beta$ in order to make the edge of the spiral ripple up and down.

Of course there is an infinite variety of artistic surfaces which can be constructed from simple formulas. Other interesting surfaces are mentioned in this section so that you can do future experiments. A particularly interesting surface, and a personal favorite, is defined by

$$z = \frac{1}{3} x^3 - xy^2 \tag{28.5}$$

This surface is called a *monkey saddle* because a monkey sitting on it would have a place for his tail as well as his legs. Another graphically interesting surface is

```
ALGORITHM: Main part of the C language code used to
          compute z=f(x,y).
```

Notes:   the atan2 function must be used instead of atan to
insure angles returned are in correct quadrant.   The term
"res" controls the resolution of the surface.   Some
suggested values are:    xmin=-1.2, ymin=-1.2, xmax=1.2,
ymax=1.2

```
#define SQR(x)  ((x)*(x))
#define SSQR(x)  ((x)*(x)*(x)*(x))
float screen[512][512];
float xmin,xmax,ymin,ymax,res;
res = 512;
printf("Enter xmin, xmax, ymin, ymax \n");
scanf("%f %f %f %f", &xmin, &xmax, &ymin, &ymax);
for(i = 0, x = xmin; (x <= xmax) && (i < res);
    i++, x += (xmax - xmin) / res)
  for(j = 0, y = ymin; (y <= ymax) && (j < res );
      j++, y += (ymax - ymin) / res){
    screen[i][j]=
    /* Equation 2 */
    3.0 * y * (3.0 * SQR(x) - 4.0 * SQR(y)) / 4.0
    /* Equation 3 */
    /* + 5*SQR(fabs(x)-fabs(y)) + 2*fabs(x*y)/(sqrt(SQR(x)
       +SQR(y))) | */
    /* Equation 4 */
    /* + 5*x*SQR(y)/(SQR(x)+SSQR(y))+ */
    /* Equation 1 */
    + cos(6.0 * 3.14156 * sqrt(SQR(x) + SQR(y)) + (atan2(x,y)));
  }
```

**Pseudocode 28.1.** *Main part of C language code used to compute z = f(x,y).*

$$z = \frac{-5x}{x^2 + y^2 + 1} \tag{28.6}$$

which has a positive and negative dimple in its smooth surface.

Care to make concentric rippling waves, like ripples in a pond, or a trumpet-horn shape? The following two formulas produce these surfaces, respectively.

$$z = \sin^2(\sqrt{x^2 + y^2}) \tag{28.7}$$

$$z = \ln(x^2 + y^2). \tag{28.8}$$

The following equation produces a surface with a rapidly rising wall, due to the cubic term, and a small, pretty ridge.

$$z = x - \frac{1}{12}x^3 - \frac{1}{4}y^2 + \frac{1}{2}. \tag{28.9}$$

The piece of C code in Pseudocode 28.1 may help you to compute the formulas used to make the surfaces in this article. The array "screen(i)(j)" contains the altitudes *(z)* as a function of *x* and *y*. The approximate range of *x* and *y* values are ( $-1.2 \leq x,y \leq 1.2$ ) for all of the plots. If 3-D surface display programs are not available, the surfaces can be viewed in 2-D with various colors representing the height of the function (see the color plates of *Computers, Pattern, Chaos and Beauty* for an example). Therefore, you can create artistic pictures without sophisticated 3-D rendering software. You may also experiment further by getting ideas for additional intricate functions from the books listed in the reference section.

## 28.1 Stop and Think

As opposed to the curves described in this chapter which lie wholly in a plane certain curves occupy three dimensions; these are called "skew curves." 3-D curves may be expressed in parametric form (Seggern, 1990): $x = f(t)$, $y = g(t)$, $z = h(t)$. Because $f$, $g$, and $h$ can be anything you like, the remarkable panoply of art forms made possible by plotting these curves is quite large. Some personal favorites are listed below.

### 28.1.1 Helical Curves

$$x = a \sin(t), y = a \cos(t), z = at/(2\pi c) \tag{28.10}$$

where $a$ and $c$ are constants. Try $a = 0.5$, $c = 5.0$, and $0 < t < 10\pi$. A plot of this

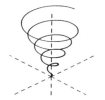

"circular helix" curve resembles a wire spring. To draw a "conical helix" try

$$x = az \sin(t), y = az \cos(t), z = t/(2\pi c) \tag{28.11}$$

where $a$ and $c$ are constants.

### 28.1.2 3-D Sine Wave

$$x = b[1 - c^2 \cos^2(at)]^{0.5} \cos(t) \tag{28.12}$$

$$y = b[1 - c^2 \cos^2(at)]^{0.5} \sin(t) \tag{28.13}$$

$$z = c \cos(at) \tag{28.14}$$

This is for a sine wave on a sphere. For a rotating sine wave, try

$$x = \sin(at) \cos(bt) \tag{28.15}$$

$$y = \sin(at) \sin(bt) \tag{28.16}$$

$$z = t/(2\pi) \tag{28.17}$$

This produces very wild effects depending on the $a/b$ ratio you use. For a toroidal spiral,

$$x = [a \sin(ct) + b] \cos(t) \tag{28.18}$$

$$y = \left[ a \sin(ct) + b) \right] \sin(t) \tag{28.19}$$

$$z = a \cos(ct) \tag{28.20}$$

If you do not have access to 3-D graphics, you can plot projections of these curves in the x-y plane simply by plotting $(x,y)$ as you iterate $t$ in a computer program. Alternatively, Seggern (1990) gives a handy formula for viewing the curves at any angle.

$$x_p = -x \sin \theta + y \cos \theta \tag{28.21}$$

$$y_p = -x \sin \theta \cos \phi - y \sin \theta \cos \phi + z \sin \phi \tag{28.22}$$

where $(x,y,z)$ are the coordinates of the point on the curve prior to projection and $(\theta, \phi)$ are the viewing angles in spherical coordinates

## 28.2 For Further Reading

1.  Peterson, I. (1987) Portraits of Equations *Science News* 132(12): 184-186.

2.  Pruoitt, M. (1975) *Computer Graphics*. Dover. New York.

3.  J. Gleick, *Chaos: Making a New Science*. Viking: New York (1987).

4.  Abramowitz, M., Stegun, I. (1970) *Handbook of Mathematical Functions*. Dover: New York.

5.  Shenk, A. (1979) *Calculus and Analytic Geometry*. Goodyear: Santa Monica.

6.  Pickover, C. (1990) *Computers, Pattern, Chaos, and Beauty*. St. Martin's Press: New York.

7.  Seggern, D. (1990) *CRC Handbook of Mathematical Curves and Surfaces*. CRC Press: Boca Raton, Florida.

8.  Ricard, G. (1989) Intricate mathematical surfaces. *J. Chaos and Graphics*. 2: 10. (This newsletter is available to any who write me.)

Leonardo's "Concatenation."

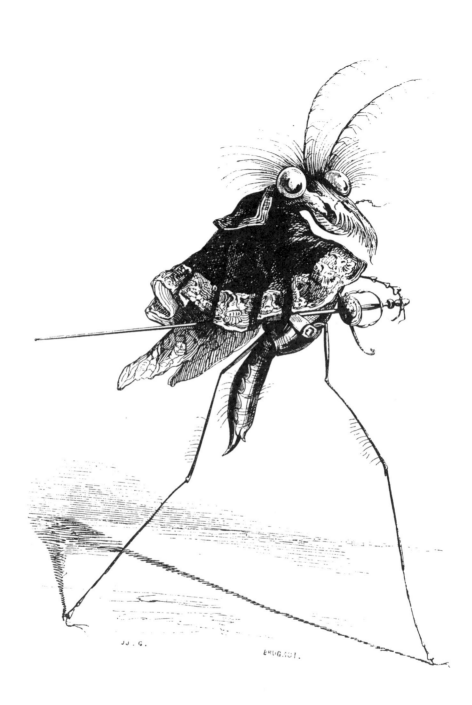

Chapter 29

# Visualization of the Gleichniszahlen-Reihe Monster

If you do not read German, the title of this chapter may conjure up visions of a strange animal from a science fiction movie. However, the "Gleichniszahlen-Reihe Monster" refers to a number sequence with some rather strange and compelling properties, and the German name will be explained shortly. Because the sequence never seems to contain a number greater than 3, you don't need large computers to begin exploring.

Consider the number-theory sequence $u_{r,n}$, where $r$ is the row number, and $n$ the column number:

```
1
1 1
2 1
1 2 1 1
1 1 1 2 2 1
    . . .
```

You probably can't guess the numerical entries for the next row. However, the answer is actually simple, when viewed in hindsight. To appreciate the answer, it helps to speak the entries in each row out loud. Note that row Two has two "ones," thereby giving the sequence 2 1 for the third row. Row Three has one "two" and one "one." Row Four has one "one," one "two," and two "ones." From this, an entire sequence $u_{r,n}$ can be generated. This interesting sequence was described in a German article, where M. Hilgemeier called the sequence "Die Gleichniszahlen-Reihe," which translates into English as "the likeness sequence." The sequence, also extensively studied by John H. Conway, grows rather rapidly. For example, row 15 is:

132113213222113311121321133112111312211213211312111322211123113112221131112311332111213211322211312113211

Row 27 contains 2012 entries (see Figure 29.4). A casual inspection of the sequence indicates a predominance of 1's, with 2 and 3 less common. For rows

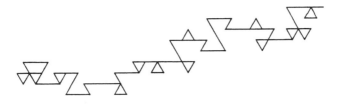

**Figure 29.1.** *Vectorgram.* This is for *u* when *r* = 15.

between 6 and 27, there are about 50% 1's, 30% 2's, and 20% 3's. As has been proved previously by Hilgemeier, the largest number *u* can contain is 3. Interestingly, the hypothesis that 3 3 3 can never occur has never been proved, although Hilgemeier has tested this for *r* = 27 and I have tested it up to *r* = 33 which has over 10,000 entries.

In this chapter, I am particularly interested in the distribution of 1's, 2's, and 3's. While one can simply compute the percentage of occurrence of each digit for a given row, this does not tell us anything about any interesting clusters or peculiar areas of concentration of one digit over another. A technique which has proved useful in overcoming this drawback involves the transformation of the digit strings into characteristic two-dimensional patterns. A single digit is inspected and assigned a direction of movement on a plane. To visualize this (and other) ternary sequences, use a 3-way vectorgram where the occurrence of a 1 directs the trace one unit at 0°, a 2 causes a walk at 120°, and a 3 a walk at 240°. Each of these angles is with respect to the *x*-axis. Figure 29.1 - Figure 29.3 show patterns for row 15, containing 102 digits, row 25 containing 1182 digits, and row 33, containing somewhat over 10,000 digits. Different scales were used to fit the graphs on a page. Notice that if the string contained only ones, the walk would be only to the right. As can be seen from the figures, *u* is far from random. The upward diagonal trend in Figure 29.1 and Figure 29.2 indicates a mixture of predominantly 1's, some 2's, and relatively few 3's. The fact that the trends are fairly linear suggests that the ratios are relatively constant throughout the row. Figure 29.1 and Figure 29.2 show occurrence of sudden upward bumps which eventually return to the diagonal base line. These bumps indicate a temporary change in the trend to more 2's.

You can understand the resulting patterns by considering the directions travelled by various combinations of entries in the sequence. For example, the sequence 1-1-1 is totally *x*-directed. 1-2-3, 1-3-2, and various cyclic permutations return to the original point (as diagramed here). For future experiments, you may wish to compute the slope of the mean-line of the vectorgram as a function of the row number, or make a plot of the slope of the mean-line versus the number of entries in a row. It appears, from just a few sample points, that the slope of the mean-line increases as a function of row-number.

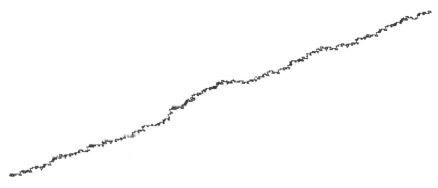

**Figure 29.2.** *Vectorgram.* This is for *u* when *r* = 25.

I hope that you will uncover or solve additional mysteries with this interesting sequence. If you are interested in the use of 8-way vectorgrams in the characterization of genetic sequences, you should see (Pickover, 1987).

[[ In closing, I mention some observations by Dr. A. Lakhtakia and myself. In 1989 we became intrigued by the fact that the likeness sequence can be generalized to the array $G(p)$ where $p \neq 1$ is either zero or a positive integer. The following is an example.

```
p
1 p
1 1 1 p
3 1 1 p
1 3 2 1 1 p
1 1 1 3 1 2 2 1 1 p
```

It is interesting to note that simply substituting $p = 1$ into $G(p)$ does not allow us to obtain a standard likeness-sequence since numbers and symbols are mixed in the construction of these arrays. It is conjectured here that the largest number occurring in $G(p)$ is max$(p,3)$. Also, if $p > 3$ then $p$ occurs only in the rightmost entry of the row.

So far, I have discussed the use of only one number or symbol to start the likeness-sequence. A further generalization is obtained by placing two symbols, $p$ and $q$, as the first entries, thus:

```
pq
1p1q
111p111q
311p311q
13211p13211q
```

It is easily observed that for $p \neq 1, q \neq 1, p \neq q$, the array obtained is simply the two copies of array $G(p)$ placed row-wise, side by side. Also, the $n$-th row $(n = 0,1,2,3, \ldots )$ of the array obtained when $p = 1, q \neq 1$ is the $(n+1)$-th row of $G(q)$. When $p = q = 1$, the $n$-th row is the same as the $(n+1)$-th row of the like-

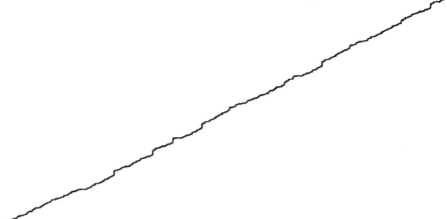

**Figure 29.3.** *Vectorgram.* This is for $u$ when $r = 33$.

ness-sequence. If $p \neq 1$ and $q = 1$, the structure is the same as that obtained by placing the usual likeness sequence to the right of $G(p)$. ]]

## 29.1 Stop and Think

I invite you to ponder several related questions:

1.  What are the properties of reverse likeness-sequences? Starting from a particular row, can one work backward and compute the starting string of symbols?

2.  Could the likeness-sequence be useful as a method of encryption? Could the military use this for scrambling messages and making secret codes? For those of you who may find difficulty in computing large likeness-sequences but wish to examine various statistical properties of the sequence, I include Figure 29.4 – a likeness sequence for row 27. (See "Notes for the Curious" on page 371 for additional information on likeness-sequences.)

## 29.2 For Further Reading

1.  Hilgemeir, M. (1986) Die Gleichniszahlen-Reihe. *Bild der Wissenschaft.* 12: 194-195.

2.  Pickover, C. (1987) DNA Vectorgrams: representation of cancer gene sequences as movements along a 2-D cellular lattice, *IBM Journal of Research and Development.* 31: 111-119.

3.  Pickover, C., Khorasani, E. (1991) Visualization of the Gleichniszahlen-Reihe, an unusual number theory sequence, *Math. Spectrum*, in press.

4.  Lakhtakia, A., Pickover, C. (1991) Observations on the Gleichniszahlen-Reihe, *Journal of Recreational Math.*, in press.

```
3113112221131112311332111213122112311311123112111331121113122
1121321131211132221123113112211121312211231131122211211133112
1113112221121113122113121113222112132113213221232112111312111
2133221123113112221131112212211131221121321131211132221123113
1122211311123113322112111331121113112221121113122113111231133
2211211131221131211132221232112111312111213322112132113213221
2112311321322112111312212321121113122122211211232221123113112
2211311123113322111213122112311311123112111301121113122112321321
1331121321132122212221113122113121111322212321121113121111213322
1121321132132211331121321132213211231132132221211131221232112
1113122122211211232221121321132132211331121321231231121113112
2211213211331121321123123211231131122211211131221131112311332
2112132113212231121113112221121321132122211322212221121123222
1123113112221131112311332111213122112311311123112111331121113
1221121321131211132221123113112211131112311332211322311311222
1131112311332211211131221131211132221112131221123113121113112111231211
2322211213211321321132211331221122311311122211211113122113111231133
2211213211312132211331122112332112131122211332113221122112221121332
2112111312211312111322212321121113121112131221121321132132221123113211
1121113122123211211131221121311121221121321132132221112311311
2221133112132123222112111312211312112213211231132132211211131
2211131211113222112131111213122112132113121113221131122311311221122213213221
1331121321232221123113112221131112311322231121113112221121321
3311213211221121332211211131221131211113222212311222122132113211321
3221123113112221133112132123222112111312211312111322212321121
1131211121332211213111213122112132113121113222112132113213221
2321121113121111213322112132113213221133112132123123112111213112
2211213211331121321122112133221123113112221131112311332111213
1221123113111123112111331121113122112132113121113222112311311
2211311112212211312211312111322211213211321321231213221113312211231
1332111213322112132113213221132231131122211311123113322112111
3122113121111322212321121113122123211231131122113221123113221
1312211213211321321112133221231132211321221
```

**Figure 29.4.** *Likeness-sequence for row 27.*

Chapter 30

# The Moire Effect: Practical
# And Pictorial Patterns

Moire patterns, the images that appear when two sets of lines or curves are super-imposed, are common in everyday life. When two fine mesh curtains happen to overlap, weird and wavy patterns of dark and light may play across them. When we pass two picket fences and look through one fence at the other, we may see vertical bars of dark and light race along them. The same effect is obtained at home simply by holding two combs together.

The name "Moire" (pronounced "mwah-ray") does not come from some famous French mathematician; rather, "Moire" is the French word for "watered" or "wetted." Many spectacular-looking Moire images can be made on computer graphics terminals. The images that I will describe here were produced on high-resolution printers and graphics terminals, but more modest equipment will also clearly show the patterns.

There have been so many pretty patterns published in the scientific and artistic literature, that I prefer to concentrate in this article on various *practical* uses for Moire patterns. Therefore, one of the goals of this chapter is to illustrate simple graphics techniques whereby the non-linearity of computer screens can be checked. In addition, a method of highlighting objects on a graphic screen is presented. Finally, I will tell you how to build your own screw tightness indicator. All of these topics make use of Moire interference techniques. For a beautiful background article on Moire methods in art and science, see (Giger, 1986); for practical applications in the field of biology, see (Pickover, 1984).

## 30.1 Non-Linear Screens

In this section, I'll use a Moire interference pattern to give a visual indication of non-linearities in beam positioning in a cathode ray tube, such as used in televison screens or computer terminals. As background, the basic arrangement of a cathode ray tube (CRT) involves an electron gun and a yoke (a system of electro-magnetic coils mounted on the outside of the tube at the base of its neck). The yoke deflects the electron beam to different parts of the tube face when currents

**Figure 30.1.** *Horizontal lines.* No non-linearity is evident.

pass through the coils. Two pairs of coils are used, one to control horizontal deflection, the other vertical. Amplifiers are used to convert small voltages received from the display controller into currents of the appropriate magnitude for the deflection system. By using a digital-to-analog converter, the voltages used for deflection are generated, by the display controller, from digital values provided by the computer.

In order to check the operation of the CRT's yoke, I suggest a simple visual method whereby the Moire effect can be used to demonstrate minute "hidden" non-linearities or periodicities. Perhaps you can think of other applications for this approach. The method (to check vertical deflection) is described as follows:

1. Draw parallel horizontal lines with equal spacings between them.

2. The obtained ruling (in Step 1) is then inclined and superimposed on the original.

The resulting pattern will reveal hidden periodicities. Pseudocode 30.1 will help you create the patterns. For best results, the top of the first inclined line should coincide with a line of the original (noninclined) pattern. In general, the higher the density of lines, the more accurate the resulting pattern. The figures demonstrate the use of this invention to check vertical deflection in a vector graphics display. In Figure 30.1, horizontal lines are drawn. In Figure 30.2, the same lines are inclined and superimposed. Note that the resultant figure reveals a sinusoidal periodicity in the spacing of the lines. This tiny periodicity is not evident by casual inspection of Figure 30.1! Figure 30.3 was generated after this non-linearity was corrected. To provide additional demonstrations in a "real" system, I ran the Moire generator on several Tektronix CRT's. Both large and small non-linearities were detected.

I would be interested in hearing from you regarding any other interesting and creative uses for this particularly simple pattern.

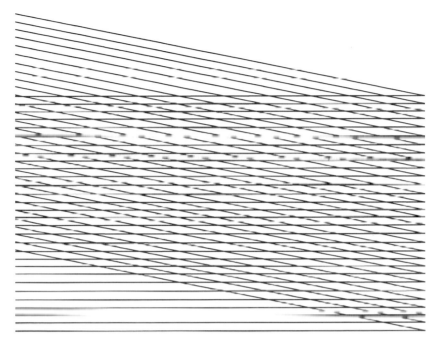

**Figure 30.2.** *Non-linearity   checker   applied   to   previous   figure.* Note that sinusoidal periodicities in the previous figured are now revealed.

## 30.2  Highlighting Objects

Often it is important to "highlight" objects, text, or other graphic items on a complicated graphics screen.  Let me give one example which I have worked with. Using an electronic circuit editor, a designer points at a drawing of a tiny transistor in a very complicated drawing of a circuit, and the transistor blinks. Sometimes a white box is drawn around the component in a VLSI (very-large scale integration) layout whenever that component is selected (by cursor, name, or other means). Unfortunately, blinking is not provided in many graphics languages for a variety of reasons, and simply placing a white border around an object superimposed on a complicated background is simply not adequate for detection of that graphics object. Therefore, I'd like to propose an aperture-frame composed of a Moire interference pattern. The frame described here is circular; however, a similar approach can be used for other highlighting shapes.  Here's how to do it. A composite pattern consists of two simpler patterns which are superimposed as follows:

1.   Pattern 1. A ring of radial striations at 1 degree intervals.

2.   Pattern 2. A ring of radial striations at 1 degree intervals, but with the outer tips of the radial striations displaced by $\theta$ degrees relative to the inner tip.

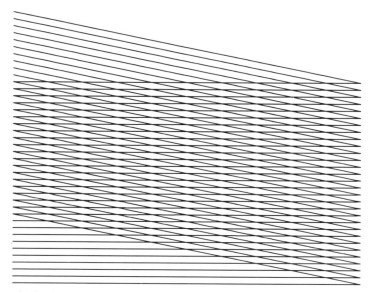

**Figure 30.3.** *Same as previous figure, after correction of non-linearity problem.*

Pseudocode 30.2 will help you draw the pattern. When superimposed, $N$ concentric rings appear. As $\theta$ increases, $N$ also increases. This is a little like superimposing two spoked bike wheels.

The key idea here is that if Pattern 2 is rotated relative to Pattern 1, the concentric interference patterns move outward or inward (depending on clockwise or counterclockwise rotation). *This eye-catching outward or inward concentric movement $M_c$ is much faster than the rotation speed $M_r$ ($M_c > M_r$).* This means the user gets a strong, rapidly moving visual effect for less CPU loading than it would take to move an "ordinary" animated pattern. For tiny amounts of movement in Pattern 2, the concentric rings move rapidly. Consider a possible scenario: a user points to a small transistor in a dense VLSI layout. The Moire rings surround the transistor, and *concentric patterns move inward, "pointing" at the transistor.* Some advantages of this method are that it is easy to implement, the direction of radial motion is controllable, and the number of concentric circles is controllable using $\theta$. The fact that $M_c > M_r$ provides more motion for the user's "CPU dollar." This would be useful on small systems.

I leave this section by asking you to speculate what would happen if the radial pattern were to be turned at the speed of light. Since we know that the Moire fringe always travels faster than the speed of rotation, and we know that nothing travels faster than the speed of light, have we arrived at an interesting paradox?

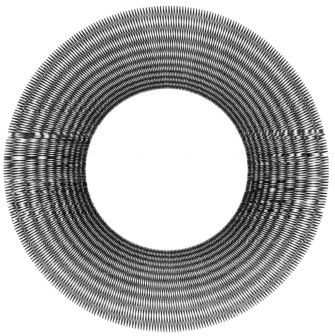

**Figure 30.4.** *Concentric rings.* These rings move outward (or inward) when one pattern is rotated relative to the other. Note that $M_c > M_r$. In this figure, $\theta = 10°$.

## 30.3  Keeping the Screws Tight

As a final idea, the perception of moire interference patterns on a screw and its mounting surface can be used to detect and characterize small relative motions occurring between the screw and its mounting. A transparent washer-like disc affixed to the screwhead contains rings of ink. When the screw is tight, the washer is then "hit," transferring ink to the mounting surface – thereby creating a pattern of identical random dots on the mounting surface and the screw-head disc. The transparent washer is free to rotate with the screw. If the screw rotates by even a small degree, an interference effect will be revealed to an observer by casual visual inspection.

I have done some tests with concentric circles – with the screw's axis off-center. This method is very sensitive (visually) to loosening over a wide range of degrees, and it is possible to get an idea of the amount of rotation by casual inspection of the screw (see Figure 30.7).

An interesting extension of this approach which requires no special hardware (just a screw with off-center concentric circles) would involve the following approach:

1.  take an initial photo of the screws, and place the pattern on a transparency,

2.  take a picture after time has elapsed, and

3.  superimpose the pictures. Loose screws will stand out "like a sore thumb."

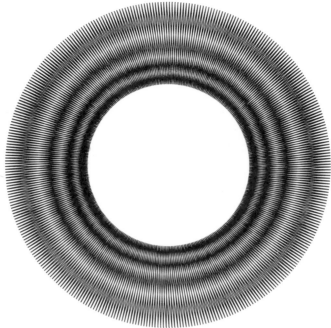

**Figure 30.5.** *Same as previous figure,* except $\theta = 4°$.

Small movements, such as in the color graphics display dials, could become apparent to the user in a visual and intuitive manner. Try something like this with jar caps as well.

## 30.4 For Further Reading

1.  Giger, H. (1986) Moires. *Computers and Mathematics with Applications.* 12B(1/2): 329 - 361.
2.  Pickover, C. (1984) The use of random-dot displays in the study of biomolecular conformation. *Journal of Molecular Graphics.* 2: 34.
3.  Pickover, C. (1990) Moire patterns. *Algorithm.* Sept. 1(6): 12.

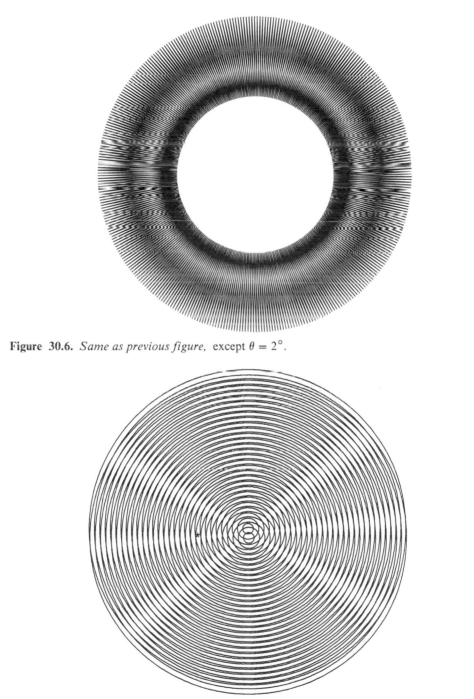

**Figure  30.6.**  *Same as previous figure,* except $\theta = 2°$.

**Figure  30.7.**  *Screw tightness patterns.*  One screw head has become loose and has rotated 10 degrees relative to the other.

```
ALGORITHM: Nonlinearity Checker
/*-----draw the first set of lines ----*/
do x = 1 to 100 by .25;
 MoveTo(x,0); PenTo(x,80);
end;
/*-----now incline the lines ---------*/
do x = 1 to 100 by .25;
 MoveTo(x,0); PenTo(x+10,80);
end;
```

**Pseudocode 30.1.** *Nonlinearity Checker.*

```
ALGORITHM:  Moire Frame Highlighting
/* ------------ Pattern 1 ---------------*/
do theta = 1 to 360;
   r= 20; x=r*cosd(theta)+50; y=r*sind(theta)+50; MoveTo(x,y);
   r= 40; x=r*cosd(theta)+50; y=r*sind(theta)+50; PenTo(x,y);
end;
/* ------------ Pattern 2 ---------------*/
/* --- Angle variable a controls the
       number of Moire lines --*/
/* --- Experiment by making a
       transparency of Pattern 2 and
       superimposing it upon pattern 1----*/
do theta = 1 to 360;
   r= 20; x=r*cosd(theta)+50; y=r*sind(theta)+50;
   MoveTo(x,y);
   r= 40; x=r*cosd(theta+a )+50; y=r*sind(theta+a)+50;
   PenTo(x,y);
end;
```

**Pseudocode 30.2.** *Moire frame highlighting.*

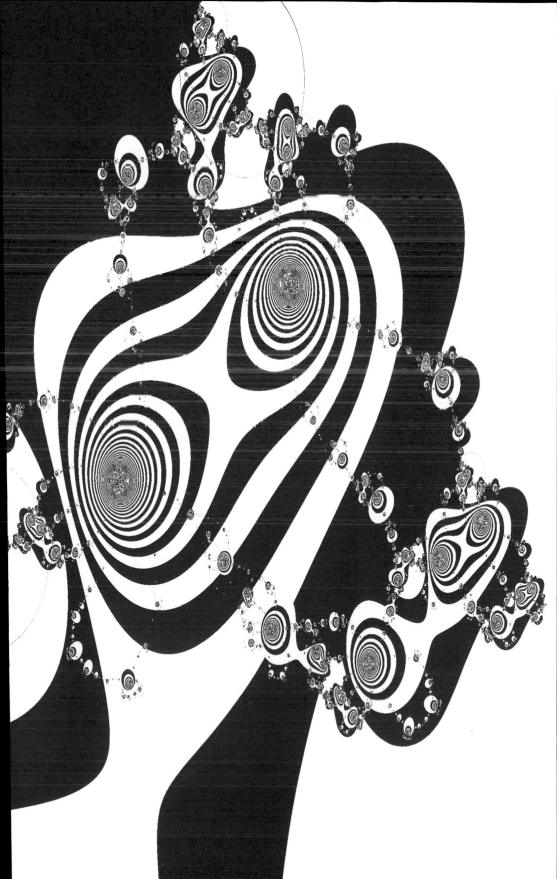

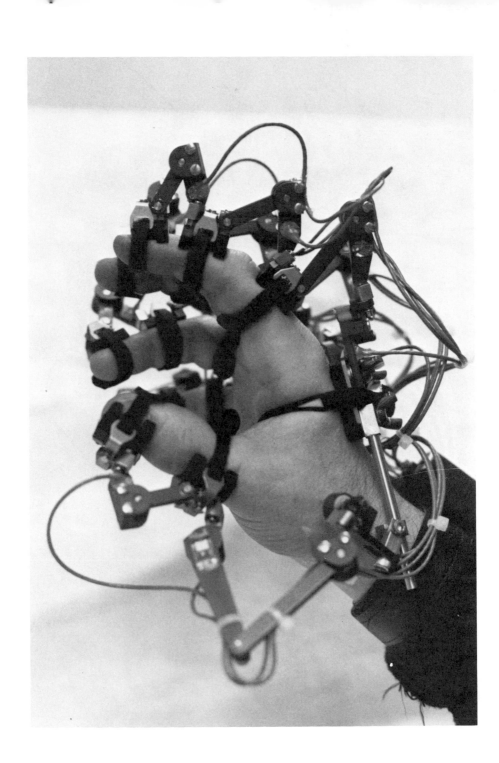

# Chapter 31

# Interlude: Computer Exoskeletons

Why should sophisticated computers be difficult to use? Most computers of the future will be responsive to human modes of communication including touch, gestures, speech, and eye movements. High-precision exoskeletons, such as the *Series 2 Dextrous Hand Master* shown in the frontispiece for this Interlude, already permit one to manipulate computer-generated images in artificial reality environments, control robotic hands, and measure hand strain. Within the next few years, musicians, dancers, artists, film-makers, sports enthusiasts, surgeons, and masseuses will have access to these devices. Applications of exoskeletons are limitless.

The device shown here uses sensors attached to each finger joint to measure three bending and side-to-side motions of each finger. Twenty joint angle measurements are collected by an IBM AT, Macintosh, or VME computer at very fast rates. The Series 2 Dextrous Hand Master is manufactured by: Exos Inc., 8 Blanchard Rd., Burlington, Massachusetts 01803 USA. (See "Notes for the Curious" on page 371 for additional information on novel computer input devices.)

# Part  V

# EXPLORATION

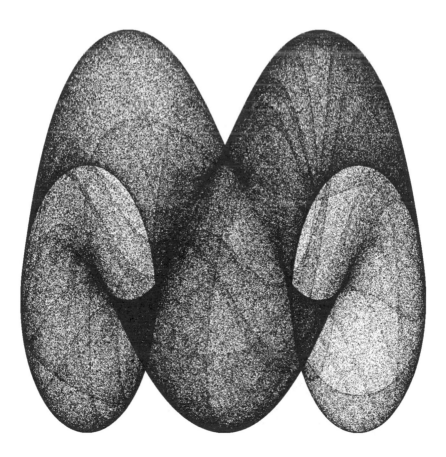

Chapter 32

# Exploration: Introduction

*"I have often been astonished to find that almost all books on philosophy and even most modern books on geometry are totally without pictures. Philosophy is supposed to be the study of thought, and I have always believed that most people thought in pictures. "* Alan L. Mackay, *In the Mind's Eye*

*"Mathematics is the only science where one never knows what one is talking about nor whether what is said is true. "* Bertrand Russell

In this section, we explore a few threads in the fabric of mathematics. Some chapters contain new concepts, while other topics in this section are based on curiosities in the literature which are taken a step further into unusual new areas. Like some of the chapters in the *Simulation* section of this book, *Exploration* is an exciting collection of mathematical curiosities and puzzles. Among the topics are: cakemorphic numbers, the Lute of Pythagoras, earthworm algebra, palindromic numbers, and the Mandelbrot set. A number of topics in this part of the book deal with number theory. Number theory – the study of properties of integers – is an ancient discipline. Much mysticism accompanied early treatises; for example, Pythagoreans based all events in the universe on whole numbers. Only a few hundred years ago courses in numerology were required by all college students, and even today such numbers as 13, 7, and 666 conjure up emotional reactions in many people. Today integer arithmetic is used in an incredible number of areas, for example, in communications, computer science, cryptography, physics, biology and art (Schroeder, 1986).

Since this *Exploration* section contains puzzles and contests, it should awaken lethargic students in a classroom. Educators Martha Boles and Rochelle Newman, in their book *Universal Patterns*, note that mathematics flourishes in an environment where there is unlimited freedom of inquiry regardless of whether the results have immediate practical application. You see this philosophy in action throughout the *Exploration* section.

## 32.1  For Further Reading

1.    Spencer, D. (1982) *Computers in Number Theory*. Computer Science Press: Maryland. (An easy-to-read book with computational recipes.)

2.    Schröder, M. (1986) *Number Theory in Science and Communication*. Springer: New York (This book is recommended highly. An interesting book, by a fascinating author.)

3.    Beiler, A. (1966) *Recreations in the Theory of Numbers*. Dover: New York.

4.    Meyer, J. (1963) *More Fun with Mathematics*. Gramercy: New York.

5.    Boles, M., Newman, R. (1990) *Universal Patterns*. Pythagorean Press: Massachusetts.

# Chapter 33

# The Lute of Pythagoras

*"Nature is relationships in space. Geometry defines relationships in space. Art creates relationships in space. "*

M. Boles and R. Newman, *Universal Patterns, 1990*

*The Lute of Pythagoras* is among mathematics' most beautiful recursive shapes, and it is constructed using only straight lines. You may wish to spend some time constructing this interesting shape and thinking about some of its properties. An example is shown in Figure 33.1. You can construct this form with or without computer graphics, although a computer can be used to generate the lute to a greater degree of recursion and fineness than shown here.

Begin your construction by drawing an isosceles triangle, such as you see marked *ABC* in Figure 33.1. Next, construct the ladder steps marked *ED*, *FG*, etc. There is a trick you must follow to locate the ladder steps: the length *AC* must equal *AE*, the length *DE* must equal *DG*, etc. Thus we have: *AC = DC = AE, DE = DG = EF*, etc. A compass may help you make these distances equal in your drawing. You may travel as far down the isosceles triangle as the resolution of your eye or graphics display permits. Next create the pentagonal, star-like figures by joining the proper ladder points. A new point *Z* is located so that *CE = AD = AZ = ZC*. You can also recursively create star-shapes for as far as your eye can see.

Mathematicians have noted that the ratio of successive sides of the ladder *CE/EG = EG/HI* ... is 1.61803. This number is also called the golden ratio. Because 1.61803 appears in the most surprising places (Boles and Newman, 1990), and has such unique properties, mathematicians have given it a special name, $\phi$. This symbol is the Greek letter Phi, the first letter in the name Phidias, the classical Greek sculptor who used the Golden Ratio extensively in his work. A golden rectangle has a ratio of the length of its sides equal to 1: $\phi$. It is considered the most visually pleasing of all rectangles, being neither too squat nor too thin. Many artistic works contain examples of golden ratios, for example: the Greek Parthenon, Leonardo da Vinci's *Mona Lisa*, Salvador Dali's *The Sacrament of*

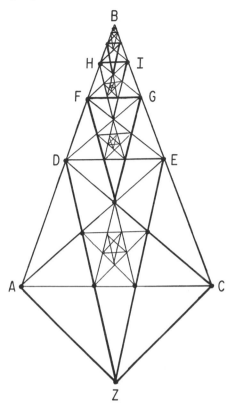

**Figure 33.1.** *The Lute of Pythagoras.*

*the Last Supper*, and much of M.C. Escher's work. Since $\phi = (1 + \sqrt{5})/2$, it has some rather amazing mathematical properties. For example,

$$\phi - 1 = \frac{1}{\phi}; \quad \phi\phi' = -1; \quad \phi + \phi' = 1; \quad \phi^n + \phi^{n+1} = \phi^{n+2} \tag{33.1}$$

where $\phi' = (1 - \sqrt{5})/2$. Both $\phi$ and $\phi'$ are the roots of $x^2 - x - 1 = 0$. In addition, we have the remarkable formulas involving the single digit, 1.

$$\phi = \sqrt{1 + \sqrt{1 + \sqrt{1 + \sqrt{1 + \cdots}}}} \tag{33.2}$$

$$\phi = 1 + \cfrac{1}{1 + \cfrac{1}{1 + \cfrac{1}{\cdots}}} \tag{33.3}$$

Equation (33.3) is an elementary example of continued fractions that have numerous uses for mathematicians and physicists. A general expression uses the letter $b$ to denote the number in each denominator in Equation (33.3).

$$\phi = b_0 + \cfrac{1}{b_1 + \cfrac{1}{b_2 + \cfrac{1}{\cdots}}}$$

(33.4)

M. Schroeder (1986) remarks, "Continued fractions are one of the most delightful and useful subjects of arithmetic, yet they have been continually neglected by our educational factions." These typographical nightmares can be more compactly written as: $[b_0, b_1, b_2, \ldots]$. And the golden ration can be represented as $[1,1,1,1, \ldots]$. We can also write this more compactly as: $[1,\overline{1}]$, where the bar indicates a repetition of the number 1. It is mind-boggling that the irrational number $e$ ($e = 2.718281828 \ldots$), unlike $\pi$, can be represented as a continued fraction with unusual regularity $[2,1,2,1,1,4,1,1,6,1,1,8,1, \ldots]$, however this converges initially very slowly because of the many 1's. In fact, the golden ratio, which contains infinitely many 1's, is the most slowly converging of all continued fractions. Schroeder notes, "It is therefore said, somewhat irrationally, that the golden section is the most irrational number." The approximation of the continued fraction to the golden ratio is also worse than for any other number. Therefore, chaos researchers (see "The World of Chaos" on page 121) often pick the golden ratio as a parameter to make the behavior of simulations as aperiodic as possible. (See "Notes for the Curious" on page 371 for additional information on continued fractions.)

## 33.1  Stop and Think

1.  Can you prove any of the interesting identities in Equation (33.1)?
2.  Can you create a lute with a greater degree of recursion (internal nesting of shapes) than shown in Figure 33.1?
3.  The lute in Figure 33.1 was created using an angle $ABC$ of about 40 degrees. What do lutes look like for other angles?
4.  Can you determine the value of the single-digit integer $n$ in the expression $\sqrt{n} = [1,2,2,2,2,2 \ldots] = [1,\overline{2}]$.
5.  The frontispiece for Chapter 32 shows a *Golden Julia Set* produced by the iteration of $z = z^2 + c$, where $Im(c) = 1/\phi$. ("Im" denotes the imaginary part of the complex number $c$.) Why should the golden ratio produce such a beautiful Julia set? (The Golden Julia Set is a collaboration with G. Adamson.)

## 33.2  For Further Reading

1.  Boles, M., Newman, R. (1990) *Universal Patterns*. Pythagorean Press: Bradford, Massachusetts.
2.  Hill, F. (1990) *Computer Graphics*. Macmillan: New York.
3.  Schroeder, M. (1986) *Number Theory in Science and Communication*. Springer: Berlin. (A goldmine of valuable information.)

# Chapter 34

# Results of the Very-Large-Number Contest

*"The study of the infinite is much more than a dry, academic game. The intellectual pursuit of the Absolute Infinite is a form of the soul's quest for God. Whether or not the goal is ever reached, an awareness of the process brings enlightenment. "*                    Rudy Rucker, *Infinity and the Mind*

*"For a human, there are gigaplex possible thoughts.[28]"*
                                        Rudy Rucker, *Mind Tools*

A *googol* is a very large number: 10 raised to the power of 100, or 1 followed by 100 zeros:

10000000000 0000000000 0000000000 0000000000 0000000000 0000000000 0000000000 0000000000 0000000000 0000000000

American mathematician Edward Kasner popularized this number in the 1930s. Most scientists agree that if we could count all the atoms in all the stars we can see, we would come up with less than googol of them.   Interestingly, the name googol was invented by Kasner's nine-year-old nephew who was asked what he would call this number.   The boy came up with the word "googol."   The same youngster also invented the term "googolplex" for an even higher number: 1 followed by a googol zeros.   Numbers such as these cannot really be comprehended by humans, with our limited brain architecture, because we have not needed to evolve this capability to insure our survival.  However, just as children slowly become able to name and appreciate larger and larger numbers as they grow, civilization has gradually increased its ability to name and deal with large numbers. This is briefly discussed in "Background" on page 208.

The numbers discussed in this chapter are often much larger than a googol, yet they are constructed with the barest of mathematical notation. I conducted

---

[28] A gigaplex is the number written as one with a billion zeros. Quotation from: Rucker, R. (1987) *Mind Tools*. Houghton Mifflin: Boston.

**Figure 34.1.** *Coffee beans.* Estimate how many beans there are with only a few seconds' glance at the photograph. Check your estimate by carefully counting the beans. When in humankind's history could such a number be articulated? Are there any cultures today which do not have a name for this number?

the "Very-large-number Contest" in February of 1989. I asked participants to construct an expression for a very large number using only the digits 1, 2, 3, and 4, and the symbols: "(," ")," the decimal point, and the minus sign. Each digit could be used only once. In a second contest, the contributors could use, in addition to these symbols, *any* standard mathematical symbol (such as the factorial symbol, "!") to produce a large number. Each symbol could be used only once in the mathematical expression. For both contest parts, the final answer had to have a finite value. Of the approximately fifty contributors, the eight top entries are listed in this chapter. As a prelude to the results, I present several related background curiosities on the topic of large numbers.

## 34.1 Background

Which number is larger: the number of possible chess games (which I will denote by $\beta$), or the number of trials needed for a monkey to type Shakespeare's *Hamlet* by random selection of keys (expressed as 1 chance in $\alpha$ trials)? How do the values of $\alpha$ and $\beta$ compare with the number of electrons, protons, and neutrons in the universe, $\delta$, or with Skewes' number $\gamma$ (which is reported to be the largest number that has occurred in a mathematical proof)? The values of these numbers are listed in the following.

Hamlet number:

$$\alpha = 35^{27,000} \sim 10^{40,000} \qquad (34.1)$$

Chess number:

$$\beta = 10^{10^{70.5}} \qquad (34.2)$$

Universe number:

$$\delta = 10^{79} \qquad (34.3)$$

Skewes number:

$$\gamma = 10^{10^{10^{34}}} \qquad (34.4)$$

The point is that today, large numbers such as $\alpha$ and $\beta$ are often contemplated, but this is a relatively recent development in man's history. For example, in biblical times, the largest number expressed as a single word was ten thousand. This occurs in the ancient Hebrew version of the Old Testament as the word "r'vavah." The word for million was an Italian invention of the 13th Century, and the English world billion was coined in the 17th century (largely as a curiosity).

## 34.2 Contest Results for Part 1

In evaluating and formulating expressions, it is important to recall some of the simple rules of exponentiation. For example, $(a^m)^n = a^{mn}$. Parentheses are often needed to resolve ambiguities. $3^{(2^3)} \neq (3^2)^{3}$. A number raised to a negative power is simply 1 over the number raised to the positive value of the power. The symbol $a^{b^c}$ is usually taken to mean $a^{(b^c)}$. To determine the number of digits $N$ in a value $X$, recall that $N = \log_{10} X + 1$.

For Part 1 of the contest exponentiation is allowed since it does not require a symbol when traditionally expressed. The following are the results for part 1.

**First place winner: Walt Hedman and Tim Greer, New York.**

$$0.3^{-(0.2^{-(0.1^{-4})})} = 3.33^{(5^{10000})} \qquad (34.5)$$

or

$$3.3^{5 \times 10^{6989}} \qquad (34.6)$$

(See "Stop and Think" on page 211 for more information on this number, including the number of digits.)

**Second place: Diana Dloughy, New York.**

$$(.1)^{-(4^{32})} = 1 \times 10^{x} \qquad (34.7)$$

where $x = 4^{32} \sim 1 \times 10^{19}$.

This second place answer has $1 \times 10^{19}$ digits. (Note: later in the course of her experimentation Diana discovered that $3^{42}$ is 1 decimal place larger than $4^{32}$ so that her answer can be changed to: $(.1)^{-(3^{42})} = 1 \times 10^x$ where $x = 3^{42} \sim 1 \times 10^{20}$.)

**Third place: Rod Davis, New York.**

$$2^{3^{41}} \tag{34.8}$$

This has $1.0979 \times 10^{19}$ digits.

**Fourth place: Rod Davis, New York.**

$$3^{4^{21}} = 3^{(4^{21})} = 3^{4398046511104} \tag{34.9}$$

His answer has $2.1 \times 10^{12}$ digits.

**Fifth place: Diana Dloughy, New York.**

$$(.1)^{(-432)} = 1 \times 10^{432} \tag{34.10}$$

Her answer has 433 digits.

**Sixth place: many people for their 201 digit entry.**

$$3^{421} = 7.37986 \times 10^{200}. \tag{34.11}$$

Submitters: Gary Hackney, Erik Tkal, Mike Shreeve, and Christine Wolak, among others.

**Seventh place: Mike Ott, Toronto.**

$$2^{(4^{(3+1)})} = 2^{256} = 1.1 \times 10^{77} \tag{34.12}$$

This has 78 digits. (Note: technically this answer should be disallowed since the plus sign was not allowed in the contest rules.)

**Eigth place: W. Gunn, North Carolina.**

$$31^{42} \tag{34.13}$$

This has 63 digits.

Can you beat the first prize winner in this contest?

## 34.3 Contest Results for Part 2

To create the prize-winning answers for the second part of the contest, contributors often simply placed factorial signs at the end of the expressions listed above. (For those of you who would like to evaluate the results with factorial symbols for themselves, the following formulas may be helpful: $n! \sim \sqrt{2\pi n}\, n^n e^{-n}$ and $\ln(n!) \sim [n \ln(n)] - n$). However, the second prize winner for this part, Dave

Challener from New York also used a gamma function symbol in the front of the first solution in Part 1. For positive integers $\Gamma(n + 1) = n!$. Note that, in general,

$$\Gamma(x) = \int_0^\infty t^{x-1} e^{-t} dt \quad x > 0 \tag{34.14}$$

or alternatively,

$$\frac{1}{\Gamma(x)} = xe^{\gamma x} \prod_{m=1}^\infty \left\{ \left( 1 + \frac{x}{m} \right) e^{-x/m} \right\} \tag{34.15}$$

where $\gamma$ is Euler's constant.

Mike Shreeve from Atlanta was the first place winner. His answer made use of a second-order Ackermann's function (Aho, 1974), which can be expressed by $A_n = 2^{A(n-1)}$ with $A(0) = 1$. The sequence progresses as follows 1, 2, 4, 16, 64000, $2^{64,000}$, ... Mike Shreeve believes that this function grows faster than any other named function.   As big as the gamma answer is, it is smaller than $A(4 + 3 + 2 + 1)$. Mike concluded his note to me with the words "I don't even want to think about $A[(3^{(4^{7})}!)]$. "

## 34.4  Stop and Think

Note that Hunter and Madachy's fascinating book *Mathematical Diversions* (1968) lists the expression in the first prize for Contest 1 as an example of a very large number. They note that this number is 3 to the $n$th power where $n$ has approximately 6990 digits. The number of cubic inches in the whole volume of space comprising the observable universe is almost negligible compared to this quantity.

[[ Although Skewes' number, mentioned earlier in this chapter, is often thought to be the largest number ever used in a mathematical proof, there is actually a more recent record-holder.  *Graham's number* is an upper bound from a problem in a part of combinatorics called Ramsey theory.  Graham's number cannot be expressed using the conventional notation of powers, and powers of powers. Let me try to explain it using the symbol "#." 3#3 means 3 cubed. 3##3 means 3#(3#3).   3###3 = 3##(3##3). 3####3 = 3###(3###3).   Consider the number 3### ... ###3 in which there are 3####3 "#" signs. Next construct the number 3### ... ###3 where the number of # signs is the previous 3###...###3 number. Now continue the process making the number of # signs in 3###...###3 equal to the number at the previous step, until you are 63 steps from 3####3. This is Graham's number, which occurred in a proof by R. L. Graham (Wells, 1987). ]]

## 34.5 For Further Reading

1. Davis, P. (1961) *The Lore of Large Numbers*. Random House: New York.

2. Berezin, A. (1987) Super super large numbers. *Journal of Recreational Math.* 19(2): 142-143. This paper discusses the mathematical and philosophical implications of the "superfactorial" function defined by the symbol $, where

$$N\$ = N!^{N!^{N!}} \ldots \qquad (34.16)$$

(term $N!$ is repeated $N!$ times).

3. Aho, Hopcroft, and Ullman (1974) *Data Structures and Algorithms*. Addison-Wesley: Massachusetts.

4. Pickover, C. (1990) Results of the very-large-number contest, *Journal of Recreational Math.*, 22(3) 166-169.

5. Hunter J., and Madachy, J. (1968) *Mathematical Diversions*. Van Nostrand: New York.

6. Wells, D. (1987) *The Penguin Dictionary of Curious and Unusual Numbers*. Penguin: New York.

7. Ellis, K. (1978) Is God a Number? In *Number Power In Nature, Art, and Everyday Life*. St. Martin's Press: New York.

In the frontispiece figure for this chapter, artist Gustave Dore (1832-1883) endeavors to show the infinite number of bodies inhabiting Hell.

# Chapter 35

# A Prime Plaid

Various patterns produced by prime numbers continue to be a source of interest and art for mathematicians and computer graphics scientists.[29] As examples, we have pleasing patterns produced by Gauss and Einstein primes (i.e., prime numbers defined in the complex number field $C$) which have been used for weaving tablecloths and tiling floors (ref. 1). Other published patterns involving prime numbers include the coprimality function (which indicates numbers which do not have a common divisor) and Ulam's square spiral primes (Stein et al., 1964). Here I add another prime pattern to the catalog of prime pictures.

Consider the prime numbers $p_i$, $i = 0,1,2,3, \ldots$ where $p_0 = 2$, $p_1 = 3$, etc. A plot of $p_i$ vs. $p_{i+1}$ for $p_i < 2000$ (not shown) yields a "dusty" (approximately) diagonal line with a slope of about 1. It is dusty due to the gaps in the prime number sequence, and roughly diagonal since $p_i \sim p_{i+1}$ at the size scale of the plot.

A visually interesting "plaid" structure (Figure 35.1) can be generated by using different shift values $\alpha$ and superimposing plots of

$$p_i \text{ vs. } p_{i+\alpha}$$

where $\alpha = 1,2,3, \ldots , 200$ for $p_i < 2000$. The bottom diagonal edge of the plaid corresponds to $p_i$ vs. $p_{i+1}$. The gaps indicate gaps in the prime number sequence.

As we go to larger and larger integers, the primes become increasingly rare, so the plaid also becomes more diffuse. When I attempt to compute a fairly good approximation for the number of primes smaller than or equal to $x$, usually designated $\pi(x)$, I prefer to use

$$\pi(x) \sim \frac{x}{\ln x - 1.08366} \tag{35.1}$$

---

[29] A prime is a positive integer that cannot be written as the product of two smaller integers. The number 6 is equal to 2 times 3, but 7 cannot be written as a product of factors; therefore, 7 is called a prime number or prime. Here are the first few prime numbers: 2, 3, 5, 7, 11, 13, 17, 19, 23, 29, 31, 37, 41, 43, 47, 53, 59.

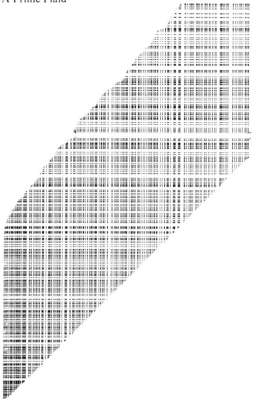

**Figure 35.1.** *A prime plaid.* The $x$-axis is $P_i$. The $y$-axis is $P_{i+\alpha}$.

This formula, given by Legendre in 1778, is much simpler to implement on a computer than the so-called Gauss and Riemann method, although this Legendre formula should be used only for prime numbers less than 5 million. Above 5 million, Legendre's formula becomes less accurate.

The primes in this chapter were computed in just a second or two using the Sieve of Eratosthenes method implemented on an IBM RISC System/6000. You can get the program code for this method from Spencer(1982) (See "Notes for the Curious" on page 371 for additional information.)

## 35.1  For Further Reading

1. Schroeder, M. (1986) *Number Theory in Science and Communication.* Springer: New York.

2. Spencer, D. (1982) *Computers in Number Theory.* Computer Science Press: Maryland.

3. Stein, M., Ulam, S. Wells, M. (1964) A visual display of some properties of the distribution of primes. *Mathematics Monthly.* 71(5): 516-520.

# Chapter 36

# Infinite Sequences in Centered Hexamorphic Numbers

Many years ago the villagers in a mideastern desert city gathered around their new war machine, a cannon. A primitive weapon by today's standards, the cannon was the supreme destructive weapon of that time. On the first day the cannon was displayed, one of the bearded men in the gathering began to meticulously arrange the new cannon balls on the hot sand amidst the parched and withered cacti. He arranged the balls in the shape of concentric hexagons, as shown in Figure 36.1. After resting for a few minutes, the wizened man groaned, knelt down, and began to count the balls starting from the center. He noted that there was one center ball, surrounded by 6 balls, surrounded by 12, and so on. On that same day, the wise man was able to determine a generating formula for the number of balls in each surrounding hexagonal layer. Can your modern mind do the same?

The sequence that the wizened warrior derived was

$$H_c = 3n(n - 1) + 1, \quad n = 1,2,3, \ldots \tag{36.1}$$

and this sequence of numbers defines the *centered hexagonal numbers*.[30]

Let's go a step further and introduce a new term. A centered hexagonal number is called *centered hexamorphic* if it terminates with its associated centered hexagonal integer. For example, $n = 7$ is centered hexamorphic because

---

[30] "Undulating Undecamorphic and Undulating Pseudofareymorphic Integers" on page 259 also deals with numbers based on the arrangement of balls.

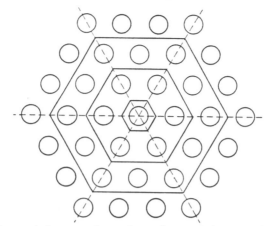

**Figure 36.1.** *Centered hexagonal numbers.* Centered hexagonal numbers are derived from the number of concentric hexagonal points in each "layer" arranged as shown here. The first hexagonal number is 1, since there is only one "ball" in the center of the figure. The next hexagonal number is 6, and so on. Figure adapted from Wells (1986).

$H_c(7)$ equals 127. 17 is also centered hexamorphic because $H_c(17) = 817$. The centered hexamorphic sequence is fascinating to study! Figure 36.3 contains a list of the first 23 centered hexamorphic integers. Note the interesting fact that all centered hexamorphic numbers end in the digits 1 and 7.

A convenient notation $a_5 = aaaaa$ can be employed where the subscript indicates the number of times the digit or group appears consecutively. I have found the following interesting infinite sequence:

$$H_c(50_k1) = 750_{k-1}150_k1 \quad k = 0,1,2, \ldots \tag{36.2}$$

For example, $k = 2$ produces $H_c(5001) = 75015001$ (see Figure 36.3). It's intriguing to note that while centered hexagonal numbers have a different generating formula from standard hexagonal numbers $(H(n) = n(2n - 1))$, the infinite sequences for hexamorphic and centered hexamorphic numbers are similar. For hexamorphic numbers, we have

$$H(50_k1) = 50_k150_k1 \quad k = 0,1,2, \ldots \tag{36.3}$$

Figure 36.4 contains a list of hexamorphic numbers. I invite your comments on the similarities between Equation (36.2) and Equation (36.3).

Additional infinite sequences in centered hexamorphic numbers are:

$$(16_k7) = 83_k16_k7 \quad k = 0,1,2, \ldots \tag{36.4}$$

and

$$H_c(6_k7) = 13_k26_k7 \quad k = 0,1,2, \ldots \tag{36.5}$$

Hexamorphic numbers do not contain any numbers ending with 7, but they do contain numbers ending with 1, and these also exist in the centered hexamorphic sequence. Those of you who wish to learn about hexamorphic numbers in various bases will enjoy Trigg (1987).

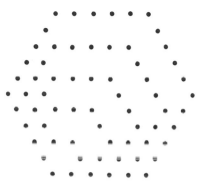

**Figure 36.2.** *Hexagonal numbers.* Hexagonal numbers are derived from hexagonal points arranged as shown here. Hexagonal numbers can be generated using $H(n) = n(2n - 1)$.

In closing, Leo A. Senneville and I have noted that there are some interesting relations between centered hexagonal and hexagonal numbers. For example, the second differences between successive terms for centered hexagonal numbers is always 6. The second differences between successive terms for hexagonal numbers is always 4. These statements condense to

$$H_c(n + 1) - 2H_c(n) + H_c(n - 1) = 6 \qquad (36.6)$$

$$H(n + 1) - 2H(n) + H(n - 1) = 4 \qquad (36.7)$$

We also have noted the following infinite series:

$$H_c(n)/H(n) = 3(1/2 - 1/(4n) - 1/(8n^2) - 1/(16n^3) - \cdots) \qquad (36.8)$$

The sum of this series approaches $3/2$ as a limit, which is also the ratio of the second differences. Finally, if one plots curves with the horizontal axis containing the natural numbers and the value of the hexagonal functions on the vertical axis, the difference in height between the two curves is always $(n - 1)^2$.

Can you find any additional patterns in these numbers?

## 36.1  For Further Reading

1.  Wells, D. (1986) *The Penguin Dictionary of Curious and Interesting Numbers.* Penguin Books: New York.

2.  Trigg, C. (1987) Hexamorphic numbers. *Journal of Recreational Math.* 19(1): 42-55.

| n | H(n)(centered) | n | H(n)(centered) |
|---|---|---|---|
| 1 | 1 | 1251 | 4691251 |
| 7 | 127 | 1667 | 8331667 |
| 17 | 817 | 5001 | 75015001 |
| 51 | 7651 | 5417 | 88015417 |
| 67 | 13267 | 6251 | 117206251 |
| 167 | 83167 | 6667 | 133326667 |
| 251 | 188251 | 10417 | 325510417 |
| 417 | 520417 | 16667 | 833316667 |
| 501 | 751501 | 50001 | 7500150001 |
| 667 | 1332667 | 56251 | 9492356251 |
| 751 | 1689751 | 60417 | 10950460417 |
| 917 | 2519917 | | |

**Figure 36.3.** *Centered Hexamorphic Numbers.*

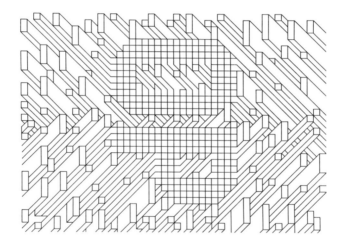

| n | H(n) | n | H(n) |
|---|---|---|---|
| 1 | 1 | 376 | 282376 |
| 5 | 45 | 500 | 499500 |
| 6 | 66 | 501 | 501501 |
| 25 | 1225 | 625 | 780625 |
| 26 | 1326 | 876 | 1533876 |
| 50 | 4950 | 4376 | 38294376 |
| 51 | 5151 | 5000 | 49995000 |
| 75 | 11175 | 5001 | 50015001 |
| 76 | 11476 | 5625 | 63275625 |
| 125 | 31125 | | |

**Figure 36.4.** *Hexamorphic Numbers.*

Chapter 37

# On the Existence of
# Cakemorphic Integers

Cake integers are a delicious low-calorie snack for health-conscious readers. Let us define *cake integers* as having the form $Cake(n) = (n^2 + n + 2)/2$. Cake integers indicate the maximum number of pieces in which a cake can be cut with $n$ slices. (The cake is represented as a flat disc.) For example, with just 2 straight slices, a cake can be maximally cut into 4 pieces. With 3 cuts, 7 pieces can result. The sequence goes as 2, 4, 7, 11, 16, 22, 29, 37, ... (see Figure 37.1). This sequence has been presented in various places in the literature, for example in Wells (1986).

A cake integer is called *cakemorphic* if it terminates with its associated cake integer. For example, if $n = 25$ and $C(n)$ were to equal 1325, $n$ would be called cakemorphic because the starting number 25 occurs as the last 2 digits.

While you can show that hexamorphic and even square pyramorphic numbers[31] are quite common, (see Figure 37.2 - Figure 37.4), I have not been able to find a cakemorphic integer even though a search was conducted for all $n \leq 10^7$.

In 1989, I developed the notion of "cakemorphic integer," and conjectured that no cakemorphic integer exists.[32] Mike Angelo of IBM has proven this conjecture by the following argument. [[ Let's examine the possible last digits of the expression $Cake(n) = (n^2 + n + 2)/2$. This is equivalent to evaluating *Cake* mod 10. If $n$ is a multiple of 10, e.g. $n = 10x$, then *Cake* mod 10 is equivalent to: $(100x^2 + 10x + 2)/2$ mod 10 which reduces to $(5x + 1)$ mod 10. This expression has only 2 different values for all $x$: 1 and 6. We conclude that all integers which are a multiple of 10 (hence, end in 0) yield cake integers that end in 1 or 6. Next we evaluate *Cake* mod 10 for integers equal to 1 mod 10, 2 mod 10, ...

---

[31] Hexagonal numbers have the form $H(n) = n(2n - 1)$ (see previous chapter). A number is hexamorphic if it terminates with its associated hexagonal number (Trigg, 1980). The number 125 is hexamorphic because $H(125) = 31125$. *Square pyramidal numbers* are related to 3-D objects rather than 2-D polygons. If cannonballs are piled so that each layer is a square, then the total number of balls in successive piles will be 1, 5, 14, 30 ... $n(n + 1)(2n + 1)/6$. Just like hexamorphic numbers, a number is square pyramorphic if it terminates with its associated square pyramidal number.

[32] Note that $Cake(n) = 1 + T_n$ where $T_n$ is the $n$-th triangular number.

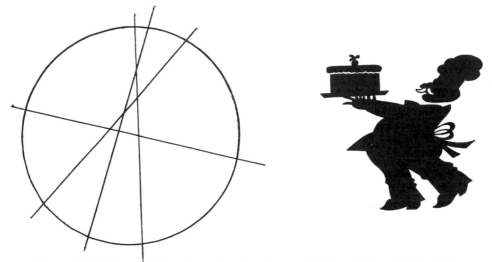

**Figure 37.1.** *Sample dissection of a cake, for n = 4.* Here $C(n) = 11$. (Left) Top view. (Right) Side view.

9 mod 10. We include one more evaluation for 1 mod 10. $n = 10x + 1$ and $Cake = (100(x^2) + 20x + 1 + 10x + 1 + 2))/2 = 50x^2 + 15x + 2$. Therefore $Cake \mod 10 = 5x + 2$. The only possible values are 2 and 7. Thus any number ending in 1 (e.g. 11, 21, 31 ...) yields a cake integer ending in 2 or 7. Hence it is impossible for an integer ending in 1 to be cakemorphic. By applying this method to the other cases we find that any value of $n$ yields a cake integer which terminates in a different integer from that which terminates $n$. Hence, there can be no cakemorphic integers. ]]

## 37.1 Stop and Think

1.  I invite you to ponder the following: Is there a *doughnutmorphic integer*? Doughnut numbers are constructed in a manner similar to cakenumbers, except that the circular pancake region has a hole in it, and hence the sequence for $C(n)$ docs not equal $D(n)$. I would be interested in hearing from those of you who have worked on this problem.

2.  What about the existence of pretzelmorphic numbers? These numbers concern the cutting of a pretzel-shaped object.

3.  See "Notes for the Curious" on page 371 for an equation giving the largest number of pieces that can be produced with $n$ simultaneous plane cuts of a 3-D doughnut, sphere, and other shapes.

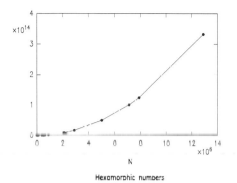

**Figure 37.2.** *Distribution of hexamorphic numbers.*

## 37.2 For Further Reading

1. Wells, D. (1986) *The Penguin Dictionary of Curious and Interesting Numbers.* Penguin Books: New York.

2. Trigg, C. (1980-81) A matter of morphic nomenclature. *Journal of Recreational Math.* 13(1): 48-49.; Trigg, C. (1987) Hexamorphic numbers. *Journal of Recreational Math.* 19(1): 42-55.

3. Pickover, C., Angelo, M. (1991). On the existence of cakemorphic integers. *Journal of Recreational Math.*, in press.

| n | H(n) | n | H(n) |
|---|------|---|------|
| 5625 | 63275625 | 609376 | 742677609376 |
| 9376 | 175809376 | 890625 | 1586424890625 |
| 40625 | 3300740625 | 2109376 | 8898932109376 |
| 50000 | 4999950000 | 2890625 | 16711422890625 |
| 50001 | 5000150001 | 5000000 | 49999995000000 |
| 59376 | 7050959376 | 5000001 | 50000015000001 |
| 90625 | 16425690625 | 7109376 | 101086447109376 |
| 109376 | 23926109376 | 7890625 | 124523917890625 |
| 390625 | 305175390625 | 12890625 | 332336412890625 |
| 500000 | 499999500000 | | |
| 500001 | 500001500001 | | |

**Figure 37.3.** *Large hexamorphic numbers.* The table here continues the table in the previous chapter which lists the hexamorphic numbers less than 63275625. Note: this table may contain the most comprehensive list of hexamorphic numbers to date. In 1987, Trigg searched only as far as $n \leq 10^4$.

| n | S(n) | n | S(n) |
|---|------|---|------|
| 1 | 1 | 960 | 295372960 |
| 5 | 55 | 1185 | 555371185 |
| 25 | 5525 | 2560 | 5595682560 |
| 40 | 22140 | 2625 | 6032742625 |
| 65 | 93665 | 4000 | 21341334000 |
| 80 | 173880 | 5185 | 46478345185 |
| 160 | 1378160 | 6560 | 94121656560 |
| 225 | 3822225 | 6625 | 96947076625 |
| 385 | 19096385 | 8000 | 170698668000 |
| 400 | 21413400 | 9185 | 258337319185 |
| 560 | 58695560 | 9376 | 274790059376 |
| 625 | 81575625 | 10625 | 399877410625 |
| 785 | 161553785 | | |
| 800 | 170986800 | | |

**Figure  37.4.**  *Square pyramorphic numbers.*

**Figure  37.5.**  *Pyramidal numbers and stacks of balls.* Pyramidal numbers are derived from the number of balls in each layer of a pyramid of balls, such as shown in this figure.

Child Solenoid

Parent Solenoid

Chapter 38

# Interlude: A Fractal Goose

Olive Schreiner in *The Story of an African Farm*, first published in 1883, gives an early, poignant description of the fractal geometry of nature:

> "*A gander drowns itself in our dam. We take it out, and open it on the bank, and kneel looking at it. Above are the organs divided by delicate tissues; below are the intestines artistically curved in a spiral form, and each tier covered by a delicate network of blood vessels standing out red against the faint blue background. Each branch of the blood-vessels is comprised of a trunk, bifurcating and rebifurcating into the most delicate, hair-like threads, symmetrically arranged. We are struck with its singular beauty. And, moreover – and here we drop from our kneeling into a sitting position – this also we remark: of that same exact shape and outline is our thorn-tree seen against the sky in mid-winter; of that shape also is delicate metallic tracery between our rocks; in that exact path does our water flow when without a furrow we lead it from the dam; so shaped are the antlers of the horned beetle. How are these things related that such union should exist between them all? Is it chance? Or, are they not all the fine branches of one trunk, whose sap flows through us all? That would explain it. We nod over the gander's insides.*"

# Chapter 39

# All Known Replicating Fibonacci-Digits Less Than One Billion

You go to a neighborhood pet store and buy a pair of small dogs and breed them. The pair produces one pair of young after one year, and a second pair after the second year. Then they stop breeding. Each new pair also produces two more pairs in the same way, and then stops breeding. How many new pairs of dogs would you have each year? To answer this question, write down the number of pairs in each generation. First write the number 1 for the single pair you bought from the pet shop. Next write the number 1 for the pair they produced after a year. The next year both pairs have young, so the next number is 2. Continuing this process, we have the sequence of numbers: 1, 1, 2, 3, 5, 8, 13, 21, 34, 55, 89, 144, 233, 377,.... This sequence of numbers, called the *Fibonacci sequence* after the wealthy Italian merchant Leonardo Fibonacci of Pisa, plays important roles in mathematics and nature. These numbers are such that, after the first two, every number in the sequence equals the sum of the two previous numbers

$$F_n = F_{n-1} + F_{n-2} \qquad (39.1)$$

Pseudocode 39.1 shows how to program this sequence on the computer.

The present chapter is about numerical world records with numbers related to Fibonacci numbers, and I challenge you to break the record discussed here. In 1989 I discovered two new *replicating Fibonacci-digits* (defined in next paragraph) in the range 100 million to 1 billion (129,572,008 and 251,133,297). These are believed to be the largest replicating Fibonacci-digits discovered to date, as evidenced by the previous 1989 world record which included all known eight-digit replicating Fibonacci-digits (Ashbacher, 1989).

```
ALGORITHM:  Print 30 Fibonacci Numbers

Dimension Fib(30)
Fib(1)=1
Fib(2)=1
For n = 1 to 28
    Fib(n+2) = Fib(n+1) + Fib(n)
Next n
For x = 1 to 30
    Print Fib(x)
end
```

**Pseudocode 39.1.** *How to compute Fibonacci numbers.*


A replicating Fibonacci-digit, or "repfigit," has the remarkable property that it repeats itself in a sequence generated by starting with the $n$ digits of a number and then continuing the sequence with a number that is the sum of the previous $n$ terms. An example should clarify this. 47 is a repfigit since the sequence (4, 7, 11, 18, 29, 47 ) passes through 47. Likewise 1537 is a repfigit since the sequence (1, 5, 3, 7, 16, 31, 57, 111, 215, 414, 797, 1537) passes through 1537.

For mathematical readers, this can be restated as follows. Consider any positive integer $N$ with $n$ digits $d_1 d_2, \dots , d_n$. Consider the sequence defined by

$$\alpha_k = d_k \quad (k = 1, 2, \dots , n) \tag{39.2}$$

and

$$\alpha_k = \sum_{i=1}^{n} \alpha_{k-i} \quad (k > n) \tag{39.3}$$

If $\alpha_k = N$ for any $k$, we call $N$ a replicating Fibonacci digit.

In 1987, Michael Keith introduced the concept of replicating Fibonacci digits and at that time the largest repfigit discovered was the 7-digit number 7,913,837. In November, 1989, three new larger repfigits were discovered, and the world's largest repfigit was 44,121,607.

Repfigits are interesting for several reasons. For one, the question of whether or not the number of repfigits is infinite is an unsolved question. It would be interesting to find that no repfigit exists for higher numbers of digits, or to find if any patterns could be discovered by obtaining more numerical data. Moreover, progress on certain famous problems has historically been used as a yardstick for measuring the growth in computer power (Wagon, 1985).

Figure 39.1 indicates all known Repfigit numbers to date. The new repfigits are all in the range from 100 million to 1 billion. In order to leverage available state-of-the-art computer hardware, computations were accomplished using a C language program running in parallel between several computing machines. Part of the computation was solved using a Silicon Graphics IRIS 4D/120GTX, while other parts were computed on a Stellar GS1000, and two IBM RT's. To get a feel for the computation time required: to find the first of the two 9-digit repfigits, 129572008, the computation used roughly three hours of elapsed time on the IRIS machine. The machine was devoted to the task (no

| | |
|---|---|
| 2 | 14 19 28 47 61 75 |
| 3 | 197 742 |
| 4 | 1104 1537 2208 2508 3684 4788 7385 7647 7909 |
| 5 | 31331 34285 34348 55604 62662 86935 93993 |
| 6 | 120284 129106 147640 156146 174680 183186 298320 355419 694280 925993 |
| 7 | 1084051 7913837 |
| 8 | 11436171 33445755 44121607 |
| 9 | 129572000 251133297 |

**Figure 39.1.** *Replicating Fibonacci digits less than one billion.* (The first column indicates the number of digits.)

other users competed for time). If the processes were not split between several machines, the IRIS machine alone would require about one week to search for all repfigits in the range from 100 million to 1 billion. To prevent loss of data due to system failure, whenever a repfigit was found, the C command "fflush" was used to insure that the data was written to disk. Standard "long integers" were used in all calculations.

Note that it is possible to speed future computations of Equation (39.3) by observing:

$$\alpha_{k+1} = 2\alpha_k - \alpha_{k-n} \tag{39.4}$$

The use of this equation may lead to an increase in speed, $\delta$,

$$\delta = \frac{T_{1\,shift} + T_{1add}}{(n-1)T_{1\,add}} \tag{39.5}$$

where $T$ is the time the computer takes for various operations. (A multiplication by 2 can be done by a C language shift operation.) This leads to a potential speed improvement of

$$\delta \sim \frac{2}{n-1} \tag{39.6}$$

Figure 39.2 in this chapter shows the actual sequence generated by 251133297.

## For Further Reading

1. Ashbacher, C. (1989) Repfigit numbers. *Journal of Recreational Math.* 21(4): 310-311.

2. Keith, M. (1987) Repfigit numbers. *Journal of Recreational Math.* 19(1): 41-42.

3. Wagon, S. (1985) The Colatz problem. *Mathematical Intelligencer.* 7: 72-76.

4. Pickover, C. (1990) All known replicating Fibonacci-digits less than one billion, *Journal of Recreational Math.* 22(3): 176-178.

| |
|---|
| 2, 5, 1, 1, 3, 3, 2, 9, 7, 33, 64, 123, 245, 489, 975, 1947, 3892, 7775, 15543, 31053, 62042, 123961, 247677, 494865, 988755, 1975563, 3947234, 7886693, 15757843, 31484633, 62907224, 125690487, 251133297 |

**Figure 39.2.** *Actual sequence for 251133297.* (This is the largest repfigit known.)

# Chapter 40

# The Juggler Sequence

One spring morning, while watching a juggler throw colored balls through the air of a circus tent, I developed a simple number sequence which some friends have since spent countless hours studying. Like a ball thrown up and down by a circus juggler, this sequence also drifts down and up, sometimes in seemingly haphazard patterns. Also like a juggler's ball, the Juggler sequence apparently always falls back down to the juggler's hand (which we represent by the integer "1").

First I will define the problem in mathematical terms and then I will explain it in simple English: The *Juggler problem*, which we might also call the $n^{(3/2)}$ problem, is defined by the function $j:N \rightarrow N$ on the set of positive integers:

$$j(n) = \begin{cases} \left[ n^{(1/2)} \right] & \text{if } n \text{ even,} \\ \left[ n^{(3/2)} \right] & \text{if } n \text{ odd} \end{cases} \tag{40.1}$$

where $n$ is any initial positive integer. The bracket signs indicate that non-integer values are to be truncated to the maximum integer equal to or smaller than the number enclosed (i.e., $4.1 \rightarrow 4$). This means that you start with any integer and raise it to either of the two choices of powers ($1/2$ or $3/2$) depending on whether or not it is even or odd, and repeat the operations over and over again. This sequence, like other sequences in this book, is produced by iterative rules: apply the rule to the current number in the sequence and you get the next one.

We can state this more mathematically. Let $j^k(n)$ be the $k$th iterate of $j(n)$. A sequence of numbers is generated by

$$j^k(n) = j(j^{k-1}(n)) \quad \text{for } k \in N \tag{40.2}$$

and can be represented by the following forumula.

$$J(n) = \{j^k(n)\} \quad k = 1,2,3, \ldots \infty \tag{40.3}$$

| n | J(n) |
|---|---|
| 1 | |
| 2 | 1 |
| 3 | 5 11 36 6 2 1 |
| 4 | 2 1 |
| 5 | 11 36 6 2 1 |
| 6 | 2 1 |
| 7 | 18 4 2 1 |
| 8 | 2 1 |
| 9 | 27 140 11 36 6 2 1 |
| 10 | 3 5 11 36 6 2 1 |
| 11 | 36 6 2 1 |
| 12 | 3 5 11 36 6 2 1 |
| 13 | 46 6 2 1 |
| 14 | 3 5 11 36 6 2 1 |
| 15 | 58 7 18 4 2 1 |
| 16 | 4 2 1 |
| 17 | 70 8 2 1 |
| 18 | 4 2 1 |
| 19 | 82 9 27 140 11 36 6 2 1 |
| 20 | 4 2 1 |
| 21 | 96 9 27 140 11 36 6 2 1 |
| 22 | 4 2 1 |
| 23 | 110 10 3 5 11 36 6 2 1 |
| 24 | 4 2 1 |
| 25 | 125 1397 52214 228 15 58 7 18 4 2 1 |
| 26 | 5 11 36 6 2 1 |
| 27 | 140 11 36 6 2 1 |
| 28 | 5 11 36 6 2 1 |
| 29 | 156 12 3 5 11 36 6 2 1 |
| 30 | 5 11 36 6 2 1 |
| 31 | 172 13 46 6 2 1 |
| 32 | 5 11 36 6 2 1 |
| 33 | 189 2598 50 7 18 4 2 1 |
| 34 | 5 11 36 6 2 1 |
| 35 | 207 2978 54 7 18 4 2 1 |
| 36 | 6 2 1 |
| 37 | 225 3375 196069 86818724 9317 899319 852846071 24906114455136 4990602 2233 10 5519 34276462 5854 76 8 2 1 |
| 38 | 6 2 1 |
| 39 | 243 3787 233046 482 21 96 9 27 140 11 36 6 2 1 |
| 40 | 6 2 1 |
| 41 | 262 16 4 2 1 |
| 42 | 6 2 1 |
| 43 | 281 4710 68 8 2 1 |
| 44 | 6 2 1 |
| 45 | 301 5222 72 8 2 1 |
| 46 | 6 2 1 |
| 47 | 322 17 70 8 2 1 |
| 48 | 6 2 1 |
| 49 | 343 6352 79 702 26 5 11 36 6 2 1 |
| 50 | 7 18 4 2 1 |

**Figure 40.1.** *Behavior of iterates of j(n)*. Each line in this table represents a juggler sequence $J(n)$ for the starting number at the left.

| n | J'(n) |
|---|---|
| 1 | |
| 2 | 1 |
| 3 | 5 11 36 6 2 1 |
| 4 | 2 1 |
| 5 | 11 36 6 2 1 |
| 6 | 2 1 |
| 7 | 19 83 756 27 140 12 3 5 11 36 6 2 1 |
| 8 | 3 5 11 36 6 2 1 |
| 9 | 27 140 12 3 5 11 36 6 2 1 |
| 10 | 3 5 11 36 6 2 1 |
| 11 | 36 6 2 1 |
| 12 | 3 5 11 36 6 2 1 |
| 13 | 47 322 18 4 2 1 |
| 14 | 4 2 1 |
| 15 | 58 8 3 5 11 36 6 2 1 |
| 16 | 4 2 1 |
| 17 | 70 8 3 5 11 36 6 2 1 |
| 18 | 4 2 1 |
| 19 | 83 756 27 140 12 3 5 11 36 6 2 1 |
| 20 | 4 2 1 |
| 21 | 96 10 3 5 11 36 6 2 1 |
| 22 | 5 11 36 6 2 1 |
| 23 | 110 10 3 5 11 36 6 2 1 |
| 24 | 5 11 36 6 2 1 |
| 25 | 125 1398 37 225 3375 196070 443 9324 97 955 29512 172 13 47 322 18 4 2 1 |
| 26 | 5 11 36 6 2 1 |
| 27 | 140 12 3 5 11 36 6 2 1 |
| 28 | 5 11 36 6 2 1 |
| 29 | 156 12 3 5 11 36 6 2 1 |
| 30 | 5 11 36 6 2 1 |
| 31 | 173 2275 108511 35744617 213705634112 462283 314312668 17729 2360622 1536 39 244 16 4 2 1 |
| 32 | 6 2 1 |
| 33 | 190 14 4 2 1 |
| 34 | 6 2 1 |
| 35 | 207 2978 55 408 20 4 2 1 |
| 36 | 6 2 1 |
| 37 | 225 3375 196070 443 9324 97 955 29512 172 13 47 322 18 4 2 1 |
| 38 | 6 2 1 |
| 39 | 244 16 4 2 1 |
| 40 | 6 2 1 |
| 41 | 263 4265 278534 528 23 110 10 3 5 11 36 6 2 1 |
| 42 | 6 2 1 |
| 43 | 282 17 70 8 3 5 11 36 6 2 1 |
| 44 | 7 19 83 756 27 140 12 3 5 11 36 6 2 1 |
| 45 | 302 17 70 8 3 5 11 36 6 2 1 |
| 46 | 7 19 83 756 27 140 12 3 5 11 36 6 2 1 |
| 47 | 322 18 4 2 1 |
| 48 | 7 19 83 756 27 140 12 3 5 11 36 6 2 1 |
| 49 | 343 6352 80 9 27 140 12 3 5 11 36 6 2 1 |
| 50 | 7 19 83 756 27 140 12 3 5 11 36 6 2 1 |

**Figure 40.2.** *Behavior of iterates of* $j'(n)$. ( $J'$ *is rounded to nearest integer.*) Each line in this table represents a juggler sequence $J'(n)$ for the starting number at the left.

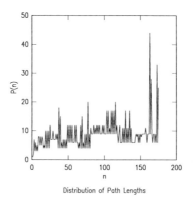

Distribution of Path Lengths

**Figure 40.3.** *Path lengths for starting integers between 0 and 175.*

What is the long behavior of such sequences? Will they settle into a cycle? If so, what sort of cycle? If you can program your computer to calculate fractional powers (and you can), you will be able to create a juggler sequence. In your program you can continue the iteration process until the juggler number returns to 1 (see Pseudocode 40.1). Was I foolish to terminate the loop in this way? What if the sequence never returns to 1? Apart from this nasty little question, the more general question of what patterns evolve is sure to delight. Consider for example what happens when the process goes to work on the number 3 as input: $J(3) = \{3, 5, 11, 36, 6, 2, 1\}$. The basic pattern is simple enough. It rises, then it falls to 1. Once the value of $J$ goes to 1, the value repeats: 1,1,1, ... . The Juggler problem is an interesting extension to the famous $3n + 1$ (or Hailstone or Collatz) problem which has been discussed extensively in the past. Collatz sequences evolve according to the rule

*if x is even*
    *then x = x / 2*
    *else x = 3 x + 1*

Juggler sequences use an analogous rule involving powers instead of multiplies. Like the Collatz sequence, the Juggler sequence drifts down and up, sometimes in seemingly chaotic patterns. You are forewarned that, unlike the Collatz sequence, Juggler numbers can reach very large values in just a few iterations. However, even though large numbers can be reached rather rapidly, such as the 9th member of the juggler sequence for 37 (i.e. $h^9(37) = 24906114455136$), it seems that these large values soon decay fairly quickly to 1. One may conjecture that, starting from any positive integer, repeated iteration of this function eventually produces the value 1. (A variety of cash awards have been offered for a proof of this conjecture for the $3n + 1$ problem.) I have checked this conjecture for the Juggler sequence for a range of $n$ ($1 \leq n \leq 200$). Figure 40.1 shows the behavior of the iterates for $1 \leq n \leq 50$. They all converge, but fairly long sequences can be generated by the Juggler procedure before the values settle back to 1. I wonder

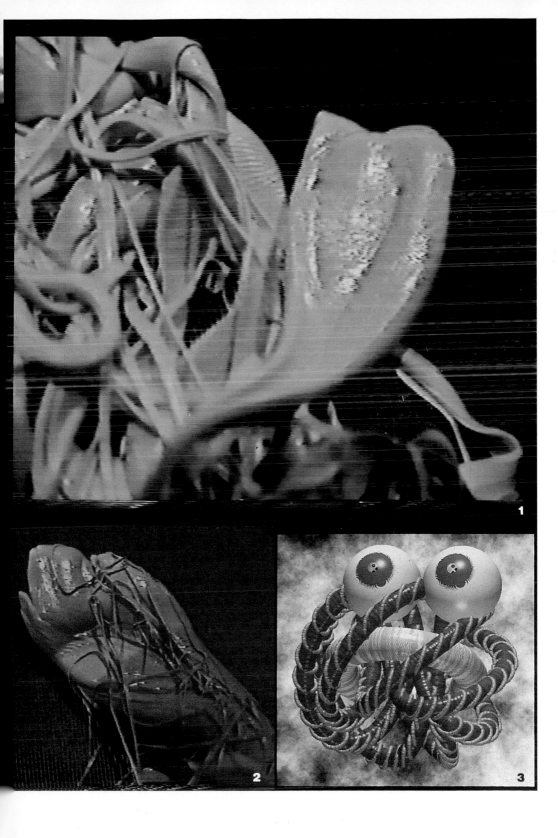

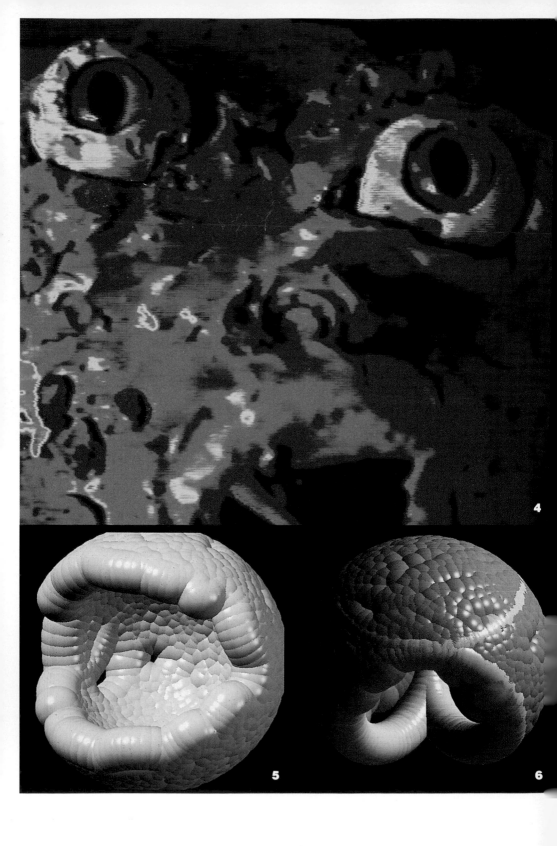

**4**

**5**

**6**

7

8

9

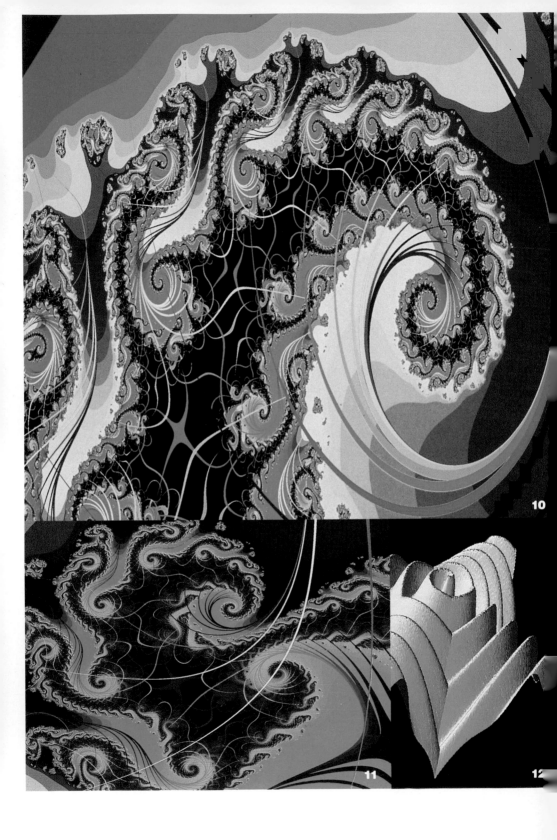

10

11

12

13

14

15

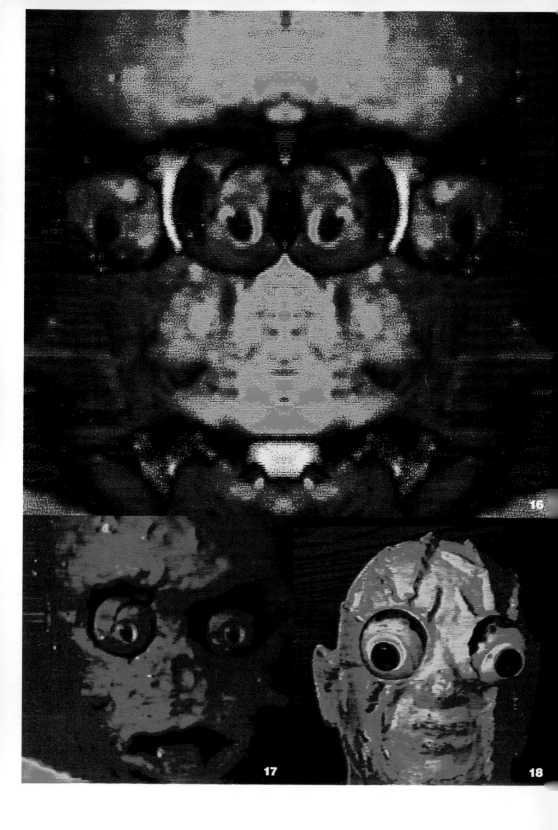

19

20

21

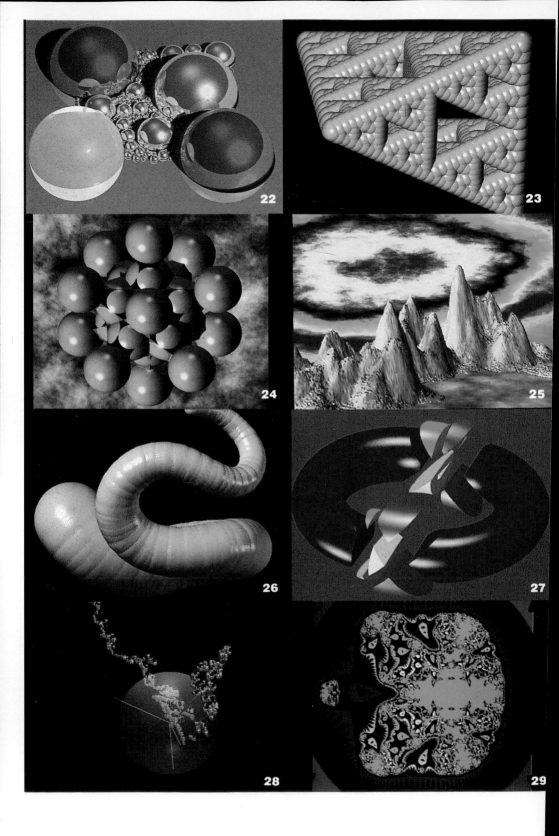

```
ALGORITHM: Juggler Geometry
```
```
Input a positive integer, x.
REPEAT
    if x is even then x = truncate ( x ** 1/2 )
    if x is odd  then x = truncate ( x ** 3/2 )
UNTIL x = 1
```

**Pseudocode 40.1.** *How to create Juggler Numbers.*

whether any of you would like to test my conjecture beyond 200. Here is an example for 77.

$J(77) = 77\ 675\ 17537\ 2322378\ 1523\ 59436\ 243\ 3787\ 233046\ 482\ 21\ 96\ 9\ 27\ 140\ 11\ 36\ 6\ 2\ 1$

$J(77)$ has a path length of 20. You can see that the pattern here is not so simple as the previous example for 3. Here there are 6 ups and 6 downs in a haphazard order. Several observations can be made. Odd starting integers generally give rise to longer path lengths. Figure 40.3 shows the path length of the sequence for starting integers between 0 and 175. The up-and-down zig zags in the line indicate highs and lows corresponding to consecutive odd and even starting integers. Usually the sequence is fairly tame, reaching its maximum value in a few steps, and returning to 1 in under 10 iterations. There are some notable exceptions: 37, 77, 103, 105, 109, 111, 113, 115, 129, 135, 163, 165, 173, 175, 183, and 193 give fairly long sequences. Also note that if a number of the form

$$2^{2^n} \tag{40.4}$$

ever arises  (e.g. 4 or 16), then the sequence must monotonically decrease to the ground state, 1. Examination of Figure 40.1 suggests that several terminating patterns are quite common; for the first 200 starting integers, there are only three terminating 3-digit patterns: (6 2 1), (4 2 1), and (8 2 1). Why only these three? Figure 40.4 shows monotonic decay paths for the end sequences observed for starting values less than 200.

## 40.1 Stop and Think

I invite you to extend the search for longer $J(n)$ sequences. In addition, $J'(n)$ sequences determined by rounding to the nearest integer (rather than simply truncating them) provide a new problem to examine (see Figure 40.2). Whether or not the Juggler sequence always settles back to 1 is not known. This is a hard challenge, no doubt, to resolve. You may find that the juggler problem is of interest because it is so simple to state yet intractably hard to solve. (See "Notes for the Curious" on page 371 for additional information.)

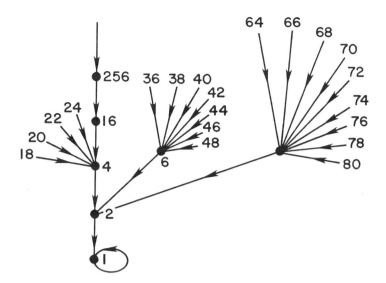

**Figure 40.4.** *Monotonic decay paths.* These are for the end sequences observed for starting values less than 200. The central trunk of the tree is comprised of numbers of the form $2^{2^n}$.

## 40.2 For Further Reading

1.    Dodge, C. (1969) *Numbers and Mathematics.* Prindle, Weber, and Schmidt: Boston.

2.    Hayes, B. (1984) Computer recreations: on the ups and downs of hailstone numbers. *Scientific American.* 250: 10-16.

3.    Legarias, J. (1985) The 3x + 1 problem and its generalizations. *American Mathematics Monthly.* January 3-23.

4.    Wagon, S. (1985) The Colatz problem. *Mathematical Intelligencer.* 7: 72-76.

5.    Garner, L.  (1981) On the Collatz 3n+1 problem. *Proceedings of the American Mathematics Society.* 82: 19-22.

6.    Crandall, R. (1978) On the "3x+1" problem. *Mathematics of Computation* 32: 1281-1292.

7.    Pickover, C. (1989) Hailstone (3n + 1) number graphs. *Journal of Recreational Mathematics.* 21(2): 112-115.

8.    Pickover, C. (1990) Juggler geometry and earthworm algebra. *Algorithm.* Nov 1(7): 11-13.

# Chapter 41

# Earthworm Algebra

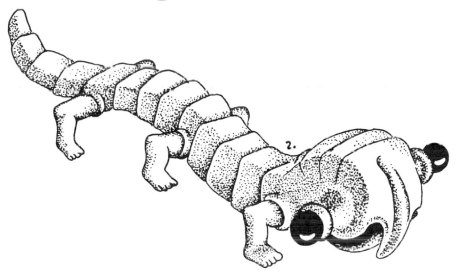

One cool November day, while digging in my garden, my wood-handled trowel inadvertently severed an earthworm's moist body. At this time in the year many of the worms in the garden seemed to have entered into a breeding period, and they were multiplying at a furious rate. An earthworm has marvelous regenerative powers, so I did not mourn for the worm: I had been taught that at least one half of the worm, and perhaps both halves, might continue to live depending on where the body was cut. After gazing for a few minutes at the leaf-shrouded soil, I developed a little problem called *Earthworm Algebra*, which, like the scenario in my garden, involves worm multiplication and severing. In fact the problem consists of the repeated multiplication and truncation of integers, and I think many of you will find it enjoyable. Start by picking any 2-digit number at random between 10 and 99. Multiply by 2, and sever the number by taking the last two digits of this result, and multiply by 2 again. Repeat the process. Program pseudocode is given in Pseudocode 41.1.

[[ For the more mathematical reader, the problem is defined by the function $h:N \rightarrow N$ on the set of positive integers:

$$h(N) = [2N] \tag{41.1}$$

where $N$ is any initial 2-digit positive integer. *The bracket signs in the equation indicate that the numbers are to contain only the last two digits.* (Sometimes this is written as $(2N)$ mod 100.) ]] Let $h^k(N)$ be the $k$th iterate of $h(N)$. A sequence of numbers is generated by

$$h^k(N) = h(h^{k-1}(N)) \text{ for } k \in N \tag{41.2}$$

and can be represented as

```
ALGORITHM: Earthworm Numbers
Note: the function trunc2 truncates the number to its last
      two digits.  You can do this by taking the remainder
      of x after dividing by 100.

Input x
REPEAT
     x = 2 * x
     x = trunc2 (x)
     Output x
UNTIL x = a previous x
```

**Pseudocode 41.1.** *How to create Earthworm numbers.*

$$H(N) = \{h^k(N)\} \quad k = 1,2,3, \ldots \tag{41.3}$$

Before reading further, consider the following: Does the sequence always return to the starting integer? If so, how many steps are needed? (Odd starting numbers will never return, so we test only even numbers.) For example 12 takes 20 steps to return:

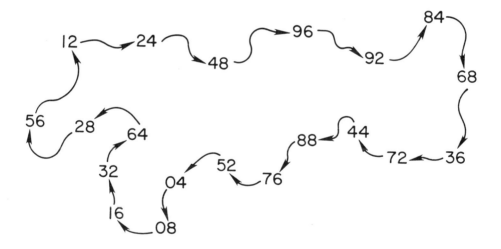

Indeed, every number in the above sequence returns to itself. You will find after much exploration that, starting with any even numbers, there are, remarkably, only 3 possible outcomes:

1. the path never returns to the starting point, but rather executes a repeating loop, or

2.   the path length is 20, or

3.   the path length is 4.

In particular note that if the starting number is a multiple of 20 it will take 4 iterations; if the starting number is a multiple of 4 it will take 20 iterations; otherwise it will loop indefinitely.

You could, if you wish, begin to analyze Earthworm algebra by noting that the truncation to 2 digits implies addition modulo 100. Denote the starting integer as $y$. It is easy to see that after $n$ successive doublings we have $(2^n)y \bmod 100$. For the sequence to repeat we require this quantity to equal $y$ for some $n$. Therefore, to produce a return cycle requires $y[2^n - 1] \bmod 100 = 0$.

Note that earthworm algebra has some similarities with a class of problems used in the field of pseudorandom number generators based on multiplicative-congruential techniques (Knuth, 1981).

## 41.1  Stop and Think

The field for exploration is wide open here. Do earthworm sequences always return to the starting point for related problems, where 3 is used as the multiplicative factor instead of 2. What graphics can you develop to show patterns? One beautiful way to summarize the behavior for all cases is to draw an iteration diagram. You can place each of the starting numbers on the $x$-axis and plot their trajectories on the $y$-axis.

## 41.2  For Further Reading

1.   Knuth, D. (1981) *The Art of Computer Programming*. Vol. 2, 2nd ed. Addison-Wesley: Massachusetts.

2.   Pickover, C. (1990) Juggler geometry and earthworm algebra. *Algorithm*. Nov 1(7): 11-13.

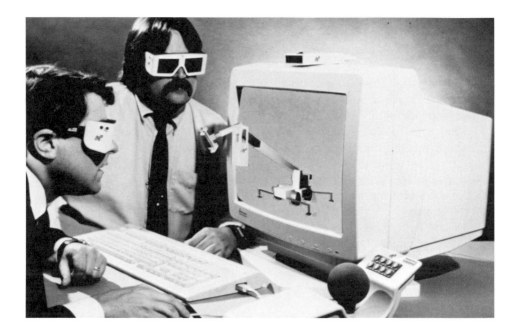

# Chapter 42

# Interlude: Friendly Technology

In the 1990s, researchers working with computer models of buildings, molecules, and mountains can "take a walk" through their 3-D structures using special goggles that receive infrared signals from a computer monitor. With the devices shown in the figure at the top of the facing page, the viewer gets a realistic impression of depth from a 2-D computer screen. Viewers can stand on an imaginary Martian mountain or dive into an infinite red sea!

Recently, personal computer users who are young at heart, or who want friendlier PCs, have a different kind of "software" to dress up their monitors. "Computer critters" are plush doll-like parts that attach to a monitor. Various animals have been manufactured, including dragons, bulldogs, and rabbits (see figure at the bottom of facing page).

Also in the 1990s, orthopedic implants can be custom-made, using 3-D CAD and numeric control to manufacture parts. In the future, more and more body parts will be replaceable by artificial parts. One interesting example, shown below, is a total wrist joint replacement, originally designed by Chr. Meuli, M.D.[33]

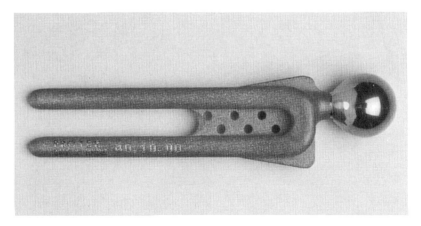

[33] The 3-D goggle picture is courtesy of Bechtel Software, 289 Great Road, Acton, Mass 01720. The "computer critters" picture is courtesy of Celsus Designs, Box 5401, Hacienda Heights, California 91745. The wrist prosthesis is made of high-strength $Ti_6Al_7Nb$ forged alloy, rough blasted with pure corundum. The spherical head is coated with titanium nitride. Photos courtesy of the manufacturer, PROTEK, Stadtbachstrasse 64, CH-3001 Bern, Switzerland.

# Chapter 43

# Palindromes on Parade

A palindrome is usually defined as a word, sentence, or set of sentences that spell the same backward and forward. I don't think there are any common English words of more than seven letters that are palindromic. Examples of seven-letter palindromes are "rotator" and "reviver." In all the major languages, the largest non-hyphenated word palindrome is *"saippuakauppias,"* a Finnish word for a soap dealer. An interesting example of a palindromic sentence in which words, not letters, are the units is:

*"You can cage a swallow, can't you, but you can't swallow a cage, can you?"*

In this chapter we are more interested in palindromic *numbers* than palindromic words or sentences. Palindromic numbers are positive integers which "read" the same backwards or forwards. For example, 12321, 11, 261162, and 454 are all palindromic numbers. Numbers of this form have often been discussed in the past; for example, see many of the issues of *The Journal of Recreational Mathematics* and the references at the end of this chapter. Dr. Akhlesh Lakhtakia (Pennsylvania State University) and I began our research by first considering the number of palindromic numbers less than or equal to the integer $P$. We call this quantity $W(P)$. For example, $W(3) = 3$, since 1, 2 and 3 are palindromes. Figure 43.1 shows the number of 1-digit palindromes, the number of 2-digit palindromes, etc. (the left-most digit is not allowed to be zero). Using this table it is easy to see that

$$W(10^n) = 2\{10^{(n-1)/2} - 1\} + 9 \times 10^{(n-1)/2} \quad \text{for } n \text{ odd}$$

$$W(10^n) = 2\{10^{(n/2)} - 1\} \quad \text{for } n \text{ even}$$

Some results in this area have been made by Schwartz who derived a similar formula for even $n$ (Schwartz, 1976).

How does the value of $W(P)$ grow with $P$? Although several researchers considered this question, our finding is that a log-log plot computed for the first 10 million integers easily illustrates how $W(P)$ grows. Figure 43.2 shows a log-log plot for the first 200 numbers. Figure 43.3 shows the same plot for the first 10

| Digits | Form | W(P) |
|--------|------|------|
| 1 digit | a | 9 (excluding 0) |
| 2 digits | aa | 9 |
| 3 digits | aba | 9 x 10 |
| 4 digits | abba | 9 x 10 |
| 5 digits | abcba | 9 x 10 x 10 |
| 6 digits | abccba | 9 x 10 x 10 |

**Figure 43.1.** *Palindromes.*

million numbers. The peculiar features indicated in Figure 43.1 are also reflected in Figure 43.3 where the plot has distinctive curves over each 2-decade span of *P*. From this plot, it can be conjectured that

$$\lim_{P \to \infty} \frac{\log W(P)}{\log(P)} = \frac{1}{2}. \tag{43.1}$$

Figure 43.4 is an interesting plot showing the distribution of the first 200 palindromes when multiplied by a constant. To create the plot, start with an integer *x* from 1 to 200, multiply it by a constant $\alpha$, and determine if the result is a palindrome. The "Multiplier" $\alpha$ on the y-axis of the plot goes from 1 to 200. A dot on the graph indicates a palindromic number. The various patterns produced are quite interesting, and a few casual observations can be made. Note that there is clearly a dense structure below some "hyperbolic" boundary. There is a conspicuous vertical line of closely spaced dots at *x* = 55 corresponding to 10 consecutive odd $\alpha$ values which produce palindromes. The products are: (55 x 91, 55 x 93, 55 x 95, 55 x 97, 55 x 99, 55 x 101, 55 x 103, 55 x 105, 55 x 107, 55 x 109). Also, when the *x*-axis value is an even multiple of 5, there are no *y*-data. When the *x*-axis value is a non-palindromic odd multiple of 5, the *y*-data are scarce. When *x* is palindromic, there are many *y*-data points. Notice the plot has symmetry: if *xy* is palindromic, *yx* is also palindromic.

There are many other interesting patterns in the plot, and you will probably find many more patterns which we have not yet discovered. For further work on palindromes, you should consult the work

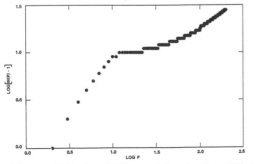

**Figure 43.2.** *Log W(P) vs. P for the first 200 integers.*

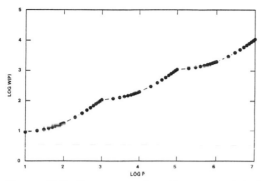

**Figure 43.3.** *Same as previous figure except* $1 < P < 10,000,000$.

of IBM researcher Shaiy Pilpel (1985) for a list of numbers which are palindromic for both their decimal and binary expressions. For example, 313 is such a "double" palindrome since 313 = 100111001 in binary notation.

## For Further Reading

1.  Pilpel, S. (1985-86) Some more double palindromic integers. *Journal of Recreational Math.* 18(3): 174-176. Also: Schmidt, H. (1988) Palindromes: density and divisibility. *Mathematics Magazine.* 61(5): 297-299.

2.  Schwartz, B. (1986) Counting palindromes. *Journal of Recreational Math.* 18(3): 177-179. Also: Calandra, M. (1985-86) Integers which are palindromic in both decimal and binary notation. *Journal of Recreational Math.* 18(1): 47.

3.  Gardner, M. (1979) *Mathematical Circus.* Alfred Knopf: New York. (pages 242-252). Also: Peretti, A. (1985) Query 386C. *Notices of the American Mathematics Society.* (May Issue).

4.  Lakhtakia, A., Pickover, C. (1990) Some observations on palindromic numbers. *Journal of Recreational Math.* 22(1): 55-60.

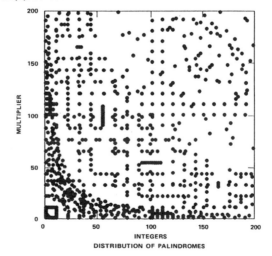

DISTRIBUTION OF PALINDROMES

**Figure 43.4.** *Distribution of palindromes.* The horizontal axis gives the integers $x$, and the vertical axis indicates the integral multiplier $\alpha$. A dot on the graph indicates that $\alpha x$ is palindromic.

58084187652859752958584966023611738926743407113271198106707607694846726048012436
86395993241133608145900661194710537936696162381047214162218407706119556629212851
92796292802440421200633744531802667949167189646248721908821587203725937425444544
20374477147681918616288860669875627211275953922247689567812524895127793586823258
81441876560899478096481634362698781836826426774416197110782139379031420666399
21471138473645134477507281172254824820223928019009123508725827419189838418792363
41825208368005058888872532950961899680417457969063267234011488427962878427463780
20456368171892958648157250651022516781725453384328066066910437933468231
29482041799734648436018949062547344969237138904029647679410895255962026889919052
68448457383874860213004205555436631028483998997305905577901586452263860360338356
36239568498297208032278217189863008170174451227351461722173793968005827244691786
72865862473337030509552869899686360505554885852119851941472933925879156940402868
87738911009601962411308566164588882590734233609418009446201420599333286958099965
25490471818619920040129699464193322791588578739824654398197491107863274554092373
37027254799083317741081826777469806463316814605150039888375091714310186321684644
21228122894137423500837524500163350821331116681941121279315277992595088757929530
88847681510649441556325069257672396268895692643430720236692048040477357585129
93658086438400082599290843963949697180993046982813764320120555650080497729718960
42931250550213964768300889339212746682259350438819437481383304843481531743926421
53170405217189047009717565083838127159205043811765041475609764556750576362016
35954483560779461475882404043451174044055119997286322513605432720565645912847658
21504940557580565988515886827829813778332668643332641999138007835389453853118375
61707420144792945950051123924751925664503994926999421583278532811310589930049048
61641457084432581894468074585848144528938858846452849367891746253498972408363214
90762753662455512724604521243344234093862121743336853161561526501732130
16046342406367768918789304528684187141604386636525290325179326655198319503225668
35974124688131132706647305606386170415926515438844306805222690464344988809
88091785796437944153970293352546801407760710832138119320843292117819002399969289
27230684945029097733703131521070786215471232990128753903849459171991254687432985
05492050586882378735216901508301069316809493192899224349483969364760530854155357
02601281736217486408339731151484282873035125478972957640045680647740240866746391
26840922241370558915878044495678257017845350191543711675514291552123702890159709
83976559597149376640661318394647350965064220402830487328863033933719899815680639
57537622643042902551481841392140555433991764538827109966126543730371183583969
17730099503538531202832117564763246875825816802639250137902890065220858473030447
37072036168372541953195273097185539284066838173029481126105571005517664878384319
05218067858580280313436051805125362062404268349858271893817536463235253501104572
39355300979932521524785670506767415624045396074947910392546785684164601570411157
90133907204654097884257770082056733572683989594389430421101524237990114059392911
93841471736848658588502309988500976287685263978375333768957093399766997305019820
57321381470899534463335845899501366853617074692090591486032825280070594835094
09384413178586205020481345467038005975193375026049280246480557201523823135124060
35570756476043811033238943455071554943348232938303667455547229176264626623335942
24646617918427756504557830819165656376115781471804443006769810379493285200190351
80209152762791068230530392110210101306052725942112012701008763279296957185540-9
53798503254199893138806254941925843424361993124864979585546368070101578394 29
17318177040838790729395360200669321788578248189596556346256655070010709765286449
57930948624290292532170463051048959928323405955520077165711993803304734239899 32
29960351848919123455430680631192491849167618491942012135986924554322018849154-99
06971127637640824330617628135401004999196718491942012135986924554322018849154069-9
22289904133740330390206562870014506065439326613036397223518210331683500298
58446935668081100694566636436555858929417867881228671019545840270878390308709237
09338387620097074424547580756743049832991744234851923945357831398992444214793
60035591660719288325790900831021124952616159210111021204034944386008825835109119
82529920014932849741097676003444190641876205846565510181278653946578239188157564
22386433157364615819218555476630373033174335055017155433894233010735167646461855
35943043143832510168649747520720496294833025686098396645431950195125857823034939
03901552749508972638120684206950129646971535966405199835764336442500897508412426
63881150369076690428058977332483780363585692580094890013194888695683774706414 93
92191938614108988413262011240338943859903773753266502896777524888014564016104309
88611041750954723765877551841087505696045393266137677149665875351252399690925540
41686401105242642265635707409073848052773404161153630507161633040829758587708215
08134947684668255000065105211949292817386714819455708012626023580462737726301618
26441403638591214709892987419539253080707529677651376365821228291135945294990 378
18703867018393834463165901167892588957780904235561402041317195046299392462268347
60335977607999027328330368833694929293022471568944836494802167135674050705856793
90168619882084212550934154672063462910535378196529865834507786189649740322300396
12035476707420477407650936760270875521530279183473421611379337936848226262920962
96634624579539574749583948534318992814049186030700929051997026378731797849403054
94893436875520901452074521588071125037111213367009305384969228
28928700041999178211823491229208401391061767032186451434029704503507246975872007
90078895536398622206239725384945050020165463061397258459659285649733113078652047 95
38665323148139025566228824141914253660943925506913978145128879189667745932447396
19212819473505626035764437212140035822125740143313433421636454372155541574472580
85222647943688943636209762849244648858399144528375848176538917633438175403-72
68399499299959042083358723512389972849930656651924653932115004865918744201480-71
66747113594538942728088231000236333442882782893882978850598955505757561385151
28458473295465650271354964042236936899214504404820443513932885840650869553953506
26201536761576535801657413951657100399535029506318375390437170074998082249441712
52246194362341953375132742836350179439440622866362130428890297746931205494 32293
39599170268004980946555130913467319280641290082795850469239092906181003734690-7564
00205858232587439850296641918134345197583590463187152365503505609492967378
91250287578914862908714139721320401767211331279532720054148380954138404092208321
24463772235710135270905827890400050516407723363609794677728181037724379889551631-7
33731913465723578110956818934564289378758861883232924638970309300300257191651944-4
15700075969333286059151917539098239163324271852788964605659131141602058001199367
88692930496618786393391740501598012595784556149536869989693549150297433742684691
66882964416296008584082722270541647220444819728002589916128722407028028047660415
36539129573669642535965098775618513797943012673455494251031195847839365-9537
73499189886212606524891138768559294089406329705426463599489206239564369080411859
21327653288440086708609273492453441723161532000471526517468602892707636551
19784636248792608138852104316733599688637140769992591493242788888615007647916380
33741879248279929038276377943329009092942202841742522820836947444145736394-11741
19035660242398838842178111070205144772170906174436084600784899090556792440
78523297852877215984253177759956532183606721127155789670588925162018675067444-730
24454254843863730278511790921695154701827608508761898284448433600201130542181-991
92471302575499206176939222550216510841615966408240184811660106408163311422906925
86342109496267475076958176008021723017933476298382053316693759691479592576813907 5

# Chapter 44

# Reversed Numbers and Palindromes

If you select an integer, reverse its digits, add the two numbers together, and continue to reverse and add, the result often becomes a palindrome – that is, the number reads the same in both directions (see previous chapter). With some numbers, this happens in a single step. For example,

$$18 + 81 = 99, \tag{44.1}$$

which is a palindrome. Other numbers may require more steps. For example, 19 + 91 = 110. 110 + 011 = 121. Of all the numbers under 10,000, only 249 fail to form palindromes in 100 steps or less. In 1984, Gruenberg noted that the smallest number that *seems* never to become palindromic by this process is 196. (It has been tested through 50,000 steps.) I have tested the starting number 879 for 19,000 steps producing a 7,841-digit number – with no palindrome resulting. The 7,841-digit number starts with the sequence 58084187... and ends with ...139075 (see the frontispiece figure of this chapter)! Statistical tests indicate an approximately equal percent occurrence of digits 0 through 9 for this large number. Similarly, I have tested 1997 for 8000 steps, with no palindrome occurring.

Are there any patterns underlying this reverse and add process? Can we make any predictions? The number of steps needed (called the "path length" and represented by $p$) is often under 5 steps. Figure 44.1 shows all path lengths for starting integers $n$ ($1 \le n \le 1000$). To produce a convenient graphical representation, Figure 44.1 is truncated in the $y$-axis direction (that is, the search for palindromes is stopped after 25 steps). Notice the interesting periodicity in the path lengths made apparent in the graph. Also notice that while patterns exist, they are not perfect or entirely regular. A Fourier-transform generated power spectrum (Figure 44.2) is a good way of quantifying periodic patterns (see Bendat, 1963, for a background to Fourier transforms). Like a prism which separates white light passing through it into its rainbow-colored components, the power spectrum gives us an idea of the hidden components in complicated input. The power spectrum gives information about the frequency spectrum of the input data and contains prominent peaks which correspond to prominent frequencies. Higher peaks indicate patterns which occur with greater regularity and/or with greater

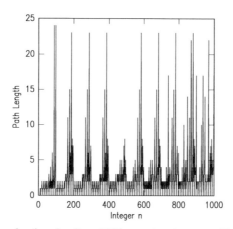

**Figure 44.1.** *Path lengths for the first 1000 starting integers.* To produce a convenient graphical representation, the figure is truncated in the *y*-axis direction (that is, the search for palindromes is stopped after 25 steps).

amplitude. The frequency axis indicates roughly how many times a pattern occurs in the 1000-integer window. For the sake of analysis, the large path lengths are also cut off at 25, as shown in Figure 44.1 The first large peak at low frequency corresponds to the periodic large path lengths occurring about every 100 integers. Other periodicities are also evident. For example, periodic paths of length 0 (corresponding to starting integers that are already palindromic) occur with periods of 10 integers, e.g., 101, 111, 121, 131, 141. This is represented by the second main peak in the power spectrum. Other peaks correspond to periodic events occurring with periods in the 10 to 1 integer length scales.

[[ Some simple observations help to predict the outcome of the reverse and add process. Let $d_n$ be the *n*-th digit in a number, and $d_n^r$ be the *n*-th digit in the reversed number. Let $p$ be the path length. Then $p \leq 1$ if, for all digits in the number, $d_n \leq 4$. Also, $p$ is greater than 1 whenever there exists a digit such that $d_n + d_n^r \geq 10$. ]]

## 44.1 Stop and Think

The graphs stimulate several questions which may not be easily answered. For example, why are the periodic large path lengths absent in the 400-500 integer range (Figure 44.1)? Also, if we were to list the palindrome values for the moderately-sized path lengths, we find a high percentage of occurrence of the digit 8. Why 8? Figure 44.3 shows the palindromic end points for some of the moderate-sized path lengths for the first 300 starting integers. Finally, you may wish to look for patterns for larger starting integers. For example, the path length graph corresponding to Figure 44.1 for $(1000 \leq n \leq 10000)$, while displaying similar interesting periodic patterns, looks quite different. One notable difference is that there are many fewer 0-length paths since there are fewer starting palindromes. There are various gaps and peaks. The resultant graph is left as a curiosity exercise for you. For those of you who wish to learn more about this palin-

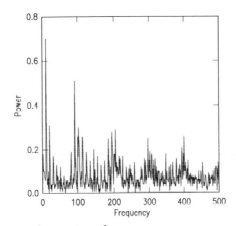

**Figure 44.2.** *Power spectrum for previous figure.*

drome problem, see Gardner and Trigg. Gardner also discusses the problem for other number systems (e.g., binary numbers).

## 44.2  For Further Reading

1. Pickover, C. (1991) Reversed numbers and palindromes. *Journal of Recreational Math.*, in press.
2. Ellis, K. (1987) *Number Power*. St. Martin's Press: New York. (pgs. 122-123)
3. Gruenberg, F. (1984) Computer Recreations. *Scientific American.* April. 19-26.
4. Bendat, J., Piersol, R. (1966) *Measurement and Analysis of Random Data.* John Wiley and Sons: New York.
5. Gardner, M. (1979) *Mathematical Circus.* Alfred Knopf: New York. (pgs 242-252).
6. Trigg, C. (1972) More on palindromes by reversal-addition. *Mathematics Magazine.* 45: 184-186; Trigg, C. (1973) Versum sequences in the binary system. *Pacific Journal of Math.* 47: 263-275.

| n | Palindrome | Path Length |
|---|---|---|
| 89 | 8813200023188 | 24 |
| 98 | 8813200023188 | 24 |
| 167 | 88555588 | 11 |
| 177 | 8836886388 | 15 |
| 187 | 8813200023188 | 23 |
| 266 | 88555588 | 11 |
| 276 | 8836886388 | 15 |
| 286 | 8813200023188 | 23 |

**Figure 44.3.** *Palindromic end points for some of the moderately-sized path lengths.*

Chapter 45

# Interlude: Chimpanzee/Man Hybrid

What would the hypothetical offspring of a chimpanzee and human look like? This arresting composite image of a chimpanzee and a man (facing page), was produced by New York photographer Nancy Burson using personal computer software developed by her husband and collaborator, David Kramlich. Burson has created other interesting hybrid images including a composite portrait of human-kind showing an Asian, a Caucasian, and a Black weighted according to recent population statistics. Burson's composite photography grew from her first efforts to transform faces by aging them. Her methods allow people to see portraits of themselves as they might appear years into the future. This work has a practical application. For example, "artificially aged" photos of lost or kidnapped children have helped law enforcement agencies, families, and entire communities to continue searching for missing children years after their disappearance. For further information: Day, C. (1990) The Ultimate CEO. *PC/Computing.* Sept. 3(9): 173-180. The chimp/man hybrid shown here is titled "Evolution II" and is courtesy of the Jayne Baum Gallery.

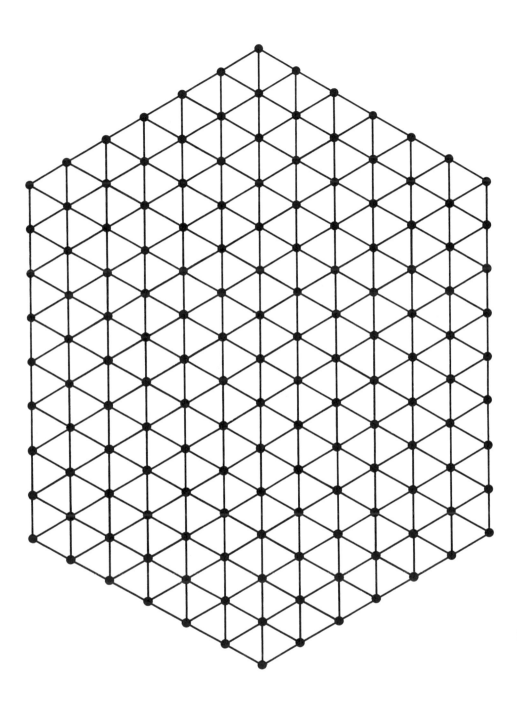

Chapter 46

# Infinite Triangular Arrays

*"Amusement is one of humankind's strongest motivating forces. Although mathematicians sometimes belittle a colleague's work by calling it 'recreational' mathematics, much serious mathematics has come out of recreational problems, which test mathematical logic and reveal mathematical truths."*      Ivars Peterson, *Islands of Truth, 1990*

One of the most famous integer patterns in the history of mathematics is Pascal's triangle. Blaise Pascal was the first to write a treatise about this progression in 1653 – although the pattern had been known by Omar Khayyam as far back as 1100 A.D. The first 7 rows of Pascal's triangle can be represented as:

```
                1
              1   1
            1   2   1
          1   3   3   1
        1   4   6   4   1
      1   5  10  10   5   1
    1   6  15  20  15   6   1
```

Each number in the triangle is the sum of the two numbers above it. The role that Pascal's triangle plays in probability theory, in the expansion of binomials of the form $(x + y)^N$, and in various number theory applications has been discussed previously (see references). If similar expansions are made for $(x + y + z)^N$ for successive powers of $N$, *Pascal's Pyramid* can be generated. Liu Zhiqing of the People's Republic of China, in 1985, reported on such a pyramid, but noted that its three-dimensionality makes it more difficult to visualize. Computer graphics is an excellent method by which patterns in Pascal's pyramid can be made obvious to both the mathematician and interested layperson.

    First we consider a 2-D representation of Pascal's triangle. Figure 46.1, for example, represent Pascal's triangle computed modulo 2; that is, points are

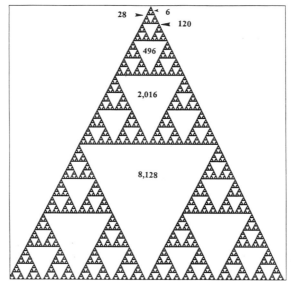

**Figure 46.1.** *Pascal's triangle (mod 2).* The numbers on the figure indicate the number of "missing" dots which make up each triangle in the central stack.

plotted for all even numbers occurring in the triangle. Each entry in the triangular array consisting of $n$ rows and $r$ columns can be denoted by the symbol:

$$\binom{n}{r} \tag{46.1}$$

For example,

$$\binom{3}{2} = 3 \tag{46.2}$$

One way these patterns can be defined is algebraically, when $n \geq 0$ and $0 \leq r \leq n$:

$$\binom{n}{r} = \frac{n!}{r!(n-r)!} \tag{46.3}$$

Other authors have extended the triangle to negative values for $n$ (Bidwell, 1973). Mandelbrot has discussed the class of gasket-like (i.e., hole-filled) structures exemplified in Figure 46.1 in his famous 1983 book.

If you were to count the number of "missing" entries in in the central white triangles starting from the top, you would find that each was made up entirely of even-numbered dots (Gardner, 1977). At the top is 1 white dot, then 6, 28, 120, 496 ... dots. 6, 28, and 496 are perfect numbers because each is the sum of all its divisors excluding itself (6=1+2+3). The formula for the number of dots in the $n$th central triangle, moving along the apex, is

$$2^{n-1}(2^n - 1). \tag{46.4}$$

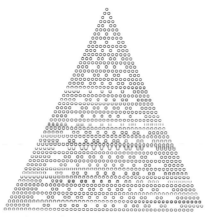

**Figure 46.2.** *Dudley's triangle (mod 2).*

Because every number of the form $2^{n-1}(2^n - 1)$, where $(2^n - 1)$ is a prime, is an even perfect number, all even perfect numbers appear in the central stacked triangular pattern in Figure 46.1.

## 46.1 The Dudley Triangle

Before progressing to the 3-D extension to Pascal's triangle, let us consider the less-known and understood Dudley triangular array, which was proposed in 1987, and can be represented as follows.

```
                        2
                     2     2
                  2     1     2
               2     0     0     2
            2     6     5     6     2
         2     6     4     4     6     2
      2     6     3     2     3     6     2
   2     6     2     0     0     2     6     2
2     6     1     9     8     9     1     6     2
2     6     0     8     6     6     8     0     6     2
2     6    12     7     4     3     4     7    12     6     2
2     6    12     6     2     0     0     2     6    12     6     2
2     6    12     5     0    12    11    12     0     5    12     6     2
```

I think it would be quite difficult for you to guess the rules for its generation, but you might want to try before reading further. As noted in (Dudley, 1987), we can denote the location of each array element by its diagonal coordinates $(m,n)$, where $m$ signifies the $m$th diagonal descending left to right and $n$ signifies the $n$th diagonal descending right to left. Every value in the array is in the range from 0 to the sum of its coordinates, $m + n$. One way the array can be reproduced is by the following formula.

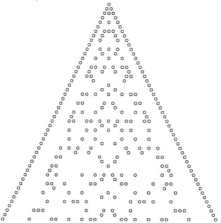

**Figure 46.3.** *Dudley's triangle, prime numbers.*

$$m,n = (m^2 + mn + n^2 - 1) \mod n + n + 1 \tag{46.5}$$

(See Glossary for "mod"). Like Pascal's triangle, the Dudley triangle is bilaterally symmetric. Notice that the triangle's values grow more slowly than Pascal's triangle and that the triangle has fewer odd-valued entries. Figure 46.2 shows the positions of even entries. Elahe Khorasani and I noticed that plotting the positions of prime-number entries yields interesting patterns (Figure 46.3). We have also noticed that as the triangle descends, certain even entries on the sides, once encountered, remain in the triangle. These values are 2, 6, 12, 20, 30, 42, ... . (The differences between these values are 4, 6, 8, 10, ... .) These entries "growing" at the sides of the triangle account for the side wings in Figure 46.2 and Figure 46.3.

## 46.2 Pascal's Pyramid

Color Plate 23 shows Pascal's pyramid, with positions corresponding to even numbered entries in the pyramid plotted as a small ball. These figures possess what is known as nonstandard scaling symmetry, also called dilation symmetry, i.e. invariance under changes of scale. Dilation symmetry is sometimes expressed by the formula ($\vec{r} \rightarrow a\vec{r}$). The crucial property of the pyramid is that each number in the pyramid is the sum of the three immediately above it. Sophisticated computer graphics systems make it possible to rapidly rotate the figure to get a better feel for its structure. This figure was generated using three programmed colored light sources to illuminate the pyramid. This helps the viewer visualize the pyramid's complicated 3-D structure.

## 46.3 Stop and Think

This introduction to infinite triangular arrays should whet your appetite. For your enjoyment, additional background references on Pascal's triangles are included in the reference section. Other interesting triangles (e.g. Bernoulli's and Vieta's) are discussed by Edwards (1988). You may wish to consider how expansions of $(x + y + z + w)^n$ can be visualized in a 4-D Pascal pyramid! Also, you may wish to plot the 3-D pyramid using a higher modulus index (e.g., mod 3 instead of mod 2), which generally yields more intricate symmetries.

### For Further Reading

1. Pickover, C., Khorasani, E. (1991) Infinite triangular arrays. *Journal of Recreational Math.*, in press.

2. Bondarenko, B. (1990) *Patterns in Pascal's Triangle.* (Recently published in Tashkent, Soviet Union, with many pictures. A bibliography lists 406 papers with topics relating to Pascal's triangle.) For more information, write Prof. B. A. Bondarenko, Institute of Cybernetics, Acad. Sci., Uzbek SSR., Ul.F. Hodgaeva 34, Tashkent - 143, 700143, USSR.)

3. Zhiqing, L. (1985) Pascal's pyramid. *Mathematical Spectrum* 17(1):1-3.

4. Gardner, M. (1977) Pascal's triangle. In *Mathematical Carnival.* Vintage Books: New York.

5. Dudley, U. (1987) An infinite triangular array. *Mathematics Magazine* 61(5): 316-317.

6. Mandelbrot, B. (1983) *The Fractal Geometry of Nature*, Freeman: New York.

7. Spencer, D. (1982) *Computers In Number Theory.* Computer Science Press: Maryland.

8. Jansson, L. (1973) Spaces, functions, polygons, and Pascal's triangle. *Mathematics Teacher.* 66. 71-77.

9. Usiskin, Z. (1973). Perfect square patterns in the Pascal triangle. *Mathematics Magazine.* Sept.-Oct. 203-208.

10. Bidwell, J. (1973) Pascal's triangle revisited. *Mathematics Teacher* 66: 448-452.

11. Holter, N., Lakhtakia, A., Varadan, V., Vasundara, V. Messier, R. (1986). On a new class of planar fractals: the Pascal-Sierpinski gaskets. *Journal of Physics. A: Math. Gen.* 19: 1753-1759.

12. Lakhtakia, A., Vasundara, V., Messier, R., Varadan, V. (1988) Fractal sequences derived from the self-similar extensions of the Sierpinski gasket. *Journal of Physics A: Math. Gen.* 21: 1925-1928.

13. Gordon, J., Goldman, A. and Maps, J. (1986) Superconducting-normal phase boundary of a fractal network in a magnetic field. *Physical Review Letters.* 56: 2280-2283.

14. Edwards, A. (1988) Pascal's triangle – and Bernoulli's and Vieta's. *Mathematical Spectrum.* 33-37.

15. Peterson, I. (1990) *Islands of Truth.* Freeman: New York. (The quote at the beginning of this chapter comes from this book.)

Stalk 27 ⟶

Chapter 47

# Undulating Undecamorphic and Undulating Pseudofareymorphic Integers

The exotic *undulating undecamorphic* and *undulating pseudofareymorphic* numbers should provide a provocative area for future computer searches and investigations, and also for recreational number theory. This chapter presents observations, computational recipes, and nomenclature, and also raises several questions for future work. Much of the material in this chapter concerns polygonal numbers, which are introduced in the following sections.

The early Greek mathematicians noticed that if groups of dots were used to represent numbers, they could be arranged so as to form geometric figures, such as:

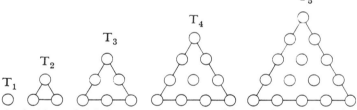

Since 1, 3, 6, 10, and 15 dots can be arranged in the form of a triangle, these numbers are called triangular numbers.[34] You may want to read more about polygonal numbers in "Infinite Sequences in Centered Hexamorphic Numbers" on page 215 before proceeding further.

Figure 47.1 shows the first five *ranks* ($r$) of polygonal numbers, graphically represented as polygonal figures, $p_n^r$ – from triangular ($n=3$) to octagonal ($n=8$). It is possible to compute $p_n^r$ (Beiler, 1964) from:

$$\frac{r}{2}\left[(r - 1)n - 2(r - 2)\right] \tag{47.1}$$

---

[34] Polygonal numbers appeared in 15th century arithmetic books and were probably known to the ancient Chinese; but they were of special interest to the Pythagoreans due to their interest in the mystical properties of such numbers.

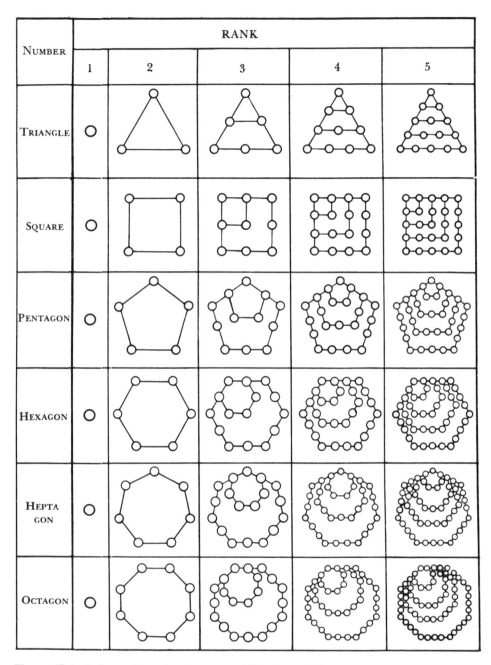

**Figure 47.1.** *Polygonal number diagrams.* (This figure is from: Beiler, A. (1964) *Recreations in the Theory of Numbers.* Dover: New York.)

| r | p(r) | |
|------|-----------|---|
| 25 | 2725 | |
| 625 | 1755625 | (r undulates, but p(r) "nearly undulates" due to consecutive 5's) |
| 9376 | 395559376 | (r undulates, but p(r) "nearly undulates" due to consecutive 5's) |

**Figure 47.2.** *Undulating undecamorphic integers less than 100,000.*

## 47.1  Undulating Polymorphic Integers

In this chapter, we are interested in polymorphic numbers, and, in particular, undulating polymorphic numbers. Professor Charles Trigg (1898 - 1989) defined a number to be *polymorphic* if it terminates with its associated polygonal number. For example, hexagonal numbers have the form $H(r) = r(2r - 1)$ (see "Infinite Sequences in Centered Hexamorphic Numbers" on page 215). The number 125 is *hexamorphic* because H(125) = 31125 . Let's now define another mathematical term. The term "smoothly undulating integer" was used by Trigg in a paper on palindromic octagonal numbers, where he defines an integer as smoothly undulating if two digits oscillate, for example 79797979. The term "smooth" differentiates this kind of number from an undulating integer where the alternating digits are consistently greater or less than the digits adjacent to them, for example 4253612 (Trigg, 1982; Pickover, 1990). For this chapter, we are interested in undulation, not smooth undulation, because smoothly undulating polymorphic numbers are so rare that even computer searches become difficult.

An undulating polymorphic number can be defined in terms of its digits, $d$,

$$[(d_\lambda - d_{\lambda-1})(d_{\lambda+1} - d_\lambda)] < 0, \; \lambda = 2,3,\dots,N-1 \qquad (47.2)$$

where $N$ is the number of digits in the number. Note that I define undulating polymorphic numbers as having an undulation in both $p_n^r$ and $r$. This means that both the rank number and the associated polygonal number must oscillate. As an example, Figure 47.2 includes the only undulating undecamorphic integer discovered for $r < 100,000$. (An 11-sided polygon is called an undecagon.)

Before attempting to find patterns in *undulating* polymorphic numbers, it is interesting to characterize the number of polymorphic numbers for a given *n*-sided figure, regardless of undulation. Notably, there are great variations in the frequency of occurrence of polymorphic numbers. Figure 47.3 shows the number of polymorphic integers $\alpha$ discovered for $2 < n < 30$, searching for all ranks less than $10^4$. The smallest and most common $\alpha$ is 5, and the largest ($\alpha = 118$) occurs for 22-morphic integers. Figure 47.4 shows an expanded version of Figure 47.3 for $2 < n \le 100$. Casual inspection of the $\alpha$ vs. $r$ plots reveals no particular patterns to me. Can you find any patterns?

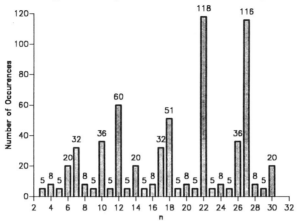

**Figure 47.3.** *The number of occurrences of polymorphic integers.* The number of occurrences $\alpha$ of polymorphic integers discovered for $2 < n \le 30$, searching for all ranks less than $10^4$. The number of integers is written above each bar.

## 47.2 Twin 27-morphic integers

We use the term *twin polymorphic integers* for polymorphic integers with consecutive rank values. For example, the 27-morphic integers follow certain notable patterns (Figure 47.6). Those numbers with 2 digits exhibit twinning with a separation distance of 7 between successive twins, e.g. (16,17), (24,25), (32,33), .... The 3-digit undulating 27-morphic integers also periodically exhibit a twinning, and the last digits repeat the patterns 5 0 1 6, 5 0 1 6, .... I challenge you to find any other examples of twin polymorphic numbers for $n \ne 27$.

## 47.3 Undulation

While polymorphic integers may exist for all polygonal numbers,[35] undulating polymorphic integers are much rarer. Like Figure 47.4, Figure 47.5 indicates the number of undulating polymorphic integers $\alpha'$ discovered for $2 < n < 100$, searching for all ranks less than $10^4$. The record-holding undulating polymorph (for $2 \le n \le 100$) is the 52-gon, which has 15 undulating occurrences (see Figure 47.7 and Figure 47.5).

---

[35] This is an unsolved question, and I invite you to prove or disprove this conjecture.

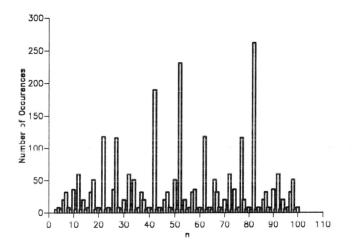

**Figure 47.4.** *Same as previous figure* (except $2 < n \leq 100.$)

## 47.4 Undulating Pseudofareymorphic Integers

We close this chapter with a final class of undulating integers, and in particular this section introduces the Pseudofareymorphic integers (Figure 47.8). Fareymorphic integers can be understood as follows. Suppose we list all the proper fractions up to some arbitrarily assigned limit in their lowest terms in order of magnitude – say with denominator not exceeding 7. We have the 17 fractions: 1/7, 1/6, 1/5, 1/4, 2/7, 1/3, 2/5, 3/7, 1/2, 4/7, 3/5, 2/3, 5/7, 3/4, 4/5, 5/6, 6/7. Let $\beta$ be the number of fractions in the Farey series of order $n$. For the previous example of order 7, $\beta_7 = 17$. This is called a Farey series, named after John Farey who lived in the Napoleonic era and worked on such numbers. It can be demonstrated (Beiler, 1964) that $\beta$ can be approximated by the expression

$$\beta' = 3n^2/\pi^2 \tag{47.3}$$

the approximation becoming more and more accurate as the value of $n$ increases. Since we know the value of $\pi$ to any desired degree of accuracy, this means we can approximate the number of terms in a Farey sequence quite easily. For $\beta_7 = 17$ we have $\beta'_7 = 14.90$, and for $\beta_{500} = 76115$ we have the approximation $\beta'_{500} = 75990.89$. I call the $\beta' = [3n^2/\pi^2]$ sequence a pseudofarey sequence (since these values approximate the number of terms in a Farey series). The brackets $[\varepsilon]$ denote the greatest integer not exceeding $\varepsilon$. From past discussions of undulating polymorphic numbers, the meaning of the term undulating pseudofareymorphic numbers should be clear. The question of the existence of pseudofareymorphic numbers is easily determined by computer computation (Figure 47.8). The question of undulation is more difficult. Except for $\beta'_{38} = 438$, I have not found any larger undulating pseudofareymorphic integers, and I would be interested in finding out if you can disprove their existence or find such a number.

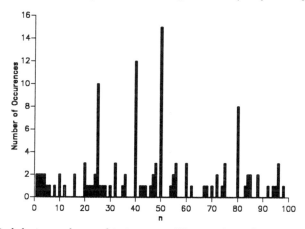

**Figure 47.5.** *Undulating polymorphic integers.* The number of occurrences $\alpha$ of undulating polymorphic integers discovered for $2 < n < 100$, searching for all ranks less than $10^4$.

## 47.5 Stop and Think

This chapter defined undulating numbers, such as 19283746, and smoothly undulating numbers, such as 101010101, where the alternating digits are consistently greater or less than the digits adjacent to them.[36] For further research, let us define smoothly gyrating numbers as those integers whose digits go up and down consecutively like a sine wave. The number of digits controlling the rise and fall determine the *kind* of number, for example

Smoothly gyrating number of the first kind: 12121212 ...
Smoothly gyrating number of the second kind: 1232123212321 ...
Smoothly gyrating number of the third kind: 1234321234321 ...

A *double* smoothly gyrating number of the *n*-th kind simply means a number which gyrates in two different bases, e.g., base 10 and base 3.

1.   Can you find a double smoothly gyrating number of the third kind?

2.   Are there any Fibonacci numbers which smoothly gyrate?

3.   Can you find a smoothly gyrating number which when multiplied by another smoothly gyrating number produces yet another smoothly gyrating number?

**For Further Reading**

1.   Beiler, A. (1964) *Recreations in the Theory of Numbers.* Dover: New York.

---

[36] For additional background information, see Pickover, C. (1990) Is there a double smoothly undulating integer? *Journal of Recreational Mathematics*, 22(1): 77-78. In this paper the term *double* smoothly undulating integer was defined as an integer that undulates in both its decimal and binary representation. The paper excluded the trivial case of double digit decimal numbers which might ordinarily fall into the category of smoothly undulating. Therefore, a number such as 21 (10101) is not included. Massive computer searches did not find a *double* smoothly undulating integer as defined above, and it was conjectured that no such number exists. Stimulated by the publication of this paper, Charles Ashbacher has since identified several numbers that smoothly undulate in more than one base. For example, $121_{10} = 171_8 = 232_7$. Also $546_{10} = 4141_5 = 20202_4 = 202020_3$.

| r | p(r) | r | p(r) |
|---|---|---|---|
| 1 | 1 * | 88 | 95788 |
| 4 | 154 * | 89 | 97989 * |
| 5 | 255 | 96 | 114096 |
| 8 | 708 * | 97 | 116497 |
| 9 | 909 * | 145 | 261145 |
| 16 | 3016 | 160 | 318160 * - |
| 17 | 3417 * | 161 | 322161 |
| 24 | 6924 * | 176 | 385176 |
| 25 | 7525 | 225 | 630225 |
| 32 | 12432 | 240 | 717240 * - |
| 33 | 13233 | 241 | 723241 * - |
| 40 | 19540 | 256 | 816256 |
| 41 | 20541 | 305 | 1159305 |
| 48 | 28248 | 320 | 1276320 - |
| 49 | 29449 | 321 | 1284321 - |
| 56 | 38556 | 336 | 1407336 |
| 57 | 39957 | 385 | 1848385 * |
| 64 | 50464 | 400 | 1995400 - |
| 65 | 52065 | 401 | 2005401 - |
| 72 | 63972 | 416 | 2158416 |
| 73 | 65773 | | |
| 80 | 79080 * | | |
| 81 | 81081 | | |

**Figure 47.6.** *Undulating 27-morphic integers.* *'s denote undulation. -'s denote three-digit twin 27-morphs.

2. Trigg, C. (1987) Hexamorphic numbers. *Journal of Recreational Math.* 19(1): 42-55.

3. Trigg, C. (1982-83) Palindromic octagonal numerals. *Journal of Recreational Math.* 15(1): 41-46.

4. Pickover, C. (1990) *Computers, Pattern, Chaos and Beauty.* St. Martin's Press: New York.

5. Pickover, C. (1991) Undulating undecamorphic and undulating pseudofareymorphic integers. *Journal of Recreational Math.* 23(2), in press

| r | p(r) |
|---|------|
| 160 | 636160 |
| 240 | 1434240 |
| 265 | 1749265 |
| 281 | 1967281 |
| 376 | 3525376 |
| 401 | 4010401 |
| 480 | 5748480 |
| 505 | 6363505 |
| 560 | 7826560 |
| 616 | 9471616 |
| 801 | 16020801 |
| 856 | 18297856 |
| 1201 | 36031201 |
| 3601 | 324093601 |
| 6576 | 1080936576 |

**Figure 47.7.** *All known undulating 52-morphic integers of rank less than 10,000.*

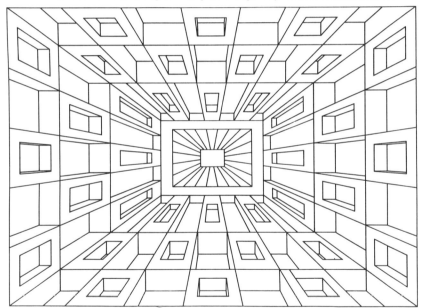

| n | F(n) |
|---|------|
| 4 | 4 |
| 38 | 438 |
| 53 | 853 |
| 245 | 18245 |
| 673 | 137673 |
| 7864 | 18797864 |
| 38861 | 459038861 |

**Figure 47.8.** *All known Pseudofareymorphic numbers less than 40,000.*

# Chapter 48

# A Pattern Based on the Mandelbrot Set

*"I wonder whether fractal images are not touching the very structure of our brains. Is there a clue in the infinitely regressing character of such images that illuminates our perception of art? Could it be that a fractal image is of such extraordinary richness, that it is bound to resonate with our neuronal circuits and stimulate the pleasure I infer we all feel. "*    P.W Atkins, *1990*

The mathematics of the iteration of algebraic functions has been studied for decades. However, the striking beauty and complexity of the patterns resulting from such iterative calculations have only recently been explored in detail, due in part to advances in computer graphics. B. Mandelbrot has been largely responsible for extending the theory and graphic presentation of iterated functions as a special class of the new geometry known as fractal geometry. Often fractals represent objects or patterns that appear "self-similar"; that is, no matter what scale is used to view the pattern, the magnified portion of the fractal shape looks similar to the original pattern.

Published algorithms for the Mandelbrot set are numerous. For example, algorithms for computing the Mandelbrot set were printed in *Scientific American* in August 1985. "Turning a Universe Inside-Out" on page 169 contains additional background information on the Mandelbrot set. In this chapter, a slight change has been made to the standard algorithm in order to produce interesting patterns which surround the set. This change occurs in line 8 in Pseudocode 48.1, and it monitors how far a point travels from its initial location rather than from the origin of the complex plane.

Fractal research often represents an effort to mathematically express the "jaggedness" of real world objects such as clouds, electrocardiogram lines, branches of the lung's bronchi, and soot generated by fires. It may interest you to know that in 1989 the world's scientific journals published about 1,500 articles with the word "fractal" in the title (Figure 48.2).

**Figure 48.1.** *A pattern based on the Mandelbrot set.*

## For Further Reading

1.  Mandelbrot, B. (1983) *The Fractal Geometry of Nature*, Freeman, San Francisco.

2.  Dewdney, A. (1988) *The Armchair Universe, An Exploration of Computer Worlds*. Freeman: New York.

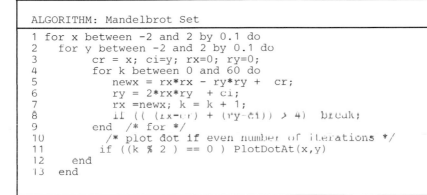

```
ALGORITHM: Mandelbrot Set

1 for x between -2 and 2 by 0.1 do
2    for y between -2 and 2 by 0.1 do
3        cr = x; ci=y; rx=0; ry=0;
4        for k between 0 and 60 do
5            newx = rx*rx - ry*ry +  cr;
6            ry = 2*rx*ry  + ci;
7            rx =newx; k = k + 1;
8            if (( (rx-cr) + (ry-ci)) > 4)  break;
9        end  /* for */
10            /* plot dot if even number of iterations */
11           if ((k % 2 ) == 0 ) PlotDotAt(x,y)
12    end
13 end
```

**Pseudocode 48.1.** *How to create the Mandelbrot variant.*

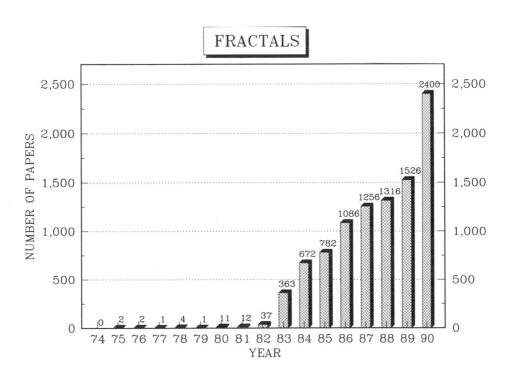

**Figure 48.2.** *Fractal Articles.* A review of the world's scientific literature shows the number of fractal articles dramatically increasing from 1980 to 1989.

$$1.37...^{\pi} = e$$

$$\frac{19^2}{\phi^2} = 137...$$

$$\frac{\phi^2}{19} = .137...$$

$$(1.9)^{\frac{1}{2}} = 1.37..$$

$$\pi^{-1.37\phi^2} = 1.37..$$

$$3.71^2 = 13.7...$$

$$\phi^{3.7^{-\frac{1}{\pi}}} = 1.37...$$

$$37! = 1.37..\times10^{43}$$

$$.037037\times37 = 1.37..$$

$$1.37... = .137.. \left(\frac{1.37\sqrt{5}}{\phi}\right)^{\frac{1}{2}} = 1.37..$$

$$\frac{\pi^{-\pi}}{.02} = 1.37..$$

$$\phi^{\frac{2}{3}} = 1.37..$$

$$\frac{(1.37...)^{\pi}}{2} = 1.37..$$

$$1.37..^{\phi} = \frac{5}{3}$$

$$Log_{10} e^{3.17} = 1.37..$$

$$\frac{\phi^2}{\sqrt{5}} \neq (1.37.)^{\frac{1}{2}}$$

$$\left(\frac{\phi}{2}\right)^2 = 1.37. \frac{\phi^3}{\sqrt{5}} = (1.37.)^2$$

$$\phi^{Ln\frac{\pi}{\phi}} = 1.37.. \frac{\phi}{\sqrt{5}} = (1.37.)^5$$

$$Log\phi \frac{\pi}{\phi} = 1.37...$$

$$\frac{20}{9\phi} = 1.37...$$

$$\phi^{1.37Ln\phi} = 1.37.$$

$$\phi^{-\frac{1}{e}\pi} = 1.37..$$

$$\pi^{1.37..^{-4}} = 1.37...$$

$$\pi^{1.5^{-\pi}} = 1.37..$$

$$\left(\frac{\pi^5}{\phi}\right)^{\frac{1}{2}} = 13.7..$$

$$163^{\frac{1}{16}} = 1.37..$$

$$\frac{\phi}{\pi} + 1.37 = (1.37)^2$$

$$\phi^{\frac{\phi}{4}} = 1.37...$$

$$\frac{20}{9\phi^2} = 1.37.$$

$$\frac{7}{\pi\phi} = 1.37..$$

$$e^{\phi^2} = 13.7..$$

$$(73\pi\phi)^2 = 1.37..\times10^5$$

$$\frac{17\phi}{2} = 13.7.$$

$$9(\pi-\phi) = 13.7..$$

$$(\pi-\phi) = (1.37.)^2$$

$$e\sqrt{1+e\sqrt{1+e\sqrt{1+e\sqrt{1+e\sqrt{...}}}}} = 1.37..$$

$$1.37.. - \frac{2.2222..}{\phi} = 1.37..$$

$$\frac{12.3456789}{9} = 1.37...$$

$$1.37..^e - 1.37... = 1.$$

$$\frac{\sqrt{e+\sqrt{e+\sqrt{e}}+...}}{\phi} = 1.37..$$

$$\frac{(11111)^2}{9} = 1.37..\times10^9$$

$$(2\phi)^{1.37..} = 5.$$

$$\frac{\sqrt[3]{11}}{\phi} = 1.37..$$

$$(111111)^3 = 1.37..\times10^{15}$$

$$\frac{\pi}{\sqrt{2}\phi} = 1.37..$$

$$(\phi^2+1)^{\frac{1}{4}} = 1.37..$$

$$(1.1)^{\sqrt{11}} = 1.37..$$

$$(\pi-\phi)^{\frac{3}{4}} = 1.37..$$

$$\frac{1.37..}{\phi^2} = 1.37.^{-2}$$

$$\phi^{1.111^{-4}} = 1.37...$$

$$\phi^{Ln\phi(1.37)} = 1.37..$$

$$\left(\frac{1.37\sqrt{5}}{\phi}\right)^{\frac{1}{2}} = 1.32..$$

$$\frac{1.37}{\phi} = 1.37..^{-\frac{1}{2}}$$

$$(1.37\phi^2)^{\frac{1}{4}} = 1.37..$$

$$(\pi\phi)^{\frac{1}{\pi\phi}} = 1.37..$$

$$\frac{137}{37} = (13.7)^{\frac{1}{2}}$$

$$1.37...^{\frac{\pi}{37}} = e$$

$$\frac{137.0137}{73} = (1.37.)^2$$

$$\frac{1}{1.37\phi^2} = 1.37..$$

$$\frac{40}{\phi^7} = 1.37..$$

$$e^{\frac{1}{\pi}} = 1.37...$$

$$e^{\frac{1}{\sqrt{10}}} = 1.37..$$

$$e^{\phi^2} = 13.7...$$

$$\phi^{1.37..} = \frac{\pi}{\phi}$$

$$\left(\frac{2\pi}{\phi^2}\right)^{\frac{1}{e}} = 1.37..$$

$$2^{7.1..} = 137.$$

$$Ln\frac{37}{\phi^2} = 1.37...$$

$$\frac{13.7^{1.37}}{\phi^2} = 13.7..$$

$$(Ln13.7)^{\frac{1}{3}} = 1.37...$$

$$(e\pi)^{-2} = .0137..$$

$$\phi^{2(\pi-\phi)} = (1.37.)\pi$$

$$\frac{10\phi}{e\pi} = (1.37.)^2$$

$$\phi^{\left(\frac{\phi^2}{4}\right)} = 1.37...$$

$$\pi^{-28} = 1.37..$$

$$\frac{\phi}{\phi} = (13.7.)^2$$

$$Ln\left(\frac{137^3}{\phi^2}\right) = 13.7..$$

$$\frac{\phi^4}{5} = 1.37..$$

$$e^{3.17} = 1.37...$$

$$e^{.317} = 1.37...$$

$$2\phi^4 = 13.7..$$

$$Log_{10}e^{\sqrt{10}} = 1.37..$$

$$\frac{\pi}{\phi}; Log_{10}1.37 = .137...$$

$$Log_{10}(2\phi e^2) = 1.37...$$

$$2^{13.7..} = 1.37\times10^4$$

$$2^{37} = 1.37..\times10^{11}$$

$$36^{1.37...} = 137.$$

$$\frac{3.6}{\phi^2} = 1.37...$$

$$3.6^{\frac{1}{4}} = 1.37..$$

$$\frac{1}{36} = 1.37..\times10^{-3}$$

$$\frac{100\frac{1}{\pi}}{\pi} = 1.37..$$

$$\left(\frac{13.7}{2}\right)^{\frac{1}{6}} = 1.37..$$

$$5^{\frac{1}{5}} = 1.37..$$

$$18^{\frac{1}{7}} = 1.37..$$

$$137^{\frac{1}{8}} = 1.37..$$

$$\frac{\pi\phi}{37^{\frac{1}{2}}} = .137..$$

$$\phi^{\frac{3}{2}} = 1.37..$$

$$(3.71)^2 = 13.7..$$

$$\phi^{\pi-\phi} = 1.37..$$

# Chapter 49

# Interlude: 1/137

*"[1/137] is one of the greatest damn mysteries of physics: a magic number that comes to us with no understanding by man. You might say the 'hand of God' wrote that number, and 'we don't know how He pushed His pencil.' "*

Richard Feynman, *QED*

The number 1/137 is a dimensionless physical parameter called the *fine structure constant*, and it plays a role in various properties of atomic and molecular systems. There are also amazing and simple numerical coincidences involving the digits 137 and other famous, dimensionless mathematical constants such as $\pi = 3.1415\ldots$, $e = 2.718\ldots$, and the golden ratio, $\phi = 1.61803\ldots$ (see "The Lute of Pythagoras" on page 203). Here I list just a few of them to stimulate your imagination.[37] Can you write a computer program to find other relationships? Is there any significance behind these coincidences?

$$\phi^{1.37\ldots} = \pi/\phi \qquad 2\phi^4 = 13.7\ldots \qquad \sqrt{10}^{\frac{2}{3}\sqrt{10}} = 1.37\ldots \qquad (49.1)$$

$$\phi^{e/10^{1/\pi}} = 1.37\ldots \qquad \frac{2\pi}{\phi^2}^{1/e} = 1.37\ldots \qquad \frac{13.7^{1.37}}{\phi^2} = 13.7\ldots \qquad (49.2)$$

$$e^{1/\pi} = 1.37\ldots \qquad \phi^{\frac{1}{\pi-\phi}} = 1.37\ldots \qquad \pi\phi^{1/\pi\phi} = 1.37\ldots \qquad (49.3)$$

$$\frac{\pi}{\phi^2}^{\frac{\pi}{\phi^2}^{\frac{\pi}{\phi^2}}} = 1.37\ldots \qquad \phi^{\frac{\phi}{e+\pi}} = 1.37\ldots \qquad \log\frac{10}{\pi-e} = 1.37\ldots \qquad (49.4)$$

$$\phi^{\ln\frac{\pi}{\phi}} = 1.37\ldots \qquad \frac{\sqrt{e+\sqrt{e+\sqrt{e+\cdots}}}}{\phi} = 1.37\ldots \qquad (49.5)$$

---

[37] These formulas come from a large list of over 200 mathematical coincidences involving 137, compiled by Gary Adamson, PO Box 16329, San Diego, California 92176-0329. A page from Adamson's notebook is shown facing this page.

Chapter 50

# The Computer Smorgasbord

*"Applications, computers, and mathematics form a tightly coupled system yielding results never before possible and ideas never before imagined. "*
Lynn Arthur Steen, *mathematician*

*"The enormous usefulness of mathematics in natural sciences is something bordering on the mysterious, and there is no rational explanation for it. It is not at all natural that 'laws of nature' exist, much less that man is able to discover them. The miracle of the appropriateness of the language of mathematics for the formulation of the laws of physics is a wonderful gift which we neither understand nor deserve. "*
Eugene P. Wigner, *physicist*

## 50.1 The Fantastic Five

Five is a remarkable number. Not only is 5 the hypotenuse of the smallest Pythagorean triangle,[38] but it is also the smallest automorphic number.[39] 5 is probably the only odd untouchable number.[40] Also, there are 5 Platonic solids.[41]

The number 5 is also remarkable for its appearance in biology and in art. Five-fold symmetry in biology is fairly common, as evidenced by a variety of animal species such as the starfish and other invertebrates. Five-fold symmetry also appears in mathematics; for example, in numerous uniform polyhedra. Five-fold symmetry is relatively rare, however, in the art forms produced by humans. Perhaps partly because pentagonal motifs do not tightly pack on the plane, they are much rarer than other symmetries in historic and artistic ornament. Never-

---

[38] A Pythagorean triangle is a right-angled triangle with integral sides.

[39] An automorphic number when multiplied by itself, terminates itself. 5 and 6 are the smallest automorphic numbers.

[40] Erdös called a number untouchable if it is never the sum of the proper divisors of any other number. The sequence of untouchable numbers starts: 2, 5, 52, 88, 96, 120.

[41] The five Platonic solids are the tetrahedron, cube, octahedron, dodecahedron, and icosahedron.

**Figure 50.1.** *Terra-cotta inlays* (from the smaller dome chamber of the Masjid-i-Jami in Isfahan (1088 A.D)).

theless, there are occasional interesting examples of pentagonal ornaments in artistic symbols and designs. The oldest and most important examples of five-fold symmetry and odd-number symmetry are the five-pointed star and triangle, first used in cave paintings and in the Near East since about 6000 BC. Since then the two have been used in sacred symbols by the Celts, Hindus, Jews, and Moslems. Later (circa 10th century AD) the five-pointed star was adopted by medieval craftspeople such as stonecutters and carpenters. In the 12th century, the five-pointed star was adopted by magicians and alchemists.

To begin this picture essay, I invite you to consider some of the Persian designs and motifs with pentagonal symmetry. Over the centuries Persia (Iran) has been periodically invaded, and elements of the invading cultures were incorporated into the native artistic transitions. Much of Persian art contains highly symmetrical designs. Examples of symmetrical ornaments appear on silk weaves, printed fabrics, carpets, ceramics, stone, and calligraphy. Occasionally, we find a five-fold symmetrical design in Persian ornament. Figure 50.1 shows terra-cotta inlays from the smaller dome chamber of the Masjid-i-Jami in Isfahan (1088 A.D). Notice that some of the figures contain an interesting mix of pentagonal and hexagonal shapes.

Religious symbols sometimes contain pentagonal symmetry, and one  example, shown here, is the five-pointed star of Bethelehem. Various symmetrical designs have also appeared in heraldic shapes. In the Middle Ages these designs on badges, coats of arms, and helmets generally indicated genealogy or family name.  Shown below the five-pointed star of Bethelehem is a badge from the Leicester family. The Japanese also had similar family symbols for the expression of heraldry. The family symbol, or *mon*, was known in Japan as early as 900 A.D., and reached its highest development during feudal times. Figure 50.2 shows several Japanese crests containing

**Figure 50.2.** *Several Japanese crests exhibiting five-fold symmetry.*

five-fold symmetry.  These kinds of crests are found on many household articles, including clothing.

To conclude this picture essay, I present a 20th Century demon mask from Bhutan (Figure 50.3).  While not displaying what is traditionally thought of as pentagonal symmetry, the number "five" plays a significant role in the mask's appearance.  There are five skulls atop the head, five protrusions on each of the eyebrows, and five ridges on each of the designs on the lower cheeks.

Symmetrical ornaments, such as those in this essay, have persisted from ancient to modern times.  It is in Arabic and Moorish design that the different kinds of symmetry have been most fully explored. The later Islamic artists were

**Figure 50.3.** *Demon mask from Bhutan (20th C.).*

forbidden by religion to represent the human form, so they naturally turned to elaborate geometric themes. To explore the full range of symmetry in historic ornament, you may wish to study the work of Gombrich, who discusses the psychology of decorative art and presents several additional examples of five-fold symmetry.

**For Further Reading**

1.  Wenninger, M. (1971) *Polyhedral Models*. Cambridge University Press: New York.
2.  Hargittai, I. (1991) *Fivefold Symmetry in Cultural Context*. World Scientific: Singapore.
3.  Dowlatshahi, A. (1979) *Persian Designs and Motifs*. Dover: New York.
4.  Lehner, E. (1978) *Symbols, Signs and Signets*. Dover: New York (1969).
5.  Lockwood, E. MacMillan, R. (1978) *Geometric Symmetry*. Cambridge: New York.
6.  Gombrich, E. (1979) *The Sense of Order: A Study in the Psychology of Decorative Art*. Cornell University Press: New York.
7.  Wigner, E. (1960) The unreasonable effectiveness of mathematics in the natural sciences. *Communications on Pure and Applied Mathematics*. 13: 1-14. (The Wigner quote at the beginning of this chapter comes from this paper.)

## 50.2  The Connell Sequence

In 1989, Dr. Akhlesh Lakhtakia (Pennsylvania State University) and I studied a weird and little-known sequence in number theory called the Connell sequence. Those of you who are not interested in technical mathematics may wish to skip this section. For those brave souls who remain after this warning: we'll begin by letting $u_n$ be the $n$th term in the sequence 1, 2, 4, 5, 7, 9, 10, 12, 14, 16, ... . This sequence, proposed in 1959, is constructed by examining the consecutive natural numbers, 1, 2, 3, 4, 5, ... , and taking the first odd number, the next two even numbers, the next three odd numbers, the next four even numbers, and so on. Practical use of this sequence in antenna theory is discussed in a recent paper by Lakhtakia et al. (1988).

One interesting question is: how fast does this sequence grow? Given the $n$-th term, what is the ratio $u_n/n$? A table of the first few entries is:

| $n$ | $u_n$ | $u_n/n$ |
|---|---|---|
| 1 | 1 | 1 |
| 2 | 2 | 1 |
| 3 | 4 | 1.3 |
| 4 | 5 | 1.25 |
| 5 | 7 | 1.4 |
| 6 | 9 | 1.5 |
| 7 | 10 | 1.43 |

Does the ratio grow increasingly large or is there some limit to its growth? One way to get a hint about the answer makes use of the interesting generating formula (Lakhtakia et al., 1988) for $u_n$

$$u_n = 2n - \{(1 + \sqrt{8n - 7})/2\} \tag{50.1}$$

where $\{\varepsilon\}$ denotes the greatest integer not exceeding $\varepsilon$. As $n \to \infty$, $u_n/n$ becomes almost $2 - \left[ 1/n - 0.5\sqrt{(8/n)} - (7/n)(1/n) \right]$. Since $(a/n) \to 0$ as $n \to \infty$, the ratio $u_n/n$ is 2 for large $n$. For example, for $n = 1000$ we have $u_n = 1955$, and the ratio is 1.955. I encouraged you to plot a graph of $u_n$ vs. $n$ and experiment with other Connell-like sequences such as those produced by taking two odd numbers, followed by four evens, followed by six odds, and so on.

Perhaps a better way of demonstrating the limiting behavior discussed in the previous paragraph is as follows. We make use of the fact that the Connell sequence is composed of subsequences:

subsequence number      subsequence
1                                    1
2                                    2,4
3                                    5,7,9
4                                    10,12,14,16

Note that there are $q$ members in subsequence $q$. Note also that the last element of each subsequence is $q^2$, thus the value of the last Connell element in any subsequence can be expressed by

$$u_{\frac{1}{2}q(q + 1)} = q^2 \tag{50.2}$$

For example, if $q = 2$ we have $u_3 = 2^2$. We also note that $u_{\frac{1}{2}q(q+1)-p} = q^2 - 2p \ \{q = 1,2,3, \ldots, \ p = 0,1,2, \ldots, q - 1\}$ where $p$ can achieve $q$ values. Let us consider the ratio:

$$\frac{u_{\frac{1}{2}q(q+1)-p}}{\frac{1}{2}q(q + 1) - p} = \frac{q^2 - 2p}{\frac{1}{2}(q^2 + q - 2p)} \tag{50.3}$$

$$= 2 \left[ \frac{1}{1 + \dfrac{q}{q^2 - 2p}} \right] \tag{50.4}$$

Since $0 \le p \le q - 1$, the limit of this ratio as $q \to \infty$ is 2.

Note also for large $q$, the sum of the first $\frac{1}{2}q(q + 1)$ Connell numbers divided by the sum of the first $\frac{1}{2}q(q + 1)$ integers also tends to 2. To be more precise, note that

$$\sum_{n=1}^{n = \frac{1}{2}q(q+1)} u_n = \frac{1}{12} q(q + 1)(3q^2 - q + 4) \tag{50.5}$$

Let $S_q = 1 + 2 + 3 + \cdots + \frac{1}{2}q(q + 1)$, i.e., $S_q$ is the sum of all integers from 1 to $\frac{1}{2}q(q + 1)$. Then

$$S_q = \frac{1}{2} \left[ \frac{1}{2} q(q + 1) \right]\left[ \frac{1}{2} q(q + 1) + 1 \right] \tag{50.6}$$

$$= \frac{1}{8} q(q + 1)(q^2 + q + 2) \tag{50.7}$$

Therefore,

$$\frac{\displaystyle\sum_{n=1}^{n = \frac{1}{2}q(q+1)} u_n}{S_q} = \frac{2}{3} \frac{3q^2 - q + 4}{q^2 + q + 2} \tag{50.8}$$

$$= \frac{2}{3} \left[ 3 - \frac{2(2q + 1)}{q^2 + q + 2} \right] \tag{50.9}$$

In the limit $q \to \infty$, this ratio also goes to 2.

**For Further Reading**

1.  Lakhtakia, A., Pickover, C. (1990) The Connell number sequence. *Journal of Recreational Math.*, in press.

2.  Lakhtakia, A., Varandan, V.K., Varandan, V.V. (1988) On Connell Arrays. In Arkiv fur Elektronische Ubertsangung (*Archive for Electronics and Communication*). Hirzel-Verlag: Stuttgart. pp. 186-189

3.  Connell, I. (1960) An unusual sequence. *American Math. Monthly.* 67: 380.

## 50.3  Pair Square Numbers

Numbers such as 4, 9, and 25 are called square numbers because $2^2 = 4$, $3^2 = 9$, and $5^2 = 25$. There exist certain *pairs* of numbers which when added or subtracted give a square number. For example, 10 and 26 are pair squares since 10 + 26 = 36 (a square number), and 26 - 10 = 16 (a square number). Stated mathematically, $n$ and $p$ are pair squares if

$$n - p = \alpha^2 \tag{50.10}$$

and

$$n + p = \beta^2 \tag{50.11}$$

where $\alpha$ and $\beta$ are integers. This section indicates interesting patterns in the *pair squares* and also provides you a simple computer program with which to generate these numbers.

How are pair squares distributed? Figure 50.4 lists several pair squares, denoted by $N$ and $P$. These were generated using the program code in Pseudocode 50.1. Figure 50.5 shows pair squares for ($0 \leq n,p \leq 1000$). The distribution is symmetric about the line $n = p$, and the lower part is not plotted. The straight line of points at $n = p$ corresponds to

$$n = \frac{\beta^2}{2}. \tag{50.12}$$

Other curves seen in the plot correspond to equations such as $n^2 - p^2 = \alpha^2\beta^2$.

[[ The program code in Pseudocode 50.1 is a fairly traditional way of finding pair squares (e.g., see Spencer (1982)). Interestingly, one can reduce the search space and computation time significantly. This is accomplished by solving for $n$ and $p$ and noting that we only need to examine pairs of integers whose difference is even.

$$n = \frac{\alpha^2 + \beta^2}{2} \tag{50.13}$$

and

$$p = \frac{-\alpha^2 + \beta^2}{2} \tag{50.14}$$

| n | p | | n | p |
|---|---|---|---|---|
| 4 | 5 | | 22 | 122 |
| 6 | 10 | | 24 | 25 |
| 8 | 17 | | 24 | 40 |
| 10 | 26 | | 24 | 145 |
| 12 | 13 | | 26 | 170 |
| 12 | 37 | | 28 | 53 |
| 14 | 30 | | 28 | 197 |
| 16 | 20 | | 30 | 34 |
| 16 | 65 | | | |
| 18 | 82 | | | |
| 20 | 29 | | | |
| 20 | 101 | | | |

**Figure 50.4.** *Pair squares.*

Note that $\beta^2 - \alpha^2 = 2p$, and hence must be even. Note also that $\beta - \alpha$ must be even. (If $\beta - \alpha$ were odd, $\beta^2 - \alpha^2$ would be odd.) Therefore, we can generate values for $n$ and $p$ from $\alpha, \delta$ values where $\beta = \alpha + 2\delta$. A faster program to compute all $n,p$ with $n \leq 1000$ is shown in Pseudocode 50.1. This faster version was developed by M. Gursky. ]]

### For Further Reading

1.  Spencer, D. (1982) *Computers in Number Theory*. Computer Science Press: Maryland.

2.  Pickover, C., Gursky, M. (1991) Pair square numbers. *Journal of Recreational Math.*, in press.

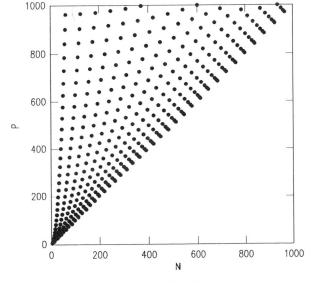

Distribution of Double Squares

**Figure 50.5.** *Pair squares.* These are for $(0 \leq n,p \leq 1000)$. The distribution is symmetric about the line $n = p$, and the lower part is not plotted.

---

ALGORITHM: Generate Pair Square Numbers

```
do p = 0 to 1000
  do n = p+1 to 1000
    root1 = sqrt(n+p)
    root2 = sqrt(n-p)
    if (root1 = trunc(root1)) & (root2 = trunc(root2)) then
      say p n
  end;
end;
```

---

**Pseudocode 50.1.** *How to generate pair square numbers less than 1000.*

## 50.4 Partition Graphs for Consecutive Integer Sums

*"Mathematical aesthetics seems more closely aligned with dance than with any time-invariant media."*                Clem Padin, *Science News*

This section describes a simple graphics technique allowing you to visualize partitions of integers. If you are not interested in technical mathematics, you may wish to skip this chapter. To help you understand the *theory of partitions*, pick an integer, for example "4." *Partitions* of 4 specify the number of ways you can sum integers to produce 4. For example, $p(4) = 5$ since $(4 = 4)$, $(4 = 1 + 3)$, $(4 = 1 + 1 + 2)$, $(4 = 1 + 1 + 1 + 1)$, and $(4 = 2 + 2)$. This problem is equivalent to finding the number of different ways in which four objects can be grouped in a row (Figure 50.6).

Given the integer $\alpha$ we say that a sequence of positive integers $n_1, n_2, \ldots, n_r$, $n_1 \le n_2 \le \cdots \le n_r$, is a *partition* of $\alpha$ if $\alpha = n_1 + n_2 + \cdots + n_r$. Let $p(\alpha)$ denote the number of partitions of $n$. In the previous paragraph I showed you why $p(4) = 5$. I am interested in the more specific problem of finding *all* series of *consecutive* positive integers whose sum is $\alpha$, where $\alpha$ is a positive integer. (I seek a partition of $\alpha$ into consecutive integers.)

As an example, there are four partitions of 10,000 into consecutive integers: $[18 + 19 + \ldots + 142]$, $[297 + 298 + \ldots + 328]$, $[388 + 389 + \ldots + 412]$, and $[1998 + 1999 + \ldots + 2002]$. $P_c(\alpha) = 4$. Figure 50.7 is a graphical representation of the distribution of all such sequences for $1 \le \alpha \le 200$. The $x$-axis contains the $\alpha$ values, and the runs of dots along the vertical $y$ direction indicate the partitions for these $\alpha$ values. (Note: this is not a plot of $\alpha$ vs $P_c(\alpha)$ but a plot of $\alpha$ vs all connsecutive partions of $\alpha$). The graph shows a number of interesting features. For example, notice, as expected, the dots never exceed $\frac{1}{2}\alpha + 1$ since the largest value possible in a series of consecutive positive integers whose sum is $\alpha$ must be $\alpha/2 + 1$. Perhaps the most apparent feature on the graph is the rising (diagonal) 2-dot cluster at the top of the graph. These dots correspond to odd values of $\alpha$ which always have $[\frac{1}{2}(\alpha + 1)] + [\frac{1}{2}(\alpha + 1) - 1]$ as a partition. For example,

```
ALGORITHM: Faster Program Code for Pair Squares
```
Note that the limits 31 and 22 can be more generally expressed as:
$a = \mathrm{trunc}(\sqrt{1000}\,)$, $d = \mathrm{trunc}(\sqrt{1000/2}\,)$.

```
do a=0 to 31
   do d=0 to 22
      b = a + 2*d
      n = (b*b + a*a)/2
      if n > 1000 then leave loop d
      p = (b*b - a*a)/2
      say p n
   end
end
```

**Pseudocode 50.2.** *How to quickly generate pair squares less than 1000.*

$$21 = \sum_{10}^{11} n. \tag{50.15}$$

Prime number values for $\alpha$ have this kind of binary partition and no others. The diagonal line of tri plet-dots in the graph represents values of $\alpha$ evenly divisible by 3, which always have as a partition $(n/3 - 1) + n/3 + (n/3 + 1)$. Interestingly, magnification of the graph reveals gaps where no parti-

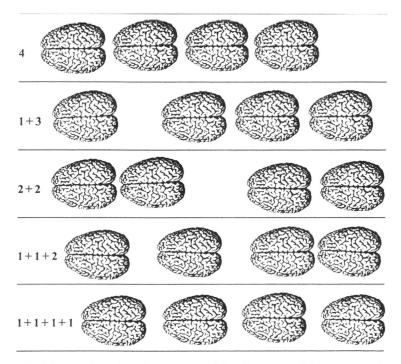

**Figure 50.6.** *The partition function.* The partition function, $p(n)$, is the number of distinct ways in which $n$ can be written as a sum of smaller or equal integers. For example, 4 can be expressed in five different ways. Hence, $p(4) = 5$. The problem is equivalent to finding the number of different ways in which four objects can be grouped in a row.

```
ALGORITHM: Compute Partition Graph for Consecutive Integer Sums
Input:
        start -    the smallest alpha value shown on the x-axis
        stop  -    the largest alpha value shown on the x-axis
scale = 100/stop;        /* this scales the x-axis for the plot */
DO alpha= start to stop;/* scan a range of alpha values         */
   looptop=alpha/2+1;     /* need to scan only to half of alpha  */
   DO i = 1 to looptop; /* search for consec. partitions for    */
   sum=0; top=i;        /*    a particular alpha value           */
   again:  sum = sum + top;
   top = top + 1;
   if sum < alpha then goto again;
   if sum = alpha then do;
      /*print out lower and upper values*/
      PrintNumbers(alpha,i,top-1);
      DO k = i to top-1;
         PlotDotAt(alpha*scale,k*scale); /* plot a dot at x,y */
      END; /*k*/
   END;    /* i */
END; /*start to end*/
```

**Pseudocode 50.3.** *How to compute a partition graph.*

tions exist. These occur at $\alpha = 2^m$, $m = 1,2, \dots$ . I urge you to find other interesting properties of the partitioning of $\alpha$ into consecutive integers by studying the graph.

As a final observation, note that since

$$\sum_1^t n = \frac{t(t+1)}{2} \tag{50.16}$$

we can express consecutive integer partitions in terms of the lower ($l$) and upper ($u$) value in the summation: $\frac{1}{2}u(u+1) - \frac{1}{2}l(l+1) + l = \alpha$. This means that values of $l$ and $u$ must lie on a hyperbolic curve of the form

$$u^2 - l^2 + u + l = 2\alpha. \tag{50.17}$$

For example, for $\alpha = 21 = 11 + 10$ we obtain $121 - 100 + 11 + 10 = 42$. Figure 50.8 shows a hyperbolic distribution for all lower and upper bounds for nearby $\alpha$ values ($95 \le \alpha \le 100$). When placed in a standard form, it becomes easier to see that Equation (50.17) represents a hyperbola shifted in the $x$ and $y$ axes

$$\frac{(u + \frac{1}{2})^2}{2\alpha} - \frac{(l - \frac{1}{2})^2}{2\alpha} = 1 \tag{50.18}$$

with distance from its center to focus equal to $\sqrt{4\alpha}$ and with an asymptote slope of 1.

I urge you to experiment with similar graphs for consecutive multiplied integers. For example, if $\alpha = 30$, then one such product is

$$\prod_5^6 n = 30. \tag{50.19}$$

To encourage your involvement, pseudocode is given for constructing the graph in Figure 50.7 and for partitioning $\alpha$ into consecutive integers. I thank Dr. Pratap Pattnaik (IBM) for useful discussions.

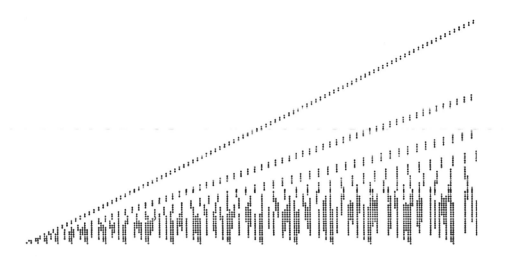

**Figure 50.7.** *Partition of alpha into consecutive integers.* This graphical representation shows the distribution of the partitions for $1 \leq \alpha \leq 200$ on the *x*-axis. The *y*-axis goes from 0 to 100.

## For Further Reading

1.  Herstein, I. (1975) *Topics in Algebra, 2nd Edition.* John Wiley: New York. Also: Andrews, G. (1976) The theory of partitions. (Volume 2 of *Encyclopedia of Mathematics and Its Applications*, Turan, P. ed.) Addison-Wesley: Massachusetts.

2.  Pickover, C. (1991) Partition graphs for consecutive integer sums, *Journal of Recreational Math*, in press.

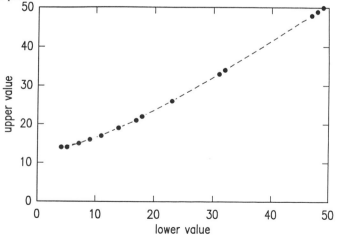

Hyperbolic Distribution for Upper and Lower Values

**Figure 50.8.** *Hyperbolic distribution for all lower and upper bounds* (for nearby $\alpha$ values ($95 \leq \alpha \leq 100$)).

# Chapter 51

# Million-Point Sculptures

*"If Leonardo da Vinci were alive today, would he forsake canvas and brush
for a computer terminal? "* 
Bob Berger, 1990

Would Leonardo dabble with fractal and chaotic graphics if he were alive today?
I think he would, and particularly with those graphics which lead to forms resembling sculpture. In this chapter, I'll show you how to create your own pointillist
"sculptures." I call them million-point sculptures because they contain precisely 1
million tiny dots – no more, no less.

Here my purpose is to illustrate some simple new algorithms whereby artistic
chaotic patterns can be clearly visualized. These computer-generated sculptures
represent mathematical objects called *attractors*, and they are scattered
throughout the book at the beginning of many of the chapters. Other chapters in
this book give a background to attractors and chaos (for example, "The Ikeda
Attractor" on page 115).

After experimenting on the computer for an hour, I finally chose the algorithms in this chapter because they exhibit mathematically complicated behavior,
but for convenience, they also require only simple numerical operations. [[ These
two properties are present in functions of two real discrete variables defined
implicitly by the recurrence:

$$x_{m+1} = F(x_m, y_m) \quad m = 1,2,3, \ldots \tag{51.1}$$

$$y_{m+1} = G(x_m, y_m) \quad m = 1,2,3, \ldots \tag{51.2}$$

You can interpret the previous equations as a mapping of a surface onto itself.
Starting from a single initial point $(x_0, y_0)$ the successive iterates $(x_m, y_m)$ are generated.

In particular, the figures show typical patterns obtained for two simple forms
of $F$ and $G$.

$$X_{m+1} = \sum_{n=1}^{\infty} \sin^n \beta_n f_n(x,y) \tag{51.3}$$

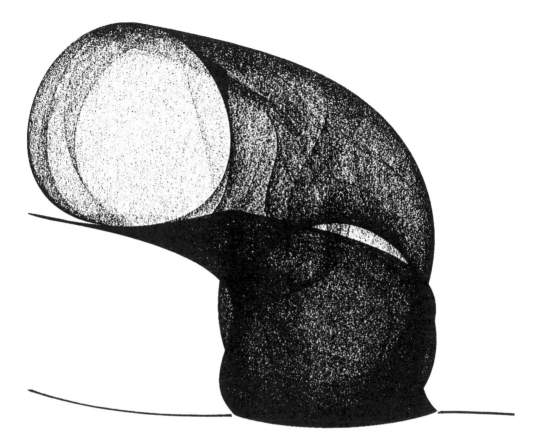

**Figure 51.1.** *A million-point sculpture.* Other sculptures generated using the methods outlined in this chapter are presented in the large chapter frontispieces throughout the book.

$$Y_{m+1} = \sum_{n=1}^{\infty} \sin^n \alpha_n f_n(y,x) \qquad (51.4)$$

where $f(u,v) = lu + (1 - l)v$, and $l$ is either 0 or 1. For simplicity, $(\alpha_n, \beta_n)$ can be integer constants. Therefore the subscripts for $\alpha$ and $\beta$ are henceforth eliminated. For the figures in this chapter, only a few terms of the summation series were used. Let me make the above equations a little more clear to you. Here is how some of them look when the terms are written out more fully:

$$x_{m+1} = \sin(y_m\beta) + \sin^2(x_m\beta),$$
$$y_{m+1} = \sin(x_m\alpha) + \sin^2(y_m\alpha) \qquad (51.5)$$

$$x_{m+1} = \sin(y_m\beta) + \sin^2(x_m\beta) + \sin^3(x_m\beta),$$
$$y_{m+1} = \sin(x_m\alpha) + \sin^2(y_m\alpha) + \sin^3(y_m\beta) \tag{51.6}$$

$$x_{m+1} = \sin(y_m\beta) + \sin^2(x_m\beta) + \sin^3(x_m\beta),$$
$$y_{m+1} = \sin(x_m\alpha) + \sin^2(y_m\alpha) + \sin^3(y_m\alpha) \tag{51.7}$$

$$x_{m+1} = \sin(y_m\beta) + \sin^2(x_m\beta) + \sin^3(x_m\beta),$$
$$y_{m+1} = \sin(x_m\alpha) + \sin^2(y_m\beta) + \sin^3(y_m\beta) \tag{51.8}$$

I have found these simple mappings of a surface onto itself particularly useful in demonstrating chaos and producing artistic sculpture-like forms. ]] Start by selecting an initial point, for example (20,30), and then iterate the equations 1 million times. For each repetition, leave a single point on the graphics screen. Note that if the dynamical system producing the figures leads to random output, then the plot would be a diffuse random scattering of points in 2-space. If the system were absolutely periodic (like a sine wave), then the figure would consist of a thin curve in 2-space. These curves are delicately poised somewhere between the two extremes and have a potential infinity of values. Although I have started with $(x_0, y_0) = (20,30)$, I find that the starting point makes little difference; this indicates that the resulting figures are attractors for the dynamical behavior. Also, the attractor is very rapidly approached so that phase portraits computed using the first 1000 points look like light and airy versions of the sculptures shown here. The point $(x_0, y_0 = 0)$ is a fixed point. [[ When $\alpha = \beta = 1$, points of the form

$$(x_0, y_0 = m\pi, m = 0,1,2, \dots) \tag{51.9}$$

map to zero – so these will not produce interesting patterns. If $\alpha = \beta$ we have the interesting map symmetry:

$$M(x,y) = M\left( x + \frac{2i\pi}{\beta}, y + \frac{2j\pi}{\beta} \right), \quad i = 0,1,2, \dots, j = 0,1,2, \dots \tag{51.10}$$

This means, for example, that the point (.1, .4) will map to the same point as $(.1 + 2i\pi, .4 + 2i\pi)$ maps. Moreover, if we represent the cartesian plane by a checkerboard whose squares are $2\pi/\beta$ in length, each square on the checkerboard maps to the same region. ]]

Simple rational ratios of $\alpha/\beta$ such as 2/1 or 1/1 produce aesthetically pleasing plots. Computation time varied between 8 seconds on an IBM RISC System/6000 to a minute or two on a Stellar GS 2000 or Silicon Graphics IRIS 4D/120GTX).

## For Further Reading

1.  Gleick, J. (1987) *Chaos: Making a New Science*. Viking: New York.

2.  Moon, F. (1987) *Chaotic Vibrations*. John Wiley and Sons, New York. (Moon gives many practical examples of chaos in real physical systems.)

3.  Shaw, A. (1984) *The Dripping Faucet as a Model Chaotic System*. Aerial Press: California.

4.  Chossat, P., Golubitsky, M. (1988) Symmetry-increasing bifurcations of chaotic attractors. *Physica D* 32: 423-426.

5.  Pickover, C. (1991) Million point sculptures. *Algorithm*. January issue. pgs. 11-12.

# Chapter 52

# Continued Roots in the Complex Plane

*"Our story has a silent and immobile hero: the digital computer. There can be little doubt that computers have acted as the most forceful forceps in extracting fractals from the dark recesses of abstract mathematics and delivering their geometrical intricacies into broad daylight."*

Manfred Schroeder, *1989*

Several chapters in this book, such as "A Pattern Based on the Mandelbrot Set" on page 267, have described the striking beauty and complexity of patterns resulting from iterative calculations and fractal theory. In order to make these kinds of patterns, your computer program repeats a mathematical operation over and over again. Simple iterated functions discussed in the literature naturally lead to curiosity about the behavior of more complicated, weirder functions. See *Glossary* for a description of the technical terms and concepts in this chapter. Dr. Lakhtakia and I have found of particular visual interest the stability plots for

$$z \rightarrow \sin(z + f^n(z)) \tag{52.1}$$

where $z$ is a complex variable, $f^n(z)$ is a continued root, and $n$ is the number of terms used in the nesting. As with other systems in this book, this equation represents a mathematical feedback loop. You start with an initial value of $z$, compute a new value, and use this new value as input to the equation again. Repeat this process many times. Let me give some background information so that you can fully appreciate Equation (52.1). Infinitely nested square roots, also known as *continued square roots*, are expressions of the form:

$$\sqrt{x_1 + \sqrt{x_2 + \sqrt{x_3 + \cdots}}} \tag{52.2}$$

and formulas such as these have sometimes appeared in the mathematics literature. For example, Ramanujan in the *Indian Journal of Mathematics* presented the following interesting equation

$$3 = \sqrt{1 + 2\sqrt{1 + 3\sqrt{1 + 4\sqrt{1 + \cdots}}}} \tag{52.3}$$

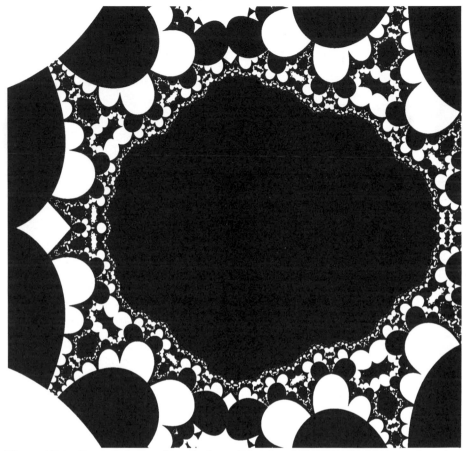

**Figure 52.1.** *Continued root fractal.* A traditional stability plot for the complex plane where $f^n(z)$ is a continued square root, and $n = 1$.

In particular, we focus on the function defined recursively by

$$f^{n+1} = \sqrt{z + f^n(z)} \ , n > 1 \tag{52.4}$$

with the initiator

$$f^1(z) = \sqrt{z} \tag{52.5}$$

Line 5 in Pseudocode 52.1 makes the meaning of this clear. Note that in the limit $n \to \infty$, $f^n(z)$ will be a solution of the quadratic $(f^\infty)^2 - f^\infty - z = 0$.

We present Julia sets for Equation (52.1). Other chapters in this book give background information to Julia sets. Figure 52.1 shows a traditional stability plot for the complex plane where $f^n(z)$ is a continued square root, and $n = 1$. The rate at which the iteration explodes is represented in alternating black and white contours. The picture boundaries are ( $-0.67$, 2, $-1.2$, 1.2) (expressed as minima and maxima in the real and imaginary directions). Figure 52.2 is the same as

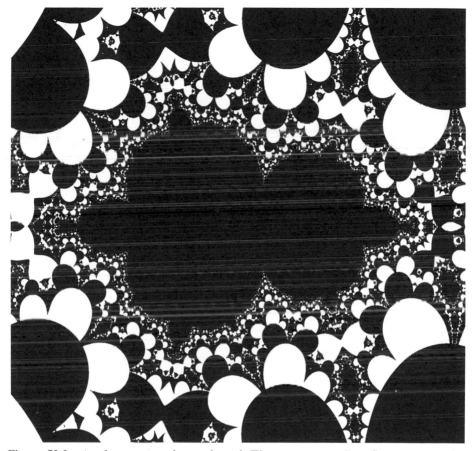

**Figure 52.2.** *Another continued root fractal.* The same as previous figure, except that $n = 3$.

Figure 52.1, except that $n = 3$. Notice that the central body (representing those initial points whose trajectories are bounded) shrinks as $n$ grows larger. The dynamical system behavior is of interest: Figure 52.3 shows a streamline representation for the flow field for $n = 1$. (The flow field is composed of a vector at each starting point indicating the direction the starting point moves.) The picture boundaries are ($-8, 8, -8, 8$). [[ Attractive and repulsive fixed points are clearly seen. Two unstable centers can be seen off the real axis. The real axis is an invariant manifold (points on the real axis line stay on the line). The origin is a fixed point because $\sin(0) = 0$. These well-behaved streamlines belie the chaotic trajectories in this discrete system.

I invite you to experiment with additional examples. For example, consider

$$f^{n+1}(z,m) = \left[\alpha_{n+1}z + f^n(z,m)\right]^{1/m}, n > 1 \tag{52.6}$$

$$f^1(z,m) = \left[\alpha_1 z\right]^{1/m} \tag{52.7}$$

**Figure 52.3.** *Continued root fractal.* A streamline representation for the flow field for $n = 1$.

where $\alpha$ may be complex. A further generalization is

$$f^{n+1}(z,m) = \left[ P_{n+1}(z) + f^n(z,m) \right]^{1/m}, n > 1 \qquad (52.8)$$

$$f^1(z,m) = \left[ P_1(z) \right]^{1/m}. \qquad (52.9)$$

where the polynomials $P_n(z)$ can be of arbitrary order. ]]

## 52.1 Recipe

In order to encourage your involvement, Pseudocode 52.1 gives an algorithmic recipe. Typical parameter constants are given within the code. I encourage you to modify the equations to create a variety of patterns of your own design. For each picture there are roughly 400 million $z$-squared operations (2000 x 2000 x 100 iterations). *You need not create the picture with such a high resolution and iteration* in order to get a visually interesting plot. Divergence tests generally follow the value of $z$ as a function is iterated. The position of $z$ in the $z$-plane after $N$ iterations determines whether or not a dot is printed in the central form on the graphics screen. Usually if $z$ grows very large, the results are considered to have

```
ALGORITHM: Continued Root Fractals
/* Pseudocode For calculation of continued-root Julia Sets    */

/* Variables: rz, iz = real, imag component of complex number */
/*             i = iteration counter                          */
/*           u, z = complex numbers                           */

/* real axis divided into 2000 pixels   */
1 DO rz = -1 to 1 by .001;
  /* imag. axis divided into 2000 pixels */
2 DO iz = 1 to 1 by .001;
3  InnerLoop: DO i = 1 to 100;  /* iteration loop            */
4   z = cplx(rz,iz);            /* cplx returns complex number */
/* The folowing line is the main computation; here the nesting */
/* is 3 deep.  Try fewer or greater terms and view the results.*/
5   z = sin(z+sqrt(z+sqrt(z+ sqrt(z))));
    /* convert to real and imag component */
6   rrz = real(z); iiz = imag(z);
7   if sqrt(rrz**2 + iiz**2) > 10 then leave InnerLoop;
8  END;                         /* InnerLoop                 */
   /* If i is evenly divisible by 2, plot a black dot.   This */
   /* creates alternating black and white contour lines.     */
9  if mod(i,2) = 0 then PrintDoLAt(rz,iz);
10 END;                         /* iz loop                   */
11 END;                         /* rz loop                   */
```

**Pseudocode 52.1.** *How to create continued root fractals.*

diverged, and no dot is printed. You can create visually interesting strips by using line 9 in the pseudocode.

## 52.2  For Further Reading

1.  Julia, G. (1918) Memoire sur l'iteration des fonctions rationnelles, *Journal of Math. Pure Appl.* 4, 47-245.

2.  Mandelbrot, B. (1983) *The Fractal Geometry of Nature.* Freeman: San Francisco.

3.  Sizer, W. (1986) Continued Roots. *Mathematics Magazine.* 59(1): 23-27.

4.  Hardy, G., Aiyar, S, Wilson, B. (1962) *Collected Papers of Srinivasa Ramanujan,* Chelsea Pub. Co., New York. p. 323.

5.  Pickover, C., Lakhtakia, A. (1991) Continued roots in the complex plane. *Journal of Recreational Math.*, in press.

# Chapter 53

# Picturing Spherical Lissajous Figures

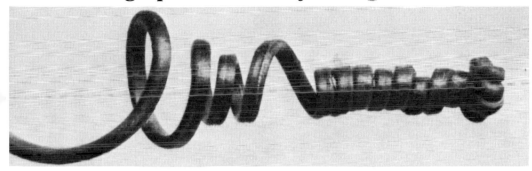

In this chapter, I urge you to create some fascinating and exquisite computer graphics images called spherical Lissajous figures. In 1857, the French mathematician Jules A. Lissajous first described these kinds of sinusoidal figures that today parade on the screens of oscilloscopes. A single Lissajous curve is traced out on the screen by a bright dot that moves up and down and side to side any number of times. It usually returns to its starting point. The classic Lissajous figures in physics can be obtained by

$$x = A_x \cos(\omega_x t + \delta) \tag{53.1}$$

$$y = A_y \cos(\omega_y t + \alpha) \tag{53.2}$$

$A$ is the amplitude, and $\alpha$ and $\delta$ are the phases of the sinusoids. If $\omega_x/\omega_y$ is a *rational* number (a number which can be expressed by the quotient of integers such as ½, so that the angular frequencies $\omega_x$ and $\omega_y$ are commensurable), then the curve is closed and the motion repeats itself at regular intervals of time.

My favorites are the spherical Lissajous curves. Spherical Lissajous figures have the same properties as their two-dimensional relatives, except that they lie on the surface of a sphere. To represent this three-dimensional curve you need three separate equations:

$$x = r \sin(\theta t) \cos(\phi t) \tag{53.3}$$

$$z = r \cos(\theta t) \tag{53.4}$$

$$y = r \sin(\theta t) \sin(\phi t) \tag{53.5}$$

These curves lie on the surface of a sphere of radius $r$ and exhibit closure when $\theta/\phi$ is rational. If $\theta/\phi$ is not rational then after a long time the curve will have passed through every point lying on the surface of the sphere. *Computers, Pattern, Chaos, and Beauty* showed some shaded 3-D sculptures based on these curves. Here I'd like to show some simple line drawings which would be easier for most personal computer users to produce. For added beauty, a second higher frequency curve winds about the initial Lissajous figure. You can best understand

**Figure 53.1.** *Spherical Lissajous figure with winding curve.* The parameters needed to reproduce this figure are given within Pseudocode 53.1.

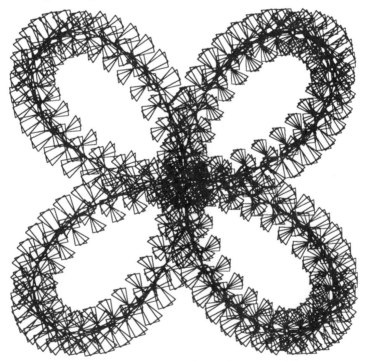

**Figure 53.2.** *Spherical Lissajous figure with winding curve.* The parameters needed to reproduce this figure are given within Pseudocode 53.1.

**Figure 53.3.** *Spherical Lissajous figure with winding curve.* The parameters needed to reproduce this figure are similar to those given within Pseudocode 53.1.

how Figure 53.1, Figure 53.2, and Figure 53.3 were generated by studying the program code in Pseudocode 53.1. Can you use Lissajous curves to model the growth of the pumpkin tendrils shown at the beginning of this chapter?

```
ALGORITHM: Spherical Lissajous figure with winding curve.

pi =3.1415926;
/* Typical Constants: */
theta = 30; phi = 12; rep = 20; r=20; r2 = 2;
theta = 60; phi = 30; rep = 20; r=20; r2 = 3;
/* Convert from degrees to radians */
theta = theta*(pi/180); phi = phi*(pi/180);

/* primary curve about which the other one winds */
do t = 0 to rep*pi by .01;
    x = r*sin(theta*t)*cos(phi*t) +50;
    z = r*cos(theta*t) +50;
    y = r*sin(theta*t)*sin(phi*t) +50;
    if (t = 0) then MovePen(x,y);
            else DrawPen(x,y);
end;

/* add 2nd wrapping curve to first curve */
do t = 0 to rep*pi by .01;
    x =  r2*sin(100*theta*t)*cos(100*phi*t)
       + r*sin(theta*t)*cos(phi*t) +50;
    z = r2*cos(100*theta*t)
       + r*cos(theta*t) +50;
    y = r2*sin(100*theta*t)*sin(100*phi*t)
       +  r *sin(theta*t)*sin(phi*t)+50;
    if (t = 0) then MovePen(x,y);
            else DrawPen(x,y);
end;
```

**Pseudocode 53.1.** *How to create spherical Lissajous figures with winding curves.* The figure is projected onto the *xy* plane, since *z* is ignored during the plotting. The screen is assumed to go from 0 to 100 in both the *x* and *y* directions. Therefore "50" is added to each of the curves in order to center the picture.

Chapter 54

# Interlude: Fractal Faces

As mentioned in "Computers and the Unexpected" on page 3, many visual artists are inspired by concepts such as fractals, scaling, repetition, and recursion — even if they do not work with a computer. Here, Warren Satter's fantastic "Fractal Faces" were molded with clay, or printed using a wood cutting. In Satter's art, there are often faces within faces, inside-out people, multiple recursive faces, and smaller and smaller people inhabiting facial orifices. For more information: Warren Satter, 7 Royal Place, Elberon, New Jersey 07740.

# Part VI

# INVENTION

I WISH WE HAD A COMPUTER
TO WORK THIS OUT FOR US.

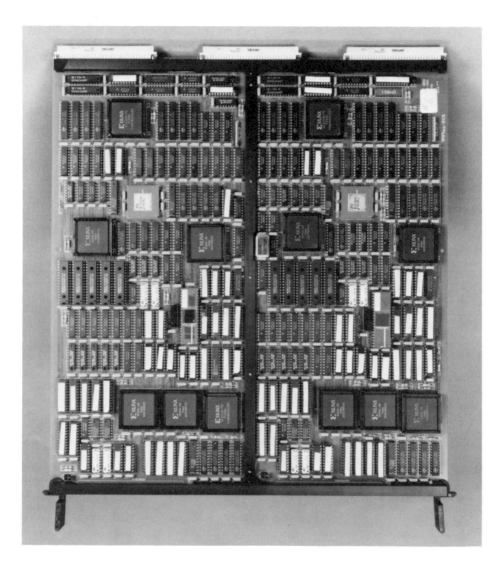

# Chapter 55

# Invention: Introduction

*"Lest humans think they have a monopoly on creative power, consider cloud formations, the spiral arms of galaxies, and the whorls and vortices that spring up spontaneously around a rock in a stream."*
Kathleen McAuliffe, *Get Smart: Controlling Chaos, 1989*

The act of creation is one of humankind's greatest gifts, and the computer is a machine which lets us realize our creative potential in ways not dreamed of only fifty years ago. As an example, the frontispiece for this chapter shows the hardware heart of one of my favorite recent inventions in the field of computer chess. The fully configured 24-processor machine can search around 10 million chess positions per second! As a comparison, Cray Blitz[42] searches at 1/40th the speed, or 250,000 positions per second, when running on a "top of the line" 8-processor Cray YMP general-purpose supercomputer.

I have personally been involved with hundreds of computer-related inventions, and some of the colorful or weird ones are briefly outlined in this part of the book.[43] Over the years I have had the good fortune of working with several creative colleagues who have added their wonderful ideas to many of the inventions which follow. Their names are mentioned in the *Acknowledgements* section of this book.

A quote from Mozart should help place you in the proper frame of mind for the inventions to come.

*"[The music] stands almost complete and finished in my mind, so that I can survey it, like a fine picture or a beautiful statue. All this inventing, this producing, takes place in a pleasingly lively dream."*
Mozart

---

[42] Cray Blitz is the name of the program that won the 4th and 5th World Computer Chess Championship in the early to middle 1980s. (Frontispiece figure courtesy of Feng-Hsiung Hsu, the developer of this hardware, IBM Watson Research Center.)

[43] See "Further Unusual Inventions" on page 391 for a partial list.

Chapter 56

# Self-Correcting Anti-Dyslexic Font

This chapter describes the invention of a font which may help people with learning disabilities, and also a changeable font which helps dyslexics. Note that this method, which represents a collaboration with Miriam Masullo of IBM, is speculative; however, it is hoped that this will stimulate other researchers to extend and further test this technique in order to assess its usefulness.

## 56.1 Background

Five to ten percent of school-age children are dyslexic. This neurologically-based reading disorder is manifest, in part, by the inability to differentiate certain subtle spatial relationships in the characters of written language. For English, this includes confusion of directional orientation in letters such as "q" and "p," "b" and "d," "m" and "w," as well as "Z" and "N." Note that these letters can be related to each other by symmetry transformations, such as rotation and mirroring.

In this invention, a new font is used which will induce certain asymmetries in hard-to-distinguish characters, such as those mentioned above, and I feel that our modified characters may enhance a dyslexic's ability to learn to read. We are developing this font by introducing new characters, and modifying them in order to arrive at a preliminary set that is accepted by the spatial dyslexic without ambiguity. The following are example asymmetries in our new font.

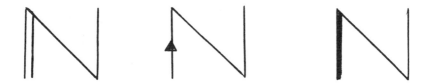

Note that in certain pictorial languages such as Japanese, dyslexia does not exist. This may be due, in part, to the fact that no character can be translated to another by simple symmetry operations.

## 56.2 A Temporal-Font

Our font will "correct" itself through time. In other words, deviations from a normal font will decrease as the child works with the language. For example, the letters which contain thickened parts will become gradually less thick. Certain serifs or balls can become smaller over the course of training. Also, the use of colors can be introduced to help differentiate confusing letters.

## 56.3 Stop and Think

In 1990, researchers showed that many children with dyslexia can improve their reading comprehension by placing plastic overlays tinted blue or gray atop the pages they are reading. Can you expand on this idea with an invention that involves the display of computer text on a blue background or with controllable shades of a blue font?

## 56.4 For Further Reading

1. Pickover, C., Massullo, M., Ennis, R. (1989) Self-correcting anti-dyslexic font. *IBM Technical Disclosure Bulletin.* November 32(6B): 131-132.

2. Pontius, A. (Harvard Medical School) Geometric figure-rotation task and face representations in dyslexia: role of spatial relations and orientation. *Perceptual and Motor Skills.* 1981, 53, 607-614.

3. Weiss, R. (1990) Dyslexics read better with the blue. *Science News.* Sept. 138(13): 196.

Chapter 57

# Speech Synthesis Grenade

Jungle warfare amidst the hot, mosquito-infested swamps is always unpleasant, and troops often go to great lengths to surprise, confuse, and camouflage themselves from the enemy. This invention describes a method which may be of some use to militarists, but which also has various peace-time applications. The *speech-synthesis "grenade"* (SSG) has several purposes. Aside from the primary military application, it is a device useful for dissemination of spoken information in hard-to-reach places. It consists of a speech synthesizer and casing. To this device you may optionally couple a heat and/or motion detector for reasons discussed later. The term "grenade" is used only to imply the fact that the SSG is hand-held and sturdy, as well as the fact that it is to be thrown in many applications.

The SSG may be used in a variety of situations. In military operations, it can be used in the field to confuse the enemy. For example, in warfare it can be carried at a soldier's side and thrown or launched into the underbrush. Upon sensing motion, the SSG will speak loudly a limited number of utterances. This may aid in confusing the enemy about the actual location of the troops. Only an "on" button may be provided to confuse and demoralize the enemy once the SSG is discovered.

Peace-time uses of the SSG include the following:

1.  The dissemination of information in hard-to-reach places such as mineshafts.

2.  A beacon carried by campers, hikers, mountaineers, and rock climbers; the SSG would be programmed and left behind (or thrown) to give specific information about the owner.

3.  Propaganda dissemination, and crisis control. (A SWAT team may toss SSG into a hard-to-reach place to provide information and warnings to the criminal in the perpetration of a crime.) The shape of the SSG would depend on the particular use.

4.  Short instructions for equipment assembly (either for the military or civilians). Often it is easier to listen rather than read, and the hands and eyes are freed. In the dark, the SSG would be especially useful. Also, there are a great number of illiterates who would find the SSG useful.

ASSEMBLED TRANSPARENT VIEW

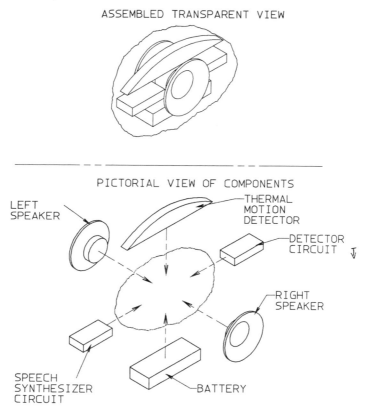

**Figure 57.1.** *Speech Synthesis Grenade.*

5. In the event of nuclear war, the SSG could be useful for information dissemination and may not be affected by the EMP interference produced by a nuclear explosion.

6. The SSG should be useful in other catastrophes such as floods or earthquakes. People buried under debris in collapsed buildings might be able to hear a dropped SSG.

## 57.1 Notes on Military Applications

In order to make the grenade sturdy and harder to defeat, the entire circuit is molded into the center of high-impact plastic. The outer shape resembles a rock, making it more difficult to localize visually.

I have done tests in which we have extracted just the prosody (pitch and duration) of sentences and find they are quite speech-like. With distance, the speech-like quality is enhanced. We therefore may need only to simulate the rhythm and inflections of speech, without the need for "real" digital recording. This may simplify the circuit and storage requirements.

We also employ *two opposed speakers* and generate varying out-of-phase (or time delayed) signals. This makes the SSG difficult to locate by ear.[44]

## 57.2  For Further Reading

1.  Sclater, N. (1983) *Introduction to Electronic Speech Synthesis*. Howard W. Sams & Co., Inc., Indiana.

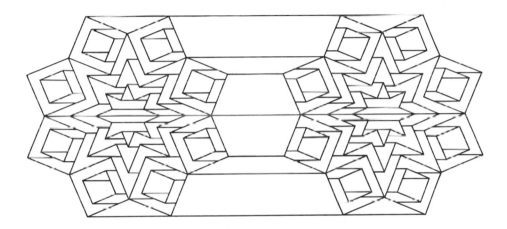

---

[44] **Implementation Details** - Many of you will want to skip this long footnote, since it contains highly technical details on the implementation of this device. Figure 57.1 shows a device consisting of two speakers, a battery, a thermal motion detector, a detector circuit, and a speech synthesizer circuit. The detector can be used to verify presence of a person within a specified radius. The detector circuit sends a signal to the speech synthesizer circuit which transfers digitally recorded sound to the speakers. The battery is used to supply power for this operation. The thermal motion detector is shown as a cut cylinder shape. Motion detection is accomplished by placing several small radius cylindrical detectors within this shape, pointing toward the outer radius. The detector circuit feeds a voltage to the detectors and waits for a change in the returned voltage. When the detector is triggered by warmth in its path, this circuit sends a current to the speech synthesizer circuit. The detector circuit continues to detect the presence of heat and turns the speech synthesizer circuit on and off accordingly. The speech synthesizer circuit is composed of an EPROM with the recorded audible utterances and a audio processor. When this circuit receives a signal, it retrieves data from the EPROM and converts this into audible sound to the speakers. The right speaker and the left speaker can receive data from separate parts of the EPROM memory. This circuit increments the memory address for retrieval and continues sending utterances to the speakers for as long as the detectors continue to detect presence or as long as the battery does not run out of power. "Incrementing" is purely for the purposes of multiple utterances. The covering material is ribbed to maintain strength around the speakers to prevent damage. The battery is the heaviest component and will keep the unit oriented with the battery down during flight. A parachute-type device or radio controlled balloon could also be added to further control position. This will also keep the detector facing up. Speaker redundancy also helps ensure sound dispersal in unknown environments with unknown blocking features such as trees and rocks. Another possible use for the speech grenade is to help troops locate the enemy troops by the sounds they trigger in the SSG. In this application, the phase-delayed presentation of sound to the speakers would not be used.

# Chapter 58

# Pictorial Password Systems

Many of the computer systems we use today require people to type in a secret password before the computer allows them to gain access, or "log on," to the system. This password consists of a special sequence of typed numbers and characters. In this chapter, an invention is described which presents a series of pictures for you to point at in order to log on to the computer. This takes the place of the standard passwords for a computer and does not even require you to have a terminal keyboard. Here's a common scenario. A computer terminal displays a complicated picture on the screen, and then you point to various parts in a particular sequence. An example pictorial password is the bridge scene in the frontispiece for this chapter and the photograph of faces at the end of the chapter. The sequence of pointing comprises a password. For example, 20 different images of human faces may be presented on the screen. You point to ten of them to gain access to a system. Note that the computer can present the twenty portraits in random order or positions during each log-on session. You can easily remember the password because the 10 faces you must choose can be faces you already know. Note that this provides a very secure system. No words are typed, nothing is written down – it is even difficult to intentionally disclose your password to another person. Even if a spy watches you as you enter your password, it is doubtful that this observer can repick 10 random faces from a line up of 20 random faces. Can you beat this with any typed password?

Another application involves the use of a scene to enter a password. A single complicated picture can be used from which the user picks certain parts (dog, man, barn). Or the user can point to a particular sequence of colors in a palate on the screen. Children, the illiterate, learning disabled, and dyslexics might use this. Quadriplegics would use this via a pointer in the mouth. This might be easier than typing. This pictorial password scheme may also be preferable to a keyboard password scheme in situations where the pictorial is readily accessible. It is easier to grab a joystick or other graphic input device in many cases, than to reach for a keyboard. Indeed, there are applications when a keyboard is inaccessible, or even totally removed from a system, and the only way to enter the password is through the pictorial. There are several other situations where this idea may be useful. For example, in medical operating theaters, the cockpit of an airplane, powerplants, cars, and large scale manufacturing. In demonstration settings (e.g. museum exhibits and shopping malls) there may be no keyboard available. It is possible that the gross movements required in a pictorial password are easier for people with certain manual dexterity deficits, since a keyboard password requires fine movements.

These pictorial passwords could allow "hidden passwords," where most users need not know that the picture can be used for password entry. While running a program the uninitiated user would do as suggested: select an option, hit enter to continue, etc. At this point, if a user were to point to parts of the picture in the password order, he could then enter a totally different part of the application program. Therefore this could be a good way to differentiate classes of users without letting one class of users even know about other classes of users.

## 58.1  Military Applications and Maps

Another application is in military intelligence. Your program would display a map of a battle zone. The person using it knows the pictorial password and enters it by pressing the different parts of the map in the correct sequence. After the password is entered, the map is refreshed and now shows where all of the troops are located. If an enemy stole the disk or cartridge and attempted to run the program, he would just assume it was an unfinished or useless piece of software and discard it without trying to break any codes.

It should be easier for the occasional user of a system to remember a picture instead of random numbers/letters that comprise traditional passwords. John Wilkins (IBM Crypto Competency Center, Manassas, Virginia) notes that if we were to consider an 8 x 8 grid of pictures, choosing 10 images in correct order would give $P(64,10) = 64!/54! = 5.5 \times 10^{17} > 2^{58}$ ordered combinations.

Chapter 59

# Interlude: Evolving Computers

Miniaturization of electronic components is responsible for sustained reduction in the cost of computing at a rate of 20 to 30 percent per year over a period of the last three decades. As these components shrink, the speed of operation increases proportionally, and the density of the elements per area of a chip rises geometrically. This chart shows the speed of computers extrapolated to the year 2020, at which point personal computers will be as fast as mainframes. Each of the bands defines a range of computing power in units of MIPS (millions of instructions per second). Obviously, we cannot be sure that speed increases will continue at current rates; however, miniaturization can be expected to continue at its current pace for another decade, and parallel processing in computing systems will also increase speeds for many applications for years to come.[45] The data for the chart in this interlude comes from: Peled, Λ. (1987) The next computer revolution. *Scientific American*. Oct 257(4): 57.

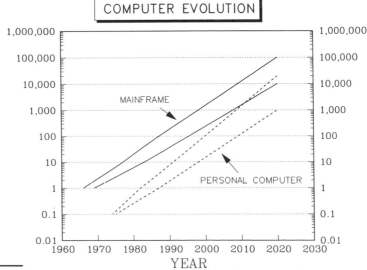

45 *Note*: Rough estimates suggest that an average small rodent is processing the computer equivalent of around 1000 MIPS per gram of brain mass.

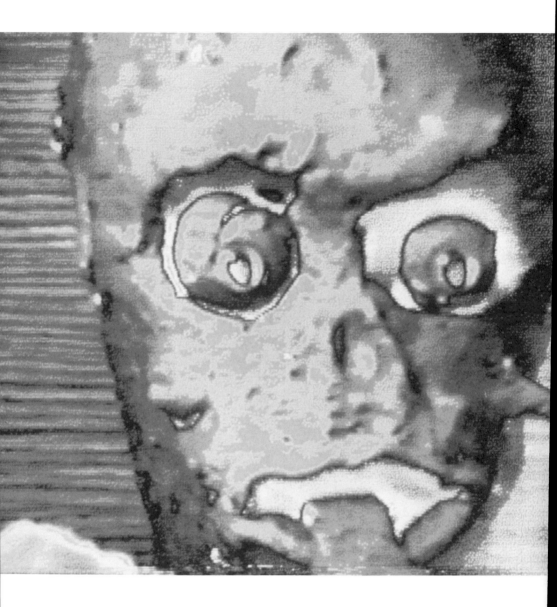

# Part VII

# IMAGINATION

*Religioso Svegliatore*

Chapter 60

# Computer-Generated Poetry

*"To me the neutrality of the machine is of great importance. It allows the spectator to find his own meanings in the association of words more easily, since their choice, size and disposition are determined at random. "*
Marc Adrian, 1968

*"Artificial Intelligence is the study of how to make computers do things at which, at the moment, people are better. "*
Elaine Rich

Experiments with the computer generation of poetry, Japanese haiku, and short stories provide a creative programming exercise for both beginning and advanced students. Computer-created poetry and text also provides a fascinating avenue for researchers interested in artificial intelligence – researchers who wish to "teach" the computer about beauty and meaning. You may wish to read about early work in the computer generation of poetry in Riechardt's book, *Cybernetic Serendipity.* Other past work includes the book *The Policeman's Beard is Half Constructed* – the first book ever written entirely by a computer. The program which generated the book was called RACTER and was written by W. Chamberlain and T. Etter.[46] Finally, there is the Kurzweil Cybernetic Poet, a computer poetry program which uses human-written poems as input to enable it to create new poems with word-sequence models based on the poems it has just read. When these computer poems are placed side by side with human poems, many humans can not judge which poems were made by humans and which by the Cybernetic Poet.

You will also find that computer-produced texts are a marvelous stimulus for the imagination when you are writing your own (non-computer generated) fictional stories and are searching for new ideas, images, and moods. If you are a visual artist in search of new subject matter, computer generated poems can

---

[46] Kurzweil, in *The Age of Thinking Machines*, comments about RACTER's book: "RACTER's prose has its charm, but is somewhat demented-sounding, due primarily to its rather limited understanding of what it is talking about."

*A Lost Sapphire*
A lost sapphire frowns at the thin kidney.
With a terrible shutter the sapphire runs.
The kidney squats in synchrony with a green unicorn.

*A Hungry Wizard*
A hungry wizard chatters far away from the dying tongue.
With great deliberation the wizard disintegrates.
The tongue oscillates above a milky limb.

*A Glass Centipede*
A glass centipede drools inches away from the shivering knuckle.
While feeding, the centipede regurgitates;
The knuckle shakes a million miles away from a buzzing flake.

*A Robotoid Wizard*
A robotoid wizard implodes on the back end of the blonde chasm.
While feeding, the wizard cries;
The chasm gyrates at the end of a crystalline prophet.

*A Wavering Kidney*
A wavering kidney disintegrates deep within the glistening wizard.
While shivering the kidney dances;
The wizard gesticulates at the tip of a dying avocado.

*A Fairylike Knuckle*
A fairylike knuckle yawns in harmony with the sensuous knuckle.
While waving its tentacles the knuckle runs;
The knuckle buzzes a million miles away from a black kidney.

*A Blonde Wizard*
A blonde wizard screams near the happy ellipse.
In mind-inflaming ecstasy, the wizard disintegrates;
The ellipse grows while grabbing at a lunar mountain.

*A Religious Ocean*
A religious ocean explodes far away from the percolating flame.
With great speed the ocean oscillates;
The flame phosphoresces while grabbing at a dying jello pudding.

*A Flying Knuckle*
A flying knuckle wanders on top of the glass unicorn.
With great speed the knuckle salivates;
The unicorn grasps while smoking a vibrating cow.

*A Glowing Tongue*
A glowing tongue laughs in spite of the wavering diamond.
Very slowly the tongue shines;
The diamond shines while crushing a frigid grasshopper.

**Figure 60.1.** *Several computer-generated poems.* (These poems were created by my program *Dreamscape*.)

*A Quivering Bone*
A quivering bone chews while touching the golden intestine.
With a terrible shutter the bone regurgitates;
The intestine yawns close to a sexy ellipse.

*A Glistening Web*
A glistening web gyrates while touching the skinny vacuum tube.
Stubbornly the web smiles,
The vacuum tube screams above a frost-encrusted jello pudding.

*A Half-Dead Avocado*
A half-dead avocado oozes while puffing the fairylike ocean.
In a frenzy the avocado grasps;
The ocean breathes while dreaming about a frigid diamond.

*A Sensuous Goose*
A sensuous goose disintegrates below the hungry ocean.
Stubbornly the goose shakes;
The ocean drools far away from a glittering knuckle.

*A Sexy Cloud*
A sexy cloud collapses while smoking the moldy soul.
Heavily the cloud frowns;
The soul evaporates behind a chocolate mouth.

*A Flawless Diamond*
A flawless diamond burns in synchrony with the lost goose.
While waving its tentacles the diamond shakes;
The goose gyrates deep within a green ellipse.

*A Religious Avocado*
A religious avocado gesticulates in between the chocolate grasshopper.
Grotesquely the avocado burns;
The grasshopper yawns while making love to a magnetic centipede.

*A Skinny Earthworm*
A skinny earthworm wriggles before the glittering brain.
Heavily the earthworm oozes;
The brain evolves while making love to a robotoid earthworm.

**Figure 60.2.** *Several computer-generated poems.*

provide a vast reservoir of original material. Let's end this short chapter with a
description of some simple programs for generating crude examples of computer
poetry. You can embellish the ideas here to create more sophisticated literary
pieces. The several sets of three-line computer poems in Figure 60.1 and in
Figure 60.2 were all generated by the random selection of words and phrases
which are then placed in a specific format, or "semantic schema." The program,
called *Dreamscape*, is written in the programming language PL/I, but you can
easily write a similar program in BASIC or the language of your choice. The
program starts by reading 30 different words in five different lists (or categories),

and storing these words in the program's memory arrays. The five categories are: adjectives, nouns, verbs, prepositional phrases, and adverbs. The program asks for a random number seed and the number of poems desired. The words are chosen and placed in the following *semantic schema*:

Poem Title: *A (adjective) (noun 1)*
*A (adjective) (noun 1) (verb) (preposition) the (adjective) (noun 2).*
*(Adverb) the (noun 1) (verb).*
*The (noun 2) (verb) (prep) a (adjective) (noun 3).*

The fact that "noun 1" and "noun 2" are used twice within the same poem produces a greater correlation – a cognitive harmony – giving the poem more meaning and solidity.

## 60.1  Stop and Think

If your computer has access to a thesaurus, you may induce further artificial meaning in the poems. This would be accomplished by using the thesaurus to force additional correlations and constraints on the chosen words. For example noun 1, noun 2, and noun 3 in the semantic schema here would all appear within the same thesaurus entry. You should also design your own semantic schema and use additional word lists. Try using probability matrices to produce the poetry. The matrices would consist of an array which makes your program more likely to pick certain combinations of words. Some entries in the matrix may be zero, which would disallow impossible combinations of words.

### For Further Reading

1.  Reichardt, J. (1969) *Cybernetic Serendipity: The Computer and the Arts*. Prager: New York. (This book has a chapter on Japanese haiku, computer texts, high-entropy essays, fairytales, and fake physics essays.)

2.  Kurzweil, R. (1990) *The Age of Intelligent Machines*. MIT Press: Cambridge, Massachusetts. (This book contains information on pattern recognition, the science of art, computer-generated poetry, and artificial intelligence.)

## 60.2  Appendix: Enhance Your Own Stories

In the previous sections, I have shown you how the computer generation of poetry and text can provide programming exercises for students and professionals – and also for those interested in artificial intelligence. There, I alluded to the fact that computer-produced text and word lists are *also* a marvelous stimulus for the imagination in *human-generated* fictional stories, books, and visual art. They can be used when you are searching for new ideas, images, and emotions. In this section, you can explore this idea in greater detail using a gigantic list of words to embellish your own fictional stories or to use as input for computer programs which write their own stories.

### 60.2.1 Language and Word Lists

Language is the primary medium with which we think and communicate ideas to others. When one reads language in written form, one is really decoding symbols. It is through the interactions of such symbols that we create new worlds, new images, new thoughts. For a long time, I have held a fascination with colorful symbols and words. Words are meant to be petted and stroked. They are meant to allow us to transcend space and time, and to inspire visions

This reference section is directed to a wide audience and intended to have a range of applications. Arranged for quick, easy reference, it contains over 1,000 descriptive phrases, commonly known as "tags" – those short, one-line descriptions which make the difference between a cold, factual fictional work and an inspired, pulsating story. Here's how:

*Without tags*: The bird flew toward the sun.

*With tags*: With wings spread and motionless, a solitary seabird glided toward the shattered crimson disc of the sun.

You may also wish to use the words and phrases in the lists which follow for inclusion within the semantic schema for the computer poems in this chapter.

Now let's continue to discuss the possibility of using this list to generate your own stories, without computers. Many fellow writers may be reluctant to accept the notion of a compendium of phrases to help make descriptions more imaginative. They may suggest that such an approach is too mechanical, too calculated. However, if tags are used occasionally and judiciously to give a little color at the right moment – and every page of a story is not littered with them – they can give a good story even more sparkle and more life. In this capacity, the list should be useful for both beginning and more seasoned writers, for even experienced authors commonly have favorite words or pet phrases they use to create a mood or define a setting. Just as an example, renowned science fiction writer Harlon Ellison in his book, *Partners in Wonder*, describes how early in his writing career he frequently used the device-image of someone shoving his fist in his mouth to demonstrate being overwhelmed by pain or horror. Similarly, S. R. Donaldson, best-selling author of the Thomas Covenant fantasy series, makes frequent use of pet words. For instance the relatively obscure word "cynosure" appears at least once, and usually more often, in each of the six books in the series.

Over the years I have accumulated phrases stimulated by my reading of a wide variety of fiction. Many of the phrases come from my own short stories. Much of the list has a science-fiction/fantasy flavor; however, the images should be useful in most forms of fiction. Possible uses for this compendium of descriptive phrases are: trigger, or "stepping-off," points for the creation of colorful environments and creatures, seasoning of bland descriptions, and creative points of departure in general. Hopefully, once your imagination is stimulated you will begin designing your own tags!

#### 60.2.1.1 The Senses

#### 60.2.1.2 Sight (Including Objects Which Emit Light)

thick vein of light; shifting veils of a mirage; pink rays of the sun; field of whiteness; shifting luminous veils; multihued light radiating from centipedes on the lake; filaments of violet light; path of light; glittering of water; darkest hole; brilliant hues of phosphorescence; glimmered like mercury; blue-green glow; mottled orange disc; edge of the glow; red-orange flicker; the color of ice; red neon lights on wet pavement; northlight flares; sky-glow; last glow of the last sunset; signs flickered; star beams; lamplit streets; glimmering aurora; burst of solar interference; dream-heavy shadows; curtains of light; a thick vein of indigo light; aurora pulsing in glacial blue and white; sky deepened from purple to sable; sky whiteness; flamboyance on fire thorn trees; brilliance of the stars; auroral light pulsed blue; brilliance

of a great star; massive red disk; shadows across the moon; sun-splashed ground; light swirls; dark-red circle of light; phosphorescent glow of crescents; iridescence; mystic visions; a point of gold; emerald spectral glow; dark gaze; vermillion moonbeam; iridescent green; winking lights; cold crimson; flood of illumination; red-dawn; slice of gold; ball of light; dark evergreen; blue stuff; blue-white glare; large, blue-white sun; dusty green; suffused sunlight; gray, nubiferous; living light; hazy, whitish light; lavender beam; dull silver; fingers of light probed the darkness; tangle of golden reflections; sacred radiance of the sun; holy light; vivid orange; beam of brilliant white; rusty brown; sun-blinded; semi-darkness; green dusk; luminescence of scavengers; swirl of dazzling light; yellow sunlight glinted; the blink of bright lights; a flood of brilliance; vastness of that blackness; visions of a long-dead planet trickled; velvet darkness; shiningness in the black; blood red hues; sun's crimson disk; faint blue glow; blue-white radiance; pools of unnatural light; pale reddish radiance; silver shining; dazzling wall of white; faint luminosity; streak of phosphorescence; dazzling light; queer, golden light; brilliant spangles; billow of white and yellow smoke; remote star; vague twilight glow suffused the ... seethed in whiteness and ice-blue; blue sparkle; blaze of light; metallic sheen; scarlet streak; blur of scarlet; blur of red; flash of scarlet; burst of unholy blue light that sparkled; a line of phosphorescence bulged; golden gleam; angular bright constellation; incredible lamp of stars; dancing glow; thick gloom; north lights; flashing neon red; dazzle of sun dots; tube of darkness; ebon; sable; turquoise.

### 60.2.1.3 Fire

of radiant fire; embers glow in the fire; twin-clouds of flaming incandescent violence; flame; tendrils of gorgeous flames; pyres; wild flames; blaze of light; shower of flames; intolerable flames of living fire; blue fire throbbed; fan-shaped flames trickled with smoke; fire; black vipers crawled through funeral pyres; embers on a living sacrifice; purple glow of the last embers; fire; holy fire; blue flame; tongues of living liquid fire; vaporous flame; green flame; flame-dazzled eyes; sourceless flame;

### 60.2.1.4 Taste and Smell

nearly liquid masses; sick odor thickened the air; murmurings; the stench of trailing vapors; amount of liquid which smelled like absinthe; pungent fluid smelling of creosol and lime; foul, hot air; rich scents; shadow of thirst; bubbling death-liquid; I believe you have a functional pizza;

### 60.2.1.5 Hearing

piercing electronic screams; dull pulse; sounded like a bassoon; all cries fade within a forest of night; terribly harsh death-whine of insects; extreme silence; chimes of doom; a thunder of fire; the last thing I heard was a mooing at one second intervals; storm of sound; sing to your death-fungi; bursts of horrid thunder; buzzing of helicopters; strange incantation; war-cry; traffic noises; dreadful moaning; mighty pulse; crickets sang in the deep grass; a deep grumbling noise; whimpering giggle; rhythm of some unheard music; rumble of traffic; full of fragrance and murmurings; bleeding noisily; gruesome growling; a high bird-like cry; clamor of wings; brook sang; whisper to us in our graves; bird fluted in the winter dusk; a soundless world; songs of men; harsh cry; wilderness of silence; dull boom; ashen tales; a thin wail out of the darkness; soundless explosion of light; chanting something; demented shriek; somber silence; silence shattered; mind whisperings; ghostly prayers; ghostly curses; celestial bells; frightful bellowing.

### 60.2.1.6 Touch

chill of dawn; tingling sensation; gentle warmth; needle-sharp; age-old tremors in the forest; heat-flicker; warmth radiated; tormenting heat; heat haze; river of pain; strange sensation; grip of hell; celestial heat; icy tendrils; his large green throat-appendage took her face and held it gently; the baboon's breath was warm and moist.

## 60.2.1.7  Environment

## 60.2.1.8  General

sky filled with unwinking eyes; the once clear streams were now homofermentative; chaotic realm of men; semi-gasiform envelope; caves of ice; island of dark blue; springtime mud filled with unwinking eyes; foggy air of a New York sky; winter-gloomy wilderness; lands of men; northern world edge; surrounded by luminous blossoms; traces of fire and broken bones; diffuse radiance of the remote heights; lushness of the forest; damned darklands; vast sheafs of leaves; enormous wilderness; sunset horizon; realms of men; garden by the poolside; patches of white powder; lunar sphere; gory icicle; innermost bowels of the earth; radiant trail; sulfurous pit, silent dust; crack of gloom; blood-red chasm; mossy cavern; shining log; flowering shrubs; flashing sands; gleaming pools; dark earth; dark extension of rock; night's lair; edge of the lagoon; strange forest; forest of spirits; grey ash; ceiling of smoke; fantastic land; pink surface of rock; deep jungles; mountain top; tall trees; darkness against the sky; red stones; pool of tears; inland sea; a world of mists and jungles; diamond haze; burning hells; primeval plant; primeval sea; steaming world; gas envelope; steamy jungle planet; jagged mass; dark air; dancing rocks; monster-inhabited jungle planets; prolific vegetation; hell-black night; dead earth; pale beach; incipient decay; mountains burning with yellow flames; darkness of the island; high sea; blackened wood and ashes; dead fire; primitive nest; disc of the sun; sliver of moon; blue flowers; blue dome; blue shadows; black and white mess; darkness full of claws; harsh cry; rays of the sun; dark earth; feather tops; dusk of the forest; looming sky; gloomy crack; forest shadows; strange varicolored flowers; sulfurous explosion; edge of the world; sun's crimson disk; wisps of smoke; glowing gas; glowing gas shells; highway of ashes; glow of dawn; shadowed wastelands; metallic hell; maelstrom; lifeless chunk of rock; crack of doom; threatening night; myriads of crystals; outcropping of crystalline matter; black deeps; blackest of black nights; afterglow; shadows of doom; glowing pools of white fire; dazzling depths; benighted crypts; luminous nodules; heavy, inky vapor; gas coiling and pouring upward; an ebony gaseous cloud; puff of greenish-white smoke; luminous greenish smoke; pools of blazing ...; tortured wisps and eddies of smoke; surrounded by glittering node of light; endless night; vague patches of light gleamed coldly; primeval mud; blazing suns; remote wisps of shiningness; sweet air; shattered, golden sun; galactic system; untold terrors in the dark; ice-sheet; white sand; silence of the forest; thick forest; shattered rocks; dank swamp; swirls of dust; scratchings on rock; ebon sky; darkness of the tree; polar waste; shattered crimson disk of the sun; cold star clouds; forest of night; ancient trees.

## 60.2.1.9  Water Environments

deep sea; bottom of the seas; vast stretches of water; glittering sea; dance of the waves; crystal streams; sunless sea; shrunken seas; gas oozing from a mistcovered swamp; a limitless sea of greenness; sluggish stream; green depths of water; plankton-swarming pool; bright water; blue waters; still water; brackish waters; flowing streams; silver pools.

## 60.2.1.10  Weather Environments

crystal wind; crystal rains; translucent, bluish cloud; dark chill winter; stormy sun; liquid air; season of mists; dark cotton cloud; death-rain; chill wind; brown cloud; eternal ripples of thunder; bursts of horrid thunder; whirlwinds caused by the eclipse; mists that swirled; foul, hot air; dull-red fog of gloom; cold dawn; grey mists; vague perpetual clouds; chill mists; revolving masses of gas; shining swirls of mist; unseen wind.

### 60.2.1.11  Surreal Environments

### 60.2.1.12  General

quantum heavens; oblivion; abyss of ages; twilight realm; imagine a world with no shadows, no sun; gates of an unknown kingdom; angular infinity; faint blue glow; a world where one need not move, and birds live forever; unbiological Christmas; scarlet hell; synthetic hell; metallic hell; lands beneath the sun; fairy land; hell upon earth; twilight kingdom; a world far from home; death's dream kingdom; half-heaven; a world far from the realm of man.

### 60.2.1.13  Outerspace Environments

island galaxy; ebon blackness of interstellar space; drifts of orbiting ice; hyperspace; stellar background; lunar dawn; cosmic void; immense night of space; infinitely distant stars; phantom suns exploded; three billion suns; three-star system; starry voids; star clusters; dwindling star; circle of worlds; patch of stars; twin-planet; deeps of space; dark waste of cosmic dusk; space-time continuum; galactic immensity; icy moons; blazing stars shrunk; silver moon; slow constellations wheeled; far-off stars; black planet; star pools; brilliance of the stars; trans-lunar pits (or) gulfs (or) wells; dark universe; red star; airless planetoid; habitual planets; stale cosmos; spaceo-temporal; stars of heaven; dull emptiness of hyperspace; angular infinity; empty universe.

### 60.2.1.14  Organisms (And Parts of Organisms)

death-spores; death-fungi; flaccid sac; nerve-complex; green blood; globular brown shape; raw celluloid; weird giant fruits; cat-like; fresh blood; gigantic armored beasts; a black, humped figure; scarred

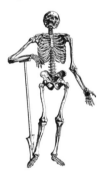

hunters; buzzing flies over spilled guts; dense black mass; unwinking eyes; soft throat; sea-spores; strange growths; dry leaves; silent hunters; a single sea bird; four unwinking eyes; black blob of flies; single organism; glittering nodes of life; brain pulsed; demonic figures; unexpected pale flowers; tendril; strange, moonbeam-bodied creature; snake-thing; cobwebbed heap; dark aromatic bushes; bright fantastic birds; whine of insects; silence of the forest; terrible lizard; man-apes; shriveled corpses; cave dwellers; slimy black tangles of ... nightmare body; the monkey will never shiver; and never gaze on the quiet men who should be bones; several crushed serpents lay at Toto's feet; oh liquid king! oh soft one!; viper, hold me in your gossamer arms; soft cattle; from its one nostril protruded a long snaking tendril; a number of thin jointed appendages sprung from beneath her eye sockets; epicycloidic monstrosity; frosted stalagmites of brown flesh; robotoid deer; an organ which resembled the man's heart sat pulsating on the dusty floor; the spider leaped through the air into my open mouth; it secreted a thin milky fluid into my esophagus; luminous nodules of plant life; a thousand golden gnats shimmered in the early evening heat; multitentacular creature; blood blackening between the teeth; an isolated nasopharynx attached to the remains of a dripping tongue; mauve men molding half-harlequins; a number of gods slowly close their eyelids; from beneath its thin, drooling mouth, a hundred throat-appendages quivered aperiodically; its several feet resembled horse-shoe crabs; its toes looked like slugs; two off-white snouts began to sniff at the air; its grey-green eyelids drooped; throbbing blood; frigid misty carp; bicornuate uterus; grey trunks; from its neck protruded a thin flexible stalk; on the end of the stalk was a tiny blue unwinking eye; permanently implant itself in four of the host's cranial nerves; frozen limbs; cold skeleton hand; fruit-bearing trees; three-fingered limb; Silurian sea creature; evanescent egg receptacles; lump of death; a creature which resembled a broomstick; the highly elongated brain filled the obscenely thin skull; the base contained several poisonous living tendrils; protruding from the hairy base were two reproductive organs which resembled bars of white soap; harpsichord phantoms; magnetic Israelites; flock of hellbats; mauve-colored women; ort-men turned to ashes; the seaworm fed on bluish grey slime; the mottled orange disk of its heat receptors; flower of flesh; dying puppets; electric superfemales; eviscerated bowl remnants; steaming guts spewed on to the ground, like apricots falling from their cellophane container; sodium chloride worms; spherical head; an earthworm stuck its head up from the ground and barked like a poodle; sprawled out on the moist forest floor were several dead elves; neon-witch; dominant race; neon-birds on an earthly chain; pink naked trunks with dark streaks; she was about the size of a chicken; eighty gossamer wings quivered on a body resembling a ball of twine; teenagers in strange mixed costumes, green closed eyelids, sinuous body; half-human beings; big silent cat; living wings; white set of wings; iridescent wings; leg-roots; half-humanlike breeds; alien flora and fauna; great race; machine civilization; small creature; whirl of frightened wings; deep-set eyes; night blue eyes; walking corpses; twisted stems; asp; spleen; mind-shield; fluid in her veins; polyhedral eyes; six-foot tall sperm creature; flute-gods eating tangerine crystals; milky red surface of its retina; his duodenum and small intestine shattered outward to angular infinity; dark veins bulged; jungle of limbs; six-veined membranous wings; wild dwarfs; twisted trees, opalescent membranes; gnats rising in the miasmic vapor; sea-spores; tiny serpentine race; hell hounds; great black wings; bones of the dead; disembodied men; gossamer wings; non-eyes; blue saurian ichor; whirling gaseous freaks; flashing eyes; floating silver-blond hair; labyrinthic tangle of roots; strange varicolored flowers; wise men with fiery eyes; black gnat; surge of blood; parasitic worms; drops of vivid blood; slender snakes; dark princess; tomb-

builders; hot bags of colored guts; gleaming tusks; supernatural creature; rotting corpse; phosphorescent creatures of the deep; carcasses of a tiny race; signs of life; tiny non-flying monsters; intricate vines; bat-like creature; tiny skeletons on bleak hillsides; bluish-gray slime; mindless monsters; marshy sea choked with fungoid growths; nightmare beasts; primeval reptile; council of war; super beasts; beast blood; reptilian creatures; eviscerated shape; vanished race; burning eyes; small-headed creatures; sun-child; black lump; stalagmites of brown flesh; white flesh; wing membrane; crimson throat-appendages quivered nervously; bodiless demons; emperor of dreams; glittering, unwinking eyes; fire-eaters; fire-colored arms; horrible phantasms; ghastly mouth shut spasmodically; frightful shape of glaring eyes; harbinger of doom; clouds of tiny sea creatures; fronds of the vermillion weed; squirming remnants of monster bodies; thick forest; enraged monster; gnarled, four-pawed things; boneless mass of flesh frosted with ...; dry web-stuff; thick white messy bulk; coal-black blood; long-dead creature; a resinous substance; huge mottled green leaves; long white hair; armored beast; shapeless worm things; primal (or) primordial (or) primeval broth (or) ooze (or) slime; alien thing; troll-creature; sea-serpents; azure vein; silver-grey human sacrifices; gnarled body; gnarled pony; green-winged; red-eyed; star-spawn; bright blue eyes; bloodsucking; smoke-belching; freakish; luminescence of scavengers; body glows; gnome-like; blue-white scar; human-born; alien strangeness; long-beaked; jelly-like; ape-like; aboriginal; vermillion spotted;

## 60.2.1.15 Artificial Objects

light-ray; gleaming metal; insanity goblet; trumpets of doom; black ancestral flute; king's flute; ghost-beam; candycane crucifix; clutter of coils and wires; horse-tambourines; cables terminating in spring clips; surrounded by heavy coils; ranks of shining equipment; glittering glass shaft; tables made of milk; pillow of rust; antlered helmet; foam plastic flutes; black coiling fragments of man's world; fountain of wreckage; torrent of debris; pithecoid prisms; black stone images; breathing death-crib; frost-covered casket; burning ray; bubble in a fog; golden gleam of a broken column; death-vial; ancient oil; fire-pot; chemistry of war; ancestral medicines; book of dreams; death ray; death cups; blue dome.

## 60.2.1.16 Architectural Structures

gleaming corridor; dark tower; alien ball; silent chambers of an ancient tomb; temple's inner shrine; trigonal biplanar stone throne; turquoise obelisk; dark planet's crypt; dome of pleasure; in the black monastery's open maw; empty halls; heaven-climbing spires; great glass globes; palace of wisdom; slopes of girders and cables; glittering emerald walls; steel flowers; dream-plagued masonry; tomb of the ages; spires of gold; ovoid; cosmic throne; glass hemispheric crypt; castles of calcite.

### 60.2.1.17 Time

maelstrom of time; lunar eternity; deserts of vast eternity; gentle acid of time; dead years; days of yore; glasses of time; tides of fortune; non-time; eternal rhythm; eerie infinitude; lonely period of timelessness; barren continuum; spawned eons ago from the stuff of dreams;

### 60.2.1.18 Actions

glistening sweep; crashes into flaming death; vegetable love; plasticene love; strange fungoid growths froth; the rabbit writhed in the blaze of unholy light; the infant crawled into her dry fossilized rib cage; burn before their shrines; love-in-a-wave; ultraviolet elephant dances; writhed in the blaze of light; blood-red fluid spewed; blood-bathing; ritual hunt; twitching of a terrible lizard; haziness swirled; worshiped the bronze god of death; rites of an Aztec sadist cult; death rites of a small city; clothed him in darkness; writhing and squirming; wings spread and motionless; writhing of her fingers in the moonlight; gleamed oily; strange sleep; shimmering in the heat; crimson-love; paralysis of the silent hunters; spasm of her soft throat; paroxysm of a snake-thing; making her death their life; dance of nodes; shuddering violently; made black love; star-blasting; spawned of an act of darkness; bloody climax of a death struggle; ritual drinking of blood; erosion sears; descent into the darkness of death; ritual death; hideous shadow loomed; frenzied ritual; primitive feast; dance of the drones;

### 60.2.1.19 Emotions, Feelings and Mind-states

chill horror; mind-inflaming ecstasy; madness of extreme terror; green lights of nausea; infinite possibility; dreams of men; with a last spasm of terror; vulnerable heart; well of sleep; spasm of terror; fire of love; numbing tendrils of madness; swirl in a rosy fog of pleasure; Electric Noel; trail of lonely feelings; man's primitive sensitivities; wave of agonized ecstasy; tidal waves of mass emotion; tears trickled; man's memory; corridors of memory; wave of awe; pool of consciousness; waters of our madness; shards of memory; waters of our despair; night of despair; mad visions pulse; flames of passion; shadow of dreams; pleasure-dreams; sleep of ages; fantastic nightmare; dream-waters obscure sleep; waters of dreams; table of dreams; night of dreams; evil dream; death-love; black omens; limbs of despair; frenzied fit of passion; memory of life; darkness of man's heart; amorphous current of the soul; dazed paralysis; trans-migration of souls; waves of agony; rings, souls, minds, of madness; a dark thought; distorted perceptions.

### 60.2.1.20 Unreal Beings

imp; sprite; Satan; sylphs; gnomes; kobolds; naid; daids; elves; satyrs; nymphs; incubi; troll-shape; almost-ghost; ghosts of our children; soft grey voice of the wind; electron priests; butterfly souls; jungle-dwarf; sand fairies dancing before a cyclopean god; elder spirit; Cinderella died screaming amidst shining voltaic coils; forest of knights; shimmering organic mirage; dim figure; two spirits in the dark; death-queen; water-demons; cancer-pianists; metal mermaids; puppet erupted on their shrine; spirits of the wind; dream-entity; chonchoidic warriors; small brown image; silver shape; dark eternal mind; slimy visitor to the world of men; idle green king; king of the grey mists; unknown men; a pulsating black presence; blob of dark; angel of death; spirit of flesh; prince of darkness; chaos-creator; twin-mind; monsters of the deep; unfamiliar shadows; wanderers of the dark; spirit of man lost; vanished race; disembodied spirits; ectoplasmic spirits; nightmare beasts; brazen, metallic god; mythical beast; angel of death; colossal minds; distorted figure; naked specters; elongated image; incredible beings.

### 60.2.1.21 Interesting Words

| | |
|---|---|
| amphicyon | - a prehistoric dog-bear |
| anacreontic | - a drinking song |
| basilisk | - a legendary reptile with fatal breath and glance |
| celadon | - yellow green |
| cenobian | - monkish |
| cenotaph | - a tomb in honor of a person whose remains are elsewhere |
| chacma | - a large African baboon |
| conchoid | - semicircular |
| condylarth | - prehistoric animal |

| | |
|---|---|
| coprolite | - petrified fecal matter |
| coprolagnia | - sexual arousal as a result of the thought or sight of feces |
| coprophobia | - fear of feces |
| coprophagous | - feeding on dung |
| cynosure | - a center of attraction or attention |
| crepuscular | - twilight |
| deliquescent | - moisture-absorbing |
| eidolon | - an unsubstantial image, phantom |
| eldritch | - weird, eerie |
| colith | - a crudely chipped flint |
| evanescent | - tending to vanish like vapor |
| glaucous | - pale yellow-green color |
| haruspication | - divination by entrail examination |
| lumbricoid | - wormlike |
| megalith | - huge stones used in prehistoric monuments |
| nacreous | - pearly |
| neolith | - stone age implement |
| nubilous | - cloudy |
| oubliette | - a dungeon with an opening only at the top |
| pithecoid | - ape-like |
| scatophagy | - the religious practice of eating excrement |
| soporific | - sleep-inducing |
| spavined | - maimed |
| spinor | - a vector-like quantity in two- or four-dimensional space |
| sudoriferous | - sweat-producing |
| surcingle | - the belt securing a saddle to a horse |
| telic | - tending towards an end |
| uxor | - wife |
| zarf | - a metallic cuplike stand |

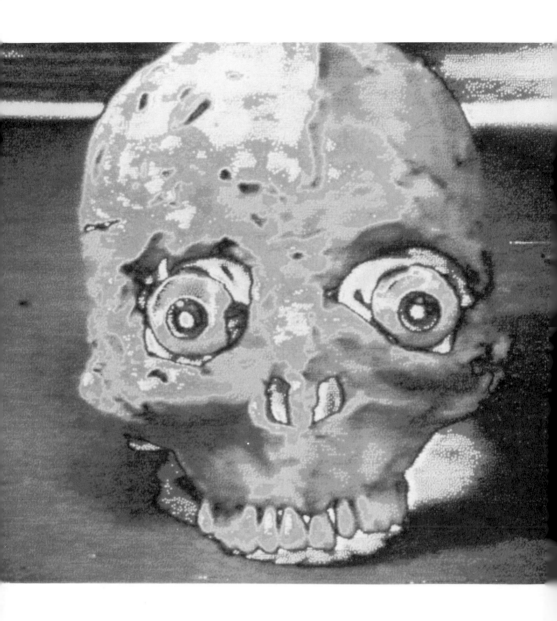

# Part  VIII

# FICTION

Chapter 61

# The Twenty-Fourth Annual Meeting
# Of the Chaos Society

If there were one place in this world I never expected trouble, it was the American Institute of Physics. Located beneath the old clock tower of the Tribune building on Nassau street, its library had the world's finest collection of Einstein's early papers. I had been visiting the library there for a long time – virtually every Saturday morning for the past five years. Today I was tempted to delay my browsing until Sunday; it was February and bitter cold. Nonetheless, I got into my car and took the one mile trip to the Institute.[47]

As I pulled next to the curb, it started to snow. Vague perpetual clouds floated overhead. I slid into a parking space in front of a pale blue Cadillac. Quickly grabbing a pen from my pocket, I rushed into the warm building. At this time in the morning, it usually wasn't too crowded. I picked up a few paper clips from the reception desk and overheard Mrs. Wright, a woman who lived several floors below me in our apartment complex, complaining to a fellow physicist. Mrs. Wright looked like a sweaty overweight child. A black purse was slung over one forearm. With her free hand, she pried open a copy of *Physics Today*.

As I walked down the narrow corridor, I passed a conference room with a big letter "A" written above the door. I poked my head into the room and saw a man in a dark suit speaking to an audience of about 50 scientists.

"I'm so glad that all of you could attend the twenty-fourth annual meeting of the Chaos Society. Today's discussion will deal with the permeability of 4-space transcendental functions." The proud audience, which appeared to be comprised solely of mathematical geniuses, eagerly awaited the lecture. The lecturer scrawled several symbols on the board:

$$\sum \sqrt{\xi \times \pi}$$

He looked at his audience for confirmation. They enthusiastically nodded, and then he continued:

---

[47] *Note:* Except for this story, which was the first *fictional* piece to be published in the scientific journal *Computers in Physics* (Sept./Oct. 4(5): 566), the stories in the *Fiction* section are from an unpublished collection of 300 short stories entitled *I Have Dreams at Night*.

$$\sum \sqrt{\xi \times \pi} \; (5\Psi) \, \frac{\chi_1}{\chi_2}$$

The audience began to discuss among themselves the relative merits of the system of equations on the board with a system they had seen presented somewhat differently at the twenty-third annual meeting. The lecturer continued.

$$\left\{ \sum \sqrt{\xi \times \pi} \; (5\Psi) \, \frac{\chi_1}{\chi_2} \int_0^1 \frac{\sqrt{32}}{\sqrt{\beta \pi}} \right\}$$

The audience wriggled with delight. Their faces were all aglow. Exclamations of surprise and praise were being expressed. Somewhere in the back of the dusty lecture room there seemed to be a small scuffle – a disagreement – or perhaps it was simply an exuberant group of scientists gesticulating in an uncharacteristically passionate manner. In another corner of the room near an open window, a distinguished-looking woman in the audience fainted, like a dying flower. I turned my attention to the proud lecturer who hit the blackboard so hard with his chalk that a few small fragments exploded outward, hitting a young man in the audience.

$$\left\{ \frac{\sum \sqrt{\xi \times \pi} \; (5\Psi) \, \frac{\chi_1}{\chi_2} \int_0^1 \frac{\sqrt{32}}{\sqrt{\beta \pi}}}{7\Omega^4 \sqrt{\pi^2} \lim_{N \to \infty} \aleph_N \left( \sum \kappa \cos \theta \right)} \right\}$$

At this point the audience began a hearty applause. The lecturer stepped off of the podium and bowed. He then paused and slowly scrutinized the audience with his wide-open eyes. Was his action simply to insure that his audience was at maximum attentiveness for the formulas to come, or was this a means to intimidate possible dissenters in the audience? For an instant, time seemed to slow, but then he jumped back onto the podium, and resumed his writing.

$$\left\{ \frac{\sum \sqrt{\xi \times \pi} \; (5\Psi) \, \frac{\chi_1}{\chi_2} \int_0^1 \frac{\sqrt{32}}{\sqrt{\beta \pi}}}{7\Omega^4 \sqrt{\pi^2} \lim_{N \to \infty} \aleph_N \left( \sum \kappa \cos \theta \right)} \right\} \sum_0^1 \frac{\sec \tau |\lambda^2|}{\chi / \omega : 3\lambda}$$

And then he added just one more symbol.

$$2 \left\{ \frac{\sum \sqrt{\xi \times \pi} \; (5\Psi) \, \frac{\chi_1}{\chi_2} \int_0^1 \frac{\sqrt{32}}{\sqrt{\beta \pi}}}{7\Omega^4 \sqrt{\pi^2} \lim_{N \to \infty} \aleph_N \left( \sum \kappa \cos \theta \right)} \right\} \sum_0^1 \frac{\sec \tau |\lambda^2|}{\chi / \omega : 3\lambda}$$

The audience went wild. Their screams of jubilant exaltation rose to a fever pitch. The lecturer's heart raced, and he wildly wrote on:

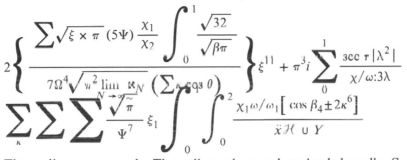

The audience screamed. They all stood up and applauded madly. Some of the mathematicians heartily congratulated the lecturer, and then picked him up and placed him on their shoulders. Whistles. Screams. Clapping. The cheering continued, adding to the exponentially increasing pandemonium. Moet champagne was poured. A three-piece musical band was brought in, and a large bearded drummer happily, but incessantly, banged on an even larger bass drum. At that point, I noticed something odd: the drummer's burly arms appeared to have various mathematical symbols and fractal curves tattooed upon them. I could not ascertain the significance of this apparent anomaly on his flesh, but I could see that his aperiodic beating was beginning to have an effect on a few normally stodgy mathematicians, who started to undulate to the syncopated rhythm. I looked towards the front of the room. As bright red streamers and mucilagenous confetti went flying through the air, a few young students rushed to the blackboard in order to record the marvelous equations in their tattered notebooks, before the nighttime cleaning staff relegated the lecturer's legacy to oblivion.

The mathematicians could hardly contain their anticipation and enthusiasm for the next annual meeting of the Chaos Society.

# Chapter 62

# The Big Black Bug

We first heard of the alien when it was trying to mate with a Unidyne 400 personal computer. Billy and I were down by the old railroad tracks eating bologna and mustard sandwiches when an old geezer came out of nowhere and started shouting at us.

"Hey kids, did you hear about what's happening on Mulberry Street? There's some kind of creature carrying on with Mr. Tyler's rusty old computer."

Billy and I looked at each other. What was this old guy trying to tell us? We were curious, and Mulberry street was about a minute away, running that is, so we got up off the grass and raced into town.

When we got there we couldn't believe it. Right on top of an old Unidyne 400 was a huge creature which looked a little like a black stag beetle and a little like a squid. I had never seen a squid, but Billy had, and I took his word for it.

"Will you look at that!" Billy whispered to me.

By now many of the townspeople had arrived and stood around gawking at the monster.

"What do you think it is?" I asked Billy.

"Dunno, maybe it's from Mars or somethin'."

I agreed that it was like nothing I'd ever seen. Billy stared at the monster.

"Looks like it's having sex with the computer!" Billy laughed.

"You're crazy," I told Billy, even though I thought he was right.

Mr. Harry, and a tall man in a hunting jacket, got a little closer to the monster. By now that overgrown insect had broken the glass screen of the computer, and one of its long arms began snaking its way into the disk drive.

"Wouldn't go any closer, Ned," Mrs. Vega from the grammar school said to the man in the hunting jacket. "It's liable to come after you."

"Don't worry, I'm not aiming to get any closer to that thing."

Billy and I took bets on what would happen next. I said that the monster would get bored on top of the computer and would move on to the modem. Billy said that it would come after us.

"If it's going to come after us, why are we standing here, Billy?"

Billy didn't have an answer for that.

"Why doesn't someone call the sheriff?" someone in the growing crowd said. We watched for another few minutes, and then there came the flashing amber lights of a patrol car.

"All right, everyone get back." It was Sheriff Sanson. He seemed to be thinking of what to say next.

"Bet you he's going to shoot it!" Billy shouted.

"Don't be crazy, Billy. Maybe the monster is friendly," I replied.

"How can it be friendly? Look what it's doing to that computer."

By now the monster had carefully removed the rear printed circuit boards and RS232 connectors. The keyboard was broken. The monster seemed especially interested in the computer's red on/off switch. It kept touching it with its hairy claws. From beneath the bug's drooling mouth, a hundred throat-appendages quietly emerged and quivered spasmodically.

Three other patrol cars came as wooden road blocks were being set up. In one backyard, a small brown dog barked and snapped as more people gathered around the strange scene. The tall man in the hunting jacket looked toward the sky and then walked up to the Sheriff. Dark cotton clouds began to drift by overhead, and all through town a mist began to descend upon the green lawns and rhododendrons. By midnight there would be a storm.

"What are you going to do about that oversized bug, Sheriff?"

"We've placed a call to the local University. They're sending a scientist down here to examine it."

"What's a scientist going to do! That thing might wreck our town by the time the University sends someone down here. Kill it while you can."

"Now hold on a minute. I grant you it's a scary thing, but it hasn't made a move off that computer for the last hour."

It was getting dark now. Crickets began to sing in the deep grass, and down by Elm Street a few children began to watch lightning bugs drift thorough the bushes. Within ten minutes, the Professor from the University was allowed past the road blocks. He drove his green Volkswagon slowly towards the creature. Billy said "Uh oh," when he saw that the Professor had a laptop computer in the back seat of his car. The monster took one look at the gleaming automobile, and began making piercing electronic screams. Then there was the clamor of wings. The Professor barely made it out of his car before the monster crashed into the back seat. From the monster's neck protruded a thin brown flexible stalk, which it suddenly thrust into the laptop's liquid crystal display.

The sky deepened to sable. The monster's movements became slower. Another two hours passed, and still no one, not even the Professor, knew what to do next. At the time it didn't seem to matter much though. You could tell the monster was dying. Its skin was turning brittle and it barely moved. Frosted stalagmites of brown flesh flaked away from the creature's membranous wings. Billy wanted to bet me when it would die. Billy liked making bets, but his bets were getting on my nerves. Before Billy could decide on exactly what to bet, the big monster died. Its blue unwinking eyes turned a shade of dark vermillion and then black. From its abdominal pores oozed a pungent fluid smelling of creosol and lime. It didn't move.

"Alright, everyone get home now. We'll clean this thing up in the morning." The Sheriff got into his patrol car. A tall woman switched on a pocket radio from which the sounds of Benny Goodman's "One O'Clock Jump" could be heard. She tapped her foot as she walked away down the dark street. The tall man in the hunting jacket was one of the last to leave. Billy and I began to walk north, down the half-lamplit streets to our homes.

"Wait, Billy – don't you hear something?"

We looked back, and we heard a thin wail out of the darkness. Then a buzzing sound, hundreds of buzzing sounds. I guess the man in the hunting jacket was right when he said we should have killed it. From beneath the wrecked computer casings on the Volkswagon's back seat, hundreds of small monsters crawled. Billy said, "Wow." We watched as the things took to the air on little leathery wings. Some had computer chips in their mouths. Others had multicolored wires. A sick odor thickened the night air, as the sky was filled with glittering nodes of light. The creatures seemed to be flying towards the bright lights of Manhattan. I swallowed hard. Billy wanted to bet on what would happen next. For the first time, I punched him in the arm.

## Chapter 63

# There Will Be Soft Cattle

I woke up in the center of an immense field of grazing cattle. Deep grumbling noises were coming from all around me, and I thought I heard the buzzing of helicopters. Hoping that my confusion would dissipate, I did not move for a few seconds. Suddenly, hundreds of white dogwood blossoms, stripped from a nearby tree by the wind, blew across my face.

Slowly rising from my prone position, I stretched my sore legs, and started to explore my peculiar surroundings. I frantically looked left and right, searching for an object or aspect of the cow field that I might recognize. I walked for hours, but to my chagrin and stupefaction, the crowded cattle continued to stretch for as far as my eye could see on a seemingly endless plain of grass, strange varicolored weeds, and a few stunted trees. Occasionally I saw gases oozing from nearby mist-covered swamps, and the movement of reeds and cattails in some of the smaller marshes. In these plankton-swarming pools stood cows of various sizes and colors. Everywhere was the smell of decay — the putrefaction of nearly liquid masses resembling the rarefying remains of long-dead cows. By comparison, this stench made the stink of a cesspool seem like a new perfume by Chanel.

How did I get here? Where was I? What do you do when something so absurd, so out of place in the scheme of everyday living, takes place? Oh, you can speculate about what you should do if this or that happens, but no one can say what action they'd take when the fabric of reality begins to tear. And when it happened to me that hot summer day, I don't think I stood there trying to figure out a rational, scientific explanation for it all. It would almost have been funny, if I were not living through the experience.

I spent the next several days in the cattle field searching for a possible escape from the warm bovine bodies that buffeted me from all sides. It didn't take me long to discover that there were two different categories of animal in my new world. One type of cow seemed to be made of some soft substance and was immobile. Its gelatinous interior was covered by a leather-like hide giving it the outward appearance of a normal cow. This "soft" cow gives milk and has a head with eyes, and a mouth that makes mooing sounds at about ten second intervals. The second type of cow appeared to be a robot. From beneath all of the robot cows' left ears dangled a tiny computer chip with the enigmatic encryption "seche vite." Removing this chip did not elicit any change in the animals' behavior or vitality. After careful dissections, I discovered that the interior of these cows contained row upon row of dark printed circuit boards, a spaghetti of shiny green wires, and an occasional rusty transformer.

Luckily for me, the milk and flesh of the soft cows provided adequate nourishment, and I now believe that I will not suffer from any major dietary deficiencies. The grass in the field is edible in small quantities. However, I can find no use for the robot cows. They provide no flesh or milk.

About a month after my awakening in the cow pasture, and after almost-unendurable frustrations, I kicked at a soft cow as hard as I could with the heel of my leather shoe. The cow bellowed in the madness of extreme terror. A robot cow charged at me as if to warn me that this action would not be permitted. Obviously it permitted me to maim soft cows for food, but not for sport. This was the only time a robot cow showed any sign of aggression towards me.

Every night I went to sleep to the eternal rhythms of the cow mooings. Sometimes my hands itched, and after a few weeks, strange fungoid growths began to appear on the palms of my hands. My nails turned black – the same color as the cow hooves surrounding me. I began to speculate that I was part of some combined genetic and electronic experiment, and that my body was regressing towards a more bovine shape. If this were true, perhaps the cows around me at one time had a human form. As my body began to slowly deteriorate, I also seemed to experience a corresponding decrease in my ability to reason in a logical manner. How could I escape from this fantastic nightmare?

One morning I felt something peculiar in my ear. I hesitated, reached into my ear, and then pulled out a computer chip that had sprouted from the base of my auditory canal. I tried to scream, but my vocal apparatus was no longer functional. A nearby cow stared intently into my eyes. Without thinking, I jumped onto its back. At first I feared some kind of aggressive reaction from the cow to the added weight upon its back, but my action did not seem to bother the cow. In fact, it permitted me to remain mounted as it quickly ran in one direction for the next few hours. The further we travelled, the more depressed I became. The cows in this area of the field were misshapen. One cow had several feet which resembled horse-shoe crabs. From the neck of another protruded several reproductive organs which resembled bars of white soap. About ten multitentacled cows with claws beneath their eyes shuffled aimlessly to my right. Perpetual amber tear drops dripped from their eyes, as if the cows were crying for some lost comrade. The "cryers" never strayed far from one another. Their tears smelled like absinthe. Suddenly, I saw a crimson cow with a long snaking tendril emanating from one of its triple nostrils, and I fainted when that greasy tendril shot out towards my face as it made barking sounds like a small poodle.

When I awoke, I determined that the triple nostril cow has implanted several peanut-sized biomechanical devices on the roof of my mouth. I could feel thick milky secretions oozing down my esophagus from these units. I ripped the little devices from my upper palate, but not before the egregious exudate began to have its soporific effects. I drifted in and out of consciousness, dreaming, travelling on a river of pain, vulnerable and spiritless, waiting to be taken away from the gates of my electronic Kingdom, where tiny dark cows dance like puppet-corpses, and ancient, twisted, winged creatures grin within their tomb of dust, as they watch me shiver and finally cry out in an endless hell-black night.

After a lonely period of about a two months, I found a large wooden spool of dirty rope in a sluggish stream. I never knew where it came from, but it was then that I embarked on what I was later to call the Soft Cow Mountain project. One motivation for this project was the fact that the "cryers" would no longer allow me to travel any further in one particular direction: they blocked every attempt by me to move. Therefore, my plan was to erect a large mountain of cows so that I could climb to the top and survey the land from a higher vantage point. I hoped the project would end the monotony of my absurd and lonely condition, and allow me to see beyond the bounds of my limited bovine world. Using the rope, I was able to coax the robot cows to drag the soft cows into one large pile. The pile constituted the base of the soft cow mountain. With a series of ropes, and after much arduous work, I began to form several layers of soft cows on top of the original square base of 40 by 40 cows. For months I worked on this project, piling soft cows one onto the other, gradually forming a huge soft cow mountain shaped somewhat like a square pyramid. The cryers stood nearby, shaking their chelicera, watching me with their unwinking eyes. I noticed that the cows on the bottom of the pile became somewhat compressed and began mooing at 5-second intervals rather than the usual 10-second intervals. Thick veins protruded from their sides. One of the cows erupted, spewing forth apricot-colored steaming guts onto the cold ground.

One night, just as twilight descended, I jumped on the back of a mobile electronic cow. While riding upon its back, I charged up the side of the slimy mountain of soft cows, reached the apex, and surveyed my kingdom. I gazed in all directions as far as my weary eye could see. Nothing but cows. I looked again. Perhaps I saw a body of water in the distance, a marshy sea, mother of life, now standing choked with fungus and goo. In that ocean, I thought I saw a cow slithering along grey shiny surfaces of rock, and with a last spasm of terror, it faded into fetid chasms of empty air. Wave upon wave of agonized ecstasy shook my oily flesh. Above me the constellations slowly wheeled as tears of laughter rippled through my body. Would the gentle acid of time destroy my mountain?

I slipped on a cow hoof, fell down the side of the mountain, and hit my head on the hard ground. The last thing I heard was a mooing at half-second intervals, and then, silence.

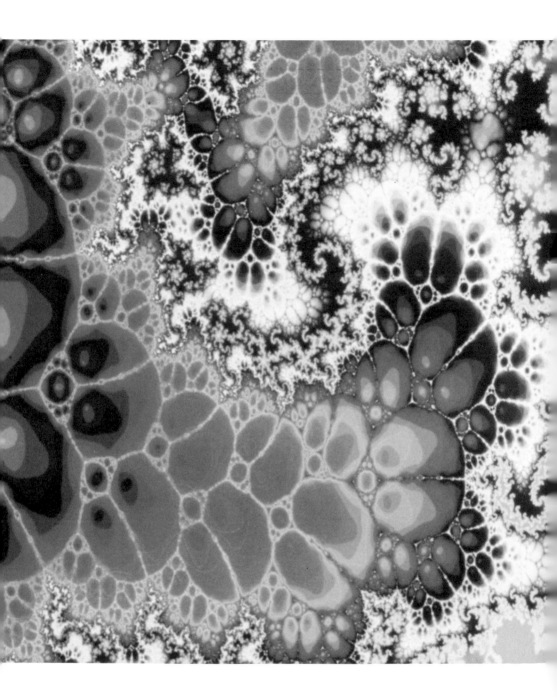

# Part  IX

## CONCLUSION

*"Those two titans of the mind, art and science, are a single human enterprise, but if I had to identify the dominant partner, I would not hesitate to name science. Science is the deeper more encompassing activity of the brain, for it elucidates the mechanisms of the world. Science encompasses art and will, one day, explain it. "*                                                      *P. W. Atkins, 1990*

We live in an age where there is increasing interplay between scientific and artistic disciplines. In the next decade, almost all advances in science and art will rely partly on the computer and advanced technology. Moreover, humans will not be able to rely on any one single field of knowledge to make significant advances. I hope that *Computers and the Imagination* will help reaffirm your interest in using the computer as a tool for simulation and discovery in a variety of fields. Indeed, it would be disappointing if human beings, as they relied more and more on computer aids, became so intellectually lazy that their powers of creative thinking were diminished.

In the 1990s, the public has a rather ambivalent attitude about science. The public distrusts science because it does not understand it. With the increasing melding of science, art, and computing, we may be able to harness and awaken an interest in science by presenting it to children in new and innovative ways.

Obviously, computers and computer-controlled robots will soon play even greater roles in the daily life of people in industrialized countries.[48] By the year 2000, says MIT electrical engineer Rodney Brooks, "we're going to see robot beings infiltrate our everyday lives – just as microprocessors have come into the toy industry, making playthings behave more like home appliances. Eventually you'll have this colony living in your house, just sitting there ready to do stuff for you." Ralph Gomory, former IBM chief scientist, predicted in 1987 that within a decade the central processing units of supercomputers will be concentrated within a space of three cubic inches. The supercomputer core of the 1990s will be suitable for a laptop.[49] This trend in computing power, coupled with the decreasing cost of hardware, makes surveys such as those in the *Speculation* part of this book more than idle dreaming. Indeed, the computer of the year 2000 will touch every aspect of our daily life, and enhance our creativity in all areas of artistic and intellectual expression. The quotation at the beginning of "Million-Point Sculptures" on page 285 provides a relevant question to conclude this book with: "If Leonardo da Vinci were alive today, would he forsake canvas and brush for a computer terminal?" Even if Leonardo could not obtain funding from the National Science

---

[48] Page 343 shows a Sulzer robot. See "Credits" for more information.
[49] The Gomory quote comes from George Gilder, in Kurzweil, R. (1990) *The Age of Intelligent Machines.* MIT Press: Cambridge, Massachusetts. The Brooks quote comes from: Suplee, C. (1991) Artificial life: the new robotics. *Breakthroughs.* February. 2(1): 42.

Foundation or the National Endowment for the Arts, he could – with just a personal computer – create, manipulate, and store fairly sophisticated art works. Colors could be mixed and chosen from a palate of millions of different hues. Screen resolution could emulate the grit of the canvas. His colleagues from around the world could receive his images over their phone lines for their comment and collaboration. Probably Leonardo would spend a large amount of his time inventing entirely new computer input devices to substitute for today's standard mouse – such as the exoskeleton shown on this page. These devices would allow him to precisely emulate his own masterful brush stokes, the viscosity and drip of wet paint, or a chisel chipping away at an imaginary chunk of shiny marble. Within the next decade, personal computers will feature hands-on manipulation of computer-generated images along with tactile sensations and force feedback. Artists such as Leonardo will work within an artificial reality, where computer sensors measure the position of the head, and track eye and hand movements. Voice recognition programs will allow Leonardo to make voice requests, and special goggles will allow him to peer into colorful new worlds limited only by computers, and the imagination.

*"When people's eyes are open, they see landscapes in the outer world. When people's eyes are closed, they see landscapes with their minds's eye. People spend hours looking at outer landscapes, but there is just as much to see in inner landscapes. The landscapes are different, but they are equally valid."*

*Seeing with the Mind's Eye:*
*This History, Techniques, and Uses of Visualization.*
Mike Samuels, M.D., and Nancy Samuels

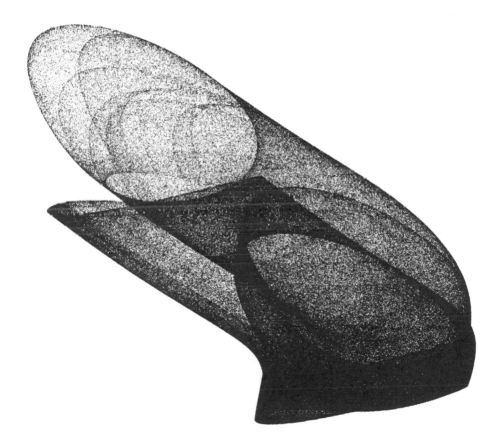

# Part X

# APPENDICES

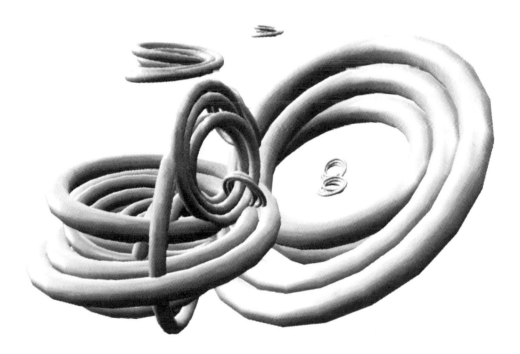

# Appendix A

# Exercises for the Mind and Eye

*"Because other planets might be physically very different from ours, scientists there might use mathematics ... very unlike ours.... Their geometry could be something rather strange, largely topological, say, and geared to flexible structures rather than fixed sizes or shapes."*

Nicholas Rescher, *1985*

## A.1 Grasshopper Sequences

The following problem was developed as an interesting exercise for imaginative programmers. The described sequence is called a *Grasshopper sequence* because it reminds one of the rapid (exponentially growing) breeding that grasshoppers undergo during their mating seasons. Grasshopper sequences are defined by the following two functions which can be visualized as a binary tree which grows increasingly in size.

$$\alpha \rightarrow 2\alpha + 2 \qquad\qquad (A.1)$$

$$\alpha \rightarrow 6\alpha + 6 \qquad\qquad (A.2)$$

where $\alpha$ is an integer. Start with $\alpha = 1$. These mappings generate a binary tree

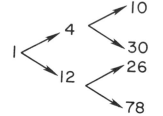

(diagrammed here). For example, after one generation we have 4 and 12 as "children" of the "parent" 1. The next generation produces 10, 30, 26, 78. All the numbers that have appeared so far, when arranged in numerical order, are: 1, 4, 10, 12, 26, 30, 78, ... . No number seems to appear twice in a row, e.g. 1, 4, 10, 10, .... Does a number *ever* appear twice? I do not know the answer to the grasshopper problem and would be interested in hearing from any of you who solve this. A colleague, Michael Clarke from England, has conducted a little study on the grasshopper problem, for the general case of

$$X = C_1 X + C_1 \text{ and } C_2 X + C_2 \tag{A.3}$$

and finds that some values of $C_1$ and $C_2$ do produce duplicates after a number of generations.

| C1 : | 1 | 2 | 3 | 4 | 5 | 6 | 7 |
|---|---|---|---|---|---|---|---|
| C2 : 1 | G2 | G4 | G5 | G6 | G7 | G8 | G9 |
| 2 | G4 | G2 | G5 | -- | G3 | -- | -- |
| 3 | G5 | G5 | G2 | G7 | -- | -- | -- |
| 4 | G6 | -- | G7 | G2 | -- | -- | -- |
| 5 | G7 | G3 | -- | -- | G2 | -- | -- |
| 6 | G8 | -- | -- | -- | -- | G2 | -- |
| 7 | G9 | -- | -- | -- | -- | -- | G2 |

Those entries with a "--" indicate that no duplicates were found when a search was conducted to the 10th generation after starting with an initial value of 1! "Gn" signifies that a duplication has in fact occurred and that it occurs in generation $n$. In order for members of the same generation to match, the two members must satisfy the condition that

$$c_1^i c_2^{(g-i)} = c_1^j c_2^{(g-j)} \tag{A.4}$$

where $g$ is the number of the generation, and $i$ and $j$ are numbers in the range $0 \ldots g$.

Since formulating this problem, I've come across similar kinds of problems, which many of you will enjoy, in: Guy, R. (1983) Don't try to solve these problems! *American Mathematics Monthly.* January 90(1): 35.

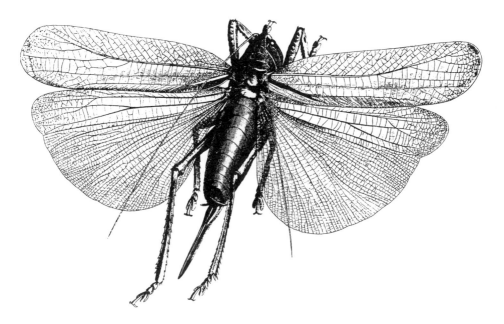

## A.2  The Amazon Skull Game

A friend of mine recently visited Itaituba, a town in Brazil's Amazon rain forest

situated near the Tapajos river, a branch of the Amazon river. The rain forest consists of enormous trees with boughs which become intricately interlaced overhead. My friend told me about a game which certain secluded tribes played with pebbles or sometimes with human skulls, when available. I suspect my friend may have been making up the entire story, or at least exaggerating, but I present the game here because it is so simple to describe, and you may wish to program it on a computer or play it with paper and pencil.

The rules are fairly simple. First I'll explain the native version, and then describe a computer implementation.

1. Start by finding a large stick.

2. Next sketch a 5-by-6 square checkerboard in the sand.

3. You and your adversary take turns placing stones (or skulls) on the checkerboard.

4. Each placed skull must be adjacent to a previous skull, so that your array of skulls trace out a continuous, connected path through the checkerboard. You can add new skulls to either end of the growing path.

5. The opponent who is forced to close the path is a loser. The diagram here shows a typical game, where the next move must be a losing one.

6. The loser donates his head to the playing collection.

I suspect there are plenty of modern versions of this game played with pencil and paper, although so far I have not discovered a winning strategy.

DASHTE KAVIR DESERT

● KASHAN

IRAN

The skull game is easily programmed on a computer. Described here is a program where the computer plays against itself, and you can make modifications to the game to have it play against a human opponent. Start with an array of dimension 5 units in the $x$ direction and 6 units in the $y$ direction. Select a random cell in the array. Let's call this array $A(i,j)$. Have the computer select an adjacent cell by randomly going up, down, right or left. For example, $A(i + 1, j)$ etc. If the cell is already occupied, or if you have traveled off the playing board, try again by selecting another random direction. When the computer cannot find a new site, then the game is over. I would be interested in hearing from any of you who compute the average number of random moves needed to finish a game played on this 5x6 board and for other sized playing boards. Also try boards which have holes in them; these are represented by disallowed array positions.

## A.3 Scorpion Geometry

*"He loved the desert because there the wind blew out one's footsteps like candle flames."*
Lawrence Durrel

Kashan, a desert city in Central Iran, is known for several things: its aromatic wild roses, its finely crafted carpets, and its plethora of small desert scorpions. The *Scorpion game* is said to have been played for centuries near Kashan in the

Dashtekavir desert.[50] Village elders play the game with black and white stones, although centuries ago it was played using the exoskeletons of the indigenous scorpion population. The game is played by two players on a "board" with a number of tiny nodes (circles) arranged as shown:

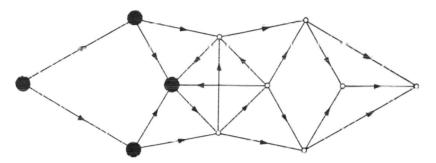

One player has three pieces, called scorpions. The other has one piece, the mouse. The scorpions are placed on any one of the large dark circles in the previous figure. The mouse is placed at the circle marked by the Farsi language character at the far right. After the first move of the scorpion, it is the mouse's move. The

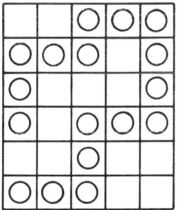

scorpion's move consists of moving one scorpion to an adjacent free circle, that is, to a circle which is connected by a line segment. A scorpion may only move from left to right: it cannot go backwards. (Ignore the arrows on the diagram for now.) After the scorpion makes its first move, the mouse may move. He moves to an adjacent circle according to the same rules, the difference being that the mouse may move backwards as well as forwards. The scorpions and mouse alternate moves. The scorpions have won when they have caught the mouse (when they have encircled him on the circle marked by the Farsi character at the right). At this point the mouse has no free position to move to. (If you wish, you may now holler "*Rafiq, aqrab-e' man tu rah shekast daad!*," which, if my knowledge of the Farsi language is correct, translates to: "My scorpion has defeated you, my friend!") The mouse wins either if he makes his way to the leftmost circle or if the scorpion and mouse continue to repeat their moves over and over again.

You may wish to play a more complex game where the scorpion's directions of movements are controlled by the arrows in the figure. How would you program this game on the computer? To simplify the game for programming purposes, you could use rules similar to those described here but played out on a square array of cells, much like in "The Amazon Skull Game" on page 355.

---

[50] Like the skull game, I suspect that the true origin for this game is more recent and probably less colorful. The playing board resembles graphs found in: Bondy, J., Murty, R. (1976) *Graph Theory*. North Holland: New York.

## A.4  The Game of Japanese Crests

*"It is a wholesome plan, in thinking about logic, to stock the mind with as many puzzles as possible, since these serve much the same purpose as is served by experiments in physical science. "*
                        Bertrand Russell, *philosopher and mathematician*

Many puzzles have been based on the problem of drawing straight lines in such a way that pictures of objects on a page are put into a separate region. *The Game of Japanese Crests* uses small circular badges which are thrown on a large piece or rice paper. (Crests or badges are the expressive form of Japanese heraldry.) Can you draw three straight lines that will divide the plane in such a way as to place each crest in a separate region? Figure A.1 shows a typical set of positions. How would a computer solve this problem?

## A.5  Hyperpower Towers

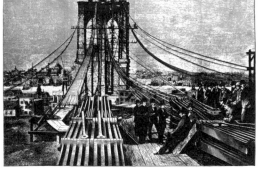

*"A mathematician is a machine for turning coffee into theorems. "*
                                                            Paul Erdos

Hyperpowers of the form
$$x = g(z) = z^{z^{z}} \tag{A.5}$$

for real positive $z$ make up a fascinating reservoir for computer study. You can define the sequence $\{z_n\}$ by
$$z_1 = z, \quad z_{n+1} = z^{z_n}, \quad n = 1, 2, \ldots \tag{A.6}$$

You can repeat this mathematical feedback loop over and over again. Whenever the sequence $\{z(n)\}$ converges we write $g(z) = \lim_{n \to \infty} z(n)$.
    You will find that the hyperpower tower diverges (gets larger and larger) for starting values greater than
$$1^{1/e} \tag{A.7}$$

You'll also find some interesting surprises when the starting value is less than

**Figure A.1.** *Japanese Crests.* Can you draw three straight lines that will put each crest in a separate region? Hint: It is possible.

$$e^{-e} \tag{$A$.8}$$

Try it.

## A.6  A Polynomial Equation with No Real Roots

The Hart equation is interesting, in part, because it is a polynomial equation with no real roots.

$$1 + x + x^2/2! + x^3/3! + \cdots x^{2n}/(2n!) = 0 \tag{$A$.9}$$

Use Newton's method to diagram the behavior of this function in the complex plane (see Glossary).

## A.7 Johnson Functions

In his article *Approximating $\sqrt{n}$* which appeared in the 19th volume of the journal *Mathematical Spectrum* (Issue 2, page 40), Simon Johnson suggests that the iterative formula

$$z \to I(z) = \frac{z + n}{z^2 + 1} \qquad (A.10)$$

applied to the rational number $z$, converges to $n^{1/3}$. Later, Irving, Richards and Sowley showed that this iteration converges to $n^{1/3}$ if $0 < n \leq 2^{3/2}$, but that if $n > 2^{3/2}$ it only converges for certain unusual initial values of $z$. Devise a graphics strategy for showing these unusual values.

## A.8 Determine the Number of Trailing Zeros in 500!

For a computer program solution to finding the number of trailing zeros in 500 factorial ($500 \times 499 \times 498 \times 497 \ldots \times 1$), without actually evaluating 500 factorial, see: Meredith, D. (1988) Meeting the challenge. *Computer Language.* November 5(11): 7-8.

## A.9 Catalan Numbers

*Catalan numbers* are defined by the following rules: The first two Catalan numbers are 1, which we can write as $C(0) = 1$ and $C(1) = 1$. The $n$-th Catalan number is defined as

$$C_n = \sum_{i=0}^{n-1} [C_i C_{n-i-1}] \qquad (A.11)$$

Can you write a program to print the first twenty Catalan numbers? The first four Catalan numbers are: 1, 1, 2, 5. A program solution to this problem appears in: Chen, S. (1989) *The IBM Programmer's Challenge.* Tab Books: Blue Ridge, Pennsylvania.

## A.10 The Schoenberg Space-Filling Curve

*"There is a discernible pattern, albeit a very complicated one. Attractive it is not. It would appear that what Arnold Schoenberg has done to music, I. J. Schoenberg has done to Peano-curves. "* Hans Sagan, *1986*

The Schoenberg space-filling curve is one of the most intricate and exotic of all space-filling curves discussed in the world's scientific literature. *Space-filling curves* are interesting patterns which grow in length without limit while they fill the region in which they lie. The two most famous are the Hilbert and Sierpinski curves. A more recent discovery is the self-similar curve, developed by Mandelbrot, which fits exactly inside a Koch snowflake (see the April 1978 cover of *Scientific American*; for a review of all these curves, see Hill, 1990). The curve discussed here was invented in 1938 by I.J. Schoenberg, and further developed in 1986 by Hans Sagan. It is certainly a challenge for mathematicians, programmers and computer graphics specialists. Or as Hans Sagan has put it: "To draw a 5th order Schoenberg curve, with no simple pattern to serve as guide, would tax the manipulative skills of a 17th century mathematician, and the mere thought of going beyond that boggles the mind." Here I give the recipe for creating these curves and you can read more about the gory details in Sagan's paper. First you must define a function $p(t)$ which looks something like a chunky sine wave (resembling a chain of trapezoids) formed with straight edges:

$$p(t) = 0 \text{ for } 0 \le t < 1/3$$
$$p(t) = 3t - 1 \text{ for } 1/3 \le t < 2/3 \tag{A.12}$$
$$p(t) = 1 \text{ for } 2/3 \le t < 1$$

This curve continues to infinity in both the $+t$ and $-t$ directions. Also $p(-t) = p(t)$, $p(t + 2) = p(t)$. To create the Schoenberg monstrosity for different orders, connect each vertex to its predecessor by a straight line using

$$x = f(t) = \sum_{k=1}^{\infty} p(3^{2k-2}t)/2^k \tag{A.13}$$

$$y = g(t) = \sum_{k=1}^{\infty} p(3^{2k-1}t)/2^k \tag{A.14}$$

Schoenberg's curve has vertices for $t_{m,m} = n/3^m$, for $m = 1,2,3, \dots$, $n = 0,1,2, \dots, 3^m$, where $m$ is the "order" of the curve. Shown here is a curve of

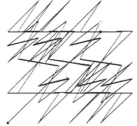

order 4. I believe that the highest order Schoenberg curve ever to be plotted in a scientific journal is 7. You can read more about his curve in: Schoenberg, I.J. (1938) The Peano-curve of Lebesgue. *Bull. Amer. Math. Soc.*, 44: 519. Additional information can be found in: Sagan, H. (1986) Approximating polygons for Lebesgue's and Schoenberg's space filling curves. *American Mathematics Monthly*. May 93(5): 361. For a general description of space-filling curves see: Hill, F. (1990) *Computer Graphics*. Macmillan: New York.

## A.11 Wither's Attractor

Wm. Douglas Withers of the U.S. Naval Academy has described an interesting attractor for

$$A(z) = z^2 - 2\bar{z} \tag{A.15}$$

where $z$ is a complex number and $\bar{z}$ is the complex conjugate ("The Ikeda Attractor" on page 115 and "The World of Chaos" on page 121 define the concept of attractors in mathematics.) Starting with any initial value for $z$ you will finally be positioned somewhere on a triangular-shaped object with vertices at $(3, -3/2 \pm 3\sqrt{3}/2)$ as you repeatedly apply Wither's formula in a mathematical

feedback loop. In other words, your new $z$ value becomes input to the equation and the mapping is repeated. For more information on this curve see: Withers, W. D. (1987) Folding polynomials and their dynamics. *American Mathematics Monthly*. 95(5) 399-407.

## A.12 Pentagonal Kaleidoscopes

In this section, we see the stunning graphics generated by symmetrical dynamical systems. Dynamical systems are also discussed in "The Ikeda Attractor" on page 115, "The World of Chaos" on page 121, and "Wither's Attractor" on page 361. (*Warning*: complicated mathematics ahead.) Kaleidoscopic forms are generated by the Chossat-Golubitsky formula:

$$f(\zeta, \lambda) = (\alpha u + \beta v + \lambda)\zeta + \gamma \bar{\zeta}^{m-1} \qquad (A.16)$$

where

$$u = \zeta\bar{\zeta} \text{ and } v = (\zeta^m + \bar{\zeta}^m)/2 \qquad (A.17)$$

and $\zeta$ is complex. $\alpha$, $\beta$, $\gamma$, $\lambda$, and $\phi$ are constants. $\bar{\zeta}$ is the complex conjugate. For those of you knowledgeable in group theory, the mapping $f{:}V \rightarrow V$ is equivariant with respect to the group $\Gamma$ acting on $V$ since $f(\gamma v) = \gamma f(v)$ (Chossat and Golubitsky, 1988). I generated Figure A.2, Figure A.3, and Figure A.4 with $m = 5$. $\lambda$ can be considered a bifurcation parameter, and low values of $\lambda$ generally correspond to smaller-sized attractors having less symmetry than the figures shown here. Figure A.2, Figure A.3, and Figure A.4 were generated by following the discrete dynamics of

$$f(\zeta, \lambda) = (\alpha u + \beta v + \lambda)\zeta + \gamma \bar{\zeta}^{m-1} + \phi \qquad (A.18)$$

where $\phi$ is a symmetry-breaking term which I have introduced and have found to produce interesting dynamics. For more information, see: Pickover, C. (1991) Pentagonal chaos. In *Five-Fold Symmetry*. I. Hargittai, ed. World Scientific: NY. Also: Chossat, P., Golubitsky, M. (1988) Symmetry-increasing bifurcations of chaotic attractors. *Physica D*. 32: 423-426.

## A.13 Graphic Design in Advertising

Various advertisers have used creative graphical methods for comparing two quantities. Figure A.5, Figure A.6, and Figure A.7 are advertisements published in various magazines. Note how the designers have used a variety of clever methods for giving simple numerical comparisons visual impact. As an interesting

**Figure A.2.** *Pentagonal chaotic attractor.* The generating equation is $f(\zeta, \lambda) = (\alpha u + \beta v + \lambda)\zeta + \gamma \bar{z}^{m-1} + \phi$. $(\gamma = 1, \lambda = -2.6, m = 9, \alpha = 4, \beta = 2, \phi = 0)$. Other parameters yield additional beautiful patterns. This pattern, as well as the following patterns in this section, represent the trajectory of a single "seed" particle as it moves on a plane. The equations are iterated one million times.

classroom exercise, students may search for other examples of how modern graphics designers communicate information through the simultaneous presentation of words, numbers, and pictures. Why are some graphics better than others? Can you change or improve the design? These figures were generated by hand, but can computer graphics be used to automate the drawing process and to add visual or emotional impact?

## A.14 Scherk's Surface

Scherk's surface, discovered in 1835, has the following form:

$$z = \ln\left( \frac{\cos y}{\cos x} \right) \tag{A.19}$$

where $-2\pi < x < 2\pi$ and $-2\pi < y < 2\pi$. Can you have your computer draw this strange surface? Stewart Dickson has actually created a 3-D physical model of

**Figure A.3.** *Another pentagonal chaotic attractor.* Same as previous figure except $\phi = 0.1 + 0.1i$. Notice that $\phi$ breaks the symmetry of the pattern in the previous figure.

this weird surface using a new process called stereolithography. This process employs a laser-based tool and a photosensitive liquid resin which hardens as it forms the 3-D object. The introduction of this book describes this process further.[51] For further information, see: Dickson, S. (1990) Minimal surfaces. *The Mathematica Journal.* 1(1): 38.

## A.15  Zenograms: Squashed Worlds

You can compress all of mathematical space from $-\infty$ to $+\infty$ into a cube that extends from -1 to 1. One way to do this makes use of the hyperbolic tangent function

$$\tanh x = \frac{e^x - e^{-x}}{e^x + e^{-x}} \tag{A.20}$$

---

[51] Interestingly, Scherk's surface is a plausible model for the structure of interacting polymers that prefer to have as little contact as possible.

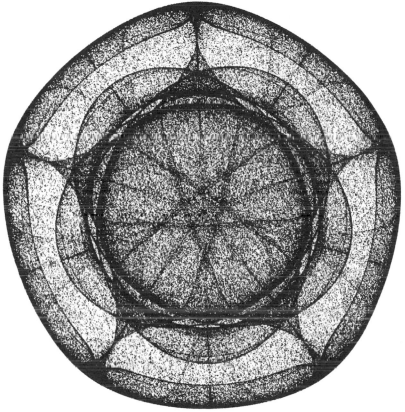

**Figure A.4.** *Another pentagonal chaotic attractor.* Same as previous figure except ($\gamma = .5, \lambda = -1.804, m = 3, \alpha = 1, \beta = 0, \phi = 0$).

I call the resulting representation a Zenogram, after the ancient philosopher who studied various properties of infinity. My graphics program, called Zenospace, allows you to explore this strange squashed world using advanced computer graphics. No matter how large your numbers are, the tanh function can only return a maximum value of positive 1 (or a minimum value of -1). Here are some observations on this weird space. In the Zenogram, diagonal parallel planes begin to curve, and meet at infinity (the sides of the box). Paraboloids ($z = x^n + y^n$, $n = 2$) become squashed in interesting ways as they near the side of the box. (What happens as you increase $n$?) Spheres deform in interesting ways as they grow larger or are pushed towards the side of the box. Figure A.8 shows a Zenogram for a sphere as it is pushed to a side wall, at positive infinity. What happens to the shape of a sphere centered at the origin as its radius grows to infinity?

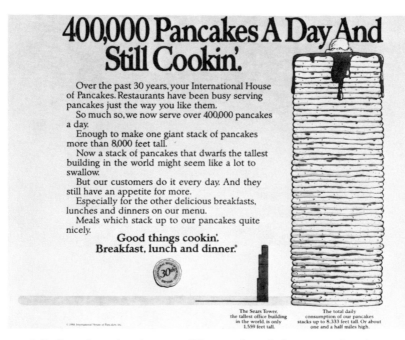

Figure A.5. *Pancake advertisement*. (Figure adapted from an advertisement for the International House of Pancakes, Inc., ©1988, IHOP; all rights reserved.)

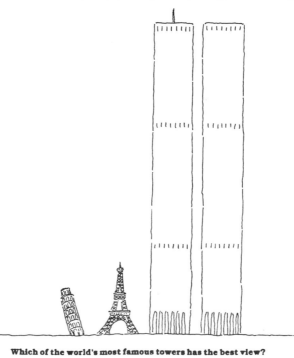

**Which of the world's most famous towers has the best view?**

Figure A.6. *World Trade Center*. (Figure from an advertisement for the World Trade Center, produced by the Port Authority of New York and New Jersey.)

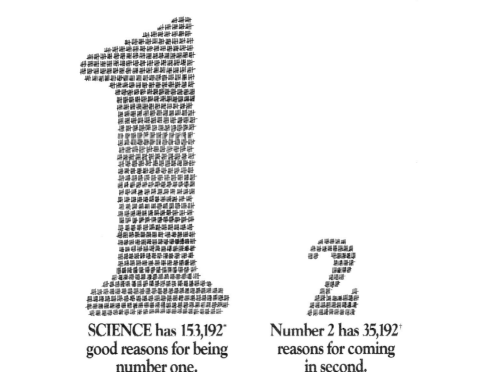

**Figure A.7.** *Magazine subscriptions.* (Figure from an advertisement for: *Science*, Vol. 242, Page 1727, Dec. 23, 1988. Original ad by Scherago Associates, Inc. ©1988 AAAS. )

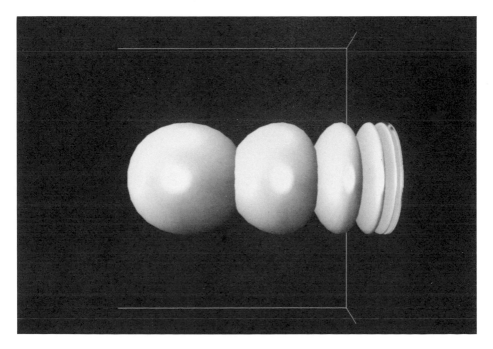

**Figure A.8.** *A Zenogram.*

# Interlude: Fractal Caves

*"Out of the vast main aisle there opened here and there smaller caves, exactly, Sir Henry said, as chapels open out of great cathedrals. Some were large, but one or two – and this is a wonderful instance of how Nature carries out her handiwork by the same unvarying laws, utterly irrespective of size – were tiny. One little nook, for instance, was no larger than an unusually big doll's house, and yet it might have been the model of the whole place, for the water dropped, the tiny icicles hung, and the spar columns were forming in just the same way. "* – H. Rider Haggard, 1885

## Appendix C

# Notes for the Curious

This section contains additional follow-up notes regarding some of the topics in this book.

• "Visualization of the Gleichniszahlen-Reihe Monster" on page 181 described an unusual number sequence. For true aficionados of this monstrous sequence, the frontispiece for this chapter contains a likeness sequence for row 33!

• "Irregularly Oscillating Fossil Seashells" on page 129 described research in the graphic representation of the unusual growth trajectories of certain bizarre fossil sea shells. You may be interested to know that there exist fossil forms much weirder than the wildly twisting *Nipponites* shell described in that chapter. In fact, if I had to single out a creature as the most unusual of all fossil invertebrate forms, the prize would go to *Anomalocaris*. Fitting no other major animal design known, this half-meter-long trilobite-killer had a mouth that actually resembled a jellyfish. Its large front feet resemble shrimp-like crustaceans. Another weird fossil form is *Hallucigenia* which supports itself by seven pairs of struts. You can read more about these and related fossil oddities in *Wonderful Life* by Stephen J. Gould (Norton, 1989). Shown here is a sketch of *Anomalocaris* (top) and *Hallucigenia* (bottom) from Gould's book. The drawings are by Marianne Collins (© 1989, Norton; all rights reserved).

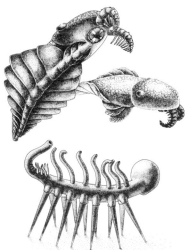

If you wish to trace out the strange growth trajectories of *Nipponites* on your personal computer, the following pseudocode may be helpful.

```
PI = 3.14159; alpha = 0.1; beta = 0.1; eps = 0.2;
gam = 3.0; f = 0.3
for(theta = -PI; theta <= 2*PI; theta=theta+PI/30.1)
   x = exp(alpha*theta) * (1+ eps * cos(2*gam*theta))
      * cos(theta - f*sin(2*gam*theta));
```

```
y = exp(alpha*theta) * (1+ eps * cos(2*gam*theta))
    * sin(theta - f*sin(2*gam*theta);
z = exp(beta*theta) * sin(gam*theta);
PlotPointAt(x,z);
```

• "Building Your Own Artificial Webs" on page 39 described natural and artificial spider webs. It might interest you to know that scientists today are stu-

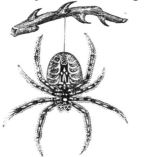

dying the chemistry of webs in order to create new kinds of artificial tendons, sutures, and bulletproof vests. Spider web strands can hold weights that would snap strands of steel of the same volume. Webs are made of proteins, some of which have been sequenced. The special arrangement of amino acids in these web proteins gives webs their remarkable physical properties. The scientific name for spiders is *Arachnids*, which comes from the Greek maiden Arachne who was turned into a spider when she defeated Athena in a weaving contest.

• The non-Newtonian fluid discussed in "The World of Chaos" on page 121 is better known as "Silly Putty."

• "Buckminsterfullerene!" on page 166 discussed a strange new example of a chemical polyhedron, an almost-spherical polyhedron known as $C_{60}$, "soccerene," "buckminsterfullerene," or "buckyball." The 60 carbon atoms in the molecule are arranged at the vertices of a truncated icosahedron, a soccer-ball form popularized by Buckminster Fuller for use in geodesic domes. In the September 27th, 1990 issue of *Nature*, several researchers announced they had developed a way to synthesize relatively large quantities of $C_{60}$ in a solid form. $C_{60}$ should make a good lubricant, because its cage-like structure is very stable and slow to react with other substances. Some scientists have predicted that the substance should make a good catalyst, or lead to a whole new class of batteries.

• "The Lute of Pythagoras" on page 203 discussed continued fractions. You may be interested in the continued fraction representation for $\pi$

$$\pi/4 = \cfrac{1}{1 + \cfrac{1^2}{2 + \cfrac{3^2}{\cdots}}} \qquad (C.1)$$

The numerator terms are: $(1, 1^2, 3^2, 5^2, 7^2, 9^2, \dots)$. The denominator terms are: $(1, 2, 2, 2, 2, 2, 2, \dots)$. For most purposes, knowing the value of $\pi$ to two decimal places is enough.[52] A recent paper discusses the use of continued fractions in "ladder" circuits, fractals, gases, optical resonators, and the characterization of rough surfaces. A continued fraction is finite in size when it represents a rational number (see Glossary). On the other hand, irrational numbers have continued

---

[52] Ivars Peterson notes that thirty nine decimal places of $\pi$ suffice for computing the circumference of a circle girdling the known universe with an error no greater than the radius of a hydrogen atom!

fractions which are infinite in size. Of these irrational numbers, *quadratic irrational* numbers, which are the solutions of a quadratic equation, have continued fractions which repeat, for example, $\sqrt{15} = [3,1,6,1,6,1,6, \ldots]$ (see the notation in "The Lute of Pythagoras" on page 203). For further information: Lakhtakia, A., Messier, R., Vasandara, V., Varadan, V. (1988) Incommensurate numbers, continued fractions, and fractal immittances. *Z. Naturforsch.* 43A: 943-955. Also: Peterson, I. (1990) *Islands of Truth*, Freeman: New York.

• "The Lute of Pythagoras" on page 203 discussed the golden ratio, $\phi =$ 1.618 .... You may be interested to know that the average ratio of a woman's height to the height of her navel is 1.618, as measured by Frank Lone of New York. David Johnson of the Philco Corporation has calculated $\phi$ to 2,878 decimal places. The unusual sequence 177111777 occurs among the first 500 decimals. For further information on $\phi$ see Gardner, M. (1961) *The Second Scientific American Book of Mathematical Puzzles and Diversions*. University of Chicago Press: Chicago.

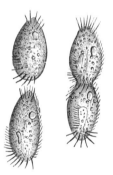

• "Desktop Evolution" on page 49 discussed the chemical evolution of life. Recently, MIT chemist Jules Rebek created an organic molecule that reproduces itself – a molecule that Rebek considers a primitive form of life. Whether or not it is truly alive, it is definitely not life as we know it. Rebek's J-shaped molecule is held together by some of the same chemical bonds as proteins, DNA, and RNA – but the molecule reproduces in a chloroform solution! (Life on earth probably evolved in water.) For those of you who are chemists, this primitive life form consists of an amino adenosine triacid ester. In a solution, Rebek's molecules can copy themselves at rates up to a dizzying million times per second. For further information: Daviss, B. (1990) Yikes! It's alive. *Discover*, 11(12): 28.

• "Interlude: Computer Exoskeletons" on page 197 and "Conclusion" on page 343 both mentioned the growing intimacy between computers and people. You may be interested to know about another new computer interface device called the "Convolvotron" developed by the NASA Ames Research Center in Moutainview, California. This computer and headphone system manipulates a listener's spatial perception of sound. For example, even though one listens through headphones, sounds seem to emanate from a particular place in a room, regardless of how you turn your head. For further information: Wright, K. (1990) An earful of 3-D music. *Discover*, 11(12): 34.

• "On the Existence of Cakemorphic Integers" on page 219 gave an equation for the maximum number of pieces that can be produced with $n$ cuts of a circular

region. Martin Gardner recently sent me a letter containing similar formulas for a doughnut and sphere cut with $n$ plane cuts. For a doughnut, the largest number of pieces that can be produced with $n$ cuts is: $(n^3 + 3n^2 + 8n)/6$. Thus a doughnut can be sliced into 13 pieces by three simultaneous plane cuts (see Figure C.1). For a sphere, the equation is: $(n^3 + 5n)/6 + 1$. For a 2-D crescent

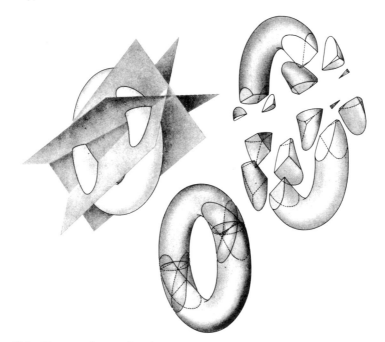

**Figure C.1.** *How to slice a doughnut into 13 pieces with only three plane cuts.* From *The Second Scientific American Book of Mathematical Puzzles and Diversions* ©1987 by Scientific American, Inc. All rights reserved. For my own computer graphical dissection of a doughnut, see Color Plate 27.

moon: $(n^2 + 3n)/2 + 1$. For further information on cutting shapes see: Gardner, M. (1961) *The Second Scientific American Book of Mathematical Puzzles and Diversions.* University of Chicago Press: Chicago. Also: Gardner, M. (1983) *New Mathematical Diversions from Scientific American.* University of Chicago Press: Chicago.

• Both "Building Your Own Artificial Webs" on page 39 and "Irregularly Oscillating Fossil Seashells" on page 129 discussed some rather unusual animal  species. How many species of animals are on earth today? Surprisingly, this is a very difficult question to answer. For example, the cephalopod shown here is among an estimated 80,000 species of mollusks. Susan Gilbert, in her April 1986 *Science Digest* article (p. 23), provides the following relevant quote summarizing Harvard biologist Edward O. Wilson: *"We know, for example, that there are 10 genes in a small virus particle and approximately 100 billion stars in our galaxy. But we don't know, even to the nearest order of magnitude, how many species live on Earth."*

• "A Wiring Problem" on page 45 discussed the task of interconnecting objects. This type of problem raises questions that pertain to the mathematical field of graph theory – the study of ways in which points can be connected. Graphs often play important roles in circuit design. One unusual problem in this field involves the following question. How does one arrange sticks in a way such

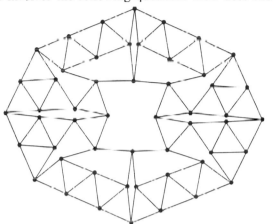

that 4 sticks meet end to end, without crossing each other, at every point in a geometrical figure on a flat surface? In the diagram here, 4 sticks meet at each vertex. This is the smallest arrangement known, but no one knows whether it's the smallest possible way to make a figure with 4 sticks meeting at each point! (Pattern discovered by Heiko Harborth; diagram from Peterson, I. (1990) *Islands of Truth*. Freeman: New York.)

• "Computers and the Unexpected" on page 3 described the work of mathematicians who are also artists. Mathematics Professor Helaman Ferguson recently created a sculpture titled *Umbilic Torus NC* which stands 27 inches high and is cast in bronze. Ferguson used a computer-programmed milling tool to emboss a fractal pattern on the sculpture's surface. Interestingly, like a mobius strip, the sculpture has only one edge. If you try tracing the edges with your finger, you'll go around the torus three times before returning to your starting point.

The simple looking twisted torus has a rather complicated looking generating formula, part of which is shown below:

$$\left( \frac{\alpha\beta}{\gamma\delta} \right) : \sum_{0 \le j \le 3} A_j x^{3-j} y^j \rightarrow \sum_{0 \le j \le 3} A_j (\alpha x + \beta y)^{3-j} (\gamma x + \delta y)^j \qquad (C.2)$$

(For further reading, see the article: "A feel for math" in *Breakthroughs*. February. 2(1): 75-76.)

• "The Juggler Sequence" on page 231 described an erratic sequence of integers. Figure C.2 shows the first few terms of a juggler behemoth for 193, which takes 74 steps before returning to 1. Cornelius Groenewoud of Bartow, Florida wrote me the following letter:

*Dear Sir:*
*You have essentially defined the juggler sequences by*

```
193 2681 138817 51720650 7191 609795 476185085
10391151638843 33496198677403032405
19386226644017681400073977497l
8535715445974697273176106626261201106667946
78860566577787233394147987499403577675976938427376583215958884528
88803472104297382249518660744695
26463356030971610422085864703771922874040048088677
136l34242643398481765860616637779751344646303632658099373147841507505327119
15883677819761122474245228321423857253871928275855318838108903965...
(continued) 5136891224470087055467097483507581305201397218
```

**Figure C.2.** *First few terms of a behemoth Juggler sequence for 193.* I performed the computation on an **IBM** 3090 using special-purpose software allowing high-precision exponentiation. To compute multi-digit square roots for a number, $x$, I iterated the following computer command several hundred times: *answer = 0.5 * (x/answer + answer).*

    *if x is even then* $x \leftarrow \lfloor x^f \rfloor$
    *else* $x \leftarrow \lfloor x^g \rfloor$
    *until x = 1*

*where f = 0.5 and g = 1.50. I think proving that every such sequence ends in 1 will be very difficult. The termination is very sensitive to the choice of f and g. As an example, let's always choose 5 as the initial value of x and then use different values of f and g very near to your choices of f = 0.50 and g = 1.50. Note what happens:*

| $f$ | $g$ | *members of sequence* |
|------|-------|-------------------------|
| 0.55 | 1.45 | 5,10,3,4,2,1 |
| 0.54 | 1.46 | 5,10,3,4,2,1 |
| 0.53 | 1.47 | 5,10,3,5, repeats |
| 0.52 | 1.48 | 5,10,3,5, repeats |
| 0.511 | 1.489 | 5,10,3,5, repeats |
| 0.510 | 1.490 | 5,11,35,199,2662,... |
|  |  | a total of 18 steps ending in ... 4,2,1 |
| 0.50 | 1.50 | 5,11,36,6,2,1 repeats |
| 0.49 | 1.51 | 5,11,37,233,3755,249839,141405711, etc. |
| 0.48 | 1.52 | 5,11,38,5 repeats |
| 0.473 | 1.527 | 5,11,38,5 repeats |
| 0.472 | 1.528 | 5,11,39,269,5160,56,6,2,1 |
| 0.471 | 1.529 | 5,11,39,270,13,50,6,2,1 |
| 0.47 | 1.53 | 5,11,39,271,5277,495738,475,12454,84,8,2,1 |
| 0.46 | 1.54 | 5,11,40,5, repeats |
| 0.45 | 1.55 | 5,12,3,5, repeats |

You may wish to make a 3-D plot showing the relationship between *f*, *g*, and the number of steps before returning to 1. Others have written to me regarding the Juggler Sequence. James Beauchamp of Quebec, Canada, notes that, in BASIC, the statement x = INT (36**(1/2)) gives the result 5, which is false. He suggests that SQR be used instead of exponentiation to the 1/2 or 0.5 power.

- "A Prime Plaid" on page 213 discusses prime numbers – integers like 11, 13, and 17 which are evenly divisible only by themselves and one. Recently Arjen Lenstra of Bellcore and Mark Manasse of the Digital Equipment Corporation found the three prime factors of a 155-digit number called the ninth Fermat number. 17th-century French mathematician Pierre de Fermat conjectured that numbers of the form $2^m + 1$ (where $m = 2^n$ and $n$ is zero or a positive integer ) are prime. This turns out to be true for $n < 5$ but not for the Fermat numbers computed for greater values of $n$. In 1990, the ninth Fermat number, shown here, was factored to 2,424,833 (a prime) and a 99- and a 49-digit prime number using 200 volunteers and nearly 1,000 computers! (For further reading, see the article: "Long, long division" in *Breakthroughs*. February. 2(1): 74-75.)

**The Ninth Fermat**:

**The number** 13,407,807,929,942,597,099,574,024,998,204,846,127,
479,365,820,592,393,377,723,561,443,721,764,030,073,546,
976,801,874,298,166,903,427,690,031,858,186,486,050,
853,753,882,811,946,569,946,433,649,006,084,097

**equals**

2,424,833

**times**

7,455,602,825,647,884,208,337,395,736,
200,454,918,783,366,342,657

**times**

741,640,062,627,530,801,524,787,141,901,937,474,059,
940,781,097,519,023,905,821,316,144,415,759,
504,705,008,092,818,711,693,940,737.

- "Picturing Randomness with Noise Spheres" on page 137 discussed the use of computer graphics to represent noisy data. Another method I've employed makes use of a pattern from Dutch artist M. C. Escher. To produce Figure C.3,

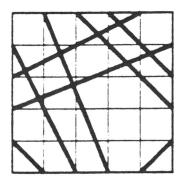

simply draw the generating tile (shown here) with a random orientation, and place it within the corner of a large square lattice. Successive adjacent tiles are added to the lattice for a particular row until it is filled, and a new row is started. When the tile is printed in any of its positions to fill out a grid of squares, a seamless plane-filling pattern is created. I used just two orientations of the tile to create this figure. You can see that there are some diamond shaped objects in the pattern. As correlations within the data become greater, the number of diamonds decreases. A completely random tiling contains the maximum number of diamonds; in this case, the *diamond fraction* is approximately 5% (number of diamonds in the pattern divided by the number of tiles). Try using this tile to represent the genetic sequence data in Figure C.4. The sequence, symbolized by the four different

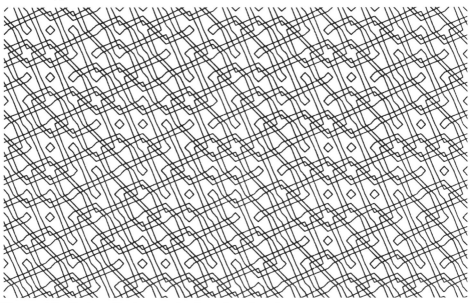

**Figure C.3.** *Escher-tile characterization of random data.*

letters G, C, A, and T, can be represented by a collection of tiles with four different orientations. What does the resulting tile pattern ("Eschergram") tell you about the patterns, and degree of randomness, within the first 1000 bases of the AIDS virus (Figure C.4)? For more information on Escher tiles see: Schattschneider, D. (1990) *Visions of Symmetry*. Freeman: New York. For information on the use of tiles to represent noisy data see: Pickover, C. (1989) Picturing randomness with Truchet tiles. *Journal of Recreational Math.* 21(4): 256-259. Also: Pickover, C. (1991) Mathematics and beauty: several short classroom experiments. *American Math Society Notices*. March, 38(3): 191-195.

- "Desktop Evolution" on page 49 discussed the folding of genetic sequences.

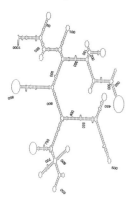

Recently two scientists from the Netherlands have applied the same kinds of computational molecular biology methods to non-biological sequences. In particular, they have constructed pseudo-RNA sequences based on the prime number series, and then used RNA-folding programs in order to analyze patterns in the prime numbers! The diagram at left is a pseudo-RNA structure obtained from the first 1000 prime pairs. A biological RNA molecule with this sequence is predicted to have a free energy of -256.9 kcal/mole. For further information on this novel and fascinating approach, contact the researchers: Mels Sluyser and Erik L. Sonnhammer, The Netherlands Cancer Institute, 1066 CX Amsterdam, The Netherlands.

```
   1 TGTAGTGGGT GGAAGGGCTA ATTCACTCCC AACGAAGACA AGATATCCTT
  51 GATCTGTGGA TCTACCACAC ACAAGGCTAC TTCCCTGATT GGCAGAACTA
 101 CACACCAGGA CCAGGGATCA GATATCCACT GACCTTTGGA TGGTGCTACA
 151 AGCTAGTACC AGTTGAGCCA GATAAGGTAG AAGAGGCCAA CAAAGGAGAG
 201 AACACCAGCT TGTTACACCC TGTGAGCCTG CATGGAATGG ATGACCCGGA
 251 GAGAGAAGTG TTAGAGTGGA GGTTTGACAG CCGCCTAGCA TTTCATCACG
 301 TGGCCCGAGA GCTGCATCCG GAGTACTTCA AGAACTGCTG ATATCGAGCT
 351 TGCTACAAGG GACTTTCCGC TGGGGACTTT CCAGGGAGGC GTGGCCTGGG
 401 CGGGACTGGG GAGTGGCGAG CCCTCAGATG CTGCATATAA GCAGCTGCTT
 451 TTTGCCTGTA CTGGGTCTCT CTGGTTAGAC CAGATCTGAG CCTGGGAGCT
 501 CTCTGGCTAA CTAGGGAACC CACTGCTTAA GCCTCAATAA AGCTTGCCTT
 551 GAGTGCTTCA AGTAGTGTGT GCCCGTCTGT TGTGTGACTC TGGTAACTAG
 601 AGATCCCTCA GACCCTTTTA GTCAGTGTGG AAAATCTCTA GCAGTGGCGC
 651 CCGAACAGGG ACTTGAAAGC GAAAGGGAAA CCAGAGGAGC TCTCTCGACG
 701 CAGGACTCGG CTTGCTGAAG CGCGCACGGC AAGAGGCGAG GGGCGGCGAC
 751 TGGTGAGTAC GCCAAAAATT TTGACTAGCG GAGGCTAGAA GGAGAGAGAT
 801 GGGTGCGAGA GCGTCAGTAT TAAGCGGGGG AGAATTAGAT CGATGGGAAA
 851 AAATTCGGTT AAGGCCAGGG GGAAAGAAAA AATATAAATT AAAACATATA
 901 GTATGGGCAA GCAGGGAGCT AGAACGATTC GCAGTTAATC CTGGCCTGTT
1001 TTCAGACAGG ATCAGAAGAA CTTAGATCAT TATATAATAC AGTAGCAACC
 951 AGAAACATCA GAAGGCTGTA GACAAATACT GGGACAGCTA CAACCATCCC
```

**Figure C.4.** *AIDS virus sequence.* Shown here are the first 1000 bases of the human immunodeficiency virus type 1. Use these data as input to the Escher-tile characterization described in the text. (Source for sequence: Muesing, M.A., Smith, D.H., Cabradilla, C.D., Benton, C.V., Lasky, L.A. and Capon, D.J. (1985) Nucleic acid structure and expression of the human AIDS/lymphadenopathy retrovirus. *Nature.* 313: 450-458.)

- "Results of the Very-Large-Number Contest" on page 207 discussed large numbers such as the Hamlet number and the Chess number. Here are a few other large numbers — all less than a googol. The *ice age number* ($10^{30}$) is the number of snow crystals necessary to form the ice age. The *Coney Island number* ($10^{20}$) is the number of grains of sands on the Coney Island beach. The *talking number* ($10^{16}$) is the number of words spoken by humans since the dawn of time. It includes all baby talk, love songs, and Congressional debates. This number is roughly the same as the number of words printed since the Gutenberg Bible appeared. The amount of money in circulation in Germany at the peak of inflation was: 496, 585, 346, 000, 000, 000, 000. The number of marks in circulation is very similar to the number of grains of sand on the Coney Island beach. The number of atoms in oxygen in the average thimble is a good deal larger: 1, 000, 000, 000, 000, 000, 000, 000, 000, 000. The number of electrons which passes through a filament of an ordinary light bulb in a minute equals the number of drops of water that flow over Niagra Falls in a century. The number of electrons in a single leaf is much larger than the number of pores of all the leaves of all the trees in the world. The number of atoms in this book is less than a googol. The chance that this book will jump from the table into your hand is not 0 — in fact, using the laws of statistical mechanics, it will almost certainly happen sometime in less than a googolplex of years.

• *Contests, Free Newsletters, etc.*:  An award of 50 dollars is hereby offered by the publisher for the most novel and aesthetically pleasing Lute of Pythagoras constructed by readers.  Lutes with a high degree of recursion will be of particular interest.  The award will be given on or about September, 1993, and the illustration may appear in subsequent editions of this book.  Please address all entries to: Pickover, P.O. Box 549, Millwood, New York 10546-0549 USA.  Readers interested in photocopies of all Lutes received may inquire at the same address.  *Juggernaut* is an informal newsletter published by the Juggler Geometry Club.  It consists of a large collection of letters written by students and researchers concerning software for, and the theory of, juggler geometry and earthworm algebra.  Inquire at the address given at the beginning of this paragraph.  An award of 50 dollars is offered by the publisher for a printout of the largest Juggler number computed by readers.  The award will be given on or about September, 1993, and the sequence will also be published in the *Juggernaut*. Currently, the largest juggler number computed is a 45,391-digit giant for the starting number 30817.  It was computed by Harry J. Smith using his own software package to perform multiple precision integer arithmetic. His package is written in the object-oriented programming language Turbo Pascal 5.5 by Borland International, Inc. His juggler package is a subset of his super-precision calculator software which computes transcendental functions to thousands of decimal places. Write him to obtain the software: Harry J. Smith, 19628 Via Monte Drive, Saratoga, CA 95070. An award of 50 dollars is also offered by the publisher for a printout of the largest likeness-sequence computed by readers.  The award will be given on or about September, 1993. *The Journal of Chaos and Graphics* is another newsletter concerning topics in mathematics and art.  Also inquire at the address given at the beginning of this paragraph.

Pictured below is MIT chemist Jules Rebek who, in the early 1990s, created an organic molecule that reproduces itself – a molecule that Rebek considers a primitive form of life. For more information, see the third page of Appendix C.

# Appendix D

# Interlude: Artistic Androids and Elephants

Robots of the future will produce paintings which rival the works of Picasso. Shown below (left) is a portrait of the author created by a portrait drawing robot which debuted at the 1985 International Science Exposition in Tskuba, Japan. The robot can interpret the outline of the face, as well as the contours of the eyes, nose and other features to create an abstract line drawing. The robotic arm dips a paint brush into paint and draws upon an easel in a startlingly human manner. These crude portraits represent the beginning of robot art which will show remarkable progress by the end of the 1990s.[53]

Can animals make art? Various researchers and artists think so. Shown below (right) is rough sketch I made from a color painting produced by an elephant. It shows just a few of the patterns in the painting. When the elephant considers one of its paintings finished, it flips up its trunk. Some authorities on abstract expressionistic art have raved about such paintings, and some elephant art sells for many hundreds of dollars. Science-writer J. Diamond notes, "If animals too have a capacity for art, what implications might that have for our own?"[54]

Today's lawyers may wonder who can grant copyright permission for art made by robots and animals.

---

[53] The portrait drawing robots use a high-speed image processor (Panasight 8X1) and a NEC PC-9801 computer.

[54] For more information on elephant art, see: Gucwa, D., Ehmann, J. (1985) *The Art of Elephants*. W. W. Norton: New York. Also: Diamond, J. (1991) Art of the Wild. *Discover*. Febr. 12(2): 78-83.

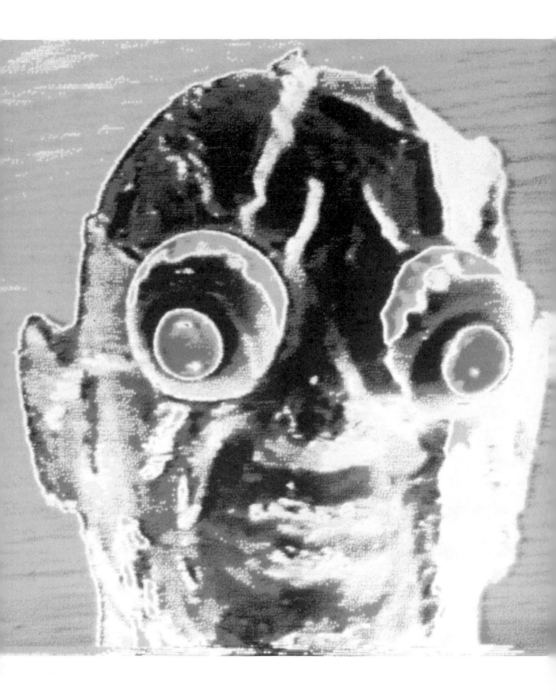

## Appendix E

# Bibliography of Computers
# In the Arts and Sciences

*"The great revolutions in science are almost always the result of unexpected intuitive leaps. After all, what is science if not the posing of difficult puzzles by the universe. Mother Nature does something interesting and challenges the scientist to figure out how she does it. "*　　　　　　　　　　　　　　　　　　　　　　Martin Gardner, *1978*

## E.1 Films

*"Human territory is defined least of all by physical frontiers."*　　　John Fowles, *The Magus*

1.  *Atoms Dance in the Amorphous World* (VHS videotape showing a computer simulation of atoms in glass; 30 min). MITA Visual Images, 3-2-12 Hongo, Bunkyo-ku, Tokyo 113 Japan.

2.  *A Non-Euclidean Universe* (1978; 25 min; color). University Media, 118 South Acacia, Box 881, Solana Beach, CA 92075.

3.  *Circle Circus* (1979; 7 min; color). International Film Bureau, 332 South Michigan Ave., Chicago, IL 60604.

4.  *Complex Numbers* (1978; 25 min; color). University Media, 118 South Acacia, Box 881, Solana Beach, CA 92075.

5.  *Cycloidal Curves, or Tales From the Wanklenberg Woods* (1974; 22 min; color). Modern Film Rentals, 2323 New Hyde Park Road, New Hyde Park, NY 11040.

6.  *Dihedral Kaleidoscopes* (1966; 13 min; color). International Film Bureau, 332 South Michigan Ave., Chicago, IL 60604.

7.  *Dragon Fold, and Other Ways to Fill Space* (1979; 7.5 min; color). International Film Bureau, 332 South Michigan Ave., Chicago, IL 60604.

8.  *Geodesic Domes: Math Raises the Roof* (1979; 20 min; color). David Nulsen Enterprises, 3211 Pico Blvd., Santa Monica, CA 90405.

9.  *Inversion* (12 min; color). International Film Bureau, 332 South Michigan Ave., Chicago, IL 60604.

10. *Sets, Crows, and Infinity* (12 min; color). BFA Educational Media, 2211 Michigan Ave., P O Box 1795, Santa Monica, CA 90406.

# E.2  Products, Classroom Aids, Art, Games, Distributors

*"There is no such thing as a problem without a gift for you in its hands. You seek problems because you need their gifts. "*                    Richard Bach

In the early 1990s, numerous computer art products and distributors came into being. Pictured above, for example, is Gregory Sams, owner of the shop *Strange Attractions*. His store is dedicated exclusively to computer art, chaos, and fractals. According to Gregory, this is Britain's first shop dedicated to chaos theory. The shop sells mugs, posters, greeting cards, badges, teeshirts, and puzzles. Although the shop's facade bears no name, you're not likely to miss the fractal swirls of green and scarlet splattered about the front walls. For more information, contact: *Strange Attractions*, 204 Kensington Park Road, London W11 1NR England. (Photo by Pete Addis.)

1.  Fractal music. (Cassette, compact disc.) Write to Botanica, Sanford Ponder, 756 S. Spring Street, 13th Floor West, Los Angeles, California, 90014.

2.  *Amber Lotus.* (Computer art, mathematics, calendars and cards.) Write to Amber Lotus, 1241 21st Street, Oakland, CA 94607.

3.  Fractal art, signed (limited-edition) color posters and catalog. Write to Fractal Generation, 2895 Biscayne Blvd, #285, Miami, Florida 33137.

4.  Mathematical metallic sculptures and tapestries by John Robinson. (Knots, DNA, bundles, beautiful ovoids. A catalog is available.) Write to Edition Limited, c/o Mrs. Anna Coyle, Trusco Management, P.O. Box 725 Carouge-Geneve, Switzerland. Or write to Mathematics and Knots, University of Wales, Bangor, LL57 1UT, UK. Or write to "Agecroft," Galhampton, Yeovil BA22 7AY, Somerset, UK.

5.  *Mathematics and Knots* by "The Mathematics and Knots Exhibition Group." (This is available as a book.) Write to Mathematics and Knots, School of Mathematics, University of Wales, Dean Street, Bangor, Gwynedd LL57 1UT, Wales, UK. Fax: (0248) 361429.

6.  Fractal Software. (Mandelbrot set, Newton's method, random walks, Julia sets, diffusion, dynamical systems.) Kenelm W. Philip, 1590 North Becker Ridge Road, Fairbanks, Alaska 99709.

7. **The Chaos Chime**. The Chaos Chime is an electromechanical analog of the classic windchime. However, the chaos chime does not require wind to activate its chimes. Instead, the Chaos Chime relies upon the chaotic (random) action of a nonlinear electromechanical engine to power the chime hammer. The principal of operation is sensitive dependence upon initial conditions. Contact: John Christensen, Christensen Designs, P.O. Box 1551 Manteca, CA 95336.

8. *POLY*. (Software which creates platonic and Archimedian solids and prisms.) Write POLY, PO Box 893, Woden, ACT, Australia 2606.

9. *Art, Science, and Technology Institute.* (This is a small, non-profit group of Eastern Europeans who teach about and sell holograms.) ASTI, 2018 R St. NW, Washington, DC 2009.

10. *BrainMaker 2.0*. (Neural network software.) California Scientific Software. 160 Montecito #E, Sierra Madre, CA 91024.

11. Fractal Software. Ian Adam, 4425 West 12th Ave., Vancouver, BC, Canada, V6R 2R3.

12. *Hallucinations 2.0*. (Software which generates non-repeating patterns.) Polymath Systems, P.O. Box 795, Berkeley, CA 94701.

13. Intricate pattern-generator. (Software and 132-page illustrated manual.) Pixel Pathways, 405 W. Washington St, # 67, San Diego, CA 92103.

14. *General Symmetrics.* (Puzzles, games, books, Engel curves.) General Symmetrics, 2935 W Chengano, Englewood, CO 80110.

15. *Blackholes in the Mandelbrot set.* (Software.) Ken Hooper, 1561 Alta Vista Drive, Vista, California 92084.

16. *The Brain.* (Software which displays real brain sections.) HyperCraft, PO Box 4582, University Park, NM 88003.

17. Koyn Software. (Fractal clip art, iterated function sets.) Koyn Software, 1754 Sprucedale, St. Louis, MO 63146.

18. Orbital Simulation. (Mandelbrot set software.) Randy Soderstrom, 7987 Altair, Anaheim, California 92808.

19. Super-precision calculators. (Software which computes transcendental functions to thousands of decimal places.) Harry J. Smith, 19628 Via Monte Drive, Saratoga, CA 95070.

20. Images, puzzles, fonts. (Software.) Write: Letterforms and Illusions, W.H. Freeman, 41 Madison Ave, New York, NY 10010.

21. Fractal art. (Software and animation.) FractalPro, MegageM, 1903 Adria, Santa Maria, CA 93454.

22. Puzzles, anagrams. (Software.) RecRoom RecWare, PO Box 307, Pacific Grove, CA 93950.

23. Checkerboard worlds, computer stories. B. V. Firner, 415 Lancaster Ct., Pisacataway, NY 08854.

24. Ray-traced faceted stones. (Slides.) Jim Gemology, Box 172, Louisville, Ohio 44641.

25. *Ariel Press.* (Books on chaos.) PO Box 1360, Santa Cruz CA 95061.

26. *Mysterious Mandelbrot Skeletons.* (Software.) Jim Gemology, Box 172, Louisville, Ohio 44641.

27. *Supermind.* (Software for Mandelbrot and Julia sets in high-resolution.) Guy Cox, Box 206, Wentworth Building, University of Sydney, NSW 2006 Australia.

28. *Ami-FX, Amiga Fractal Exchange.* Freely distributable magazine of animations, art, and software. Cade Roux, Gonville and Caius College, Cambridge CB2 1TA England.

29. Self-learning space machine. (Software.) Cognitech, PO Box 5034, Station F, Ottawa, Canada K2C 3H3.

30. *Moby worlds.* (530,000 English words plus software.) Illumind, 571 Belden St, Ste A., Montery, California 93940-1307.

31. Mandelbrot and Life software. SpeedGraoh Tiistilankuja 1 E 50, SF-02230, Espoo, Finland.

32. Minimalist art by rapid tesselation. (Software.) Christopher Computer, 28 Anderson St., Boston, MA 02114-3648.

33. Cellular Automata. (Software.) Charles Platt, PO Box 556, Chelsea Station, New York, NY 10113.

34. Neural net software. California Scientific Software, 160 Montecito #E Sierra Madre, CA 91024.

35. *CrystalEyes* (Goggles permitting viewers to see 3-D effects from a 2-D computer screen.) Stereo-Graphics, 2171-H E. Francisco Blvd. San Rafael, California 94901.

36. Fractal software. Allows $10^{72}$ magnification of fractals. Andromeda Research, 6441 Enterprise Lane, Madison, WI 53719.

37. *Explor-I.* (Chaos software which computes Biomorphs, termites, and dunes.) Turing Omnibus, PO Box 1456, London, Ontario, Canada N6A 5M2.

38. Cryptographic program for PC. Alex J. Smith, #1419-3240-66 Ave. SW, Calgary, Alberta Canada T3E 6M5.

39. Fractal Aggregation. (Software.) Fractal Recreations, 21 Wichard Blvd., Commack, NY 11725-1706.

40. *CHAOS* (Software.) EduTech, 1927 Culver Road, Rochester, NY 14609.

41. *Everglade.* (Computer poet.) Hyperion Softworld, 535 Duvernay, Sherbrooke, QC, Candada J1L 1Y8.

42. Fractal software. Ian Adam, 4425 West 12th Ave., Vancouver, British Colombia, V6R 2R3, Canada.

43. *Boston Computer Museum.* 300 Congress Street, Museum Wharf, Boston, MA 02210.

44. *ART COM.* (Computer art publications, video, oddities and catalog.) Write ART COM / Contemporary Arts Press, PO Box 193123 Rincon Center, San Francisco, CA 94119-3123 USA. Tel: 415 431-7524. Fax: 415 431-7841.

45. Fractal image compression. Write to Iterated Systems, Inc., 5550 Peachtree Parkway, Building A, Suite 545, Norcross, GA 30092.

46. *Lascaux Graphics.* (Distributor of computer math/graphics books, fractal videos, issues related to the 4th dimension, and software.) *Lascaux Graphics*, 3220 Steuben Ave., Bronx, New York 10467 USA.

47. Creativity/Recreation. (Software and catalog.) Rosemary West, P.O. Box 8059, Mission Hills, CA 91346.

48. *Visual Music.* (Videotape.) Information from Music Animation Machine, 1850 Arch Street #5, Berkeley, CA 94709.

49. *Annual Symposia on Electronic Arts.* Write to: SISEA, Westerhavenstraat 13, 9718 AJ Groningen, The Netherlands.

50. *The Math Group.* (Unique puzzles and math games.) Write to The Math Group, 396 East 79th Street, Minneapolis, MN 55420.

51. *Lano Company.* (Mathematical visual aids. Solids, transparencies, graphing aids.) Write Lano Company, 9001 Gross Road, Dexter, MI 48130.

52. *Creative Publications.* (Math books, models, games, posters, and catalog.) Creative Publications, 3977 East Bayshore Road, Box 10328, Palo Alto, CA 94303.

53. *Rite Item.* (Software for pattern-generator based on a Scientific American article.) Rite Item, 1622 N. Xerxes Ave, Minneapolis, MN 55411.

54. Astronomical software. Neutron Stars. Koen Vyverman, Leopold I-Straat 480, 1090 Brussels, Belgium.

55. *Math Shop.* (Games, math puzzles.) Math Shop, 5 Bridge St. Watertown, MA 02172.

56. Chaos made to order. *FracTools* graphics software. Also, *FracTunes* (chaos put to music). Bourbaki, PO. Box 2867, Boise, Idaho 83701.

57. *FraChaos.* (Fractal art.) Higher, Trengove, Constantine, Falmouth, Cornwall TR11 5QR.

58. *Fractal Attraction.* (Fractal software using iterated function systems.) Sandpiper Software, PO Box 8012, St. Paul, MN 55108.

59. *CSSRBB Project.* (Computer simulation and scientific recreation bulletin board project.) CSSRBB Project, PO Box 20714, Seattle, WA 98102.

60. Computer Go. (A journal on artificial intelligence issues for the game of Go.) 71 Brixford Crescent, Winnipeg, Manitoba, R2N 1E1, Canada.

61. *Just Puzzles.* (Mechanical puzzles. Rubik cube.) Just Puzzles, Dept. A. 54 Richwood Place, Denville, New Jersey 07834 USA.

62. *Math Workhorse.* (Software for geometry, complex numbers, large numbers.) Spence Barnshaw, Box 35032, Vancouver, B.C., Canada V6M 4G1.

63. *Mandelbrot Magic.* (Fractal software.) Steve Wagner, Left Coast Software, PO Box 160601 Cupertino, CA 95016-0601.

64. *Fractal Magic and Cell Master.* (Software for beautiful fractal graphics.) Sintar Software, 1001 4th Ave, Suite 3200, Seattle, Washington 98154.

65. *VGAMBROT.* (Software for fractals.) Michael Freeman, 4777 Hoskins Road North, Vancouver, B.C. Canada, V7K 2R3.

66. *Mathemagical Farrago.* (Software for mathematical recreations: prime numbers, paradoxes, games, fractals.) Mike Ecker, 909 Violet Terrace, Clarks Summit, PA 18411.

67. *Magic Math Plus.* (Software: Fibonacci numbers, mind-reading, games.) Mike Ecker, 909 Violet Terrace, Clarks Summit, PA 18411.

68. *Mandelbrot Microscope:.* (Fractal software.) Public Software Library, PO Box 35705, Houston, TX 77235-5705.

69. *Thinking Software.* (Artificial intelligence software. Neural nets.) Thinking software, 46-16 65th Place, Woodside, NY 11377.

70. *Camelot Publishing.* Excellent textbooks, teacher aids, and materials for computer science, computer graphics, and mathematics education. Camelot Publishing, P.O. Box 1357, Ormond Beach, FL 32175.

71. *MEDIA MAGIC: The Fractal Universe Catalog*, PO Box 507, Nicasio, California 94946. This fine company distributes books, videos, prints, and calendars.

72. *ART MATRIX*, creator of beautiful postcards and videotapes of exciting mathematical shapes. Write to ART MATRIX, PO Box 880, Ithaca, New York 14851 for more information.

73. *Cellular Automata Laboratory*, by Dr. Rudy Rucker. This set of software allows the user to produce stunning animated computer graphics with ease, and simulate physical and biological phenomena. Write Autodesk, Inc., 2320 Marinship Way, Sausalito, CA 94965.

74. Mandelbrot and Julia Set Generator. (Fractal software.) Charles Platt, PO Box 556, Chelsea Station, New York, NY 10013.

75. *Desktop Fractal Design System.* (Fractal software.) Academic Press, 1250 Sixth Ave, San Diego, CA 92101-9665.

76. *Fractal Programming in C.* (Fractal software and book.) M&T Publishing, 501 Galveston Drive, Redwood City, CA 94063.

77. *ARTPACK.* (Fractal software.) Zephyr Services, 1900 Murray Ave., Pittsburgh, PA 15217.

78. *Fractal GRAFICS.* (Fractal software for designing your own fractals interactively.) R1 Box 5140, Morrisville, VT 05661.

79. *Fractal Illumination* (Video cassette, fractal animation set to music). Rock Art Video, 20 Sunneyside, #304 Mill Valley, CA 94941.

80. *Fractal Calendar.* Address inquiries to J. Loyless, 5185 Ashford Court, Lilburn, Georgia 30247.

81. Math Products Plus. (Math books, T-shirts, puzzles, sculptures, games, and catalog.) Write to Math Products Plus, PO Box 64, San Carlos, CA 94070.

82. *Glimpses of a Future Universe.* (Fractal slides and Cibachrome prints at 2046x1366 resolution.) AMYGDALA, Box 219, San Cristobal, New Mexico 87564.

# E.3 Newsletters, Columns, Associations

*"No live organism can continue for long to exist sanely under conditions of absolute reality.*
*Even larks and katydids are supposed, by some to dream. "*                    Shirley Jackson

1.   *Amphotographer.* An eight issue per year newsletter covering figurative tiling and other Escher-like art. John Osborne, 250 Donegal Way, Martinez, California 94553.

2.   *Fractal Report,* a newsletter on fractals. Published by J. de Rivaz, Reeves Telecommunications Lab. West Towan House, Porthtowan, Cornwall TR4 8AX, United Kingdom.

3.   *AMYGDALA,* a fascinating newsletter on fractals. Write to AMYGDALA, Box 219, San Cristobal, New Mexico 87564 for more information.

4.   *The Cellular Automatiste,* a newsletter on cellular automata. Write to AMYGDALA, Box 219, San Cristobal, New Mexico 87564 for more information.

5.   *Mathematical Recreations* column, by A. K. Dewdney, in *Scientific American.*

6.   *Algorithm - The Personal Computer Newsletter.* P.O. Box 29237, Westmount Postal Outlet, 785 Wonderland Road S., London, Ontario, Canada, N6K, 1M6. Topics include fractals and recreational mathematics.

7.   *The Journal of Chaos and Graphics,* an informal newsletter on aesthetic and unusual graphics derived from mathematics (write to me).

8.   I. Peterson's interesting columns, frequently on topics in mathematics and graphics, in *Science News.*

9.   *Recreational and Educational Computing Newsletter.* Dr. Michael Ecker, 909 Violet Terrace, Clarks Summit, PA 18411.

10.  *Quantum Quarterly.* This newsletter lists scientific books on fractals, mathematical recreations, etc. Contact Quantum Books, One Kendall Square, Cambridge, MA 02139.

11.  *YLEM – Artists using science and technology.* This newsletter is published by an organization of artists who work with video, ionized gases, computers, lasers, holograms, robotics, and other non-traditional media. It also includes artists who use traditional media but who are inspired by images of electromagnetic phenomena, biological self-replication, and fractals. Contact: YLEM, Box 749, Orinda, CA 94563.

12.  *Powell's Technical Bookstore Newsletter.* (Great newsletter for computing, electronics, fractals, engineering.) 33 NW Park Ave., Portland, OR 97209.

13.  *John's Picks.* A great 30-page publication which describes and markets books, and a range of products, on the subjects of: fractals, chaos, neural networks, mathematical puzzles, computer graphics, cellular automata, Escher, computer physics, games, curiosities, etc. This is published three times a year. Contact Microcomputer Applications, P.O. Box E, Suisun City, California 94585-1050.

# E.4 Journals, Bibliographies, Papers

*"The eye is indeed the window of the mind, but we must now try to look through it in both*
*directions, although God did not give us an output organ to match the visual input organ. "*

Alan L. Mackay, *In the Mind's Eye*

1.   Reference list for complex systems. Prof. Ali Bulent Cambel, 6155 Kellogg Drive, McLean, Virginia 22101 USA.

2.   Computerized bibliography on chaos. Ms. Zhang Shu-yu, The Institute of Physics, Group 201, PO Box 603, Beijing 100080. People's Republic of China.

3. *Factsheet Five.* (Unusual magazine/review of books.) This magazine is not copyrighted, and you may reprint whatever you wish. Write to Factsheet Five, 6 Arizona Ave, Rensselaer, New York 12144-4502.

4. *The American Journal of Computer Art in Education.* Write: 258 Pelican Ave., Daytona Beach, Florida, 32118 USA.

5. *Idealistic Studies.* An international philosophical journal. Dept. of Philosophy, Clark University, Worcester, MA 01610.

6. "Hindu Temples. Models of a Fractal Universe." A fascinating scholarly journal article. Write to Kirti Trivedi, Industrial Design Center, Indian Institute of Technology, Powai, Bombay 400 076 INDIA.

7. *Cryptologia Journal.* Computer security, codes. Dr. Brian Winkel, Rose-Hulman Institute of Technology. Terre Haute, IN 47803.

8. "The Fractal Structure of Evolution." Scholarly journal article. Write to Gerd Binnig, IBM Research Division, Physics Group Munich, c/o Physics Section of the University, Schellingstrasse 4, D-8000 Munich 40, Fed. Rep. Germany.

9. The computer art of Herbert W. Franke and Horst Helbig. 26-page color pamphlet (ISBN 0-387-15633-X). Write to: Springer-Verlag Postfach 105280, Tiergartenstrasse 17, 6900 Heidelberg 1, FR Germany.

10. *The Yates Collection.* Softbound books, with titles such as *Repunits and Reptends*, dealing with mathematical curiosities. The books are not for the beginner. Write to Samuel Yates, 157 Capri-D, Kings Point, Delray Beach, Florida 33445.

11. *Fractals, and the Cat in the Hat.* This is actually a scholarly paper to be published in *The Journal of Recreational Mathematics.* Describes scaling laws and the recursive structure of the infinitely nested cats in a book by Dr. Seuss. Preprint available from: Dr. A. Lakhtakia, Pennsylvania State University, 227 Hammond Bldg, University Park, PA 16802.

12. *Leonardo*, published by Pergamon Press, Headington Hill Hall, Oxford OX3 0BW, UK. This fascinating interdisciplinary journal combines arts, science and technology.

13. *Computer Music Journal*, published by MIT Press, 28 Carleton Street, Cambridge, MA 02142.

14. *Complex Systems*, published by Complex Systems Press, P.O. Box 6149, Champaign, IL 61821-8149. This mathematically sophisticated journal is primarily devoted to cellular automata.

15. "Chaos and Graphics Section" of *Computers and Graphics*, published by Pergamon Press, Headington Hill Hall, Oxford OX3 0BW, UK.

16. *Journal of Recreational Mathematics*, published by Baywood Publishing Co., 26 Austin Ave, P.O. Box 337, Amityville, NY 11701. This journal is a must for those of you interested in mathematical curiosities.

17. *Journal of the British-American Scientific Research Association.* Avante garde science and speculations. BASRA, 13 Durwood Place, Madison, NJ 07940.

18. *Speculations in Science and Technology.* A journal filled with interesting speculative papers in the physical, mathematical, biological, medical and engineering sciences. Science and Technology Letters, PO Box 81, Northwood, Middlesex HA6 3DN England.

19. *21st Century Science and Technology.* A journal dedicated to providing information on advanced technologies and science policies. 21st Century Science, 60 Sycolin Road, Suite 203, Leesburg, VA 22075.

# E.5 Further Unusual References

*"Consider the true picture. Think of myriads of tiny bubbles, very sparsely scattered, rising through a vast black sea. We rule some of the bubbles. Of the waters we know nothing...."*

Niven and Pournelle, *The Mote in God's Eye*

1.  Schattschneider, D. (1990) *Visions of Symmetry*. Freeman: New York. (Probably the best book available on the mathematics behind Escher's work.)

2.  Briggs, J. (1990) *Fire in the Crucible*. Tarcher: New York. (An interesting book on creativity, genius, and scientific discoveries.)

3.  Rothman, T. (1988) God takes a nap. *Scientific American*. October, 259: 20. (Describes pluto's chaotic orbit.)

4.  Denes, A. (1989) *The Book of Dust* Visual Studies Workshop: New York. (A book covering topics such as art, evolution, computer graphics, dust, and alien life.) For information, write Visual Studies Workshop, 595 Broadway, New York, NY 10012.

5.  *The Planiverse*. (A book about 2-D creatures.) A. K. Dewdney, 42 Askin Street, London, Ontario CANADA N6C 4E4.

6.  Grossman, S., Mayer-Kress, G. (1989) Chaos in the international arms race. *Nature*. February. 337(4): 701.

7.  MacKinnon, N. (1989/1990) Modelling Monopoly. *Math Spectrum*. 22(2): 39. (Describes computer simulations of the famous Monopoly game.)

8.  Olsen, L., Schaffer, W. (1990) Chaos versus noisy periodicity: alternative hypotheses for childhood epidemics. *Science*. August 249: 499-503. (Discusses the chaotic recurrence of diseases such as measles.)

9.  Lipton, L. (1982) *Foundations of Stereoscopic Cinema*. Van Nostrand: New York. (Topics: 3-D cinema, psychology of binocular depth perception, etc.)

10. Reid, W. (1967) Weight of an hourglass. *American Journal of Physics*. April 35(4): 351-352.

11. Mackay, A. (1990) A time quasi-crystal. *Modern Physics Letters B*. 4(15): 989-991.

12. Tennenbaum, J. (1990) The metaphysics of complex numbers. *21st Century Science*. Spring 3(2): 60.

13. Keller, J., Chen, S. (1989) Texture discrimination and segmentation through fractal geometry. *Computer Vision, Graphics, and Image Processing*. 45: 150-166.

14. Villiers, J., Robinson, P. (1987) The interval of convergence and limiting functions of a hyperpower sequence. *Am. Math. Monthly*. January 93(1): 13.

15. Schroeder, M. (1989) Self-similarity and fractals in science and art. *J. Audio. Eng. Soc.* Oct 37(10): 795-808.

16. West, B. (1990) *Fractal Physiology and Chaos in Medicine*. World Scientific: Singapore.

17. Briggs, J., Peat, F. (1989) *The Turbulent Mirror: An Illustrated Guide to Chaos Theory and the Science of Wholeness*. Harper and Row: New York.

18. Basar, E. (1990) *Chaos in Brain Function*. Springer: New York.

19. Devlin, K. (1988) *Mathematics: The New Golden Age*. Penguin: New York.

20. Pool, R. (1990) Fractal Fracas. *Science*. July 27th, 249: 363-364. ("The math community is in a flap over the question of whether fractals are just pretty pictures, or more substantial tools.")

21. Barrow, J., Tippler, F. (1986) *The Anthropic Cosmological Principle*. Oxford University Press: New York. (Discusses the fine structure constant 1/137.)

22. Scott, R., Bernstein, R. (1990) *Discovering*. Harvard University Press: Cambridge, Massachusetts. (Describes the thought processes involved in scientific discovering.)

23. *Exquisite Corpse, 1990*. Surreal computer collages on a disk. Your contributions invited. Beverly Resier, 6979 Exeter Drive, Oakland, CA 94611.

24. Batty, M, Longley, P., Fotheringham, A. (1989) Urban growth and form: scaling, fractal geometry and diffusion-limited aggregation. *Environment and Planning A*. 21:1447-1472

25. Hsu, K., Hsu A. (1990) Fractal geometry of music. *Proceedings of the National Academy of Science*. 87(3):938-941

26. Schaffer, W., Kot, M. (1985) Do strange attractors govern ecological systems? *BioScience,* 35: 342-350.

27. Letter in *New Scientist*, 6 October 1990, page 66, reporting that Beardsley's illustration to Pope's 1896 *Rape of the Lock* is reminiscent of *M*-Set.

28. M. Batty (1985) Fractals: Geometry between dimensions, *New Scientist*, 105(1450): 31-35.

29. M. Batty and P. Longley (1986) The fractal simulation of urban structure. *Environment and Planning A*. 1:, 1143-1179.

30. M. Batty and P. Longley (1987) Fractal description of urban form. *Environment and Planning B*. 14: 123-134.

31. M. Batty and P. Longley (1987) Urban shapes as fractals, *Area*. 19: 215- 221, 1987

32. P. Longley and M. Batty (1987) Using fractal geometry to measure maps and simulate cities. *Computer Education*. 56: 15-19.

33. P. Longley and M. Batty (1989) Fractal measurement and line generalization, *Computers and Geosciences*. 15: 167-183.

34. P. Longley and M. Batty (1989) On the fractal measurement of geographical boundaries. *Geographical Analysis*. 21: 47-67.

35. M. Batty (1990) Cities as fractals: simulating growth and form, in R. A. Earnshaw and T. Crilly (Editors). *Fractals and Chaos*. Springer-Verlag: New York, in press.

# E.6 Further Unusual Inventions

In the interest of reducing the size of this book, several of my computer inventions, which were originally intended for the *Invention* section, have been omitted. Their titles are listed in the following and should stimulate your imagination. *ITDB* stands for *IBM Technical Disclosure Bulletin*. *RD* stands for *Research Disclosure*. For further information, contact me.

1. Chess, D., Peevers, A., Pickover, C., Reed, A. (1989) Car radio scanner differentiating music from speech. *ITDB*. October 32(5B): 12-13.

2. Pickover, C., Keithley, D. and Reed, A. (1988) Triangular toggle keys for touch-tone phones. *ITDB*. June 31(1): 47-49. (Synopsis: The standard push-button telephone keypad has 12 buttons. Eight of these buttons (2-9) each display three letters. This three to-one mapping presents a serious limitation for using a telephone as a general text input device. For example, on-line phone directories require that a person key-punch a last name. As the standard American telephone is now configured, the same button is pressed to send an "A," "B," or "C." The touch-tone system used to encode each button for transmission is a four-by-four array of pairs of high and low tones. At present, twelve of the 16 possibilities are in use to encode the buttons. We solve this letter ambiguity problem by using a triangular key. This allows the user to enter 4 different inputs with one key. The center position has the usual numeric interpretation.)

3. Capek, P., Hanthorn D., Johnson, F., Pickover, C., Rogers, J. (1989) Mouse with geodesic ball. *RD* (K. Mason Publications, Ltd, England) July, No. 303. (30357). (Synopsis: This invention pertains to an analog input device for a computer and more specifically to a mouse. A mouse is a device for moving a cursor or other object around the display screen. Mouse input devices generally have a small tracking ball to convey position information. In 1989, I described a geodesic mouse ball which has many flat sides (like a soccer ball), providing for readings from the mouse that are discrete rather than continuous. The ball provides a tactile click (detent) so that the user is sure the ball is moving. The tactile feedback might make a mouse usable by a blind person.)

4. Kugel, L., Marks, L., Pickover, C., Reed, A. (1989) Mouth-interpreter via optical fibers and infrared link. *ITDB*. Sept. 32(4B): 10 - 13. (Synopsis: "You have a big mouth!" your friend yells at you as he steps into your office. Your friend is right. On your lips, you are wearing the "artificial mouth" which translates mouth and lip movements into electrical signals. By monitoring these motions, the artificial mouth aids in speech recognition in noisy environments. You can use it for other applications as well.)

5. Kesling, D., Marks, L., Pickover, C., Reed, A. (1989) Watch with patterns for visually impaired *ITDB*. Aug. 32(3A): 218-220.

6. Pickover, C., Reed, A., Keithley, D., Kesling, D. (1988) Personal data bank information exchange. *ITDB*. November 31(6): 231-235. (Synopsis: In this invention, I describe an interface for information exchange between one digital wrist-watch and another. This should be useful for transferring the contents of "data bank" watches which are currently becoming popular, and which store many pages of alphanumeric data such as phone numbers and names. Currently it is difficult to input information with the limited number of buttons on watches.) With this invention, two watches can interlock, and twist together, so that one person can send information to another person's watch. Data is transferred either by electrical connections or blinking LEDs (light-emitting diodes). In the future, when data-bank watches become more sophisticated, they will store not only alphanumeric data, but also maps and drawings. Owners will want to exchange information with one another without the tedium of re-entering the data.)

7. Pickover, C., Ditlow, G. and Keithley, D. (1987) Passwords for computer systems and cipher locks containing rhythm patterns. *ITDB*. 30(5): 258.

8. Pickover, C. and Ditlow, G. (1988) Self-adjusting audio speaker *ITDB*. February 30(9): 460-462.

9. Pickover, C., McLean, J., Reed, A., (1989) Variable grid pattern pads for optical mouse contact surfaces. *ITDB*. Jan. 31(8): 237-240.

10. Grossman, B., McLean, J., Pickover, C., Reed, A. (1989) Space bar that rolls. *ITDB*. Aug. 32(3B): 122-123.

11. Pickover, Reed (1989). Terminal keys with antistatic pads. *ITDB*. Sept. 32(4B): 109-110.

12. Marks, L., Pickover, C., Reed, A. (1989) Labels with conductive ink. *ITDB*. Aug. 32(3A): 306-308.

13. Pickover, C., McLean, J., Reed, A. (1990) Three-dimensional joystick via cavity. *ITDB*. Febr 32(9B): 180-181.

14. McLean, J., Pickover, C., Reed, A. (1990) Liquid crystal diode bar code unit. *ITDB*. December 33(7): 363-364.

15. Pickover, C., McLean, J., Reed, A. (1990) Disposable keyboard. *ITDB*. Febr 32(9A): 411-413.

16. Pickover, C., Reed, A., Segall, M. (1989) Computer and peripheral device pole stand. *ITDB*. Aug. 32(3B): 106-109. (Synopsis: Look about you. Your computer terminals, keyboards, printers, papers, and phones are scattered all about you in a haphazard manner! The cables are difficult to follow, and frequently they get tangled. The invention described in this chapter is a stand for personal computers and peripherals. The stand resembles a pole lamp or pole plant stand. The peripherals are placed on arms protruding from the central pole. Cables are internal to the pole. The central bus architecture of the pole is discussed.)

17. Pickover, C., Kugel, L., McLean, J., Reed, A. (1990) CRT screen byte optical information interface ("Screen Suckers") *ITDB*. Febr 32(9A): 443-445. (Synopsis: Imagine a patient in a cold operating room strapped to a hard stretcher with various heart-monitoring wires stuck to his naked chest. Recently, I explored the idea further with a few colleagues. We developed a quick, inexpensive, and versatile method and hardware for data transfer from a computer or TV screen. The computer screen looks a little like the hospital patient, except here the wires emanate from small suction cups attached to the screen. All one needs to do is apply a suction cup device to the glass of a terminal screen, and information is "sucked" away to a receiving device. In this invention, a small suction cup which contains a postage-stamp-sized scanner. Two or three suckers are attached to a computer screen at particular locations on the glass to scan for information. Protruding from each sucker is a wire which conveys the information to another device.)

18. Jackman, T., Pickover, C. (1990) Novel 3-D Ramachandran plot. *ITDB*. Aug 33(3A): 165-166.

# Appendix F

# Descriptions of Color Plates And Frontispieces

*"Our normal waking consciousness is but one special type of consciousness, whilst all about it, parted from it by the filmiest of screens, there lie potential forms of consciousness entirely different. No account of the universe in its totality can be final which leaves these other forms of consciousness quite disregarded. They may determine attitudes though they cannot furnish formulas, and open a region though they fail to give a map."*

James, *1904*

## F.1 Color Plates

I used a variety of computers to produce the color plates in this book. Some were produced on an IBM 5080 graphics display at a resolution of 1024 × 1024 pixels. The programming language was usually PL/I, and an IBM 3090 mainframe computer was often used to compute the images. For some of the 3-D images, a Stellar GS 1000 or IBM RISC System/6000 computer was used, and the programming language was C. Note that many of the color plates can be rapidly created using personal computers if a lower resolution picture is computed. The following gives a description of each color plate, in order of its appearance:

1.  Image-processed portrait of a non-Newtonian fluid. For more information, see "The World of Chaos" on page 121.

2.  Same as previous figure, except that a different region of the fluid is shown. For more information, see "The World of Chaos" on page 121.

3.  *A Flying Dream Creature.* A shape composed of three recursively nested, trigonometric curves. These kinds of curves are discussed in "Picturing Spherical Lissajous Figures" on page 295. The background "clouds" are also computer-generated.

4.  *Digital monster.* To produce this image, my clay sculpture was first videotaped. A frame from the tape was digitized and captured using an IBM AT equipped with a MATROX MVP board. The image was subsequently image-processed using an IBM 3090 to achieve unusual color highlights and, in some cases, mirror symmetry.

5.  A trajectory traced out by the irregular motions of a conical pendulum, rendered on a graphics supercomputer.

6.  *Death's Helmet*, rendered on a graphics workstation using simple formulas.

7.  Lissajous-like curves. These kinds of curves are discussed in "Picturing Spherical Lissajous Figures" on page 295.

8.  Buckminsterfullerene, an example of a chemical polyhedron made of carbon atoms, surrounds a fossil seashell shape. See "Buckminsterfullerene!" on page 166 for more details.

9.  Lissajous-like curves. These kinds of curves are discussed in "Picturing Spherical Lissajous Figures" on page 295.

10. A Phoenix-like Julia set. For more information, see "The World of Chaos" on page 121.

11. A Phoenix-like Julia set. For more information, see "The World of Chaos" on page 121.

12. Strange saddle surface. For more information, see "From Math Comes Beauty: Monkey Curves and Spirals" on page 175.

13. Mandelbrot set for Newton's method. A long time ago, Isaac Newton suggested a method for finding the zeros of a function by a simple iteration scheme. You can read more about this method and Halley's method in *Computers, Pattern, Chaos, and Beauty*. This was computed for $f(z) = z^3 - 0.75z + \lambda^2 - \lambda^2 z - 0.25$, where $z$ is a complex number.

14. Halley's method for $z^7 - 1 = 0$, where $z$ is a complex number. (See also previous description.)

15. *Cantor Cheese*. For more information, see "Visualizing Cantor Cheese Construction" on page 141.

16. *Digital monster*. See description for color plate 4.

17. *Digital monster*. See description for color plate 4.

18. *Digital monster*. See description for color plate 4.

19. A computer graphics simulation of the irregular and unstable growth pattern of an extinct fossil seashell (*Nipponites mirabilis*) For more information, see "Irregularly Oscillating Fossil Seashells" on page 129.

20. Graphics simulation of a fossil sea shell (*Nipponites occidentalis*). For more information, see "Irregularly Oscillating Fossil Seashells" on page 129.

21. Graphics simulation of a fossil sea shell (*Madagascalites ryu*). For more information, see "Irregularly Oscillating Fossil Seashells" on page 129.

22. Fractal foam. For more information, see "Osculation" on page 153.

23. Pascal's pyramid. For more information, see "Infinite Triangular Arrays" on page 253.

24. Polyhedron floating amidst digital clouds. For more information, see "Polyhedral Paradise" on page 163.

25. Computer graphics of a landscape and exotic sky. The simple mathematical methods used to produce both the terrain and sky are given in *Computers, Pattern, Chaos, and Beauty*.

26. Juvenile *Nipponites* fossil seashell simulation. For more information, see "Irregularly Oscillating Fossil Seashells" on page 129.

27. How to slice a doughnut into 13 pieces with only three plane cuts. (Computer graphic created in collaboration with Dr. Mike Henderson.) For more information, see "Notes for the Curious" on page 371.

28. DNA Tetragram. Among the methods available for characterizing information-containing sequences in biology, computer graphics is emerging as an important tool. I produced the representation in this color plate by mapping DNA sequence data to a three-dimensional pattern on connected tetrahedra. Here two cancer-causing viral sequences are represented, allowing the human observer to detect important patterns and trends in the genetic information. The two transparent spheres indicate where the termini of the tetragrams would be if the DNA sequences were each composed of a random string of bases. For information on 2-D patterns representing DNA, see *Computers, Pattern, Chaos, and Beauty*.

29. Biomorph computed from a Julia set. For information on these kinds of patterns, see *Computers, Pattern, Chaos, and Beauty*.

## F.2 Chapter Frontispieces

*"Why is philosophy so complicated? It ought to be entirely simple. Philosophy unties the knots in our thinking that we have, in a senseless way, put there. To do this it must make movements that are just as complicated as these knots. Although the result of philosophy is simple, its method cannot be if it is to succeed. The complexity of philosophy is not a complexity of its subject matter, but of our knotted understanding. "* Ludwig Wittgenstein

Some of the large illustrations preceding the chapters in this book are briefly described in this section. The pointillist sculptures composed of 1 million dots are described in "Million-Point Sculptures" on page 285.

1.  The computer graphics image on the dedication page is a Phoenix-like Julia set. See "The World of Chaos" on page 121 for more information.

2.  The image on the reverse side of the dedication page is a Lissajous-like curve. These kinds of curves are discussed in "Picturing Spherical Lissajous Figures" on page 295.

3.  The image on the reverse side of the Goethe page is a *Digital monster*. To produce this image, I first videotaped my clay sculpture. A frame from the tape was digitized and captured using an IBM AT equipped with a MATROX MVP board. The figure was subsequently image-processed using an IBM 3090 to achieve unusual highlights and, in some cases, mirror symmetry. You can get a feel for the size of the original sculptures from the figures below.

4.  The figure on the bottom of the last page of the Table of Contents shows a computer-hand interface. See "Interlude: Computer Exoskeletons" on page 197 for more information.

5.  The kidney-like, tree-filled object in the frontispiece for Part I is a *Glynn function* computed for the iteration of $z \to z^{1.5} - 0.2$ where $z$ is a complex number. I produced this at a resolution of 2000 x 2000 dots. For more information, contact the Glynn Function Study Center, Earl Glynn, 10808 West 105th St, Overland Park, KS 66214-3057.

6.  The frontispiece for Chapter 1 is a million-point sculpture. See "Million-Point Sculptures" on page 285 for more information.

7.  The image on the last page of Chapter 1 is a Julia set for $z \to z^2 + \mu$, $\mu = (-0.745, 0.113)$.

8.  The frontispiece for "Simulation: Introduction" shows a Julia set, with 3-fold symmetry, for $z \to z^3 + \mu$, $\mu = (-0.574, 0.27)$.

9.  The image at the end of "Simulation: Introduction" is a *Digital monster*. (See previous description for number 3.)

10. The frontispiece diagram for Chapter 4 shows a dissection of the entire portal (liver) vein system in a human, and all the veins which feed into this system from the intestines and other organs.

11. The frontispiece for Chapter 7 shows a silk spider from Malaysia of the genus *Nephila* (male above, female below).

12. The Celtic art in Chapter 8 comes from: Bain, G. (1973) *Celtic Art*. Dover: New York.

13. The frontispiece for Chapter 11 is a magnification of the frontispiece for the "Simulation" section which shows a Julia set for $z \rightarrow z^3 + \mu$, $\mu = (-0.574, 0.27)$.

14. The frontispiece for Chapter 15 is a million-point sculpture. See "Million-Point Sculptures" on page 285 for more information.

15. The figure on the last page of Chapter 15 is an image-processed portrait of a non-Newtonian fluid. For more information, see "The World of Chaos" on page 121.

16. The computer graphics image on the frontispiece for the "Visualization: Part IV" is a Phoenix-like Julia set. See "The World of Chaos" on page 121 for more information.

17. The frontispiece for Chapter 18 is a million-point sculpture. See "Million-Point Sculptures" on page 285 for more information.

18. The frontispiece for Chapter 22 shows various species of marine snails of the subclass Prosobranchia.

19. The 3-D Mandelbrot set artwork in the frontispiece for Chapter 27 was drawn by A. K. Dewdney. It appeared in his newsletter *Algorithm - The Personal Computer Newsletter*, P.O. Box 29237, Westmount Postal Outlet, 785 Wonderland Road S., London, Ontario, Canada, N6K, 1M6.

20. The figure at the end of Chapter 29 is a modified Halley map used for finding the zeros of a function by a simple iteration scheme. You can read more about Halley's method in *Computers, Pattern, Chaos, and Beauty*. This was computed for $z = z^7 - 1$ where $z$ is a complex number.

21. The frontispiece for Chapter 32 is a *Golden Julia Set*. See "The Lute of Pythagoras" on page 203 for more information. The previous page shows a million-point sculpture.

22. In the frontispiece figure for Chapter 34, artist Gustave Dore (1832-1883) endeavors to show the infinite number of bodies inhabiting Hell.

23. The frontispiece for Chapter 47 is a Phoenix-like Julia set. See "The World of Chaos" on page 121 for more information.

24. The frontispiece for Chapter 51 is an image-processed portrait of a non-Newtonian fluid. For more information, see "The World of Chaos" on page 121.

25. The image facing Chapter 52 is a *Digital monster*. (See previous description for number 3.)

26. The frontispieces for the "Imagination" and "Fiction" section are *Digital Monsters*. (See previous description for number 3.)

27. The frontispiece for "Part IX: Conclusion" shows a Mandelbrot set for Newton's method. A long time ago, Isaac Newton suggested a method for finding the zeros of a function by a simple iteration scheme. You can read more about this method and Halley's method in *Computers, Pattern, Chaos, and Beauty*. This was computed for $f(z) = z^3 - 0.75z + \lambda^2 - \lambda^2 z - 0.25$, where $z$ is a complex number.

28. The frontispiece facing the text of the "Conclusion" is a Julia set for $z = z^2 + 0.05$. Some of the contours indicate the minimum value of an orbit. I computed the image on an IBM 3090 and rendered the original figure using a grid of 2000 by 2000 dots. Note how the pattern is reminiscent of the hyperbolic repeating patterns of M. C. Escher. (Function suggested by James Loyless.)

29. The page after the Conclusion shows a Mandelbrot set.

30. The figure under the "Seeing with the Mind's Eye" quote is a million-point sculpture. See "Million-Point Sculptures" on page 285 for more information.

31. The frontispiece for "Part X: Appendices" shows wall tiles from 13th and 14th C. Persia.

32. The frontispiece for the "Glossary" is a Mandelbrot set with stalks.

33. The frontispiece for the "Credits" is a magnification of the frontispiece for the "Conclusion."

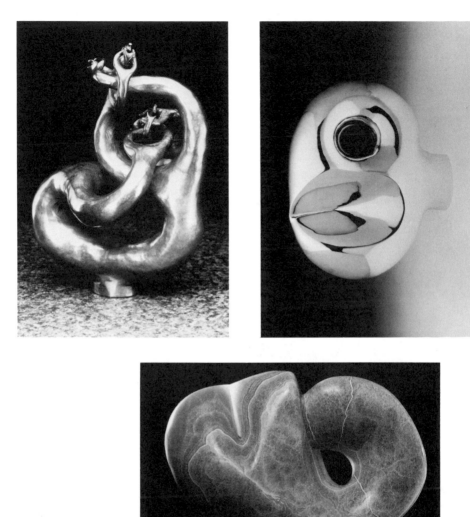

# Interlude: Stone Math

*"Paintbrushes are ancient tools, as are eyes, fingers, and neurons. Finding new uses for reliable tools is part of the artist's job. "*

Mary Jane Kenton, 1990

As mentioned in the introduction of this book, there are several modern-day artists inspired by mathematics. One notable example is mathematician Helaman Ferguson who creates mathematically inspired stone and bronze sculptures as a way of conveying the beauty of theorems. Professor Ferguson has an interesting past. At the age of 6 he was adopted by a stonemason, and later he studied painting while in college. Today he is a Professor of Mathematics at Brigham Young University. Ferguson is in the 1988 and 1989 *Guinness Book of World Records* for juggling a distance of fifty miles. His wife is an artist and claims to understand mathematicians very well, observing that: "I know what you guys are doing. First you shoot the arrow and then you draw the bull's-eye."

Shown here are some of Ferguson's sculptures. These include "Torus with Cross-Cap" (silicon bronze, upper right), which he says "contains the germ of the fundamental theorem of the topology of surfaces," "Wild Sphere, Six Bifurcation Stages, 127 Branches" (silicon bronze, upper left), and "Klein Bottle with Cross-Cap" (polished onyx, bottom). Ferguson can be reached at 10512 Pilla Terra Court, Warfield's Range and Forest, Laurel, Maryland 20723-5728. For more information, see: Ferguson, H. (1990) Two theorems, two sculptures, two posters. *American Mathematical Monthly*. August-September 97(7): 589-610.

# Glossary

This is an informal and brief reminder of the meanings of terms (for more detailed descriptions, see the relevant references in the bibliography).

**Abacus** Instrument for performing calculations by sliding beads along rods or grooves.

**Analog-to-digital converter** Electronic device that transforms continuous signals into signals with discrete values.

**Amino acid** Basic building blocks of proteins.

**Attractor** *Predictable attractors* correspond to the behavior to which a system settles down or is "attracted" (for example, a point or a looping closed cycle). The structure of these attractors is simple and well understood. A *strange attractor* is represented by an unpredictable trajectory where a minute difference in starting positions of 2 initially adjacent points leads to totally uncorrelated positions later in time or in the mathematical iteration. The structure of these attractors is very complicated and often not well understood.

**Bifurcation** Any value of a parameter at which the number and/or stability of steady states and cycles changes is called a bifurcation point, and the system is said to undergo a bifurcation.

**Binomial coefficients** The coefficients in the expansion of $(x + y)^n$. For example, $(x + y)^2 = x^2 + 2xy + y^2$ so that the binomial coefficients of order 2 are: 1, 2 and 1.

**CAD** Computer-aided design. This computer graphics process occurs when a computer is used for design work in fields such as engineering and architecture.

**CAM** Computer-aided manufacturing. For example, computers can store a 3-D representation of an object, and then control the manufacture of the object.

**Cellular automata** A class of simple mathematical systems that are becoming important as models for a variety of physical processes. Though the rules governing the creation of cellular automata are simple, the patterns they produce are complicated and sometimes seem almost random, like a turbulent fluid flow or the output of a cryptographic system. Cellular automata are characterized by the fact that they act on a discrete space or grid as opposed to a continuous medium.

**Center** See *limit*.

**Chaos** Irregular behavior displaying sensitive dependence on initial conditions. Chaos has been referred to by some physicists as the seemingly paradoxical combination of randomness and structure in certain nonperiodic solutions of dynamical systems. Chaotic behavior can sometimes be defined by a simple formula. Some researchers believe that chaos theory offers a mathematical framework for understanding much of the noise and turbulence that is seen in experimental science.

**Chaotic trajectory** A chaotic trajectory exhibits three features. 1) The motion stays within a bounded region – it does not get larger and larger without limit. 2) The trajectory never settles into a periodic pattern. 3) The motion exhibits a sensitivity to initial conditions. See also *Chaos*.

**Complex number**   A number containing a real and imaginary part, and of the form $a + bi$ where $i = \sqrt{-1}$ .

**Continued root**   Expressions of the form $\sqrt{x_1 + \sqrt{x_2 + \sqrt{x_3 + \cdots}}}$ . Also known as nested roots.

**Converge**   To draw near to. A variable is sometimes said to converge to its limit.

**CRT**   CRT stands for Cathode Ray Tube – a device whereby electrons are sprayed onto a viewing screen.   Examples include television screens and computer terminals.

**Cycle**   The cycle describes predictable periodic motions, like circular orbits. In phase plane portraits, the behavior often appears as smooth closed curves.

**Differential equations**   Equations often of the form $dx_i/dt = f_i(x)$ where $x_i(t)$ represents the $i$th variable and the function $f_i(x)$ gives the time, or spatial, evolution of $x_i(t)$. Mathematical models in the physical and biological sciences are often formulated as differential equations.

**Dimension**   See *Fractal dimension*.

**Dynamical systems**   Models containing the rules describing the way a given quantity undergoes a change through time or iteration steps. For example, the motion of planets about the sun can be modeled as a dynamical system in which the planets move according to Newton's laws. A discrete dynamical system can be represented mathematically as $x_{t+1} = f(x_t)$. A continuous dynamical system can be expressed as $dx/dt = f(x,t)$.

**EPROM**   Erasable Programmable Read-Only Memory, which can be erased under high-intensity ultraviolet light, then reprogrammed.

**Feedback**   The return to a system's input of part of its output.

**Fibonacci sequence**   The sequence 1,1,2,3,5,8,13 ... ($F_n = F_{n-2} + F_{n-1}$), which governs many patterns in the plant world.

**Fixed point**   A point which is invariant under a mapping (i.e., $x_t = x_{t+1}$ for discrete systems, or $x = f(x)$ for continuous systems). A particular kind of fixed point is a *center*. For a center, nearby trajectories neither approach nor diverge from the fixed point. In contrast to the center, for a *hyperbolic fixed point*, some nearby trajectories approach and some diverge from the fixed point. A *saddle point* is an example of a hyperbolic fixed point. An *unstable fixed point* (or repulsive fixed point or repelling fixed point) $x$ of a function occurs when $f'(x) > 0$. A *stable fixed point* (or attractive fixed point) $x$ of a function occurs when $f'(x) < 0$. For cases where $f'(x) = 0$ higher derivatives need to be considered.

**Font**   A collection of characters with a consistent size and style.

**Fourier analysis**   The separation of a complex wave into its sinusoidal components.

**Fractals**   Objects (or sets of points, or curves, or patterns) which exhibit increasing detail ("bumpiness") with increasing magnification. Many interesting fractals are self-similar. B. Mandelbrot informally defines fractals as "shapes that are equally complex in their details as in their overall form. That is, if a piece of a fractal is suitably magnified to become of the same size as the whole, it should look like the whole, either exactly, or perhaps only after slight limited deformation."

**Fractal dimension**   A quantitative property of a set of points which measures the extent to which the points fill space. A line is one dimensional and a plane is two dimensional, but a bumpy curve with infinite length, such as a Koch snowflake curve, has a dimension between 1 and 2. The snowflake curve is obviously more crinkly – better at filling space – than a smooth curve which has dimension one.

**Gasket**   A piece of material from which sections have been removed. *Mathematical gaskets*, such as Sierpinski gaskets, can be generated by removing sections of a region according to some rule. Usually the process of removal leaves pieces which are similar to the initial region; thus the gasket may be defined recursively.

**Geode**   A nodule of stone having a cavity lined with crystals.

**Halley's method**   See Newton's method.

**IC**  Integrated circuit. A complex electronic circuit fabricated on a simple piece of material, usually a silicon chip.

**Iteration**  Repetition of an operation or set of operations. In mathematics, composing a function with itself, such as in $f(f(x))$, can represent an iteration. The computational process of determining $x_{i+1}$ given $x_i$ is called an iteration.

**Julia set**  Set of all points which do not converge to a fixed point or finite attracting orbit under repeated applications of the map. Most Julia sets are fractals, displaying an endless cascade of repeated detail. An alternate definition: repeated applications of a function $f$ determine a trajectory of successive locations $x$, $f(x)$, $f(f(x))$, $f(f(f(x)))$, ... visited by a starting point $x$ in the complex plane. Depending on the starting point, this results in two types of trajectories, those which go to infinity and those which remain bounded by a fixed radius. The Julia set of the function $f$ is the boundary curve which separates these regions.

**LED**  Light Emitting Diode, a commonly used, small display unit that glows when supplied with a voltage.

**Limit**  In general, the ultimate value towards which a variable tends.

**Lyapunov exponent**  A quantity, sometimes represented by the Greek letter $\Lambda$, used to characterize the divergence of trajectories in a chaotic flow. For a 1-D formula, such as the logistic equation, $\Lambda = \lim\limits_{N \to \infty} 1/N \sum\limits_{n=1}^{N} \ln |dx_{n+1}/dx_n|$.

**Mandelbrot set**  For each complex number $\mu$ let $f_\mu(x)$ denote the polynomial $x^2 + \mu$. The Mandelbrot set is defined as the set of values of $\mu$ for which successive iterates of 0 under $f_\mu$ do not converge to infinity. An alternate definition: the set of complex numbers $\mu$ for which the *Julia set* of the iterated mapping $z \to z^2 + \mu$ separates disjoint regions of attraction. When $\mu$ lies outside this set, the corresponding Julia set is fragmented. The term "Mandelbrot Set" is originally associated with this quadratic formula, although the same construction gives rise to a (generalized) Mandelbrot Set for any iterated function with a complex parameter.

**Markov process**  A stochastic process in which the "future" is determined by the "present."

**Michelson contrast**  A measure used for comparing gray shades, where 1 is full contrast (e.g. pure black stripes against a pure white background), and 0 is no contrast (e.g. a black line on a black background).

**Mod**  Also *modulo*. A mathematical function that yields the remainder after division. A number $x$ mod $n$ gives the integer remainder of $x/n$. For example, 200 mod 47 = 200/47 − 12.

**Mouse**  A device for moving a cursor or other object around on the display screen.

**Newton's method**  A method for approximating roots of equations. Suppose the equation is $f(x) = 0$, and $a_1$ is an approximation to the roots. The next approximation, $a_2$, is found by $a_2 = a_1 - f(a_1)/f'(a_1)$, where $f'$ is the derivative of $f$. Halley's method is a related method which uses the second derivative to find the roots of an equation.

**Nonlinear equation**  Equations where the output is not directly proportional to the input. Equations which describe the behavior of most real-world problems. The response of a nonlinear system can depend crucially upon initial conditions.

**NP-complete**  A group of decision and search problems which are difficult for computers to solve since they take an unreasonable amount of time. An example of this kind of problem is the *travelling salesman problem*. The task is to find the shortest route by which a salesman can visit a particular set of cities. As the number of cities grows, the number of possible paths skyrockets. Even the fastest computers available would require years to handle the roughly $10^{62}$ paths of a 50-city itinerary.

**Penrose tiles**  In the 1970s, Roger Penrose assembled diamond-shaped tiles into patterns which fill the plane but do not repeat themselves at regular intervals. Penrose tiling patterns have a five-fold symmetry.

**Perfect numbers**  An integer which is the sum of all its divisors excluding itself. For example, 6 is a perfect number since 6=1+2+3.

**Period**  The time taken for one cycle of vibration of a wave.

**Periodic**  Recurring at equal intervals of time.

**Phase portrait**    The overall picture formed by all possible initial conditions in the $(x, \dot{x})$ plane is referred to as the phase portrait. Consider the motion of a pendulum which comes to rest due to air resistance. In the abstract two-dimensional *phase space* (with coordinates $x$, and velocity, $\dot{x}$) motions appear as noncrossing spirals converging asymptotically towards the resting, fixed state. This focus is called a *point attractor* which attracts all local transient motions.

**Pixel**    A picture on a CRT screen is made up of tiny elements called pixels.

**Polygon**    A closed plane figure bounded by straight lines.

**Polynomial**    An algebraic expression of the form $a_0 x^n + a_1 x^{n-1} + \cdots + a_{n-1} x + a_n$ where $n$ is the degree of the expression and $a_0 \neq 0$.

**PTX**    Photodetector.

**Quasiperiodicity**    Informally defined as a phenomenon with multiple periodicity. One example is the astronomical position of a point on the surface of the earth, since it results from the rotation of the earth about its axis and the rotation of the earth around the sun.

**Quaternion**    A 4-dimensional "hyper" complex number of the form $Q = a_0 + a_1 i + a_2 j + a_3 k$.

**Rational function**    A function which can be expressed as the quotient of two polynomials. A *rational number* can be expressed as a ratio of two integers.

**Recursive**    An object is said to be recursive if it partially consists of or is defined in terms of itself. A *recursive operation* invokes itself as an intermediate operation.

**ROM**    Read-Only Memory. A solid state storage chip that is programmed at the time of its manufacture and that cannot be reprogrammed by the computer user.

**Sierpinski gasket**    See *gasket*.

**Steady state**    Also called equilibrium point or *fixed point*. A set of values of the variables of a system for which the system does not change as time proceeds.

**Strange attractor**    See *attractor*.

**Trajectory**    A sequence of points in which each point produces its successor according to some mathematical function.

**Transcendental    functions**    Functions which are not algebraic, for example, circular, exponential, and logarithmic functions.

**Transformation**    The    operation    of changing (as by rotation or mapping) one configuration or expression into another in accordance with a mathematical rule.

... AND IN HERE IS THE PROGRAMMER THAT JUST FOUND AN ERROR IN HIS PROGRAM.

# Index

Michelangelo's design of a continuous pathway in quadrangle of the Capitol, Rome, from an engraving by DuPérac in 1569.

# Credits

*"All the technological knowledge we work with today will represent only one percent of the knowledge that will be available in 2050. "*

Marvin Centron, President, *Forecasting International*

Except for the four figures at the beginning of the Visualization section, all of the computer graphics presented in this book were created by the author. Some of the computer graphics and written material have appeared previously in the author's published journal papers. The journals' names are listed here to thank them and give credit to the source publication: *The Visual Computer, Communications of the ACM, Leonardo, The Journal of Recreational Mathematics, Computer Language Magazine, Computers and Graphics, Computers in Physics, IBM Technical Disclosure Bulletin, IBM Journal of Research and Development, Algorithm: The Personal Computing Newsletter, Technology Review, Supercomputing Review, Speculations in Science and Technology, IEEE Computer Graphics and Applications, The History and Social Science Teacher, IEEE Computer, American Mathematical Society Notices*, and *Symmetry*. Some figures have previously appeared in *OMNI, Science News, Computer Graphics World*, and *Scientific American*.

Many of the interesting drawings of animals and other fanciful pictures are from the *Dover Pictorial Archive*, Mineola, New York. One excellent source is: Harter, J. (1979) *Animals*, Dover: New York. Two others are: Appelbaum, S. (1974) *Fantastic Illustrations of Grandville*, and Horemis, S. (1973) *Visual Illusions Coloring Book*. Figure 1.2 is from a surface discovered by C. Costa in 1984. The image is © David Hoffman, James Hoffman, and Stewart Dickson. The jacket photo of the author is by John Christin, Peekskill, New York.

The quotations interspersed throughout the book come from a variety of sources. The quotations by P.W. Atkins, Lincoln College, Oxford, come from an article in *The Daily Telegraph* (Friday, August 17, 1990) titled "Art as Science." The Alan Watts quotations come from *Nature, Man, and Woman* (1975, Vintage: New York). The quotation by Bob Berger at the beginning of "Million-Point Sculptures" on page 285 is from: (Berger, B. (1990) Tracing the master's strokes: computer art by Lillian Schwartz, *OMNI*, October Issue, page 59.) The quotation by Manfred Schroeder at the beginning of "Continued Roots in the Complex Plane" on page 289 comes from: (Schroeder, M. (1989) Self-similarity and fractals in science and art. *J. Audio. Eng. Soc.* Oct 37(10): 795-808.) The "fractal goose" quotation comes from: (Schreiner, O., *The Story of an African Farm*, A. L. Burt: New York, pp. 138-139), first published in 1883 in London. The "fractal cave" quotation comes from a description of the cave at the entrance to The Place of Death in *King Solomon's Mines*, by H. Rider Haggard. I thank Ken Philip for bringing these two quotations to my attention. The quotations of Paul Rapp come from an article in the February 1990 issue of *OMNI* magazine titled "Get Smart: Controlling Chaos" (page 43). The author of the article is Kathleen McAuliffe. The quotation by Clem Padin comes from: (Padin, C., The mathematical aesthetic. *Science News* 138(17): 259). The Alan Mackay quotes come from: (Mackay, A. (1989) In the mind's eye. In *Computers in Art, Design and Animation*. Springer: New York). The David Larkin quote comes from: (Larkin, D. (1973) *Fantastic Art*. Ballantine Books: New York). The Lynn Steen quote comes from: (Peterson, I. (1990) *Islands of Truth*. Freeman: New York). The quote regarding the number 137 comes from: (Feynman, R. (1985) *QED*. Princeton University Press: New Jersey. page 129). The quote by Marvin Centron comes from: (Centron, M. (1991) Retiring Baby Boomers. *OMNI* Jan 13(4): 8.) The quote by Mary Jean Kenton comes from an electronic bulletin board called *Fine Art Forum*, published by the International Society for Art, Science and Technology. Kenton, an artist, is currently working on two interesting projects: *The Engineers' Notebooks* and *The Geometry of Color*. The first project consists of notebooks containing graph pages that have been filled with thousands of painted marks. *The Geometry of Color* is an ongoing installation of horticulture, naturally occurring materials, and paint. The Geometry of Color is limited only by the boundaries of the farm on which Mary Jean Kenton lives and works. In the fall of 1990, these works were shown/documented in a retrospective of Kenton's work at Allegheny College, Meadville, PA. Kenton can be reached at: Box 42, Merrittstown, PA 15463. The rough estimate for the computational power of a rodent brain comes from: (Suplee, C. (1991) Artificial life: the new robotics. *Breakthroughs*. February. 2(1): 42.) The source for the facts on the *ice age number*, *Coney Island number* and related large numbers is: (Kasner, E., Newman, J. (1989) *Mathematics and the Imagination*. Tempus: Redmond, Washington). The source for the Frankowski quote is the science-fiction book: (Frankowski, L. (1989) *Copernick's Rebellion*. Del Rey: New York.) The pictures of Leonardo da Vinci, Grace Hopper, Pascal, the Pascaline, and several cartoons come from Camelot Publishing, P.O. Box 1357, Ormond Beach, FL 32175 (see "Products, Classroom Aids, Art, Games, Distributors" on page 384). The various robot photographs at the beginning of several book parts are courtesy of B. Amman, Sulzer Robot Systems, CH-8401 Winterthur, Switzerland. The picture at the beginning of *Credits* shows a manipulator for docking a drug in a protein molecule receptor. With the device, users can "feel" the binding forces. (Photo by Bo Strain, courtesy of W. Wright, Department of Computer Science, University of North Carolina at Chapel Hill.)

# Acknowledgements

A few of the roughly 50 different articles included in this book represent collaborations with other researchers, and I thank them for giving me permission to include these collaborative pieces in the present book. For example, "Irregularly Oscillating Fossil Seashells" on page 129 is a joint research project with Chris Illert, Science-Art Center, Department of Theoretical Conchology, 2 Tern Place, Semaphore Park, S.A. 5019 Australia. "The Connell Sequence" on page 276, and a few other chapters, represent collaborative work with Professor Akhlesh Lakhtakia, Engineering Dept., Pennsylvania State University, University Park, PA 16802. Alvin E. Reed of IBM drew the engineering diagrams for the speech grenade in the *Invention* part of the book and provided many of the details for the hardware implementations. Another frequent invention collaborator is Jim McLean, from Boca Raton, Florida. George Runger provided helpful suggestions regarding the earthworm algebra problem. Other collaborators are mentioned within the text of several chapters.

I owe a special debt of gratitude to Shirley Ulrich, Carl Reynolds, and Dawn Friedman for various helpful suggestions regarding the book. A. K. Dewdney, M. Gardner, P. Longo, E. Khorasani, A. Lakhtakia, B. Grossman, and J. Leonard provided helpful comments over the years.

# About the Author

Clifford A. Pickover received his Ph.D. from Yale University's Department of Molecular Biophysics and Biochemistry. He graduated first in his class from Franklin and Marshall College, after completing the four-year undergraduate program in three years. He is author of the popular book *Computers, Pattern, Chaos, and Beauty* (St. Martin's Press, New York, 1990). He is also author of over 200 articles concerning topics in science, art, and mathematics. Pickover is currently an associate editor for the international journal *Computers and Graphics* and is a member of the editorial board for *Computers in Physics* and *Speculations in Science and Technology*. He is a guest editor for *Computers in Physics* for a special issue on chaos, a guest editor for *Speculations in Science and Technology* for a special issue on the future of computing, and a member of the Book Review panel for *Leonardo*, an international journal on topics in art and science. Editor of *The Pattern Book: Recipes for Beauty* (M&T Books, 1991) and *Future Watch: Art, Technology, and Computing in the Next Century* (Science and Technology Letters, 1992), and coeditor of the books *Spiral Symmetry* (World Scientific, 1991) and *Frontiers in Scientific Visualization* (Plenum, 1991), Dr. Pickover's primary interest is in scientific visualization.

In 1990, he received first prize in the Institute of Physics' "Beauty of Physics Photographic Competition." His computer graphics have been featured on the cover of several popular magazines, and his research has recently received considerable attention by the press – including *CNN*'s "Science and Technology Week," *Science News*, and *The Washington Post* – and also in international exhibitions and museums. *OMNI* magazine recently described him as "Van Leeuwenhoek's twentieth century equivalent." The July 1989 issue of *Scientific American* featured his graphic work, calling it "strange and beautiful, stunningly realistic." Pickover has received several awards for various inventions in the areas of novel computer input devices and display methodologies. He can be reached at P.O. Box 549, Millwood, New York 10546-0549 USA.

## GALLERY OF COMPUTER GRAPHICS

The following pages show a range of the author's recent computer graphics. Shapes include fractals from complex geometry, and 3-D lava simulations produced from mathematical models of fluids.

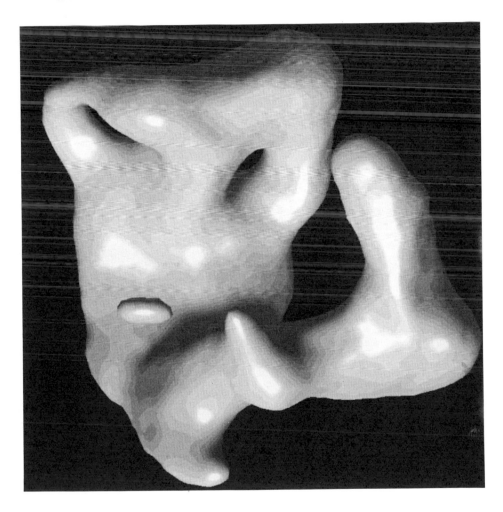

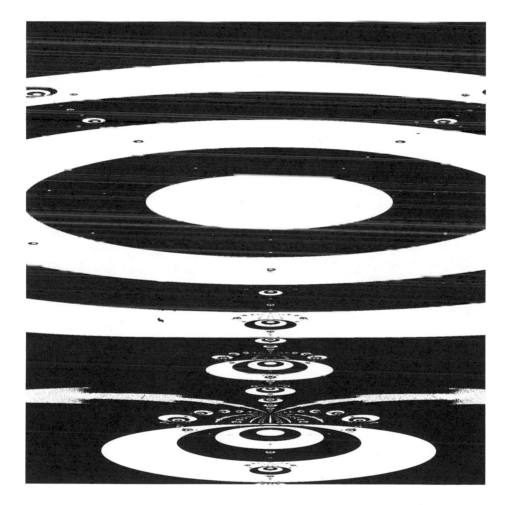

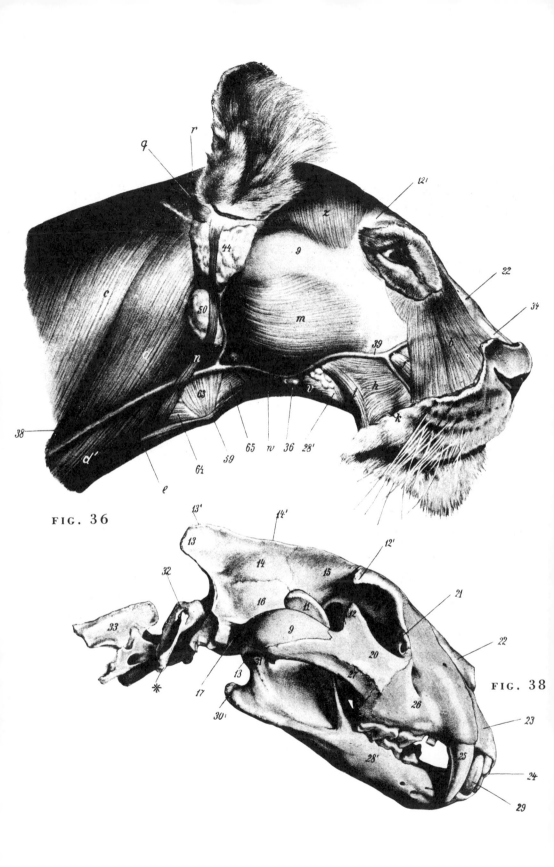

FIG. 36

FIG. 38